German Writing, American Reading

German Writing, American Reading

Women and the Import of Fiction, 1866–1917

LYNNE TATLOCK

THE OHIO STATE UNIVERSITY PRESS | COLUMBUS

Copyright © 2012 by The Ohio State University.
All rights reserved.

Library of Congress Cataloging-in-Publication Data

Tatlock, Lynne, 1950–
  German writing, American reading : women and the import of fiction, 1866–1917 / Lynne Tatlock.
    p. cm.
  Includes bibliographical references and index.
    ISBN 978-0-8142-1194-6 (cloth)—ISBN 978-0-8142-9295-2 (cd-rom)
  1. American literature—German influences. 2. German literature—Translations into English—History and criticism. 3. German literature—Women authors—History and criticism. 4. German literature—Appreciation—United States. 5. Literature and society—United States. I. Title.
  PS159.G3T38 2012
  810.9'3243—dc23
                          2012018741

Paper (ISBN: 978-0-8142-5694-7)
Cover design by Laurence J. Nozik
Text design by Juliet Williams
Type set in Adobe Minion Pro

For Joe

CONTENTS

List of Illustrations — ix
Preface — xi
Acknowledgments — xiii

PART ONE · German Writing, American Reading

Chapter 1 Introduction: Made in Germany, Read in America — 3
Chapter 2 German Women Writers at Home and Abroad — 28

PART TWO · German Texts as American Books

Chapter 3 "Family Likenesses": Marlitt's Texts as American Books — 53
Chapter 4 The German Art of the Happy Ending: Embellishing and Expanding the Boundaries of Home — 83
Chapter 5 Enduring Domesticity: German Novels of Remarriage — 121
Chapter 6 Feminized History: German Men in American Translation — 156

PART THREE · Three Americanizers: Translating, Publishing, Reading

Chapter 7 Family Matters in Postbellum America: Ann Mary Crittenden Coleman (1813–91) — 199
Chapter 8 German Fiction Clothed in "so brilliant a garb": Annis Lee Wister (1830–1908) — 216
Chapter 9 Germany at Twenty-Five Cents a Copy: Mary Stuart Smith (1834–1917) — 236
Conclusion — 263

Appendices

A	American Periodicals Cited	267
B	Late Nineteenth- and Early Twentieth-Century U.S. Library Catalogs and Finding Lists Consulted as an Index of Enduring Circulation	269
C	Total German Novels Translated in America (1866–1917) by Woman Author	270
D	Total Number of Translations of German Novels in the United States (1866–1917) by Woman Author	271
E	Total American Publications (1866–1917) by Woman Author	272

Notes   273

Bibliography   322

Index   331

ILLUSTRATIONS

Figure 1.1 Centered Moving Averages of the Total Number of New Translations of German Novels by the 17 Women in the Dataset Published in the United States. 15

Figure 1.2 Centered Moving Averages of U.S. Publications (New Translations, New Editions, and Reprint Editions) of German Novels by the 17 Women in the Dataset. 15

Figure 3.1 E. Marlitt, *Gold Elsie* (New York: Chatterton-Peck, n.d.). Author's copy. 60

Figure 3.2 Front Cover and Spine, E. Marlitt, *The Old Mam'selle's Secret* (New York: Hurst & Company, n.d.). Author's copy. 66–67

Figure 5.1 W. Heimburg, *A Maiden's Choice* (New York: R. F. Fenno & Company, 1899). Author's copy. 135

Figure 5.2 W. Heimburg, *Misjudged* (Chicago: M. A. Donohue & Co., n.d.). Author's copy. 142

Figure 8.1 Annis Lee Wister. From the Furness Manuscripts, Annenberg Rare Book and Manuscript Library, Van Pelt-Dietrich Library, Philadelphia. 221

Figure 8.2 Adolf Streckfuss, *The Lonely House* (Philadelphia: J. B. Lippincott Company, 1907). Author's copy. 232

Figure 9.1 E. Marlitt, *Gold Elsie*, (New York: Munro, 1887). Copy held by Rare Books and Manuscripts in The Ohio State University Libraries. 245

Appendices

C   Total German Novels Translated in America (1866–1917) by Woman Author   270

D   Total Number of Translations of German Novels in the United States (1866–1917) by Woman Author   271

E   Total American Publications (1866–1917) by Woman Author   272

PREFACE

When in 2007 Rochester University launched its online destination for "readers, editors, and translators interested in finding out about modern and contemporary international literature," the site was polemically named "Three Percent." Three percent corresponds to the estimated percentage of all books published in translation in the United States. As further noted on the website's home page, the total number of books of poetry and fiction amounts to a much lower percentage of the total titles published, that is, around 0.7%.[1] We, however, mistake past American reading if we draw conclusions based on the present state of things. In the Gilded Age a significant percentage of books published in the United States consisted of books in translation, and Americans read internationally even at a moment of national consolidation after the divisive Civil War. A subset of Americans' international reading—nearly a hundred original texts, approximately 180 American translations, more than a thousand editions and reprint editions, and hundreds of thousands of books strong—consisted of popular German fiction written by women and translated by American women. The adventures of this fiction in the United States concern us here.

ACKNOWLEDGMENTS

This study emerges from a glimmer of an idea I had longer ago than I care to remember. It only gradually became feasible as I returned to it intermittently over many years and began to uncover information that I had not previously suspected existed, in particular, the historical record left behind by the three translators, Ann Mary Coleman, Annis Lee Wister, and Mary Stuart Smith. I would like to thank three former graduate research assistants, Shelly Stumme Schrappen, April Seager, and especially Alyssa Howards, who early on aided me in assembling material and locating archives that were to become critical to my work. Since their early work, I have been aided in various ways and in various phases of this project, thanks to the Graduate School of Arts and Sciences and the Department of Germanic Languages and Literatures, by research assistants including Amy Cislo, Benjamin Davis, Anne Fritz, Magdalen Stanley Majors, Faruk Pašić, Shane Peterson, and Brooke Shafar.

When I began the task of assembling and managing a database that currently holds nearly 1,000 detailed entries, I turned to the Humanities Digital Workshop at Washington University. Under the able supervision of Perry Trolard, the assistant director of the workshop, student fellows and assistants, including Stephen Aiken, Catherine Coquillette, Erika Deal, Linda Donaldson, Courtney LeCompte, Anna Leeper, Ervin Malakaj, Corey Twitchell, Petra Watzke, and Magdalen Stanley Majors, helped compile, enter, and find ways of managing and visualizing the data. Maggie deserves special recognition for her work in cleaning up the data in preparation for generating the graphs included in this book. I thank all of these student researchers for so willingly sharing my enthusiasms during their time working with me. I am greatly indebted to Stephen Pentecost, who designed the template for data entry, generated the graphs in chapter 1 and in Appendices C, D, and E, helped prepare scans for the black-and-white illustrations, and otherwise assisted Perry Trolard in guiding the student teams in the Humanities Digital Workshop. Perry's successor in late 2011, Douglas Knox, immediately provided invaluable support by, among other things, pointing me toward the online historical database of the Muncie Public Library. Sabbatical leave promised by then Dean of Arts and Sciences Edward S. Macias and subsequently granted by Acting Dean of Arts and Sciences Ralph S. Quatrano allowed me the time I needed in the academic year 2009–10 finally to make sense of and give form to the data I had collected over the years.

I gratefully acknowledge the following libraries and archives for the permission to quote from materials from their holdings and their librarians who facilitated my access to this material: John Jordan Crittenden Papers Rare Book, Manuscript, and Special Collections Library, Duke University, Durham, North Carolina; Filson Historical Society, Louisville, Kentucky; Schlesinger Library, Radcliffe Institute for Advanced Study, Harvard University; Annenberg Rare Book and Manuscript Library, Van Pelt-Dietrich Library, Philadelphia, Pennsylvania; College of Physicians of Philadelphia, Pennsylvania; and Rare Books and Manuscripts at The Ohio State University.

I am obliged to many friends and colleagues who offered encouragement and advice along the way, among others Lisabeth M. Hock, Jana Mikota, Renate Schmidt, Jim Walker, and Alexandra K. Wettlaufer. Lorie A. Vanchena deserves special appreciation for her supportive reading of a draft of the manuscript. I thank Kirsten Belgum for many a stimulating conversation about the project and the challenge of transatlantic scholarship. My dear friend and colleague Michael Sherberg provided a patient and willing ear and eye, optimism, and good advice from start to finish. Most of all, he was always ready to share my excitement and give me an occasional push.

I would also especially like to thank Sandy Crooms, Senior Editor at The Ohio State University Press, for supporting and shepherding the book and Maggie Diehl for overseeing the copyediting of the manuscript. The anonymous readers for the press offered useful suggestions and asked helpful questions that inspired my final revisions of the manuscript. It has been a privilege and pleasure to work with the staff at the press.

Finally, I am grateful to my husband and colleague, Joseph F. Loewenstein, who was interested in the project from its earliest beginnings, asked hard questions, and saw to it, when the data became so extensive, that I worked with the Humanities Digital Workshop at Washington University. Without our many years of conversation, this work would likely have been a different one. I dedicate this book to him with love and gratitude.

PART ONE

German Writing, American Reading

CHAPTER 1

Introduction

Made in Germany, Read in America

IN 1905 Otto Heller, professor of German language and literature at Washington University in St. Louis, considered the work of German women writers mostly outside the "legitimate domain of letters."[1] As Heller discredits one author after another in his comprehensive essay on German women writers, one reason for his vehemence becomes usefully visible for the present undertaking. Much of this disdained work belongs to what Heller terms "amusement fiction."[2] His English label renders the derisive German term "Unterhaltungsliteratur," the bane of late nineteenth-century German intellectuals who sought a national literature of pretension and who found popular fiction suspect, in part because it was often written by women and principally read by women. Still more detrimental to the project of German national literature and its international reputation was the popularity of this fiction—not only in Germany but also in America, where Heller had settled on the Mississippi as an arbiter of all things German for his university and the local community. Heller deplored the "widespread though unpardonable American ignorance of contemporary German literature."[3] One reason for this ignorance, he believed, was the ready availability of American translations of this shoddy German amusement fiction.[4] A certain Mrs. Caspar Wister, a translator who plays a central role in my account of American reading and German cultural transfer, met with his particular disapprobation. Her American renderings of German authors had served, Heller grumbled, as the conduit through which a clichéd and false view of German womanhood had entered American culture.[5]

Writing in a moment of national canon formation in imperial Germany, a canon that excluded most women writers, Heller, with this critical essay, participated in the segmentation of reading that was taking place *internationally* at the turn of the century.[6] Yet the translated German books he despised had circulated in America for nearly four decades in a somewhat less divided reading culture. Even if in the postbellum literary field, as Richard Brodhead argues, three strata of literary production, corresponding roughly to the later categories lowbrow, middlebrow, and highbrow, were in the process of segmentation and institutionalization, American readers continued to read across these divisions.[7] As "light" or "wholesome" reading, translated novels by German women belonged to Americans' eclectic reading, marketed and enjoyed side by side with novels now considered literary classics. These translated books rewarded virtue and upheld marriage while entertaining readers with plots that sometimes shared elements of sensation fiction. Widely advertised, sold at a broad range of prices, available in multiple translations with different publishers of varying reputation, variously reviewed, and appearing prominently in the holdings of public libraries, they became standard, reliable, and popular American reading, enjoyed, recommended, and even esteemed by American readers up to the First World War.

Over the course of this study I will have occasion to return to Heller, for his backward glance at the nineteenth century speaks eloquently to the project at hand, if not precisely in the manner he intended. If he worried in 1905 that a feminized view of his country, its people, its literature, and its culture had penetrated more deeply and broadly into American habits of reading than had the male-authored literary work that he favored, he was not far from the mark.

WHEN IN 1892—just over a decade before Heller wrote his essay—W. M. Griswold compiled a *Descriptive List of Novels and Tales Dealing with Life in Germany,* translated novels by German women—and in particular the women novelists who will interest us here—predominated.[8] Griswold's title, moreover, asserted that Americans would learn about life in Germany from reading this fiction, and the editor stated his intention to make certain that readers could use the list to be reminded of "superior old books, equally fresh to most readers," that might serve this purpose.[9] By "old books" he meant the fiction of the preceding forty years. This meritorious fiction could and should endure, he thought. Although, he feared, such books were often read only a short time after their publication, they remained in libraries accessible to patrons who would surely deem them to be as good as or better than brand-new works.¹⁰ However, Griswold's notion of "superior fiction" that deserved an afterlife hardly matched the idea that academics such as Heller had of important nineteenth-century German literature; Griswold had a penchant for the popular.

Thirty years later, after assembling a voluminous bibliography of German literature in English translation, another academic, Bayard Quincy Morgan, agreed with Heller, asserting that "the English-speaking public has not been getting a faithful picture of 19th century literary production in Germany."¹¹ Likewise, in 1935, in her study of the reception of German literature in England and America, Lillie V. Hathaway bemoaned "this indiscriminate vogue of third-rate writers or less at a time when Keller, C. F. Meyer, Raabe and Fontane were hardly noticed."¹² Although they observed the American rage for certain German novels, neither Morgan nor Hathaway investigated the phenomenon further, assuming that by pointing to economically motivated pandering to the "taste of the multitude," they had said all that needed to be said.¹³ Hathaway in fact could not contain her scorn for the "'Gartenlaube' ladies" and their American readers. She not only made factual errors in her account but also, as a researcher in an era in which popular reading was not taken seriously in the academy, offered unexamined opinions and value judgments about this literature. Unfavorable reviews of these novels were, in her estimation, those that recognized "their true value," that is, their lack of literary merit.¹⁴

My study starts where Morgan and Hathaway stopped long ago; it investigates not the German literature that Americans should have been reading in the view of academics and cultural pundits interested in highbrow literature, but rather some of the novels they *did* read in a period in which "everybody [read] more or less daily."¹⁵ This was a German literature that seeped into American culture via popular reading in translation; it brought with it a host of beliefs and values that reinforced and sometimes expanded the boundaries of American domesticity, upholding marriage with emotionally satisfying stories in which wedlock is often embedded in an idea of nation. In translation this literature forfeited many of its national cultural valences only to highlight, as points of international entry, the plots with their inevitable happy endings, emotional appeal, and social and moral messages. Still, many of the novels were known to be "made in Germany" and sometimes they *therefore* sold.

In focusing on popular fiction, I follow William St Clair's call for the broader study of reading, found in his seminal work on reading culture in England in the romantic period. "Any study of the consequences of the reading of the past ought to consider the print which was actually read," St Clair maintains, and "not some modern selection, whether that selection is derived from judgments of canon or from other modern criteria."[16] Patterns of reading depend on the availability and the affordability of books. As he demonstrates, tracing print and "understanding how certain texts came to be made available in printed form to certain constituencies of buyers and readers" can aid us in writing a history of reading as it affects cultural formations and—importantly for the present study—cultural transfer.[17]

In the nineteenth-century American case, what Hathaway derisively labels the work of "third-rate [German women] writers" inhabited some of the same publication and reading venues as did that of now canonical writers; they appeared in the same American publishers' series and in the same American libraries. Interested Americans thus could read German women's novels alongside English, American, French, and other foreign classics as well as works by the iconic Goethe.[18] A list of "Suggestions for Household Libraries" in *Hints for Home Reading* from 1880 gives a sense of the proximity of books that we might now consider worlds apart. Goethe's name appears in various categories in the first and second lists but not under fiction. Although fiction is accorded relatively little space on these three lists to begin with, two popular women authors, E. Marlitt and E. Werner, do appear on the third and lowest ranking list alongside German male novelists and the likes of Thomas Hardy, Sarah Jewett, Wilkie Collins, Bret Harte, and other American, British, and French authors, both classic and popular.[19]

While attempting to answer the question of what to read in a world inundated with books of all sorts, *Hints for Home Reading* prescribes, ranks, and categorizes. Even so, it provides readers with some encouragement to enjoy their reading. Offering a tempered consideration of Emerson's prescriptions and proscription against recent, popular literature, Fred B. Perkins admits in his essay for this volume that these sorts of dicta amount to "a record of what the codifier has found to suit his individual character." He suggests that if one simply added to Emerson's rules a mitigating "unless you like," they would work perfectly well.[20] He thus acknowledges multiple pressures on choices of reading and grants readers some autonomy. Of course Americans did not need to wait for his permission.

Novels of all kinds, sanctioned and otherwise, filled library shelves. Novels by German women often claimed more shelf space than now-recognized German authors of literary pretension. In 1889 a patron of the Chicago Public Library, for example, more readily encountered German culture in novels by Luise Mühlbach than those by Goethe. The prolific Mühlbach was represented there by eleven novels; Goethe, who had only written four novels to begin with, by only three.[21] Some American readers—such as Emerson—of course had a keen sense of the cultural and intellectual pretension of reading Goethe and may have reached first for Goethe and then only Goethe; for others, reading Goethe did not necessarily preclude enjoying the highly accessible and entertaining Mühlbach.

In conceiving of these translated books as *American* products and *American* reading, I adhere to the descriptive turn in translation studies that views such works as "'facts of the culture which hosts them' and as agents of change in that culture."[22] A review of finding lists and catalogues of public libraries across the United States from the period 1870 to 1917 reveals that these books had indeed been naturalized as artifacts "of the culture which hosts them"; the libraries routinely list them alongside American, English, and other novels in translation, that is, not according to their national origins but as "English fiction" or "English prose fiction." These catalogues in no respect mark any of the translated books as foreign literature, whereas holdings in narrative fiction in the foreign language in which it was originally written are so designated and overtly separated from "English fiction." Available American translations occasionally overlap with available works in the original German, but often they do not. In 1907, for example, those patrons of the Carnegie Library of Pittsburgh who could read both English and German could have enjoyed ten novels by the perennially popular E. Marlitt and one by Goethe in either language under the alternate labels of "English Fiction" and "German Fiction." Patrons, however, had access to Fanny Lewald's *Die Erlöserin* (translated as *Hulda*) and Wilhelmine von Hillern's *Arzt der Seele* (translated as *Only a Girl*) and eighteen novels by Mühlbach only in translated works listed under "English Fiction."[23]

The great bulk of North American translation of German fiction and of the publishing of new and reprint editions of these translations occurred in the Gilded Age, coinciding with years in which the greatest annual output of titles in the United States was uniformly fiction. Fiction maintained the largest share of titles through 1916, not to be surpassed until 1917, when books and editions in the category of religion and theology moved into first place.[24] The great American book historian John Tebbel identifies a "great fiction boom" that began in the early 1870s and reached its zenith between 1890 and 1914, when reading fiction in America was "something of a mania," or, as W. D. Howells put it, the novel was "easily first among books that people read willingly."[25] The American audience was enormous. As Mary Kelley emphasizes, "by the 1840s America had the largest reading audience ever produced due to high literacy rates among white men and women early in the century." Ten years later publishing was, in Kelley's words, "becoming 'big business.'"[26] In the antebellum period women and girls sometimes only sheepishly admitted to reading novels, but they read them nonetheless, moving "back and forth across a wide spectrum of literature." [27] After the Civil War popular novels became ever more standard reading, often overtly marketed specifically to women and girls and hardly to be kept from them. With ornamental covers and in various handy sizes, novels were designed to be displayed and not hidden as forbidden fruit. Postbellum publishers, in search of a profit, stimulated and fed Americans' voracious appetite for novels in various ways, sometimes with foreign food, some of it German.

FROM 1865 TO 1917, as contemporaries frequently noted, hundreds of thousands of German books circulated in the United States, both in the original German and in English translation.[28] Reacting in 1869 to this boom in German letters in America, the *Christian Examiner* supposed that books such as E. P. Evans's history of German literature, *Abriß der Deutschen Literaturgeschichte,* would interest "a public numbered by millions, and . . . be sent to all parts of the land."[29] As the reviewer further observed, no bookstore was "so small or so remote that German books [did] not make part of its stock, and help in its profits."[30] The presence of these many books in the everyday life of American readers has, however, not typically been accorded much attention in mainstream American literary and cultural histories. Just as Heller feared the contamination of German national literature by such popular literature, Americans, who were creating their own national literature and its still very short story, had reason to turn a blind eye to international reading.

In his recent study of German and American literature, Hugh Ridley presents a compelling case for structural similarities between the development of the national literatures of Germany and the United States and at the same time demonstrates how national literary studies can be rethought by comparative study.[31] Eschewing influence studies, Ridley focuses instead on what he identifies as parallel developments, in particular, during the formative years of the growth of both nations: in Germany, the anticipation and formation of empire; in the United States, the struggle of a young democracy for cultural literacy with the special problem of the postbellum years in which the nation had to be rethought and knit together again. As Ridley argues, these "nations needed national literature"; that is, both nations sought "major writers, figures who would impress other states and bestow identity and prestige on the nation."[32]

As Ridley outlines concerning the American side, the national project led both to encouragement of American writing in the nineteenth century and to an exclusionary focus on that writing afterward in the creation of national literary history. Those pundits concerned with forming that canon of internationally impressive national work increasingly made judgments according to aesthetic criteria while summarily and scornfully dismissing popular writing. At the same time, Ridley observes, American readers and publishers presented an unruly obstacle to American efforts toward producing a national literature of pretension, since the actual practices of these readers and publishers were guided not necessarily by national interests but rather by such concerns as pleasure and profit. Popular reading in the Gilded Age therefore often ran counter to the aims of those who wished to promote national literature. American readers, Ridley maintains, read internationally and in translation—just as their European counterparts did.

Ridley's observation about the internationalism of the "reading nation" is generally absent from American accounts of this period of nation formation, which focus on American production or which, when they do take a broader view, tend to expand the focus only to British literature that influenced American production. Useful basic scholarship does, however, exist on German culture in America. I have turned repeatedly in the present study to the information assembled in Morgan's weighty *Bibliography of German Literature in English Translation* (1922). Henry A. Pochmann's voluminous study of the philosophical and literary influences of *German Culture in America* (1957) also provides useful information on translation, as does his collaborative volume with Arthur R. Schultz, *Bibliography of German Culture in America to 1940*.[33] In 1935 the above-mentioned Hathaway revised and expanded her painstakingly researched dissertation, an account of English and American reception of nineteenth-century German literature.[34] Here she includes some of the same reviews that figure in my research but, as noted above, has little regard for popular novels by women. Robert E. Cazden's *A Social History of the German Book Trade in America to the Civil War* provides a meticulous account of books published and/or reprinted in the United States. All of this work emerges from the realm of German studies; scholarship in book history and print culture based in American studies, however, has hardly taken notice of it, let alone the material it treats.

While studies in nineteenth-century American literature, reading, and book culture long focused largely on cultural materials originally written in English and particularly those of American origin, some recent trends in American studies support a broader view. Inspired and supported by the work of Werner Sollors and Marc Shell, scholarship that emerged from new interest in multiculturalism in the 1990s, American studies has especially since 2000 begun to look beyond its traditional Anglophone focus to examine literature written in the United States in languages other than English.[35] This innovative work makes a case for rethinking American literature as polyglot and emerging from a mix of immigrant and native cultures. Sollors's collection of essays *Multilingual America: Transnationalism, Ethnicity, and the Languages of American Literature* (1998), Shell's anthology *American Babel: Literatures of the United States from Abnaki to Zuni* (2003), and M. Lynn Weiss's *Creole Echoes: The Francophone Poetry of Nineteenth-Century Louisiana* exemplify scholarship that attempts such new approaches to American studies.[36] Shell and Sollors institutionalized this multilingual reframing of national literature in 2000 with *The Multilingual Anthology of American Literature,* a polyglot reader containing original texts with English translations intended for instructional purposes.[37] Sollors's inclusive reader of *Interracial Literature: Black-White Contact in the Old World and the New,* in turn, disrupts the national paradigm and moves toward an idea of world literature whose thematic transcends national boundaries, making available in the English language literature never before translated into English.[38] The founding of the online *Journal of Transnational Studies* in 2008 in the wake of Shelley Fisher Fishkin's presidential address on the "transnational turn" likewise harbingered new framings and impulses.[39] In that same year, in the vein of global studies in the new millennium, Caroline F. Levander and Robert S. Levine reconceived the field so as to de-center the U.S. nation and counter the idea of American exceptionalism with their anthology, *Hemispheric American Studies.*[40]

In the particular case of German culture in America, Sollors pointed in 2001 to German language writing in the United States as an opportunity and challenge to rethink American studies. His coedited volume with Winfried Fluck, *German? American? Literature? New Directions in German-American Studies* (2002)[41] answers his own challenge as the second book in his New Directions in German-American Studies, an undertaking that has, among other things, supported translations and editions of German and German-American writing of interest to American studies. Sollors's work remains one of the few impulses emerging from American (as opposed to German) studies in the United States to rethink American national literature by including the German element.[42]

Despite these and other important new impetuses, nineteenth-century American studies tends to overlook the significance of the foreign contingent to American publishing and reading—with the exception of books in English from Great Britain. Even Sollors's richly inclusive coedited *New Literary History of America* surprisingly does not accord much attention to international reading or multilingual America.[43] Recent important projects in American book history—book history by its very nature having the potential to be more inclusive than literary history—also omit the publication, translation, and reading of foreign books in the United States. Volumes 3 and 4, the pertinent volumes of the newest history of book publishing in the United States, *History of the Book in America*, for example, pay no attention to books in translation, and translation itself scarcely merits mention as a subject heading in the index of either volume.[44] The older book histories by John Tebbel likewise accord scant attention to the phenomenon of translation, publishing, and reading of foreign books, although Tebbel at least acknowledges it.

Meredith McGill's *American Literature and the Culture of Reprinting, 1834–1853*, with its interest in literary property and cultural production, importantly argues against understanding literary culture as national, pointing instead to the emergence of classic works of mid-nineteenth-century American authors "from a literary culture that was regional in articulation and transnational in scope."[45] Nevertheless, McGill understands transnational in this study only in a limited sense; that is, transnational refers to books written in English and thus to the British-American cultural axis: American reading of books written in other languages, unauthorized translations of books written in languages other than English, books written in America by immigrants in languages other than English, and American foreign language presses that reprinted books written in languages other than English play no role in her analysis. McGill's anthology *The Traffic in Poems* likewise aims to contribute to "transatlantic literary study" as a challenge "to the reflex sorting of literary texts according to the national identity of authors," yet here too that challenge is not framed in terms that make it as great as it might be, consisting as it does largely of examination of British and American texts, that is, mostly texts originally written in English.[46] Yet in its recognition of "social and cultural systems that operate beneath and beyond the nation-state" and in its assertion of the importance of women to transatlantic cultural transfer, McGill's project encourages the present undertaking.[47]

In short, American studies appears to have forgotten—or at least to consider unworthy of investigation—what nineteenth-century Americans themselves knew: many foreign texts were available in translation in the United States, and their fellow Americans enjoyed reading them, even sought them out, in their leisure hours. In later historical accounts of these periods, especially the German books under scrutiny here lent themselves to multiple marginalization: they were popular, foreign, read in translation, authored by women, and largely consumed by women. Yet, as Ridley asserts of both popular literature and women's writing, "these 'books' and the authority they exert over the imagination" were "a force to be reckoned with throughout the century on both sides of the Atlantic."[48]

Nineteenth-century America of course had a large population that could read German books in the original as a result of immigration and education. Some of the works examined below were also reprinted in German in the United States in German-language newspapers and in book editions for an immigrant population and were available in the original German at public libraries and even on newsstands from coast to coast. Moreover, some popular literature by women—Wilhelmine von Hillern's *Höher als die Kirche*, for instance—was edited for the purpose of teaching German in American schools and colleges. Teachers considered popular literature more likely to appeal to a young audience than weightier German writing, thus providing an attractive payoff for learning conjugations and declensions.

Reading German in the original in America is, however, precisely not what stands at the center of my investigation; the books that figure here are German books read in translation. My project thus concentrates on nineteenth-century American enjoyment of a hybrid product, hybrid because it came to the consumer altered by a process of Americanization. Americanization refers in my usage to "the processes . . . by which Americans took up, responded to, and adapted German cultural material for their own purposes," that is, the "creative adaptation" of these books as they were translated, published, and marketed. While in twentieth-century German studies "Americanization" signifies the flow of American ideas, values, and products into Europe, here Americanization refers to the "productive re-signification, transformation, or re-packaging of German ideas, values, and products in the United States."[49] I examine these processes even as I also consider the degree to which these translated books could and still did register with the reading public as German. In short, I demonstrate how the translating, marketing, reviewing, and reading of this material could de-center and disrupt the national while still transferring certain elements of national culture. Furthermore, I trace how Americanization of German-authored works in a market culture destabilized authorship. Indeed, books in translation invite us to rethink cherished notions of "individualism and individual creativity," calling into question the "empathic celebration of a narrowly interpreted uniqueness and originality."[50]

IN THE NINETEENTH century the United States notoriously reprinted foreign books. McGill has outlined the American defense of the system of reprinting and the identification of print with public property in the nineteenth century, particularly as articulated in the years 1835–53.[51] No law recognizing the principle of international copyright was passed in the United States until 1891, and indeed, no law with teeth until 1909.[52] In the absence of a legal obligation to honor the rights of foreign authors and publishers, enterprising American publishers could exploit reprints of books by foreign authors to feed the demand in the United States for novels.

Whatever their intrinsic appeal and merit, in this print landscape English novels were especially desirable to publishers as they needed only to be reprinted and repackaged for the American reading public and thus potentially involved no author's royalties or translator's honorarium. By the 1860s Great Britain had long been a source of fiction in the form of American (pirated) reprints. While publishers continued to reprint British favorites to expand their catalogues and profit from Americans' wish for leisure-time reading, some publishers also sought a fresh product in new fiction originally written in languages besides English. Thus Germany began unwittingly to supply America with stories, stories both oddly familiar and pleasantly foreign.

Some American pundits viewed the reading and expanding publication of foreign fiction—including fiction from Great Britain—with suspicion, even alarm, warning against the noxious effects of this foreign entertainment. In effect, they cautioned against what we now call "soft power," that is, the potential of the attractiveness of entertainment for "shaping the preferences of others."[53] In 1887 Brander Matthews, for example, objected in nationalist tones: "It is not wholesome . . . for the future of the American people that the books easiest to get, and therefore most widely read, should be written wholly by foreigners . . . who cannot help accepting and describing the surviving results of feudalism and the social inequalities we tried to do away with once."[54] Germany, as portrayed in these novels, did capture reader attention with its enduring aristocratic privilege and crumbling castles, yet it remains to be seen whether the values thus transmitted differed radically from Americans' own.

Beginning in the 1880s, imperial Germany generated an unparalleled supply of books for American publishers to mine. By 1910, thirty-nine years after unification, Germany could boast 31,281 book titles published in a single year, an output that far surpassed that of other leading industrial nations—for example, France at 12,615, England at 10,804, and the United States at 13,470.[55] In 1913, a year before the outbreak of the First World War in Europe, Germany led the world with 34,871 titles published in a single year.[56] Literature constituted a significant subgroup of these titles. Of the 14,941 books published in Germany in 1880, 1,521 belonged to the category that included fiction, "schöne Literatur" (*belles lettres*), that is, 10.2% of the total output; by 1910, that percentage had risen to 13.2% of 31,281 books, a total of 4,134 titles.[57]

In the Gilded Age in the United States, meanwhile, English works maintained their sizable lead in imported entertainment in the United States, yet the American market also experienced a significant influx of books from Germany, the number of translations from German "humane letters" into English climbing to the three peak years of 1882, 1887, and 1901, each of which logged more than 140 titles. In 1914 translations from German reached a record prewar high of more than 180.[58] "More than 140 titles" was a significant number in these decades. A comparison of Tebbel's and Morgan's figures from 1882, for example, yields a rough estimation of new English-language editions of German humane letters as 7% of American literary publication.[59] This first peak in 1882 may register the impact of the general growth of the German book industry on American translation and publishing: the previous year, 1881, marked a forty-two-year high in German book production with 15,191 titles.[60]

Translations of fiction by the seventeen women who figure in my study constitute a highly visible part of the American boom in German humane letters in translation. Figure 1.1 represents the centered five-year moving averages (each bar represents the average of the corresponding year, the two years immediately preceding it, and the two immediately following it) of the total per year of first-time book publication in the United States of translations by these seventeen authors.[61] As Figure 1.1 indicates, the appearance of these novels in American translation began with a burst in the late 1860s. Translation and publishing of them thereafter moved forward fitfully with a sharp rise just over twenty years later, then dropped off rapidly at the end of the new century, and nearly ceased altogether after 1903. The greatest translation activity clustered in the long decade centered in 1890–91. Figure 1.2 represents the centered five-year moving averages of the number of total book publications (discrete editions of new American translations and American reprints of translations) of these novels per year in the United States.[62] As this bar graph makes clear, the publication and reprinting of translations endured a decade longer (1885–1914) than did translation of new works by these authors, with peaks in the early 1890s and especially the first years of the new century. Figure 1.2, however, only provides a partial picture of the proliferation of reprints since it cannot take account of the undated editions and reprints produced over these years. When undated editions are included, numbers rise significantly. For example, of the 101 discrete editions and reprint editions of *The Old Mam'selle's Secret* that I have been able

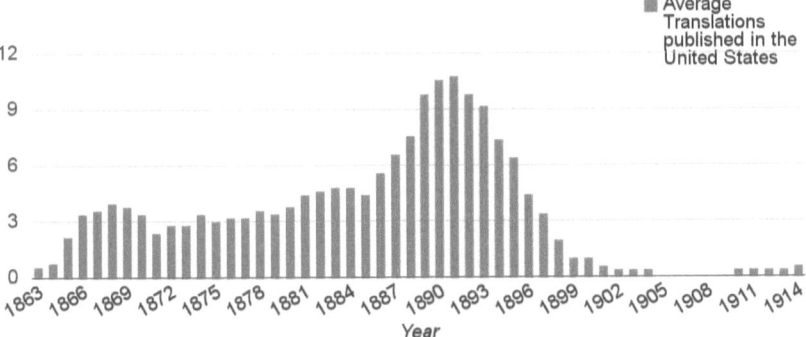

Figure 1.1 Centered Moving Averages of the Total Number of New Translations of German Novels by the 17 Women in the Dataset Published in the United States

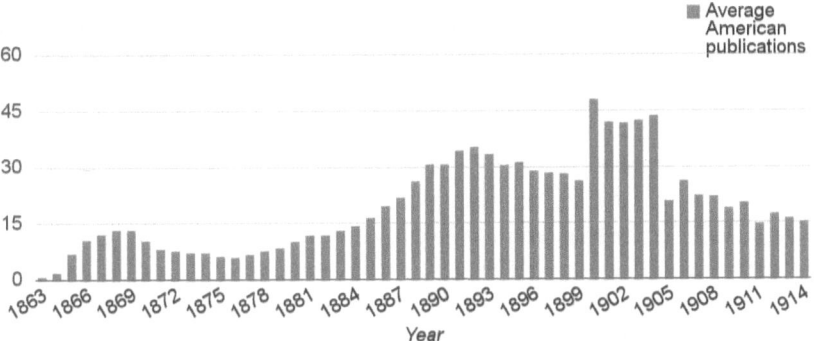

Figure 1.2 Centered Moving Averages of U.S. Publications (New Translations, New Editions, and Reprint Editions) of German Novels by the 17 Women in the Dataset

to document, forty-eight have no date and therefore play no role in the tallies in Figure 1.2.

Below, closer examination of the ramified publishing history of individual novels offers a more articulated view of the high profile and broad availability of German novels by women in this period that cannot be adequately conveyed by numbers alone. As will become clear, the names of many of these novels and their women authors, even their translators, were household words with nineteenth-century American readers. This closer scrutiny of the fate of specific works in the United States will also explain some of the lows and highs in the bar graphs shown in Figures 1.1 and 1.2. The peaks in the late 1860s indicated in Figure 1.1, for example, mark the rapid translation of eighteen novels by Luise Mühlbach, some of which had been written in the previous decade, and the translation of two best-selling novels by E. Marlitt, one of which had first appeared three years earlier; that is, Americans translated successful novels that had, as it were, accumulated. Thereafter, translation of the domestic fiction by German women included in my dataset tended to occur soon after the first publication of these novels in Germany either as serializations or as books. The spikes in translation around 1890, as a further example, have in part to do with the slightly belated discovery by American translators and publishers of Wilhelmine Heimburg and the rapid translation of several of her hitherto untapped novels.

The presence of German novels of all kinds was in any case duly noted by the "literary system," to use Andre Lefevere's term for the broader cultural context in which translation occurs, and specifically by the culture of reviewing books and commenting on reading.[63] So prominent were German novels in English translation in postbellum America that the *Christian Examiner* asserted in 1869: "The most popular of all romances, historical, local, of costume and of character, of life in the city and life in the country, are translations from the German."[64] The translations of novels from German, he further maintained, had begun to dissipate a "delusion about German literature," namely, that German novels were "generally dull enough to make the romances of James even brilliant in the comparison and that to read one of them was such a punishment as Lowell assigns to murderers in his 'Fable for Critics,'—'hard labor for life.'"[65] In short, Americans liked them. In 1874 another reviewer confirmed the American liking for this foreign fiction when he grumbled, "still [*The Second Wife*] is from the German, and will be read."[66]

In 1895 the *New York Ledger* maintained that German women writers had proven to be the equals of their British and American female counterparts. While *The Ledger* here named women whose works would later belong to the German literary canon (e.g., Marie von Ebner-Eschenbach and Annette von Droste-Hülshoff) as well as prominent women writers whose work was recovered in the twentieth century by second-wave feminist scholars (e.g., Fanny Lewald), the article also honored popular authors. Four German women authors in particular had provided an "exceedingly large public bright and agreeable reading, even if it may be deficient in depth." Marlitt was "the first of the coterie," along with E. Werner, Wilhelmine Heimburg, and Nataly von Eschstruth: "Their novels which form a miniature library by themselves have the knack of interesting readers—a trait which is so often absent in weightier works." Furthermore, the reviewer maintained, their popularity was attested by their availability in English translation.[67] In other words, American readers had received these German novels warmly, despite what the critics might have had to say about their literary merit.

BEFORE WE TURN to the authors, books, and texts, some final considerations concerning foreignness and its impact on reading are in order, especially since foreignness always remains to some degree in the eye of the beholder. In present-day North America, the case for translating literature into English tends to be based not in assertions of the universality of foreign texts but in deeply held beliefs about the importance of engagement with the Other or, as Edith Grossman advocates in *Why Translation Matters*, to free us from "our tendency toward insularity and consequent self-imposed isolation" and to "explore through literature the thoughts and feelings from another society or another time. It permits us to savor the transformation of the foreign into the familiar and for a brief time to live outside our own skins, our own preconceptions and misconceptions."[68] This argument, however appealing, perforce raises the question as to how consciously real readers register the Other when they read fiction in translation. Popular literature in particular may lack or at least lose its national markers when it is read and enjoyed abroad: "under a certain level," Ridley observes, "popular literature loses any element of national reference and shows itself to be not only international in conception and production, but also both at home in and foreign to every culture within which it is read."[69] "Transformation of the foreign into the familiar" may therefore be as much a process of appropriating the foreign as acknowledging it.

In what sense, then, does reading a translated text force an engagement with the Other if that other has already been made less foreign through the very process of translation and through subsequent widespread reading and acceptance in a given culture? The degree of engagement necessarily depends on the occasion for reading, the nature of the reader, her education, experience, and reading socialization, and her predisposition toward the cultural information that is mediated in a given text as well as on the cultural surround, the packaging, marketing, and reviewing of the translation.

Current translation theory and practice distinguish between translations that naturalize the original by striving for as fluent a rendering as possible, that is, texts that mask or minimize their foreign origins, and translations that in some respect attempt to preserve the linguistic foreignness and cultural distance of the original. Lawrence Venuti, for one, has famously argued for "foreignized" translations, translations that deliberately render the translated text alien.[70] Yet while translators can, through their choices, attempt to influence readers' perceptions of and intellectual engagement with the culture of origin, they cannot control them. As Mary Kelley, Kate Flint, Barbara Sicherman, and other historians of books and reading have demonstrated, real readers have done different things with books and made various meanings with them. In Kelley's words, "in the space between reader and text, they produced pluralities of meanings."[71]

While nineteenth-century women translators did not translate with the idea of programmatically highlighting linguistic and cultural foreignness favored by Venuti, there certainly are differences in the translations. These differences range from Annis Lee Wister's charming preservation of linguistic features of German—deliberate or not—to Mary Stuart Smith's competent renderings, to obvious misreadings, to clumsy verbatim translations that suggest a lack of versatility in English. Likewise important to the American perception of these novels as foreign were paratextual markers and the literary system in which the books circulated. For a variety of reasons that we shall explore below, the translations occupied different places on a spectrum of foreignness that changed over the course of time.

Nineteenth-century reviews, marketing, advertising, library cataloging, and advice on reading make clear that nineteenth-century American readers could read and were encouraged to understand the "German" in the fiction under scrutiny here variously. German could guarantee German settings, indicating that the novels provided a picture of German history or contemporary life in Germany. In its day, Griswold's above-mentioned *Descriptive List*, for example, asserted and valorized the function of novels to mediate "German life." More subtly, German could indicate to Americans that the novels were rooted in specific values or in a specific mindset or that they reflected taste. American reviews in fact sometimes base clumsy and opinionated attempts to formulate what these elements of Germanness might be in reductive reading of the novels. There is, furthermore, evidence that the designation "German" could serve as a guarantee of a good read—even of a happy ending—because that story was "made in Germany."

Despite the apparent national specificity of the label "German," some readers may have read some of this fiction merely as vaguely "not from here," that is, as European, and thus merely just a little—and thus pleasantly and harmlessly—exotic. At the same time, the more popular the books became, the more frequently they were read, and the more widely available they were as "English fiction," the more they became a part of American horizons, the facts of American culture, and thus less German stories than American entertainment. What, then, remained legible to influence readers' ideas of Germany?

These novels by women were originally written by Germans for Germans in a period of consolidation of German national identity. In Germany the national cultural, often patriotic, references were manifest; abroad, much less so. In considering these translated German texts as repackaged American entertainment, I examine images of Germans and Germany at stages of removal. While most of the novels rendered for American audiences betrayed their German origins in some respect—through their content or their packaging—the ability of American readers (even German Americans) to read a work in translation as did German readers the original was necessarily limited. Nevertheless—and this point was critical to the popularity of this German fiction in America—Americans could experience the pleasure of reading, follow a romance plot, or comprehend a moral lesson without possessing a strong sense of the local historical meanings of a given text. In the end, they could associate what they gathered from their reading with a place called Germany, whether or not their understanding had any basis in fact.

Yet, from the start, some texts invested more than others in urging a sense of place with its attendant history upon readers. Chapter 6 examines eleven such novels, in which German history insistently figures, and proposes what the texts might have communicated to Americans about Germany. However, it is also possible that many readers persistently read past what was for them unintelligible cultural material and instead picked up on elements that resonated more immediately with their own situation and values; in short, their reading may have had more to do with living happily in America than with learning about Germany. We shall thus have repeated occasion to consider the balance between domestication and foreign encounter in reading.

If foreignness depends, as I assert, in part on the eye of the beholder, we must also interrogate the beholder. Who were the Americans who read these nearly one hundred German novels in translation? I will be concerned with readership throughout and yet will not be able to answer questions about readership with complete certainty. Nevertheless, as will become clear, my research overwhelmingly indicates that the translations were marketed to a general Anglophone audience (and not to a niche market consisting of ethnic Germans). They were sold in international lists alongside American, British, and French favorites by mainstream and cheap publishers and reviewed in mainstream periodicals by reviewers who wrote from vantages outside of German and German-American culture. These books circulated, in the terms of one American advertisement from 1902, as "standard books for everybody."[72] Even Annis Lee Wister's translations, the set that was routinely advertised as "from the German," were repeatedly touted not as books for people interested in Germany per se but as entertaining books from Germany that had been Americanized so as to appeal to *American* reading tastes. None of the three translators whose activity will be examined in chapters 7–9 was ethnically German, and none of them anywhere remarks on ethnic Germans and certainly not as their potential audience.

Did, however, the massive German emigration to the United States in the nineteenth century make a difference in the circulation and popularity of this reading material? It would be hard to imagine that it did not at some level. For one thing, the above-mentioned import and publication in America of books in the German language meant that American translators had ready access to fiction in German to translate. Wister and her sister translators combed, for example, the popular German family magazine *Die Gartenlaube,* which circulated widely in the United States, for stories likely to appeal to their American audiences. The cheap editions of Munro's Deutsche Library, inaugurated in 1881 and aimed at German readers in America and available "at any news stand for a few cents," as a further example, provided Mary Stuart Smith and her son Harry with the German texts from which to translate for the Seaside Library.[73]

It may be useful to reflect on Munro's Deutsche Library as a source upon which publishers wishing to cater to the taste of ethnic Germans with works in English translation could have drawn. Forty of the 236 novels in Munro's Deutsche Library overlap with the ninety-six novels by German women in my dataset. The remainder of 196 works of fiction, eleven of which are international novels translated *into* German and 145 of which are German novels never translated into English, suggests that if the American publishers of the novels in my dataset had wished to target an ethnic German audience with German books in translation, they would and could have offered a much larger and more diverse set of novels; the genre would by no means have been confined to domestic fiction.[74] The presence of eleven novels in German translation in the Deutsche Library, moreover, underlines yet again that the reading preferences of a particular ethnic group or nation are not uniformly determined by the point of origin of the fiction in question.

Did Americans of German descent comprise a fraction of the reading audience for this translated fiction by German women? No doubt they did, given that between 1870 and 1910, the number of German-born Americans fluctuated between 2.7 and 4.5% of the total U.S. population, and in 1910, moreover, 4.2% of the total American-born population claimed two parents born in Germany.⁷⁵ However, since these *translated* novels overtly target a *general* reading public, there is little reason to assume that Anglophone Americans of German descent flocked to them more than they did to beloved English-language novels of a similar ilk. Of the 147 borrowers of the Public Library of Muncie, Indiana, who checked out *The Old Mam'selle's Secret* (1891–1902) and for whom census data exists, only five had a parent born in a German-speaking country; two additional borrowers were born in German-speaking countries, Germany and Switzerland. In the aggregate, the other books checked out by these seven borrowers indicate no special preference for books that were German in origin.⁷⁶

Given the complicated and diverse ways in which ethnic origin can shape the preferences of succeeding generations, it is impossible to know whether the descendent of a German family that emigrated to the United States in the 1830s chose in the 1880s to read a "romance after the German" because it was German or because it was romantic. But who was ethnic German, anyway?

The surname of the book owner Amanda A. Durff, for example, may appear to be German. What, however, does this putatively German name signify about Amanda's reading preferences, and what does it say about her affiliation with a specific ethnic group in the 1880s and 1890s? Amanda may have been the daughter of a father of German descent or the wife of a man of German descent. Neither possibility necessarily equates to a specific interest in things German on her part. But perhaps "Durff" is not German at all, but Swiss, or Austrian. Perhaps it originates in another language group altogether or is a corruption of, for example, Durfee. In short, it is impossible to determine what the surname signifies in the case of this particular book owner. The feminine given name may, however, be more telling, as it corresponds, in the gender codes of the time, to the hearts and flowers covers of the books Amanda acquired. There were in short other, more compelling personal reasons than ethnic origin for American readers to pick up, read, and reread these books in the years 1866–1917.

Indeed, while there is little in the marketing and packaging of these translations signaling their target audience as ethnic Germans, there is ample evidence to conclude that women and girls constituted their chief readers in the United States. This female readership will become ever more visible as we examine the packaging and marketing of particular books, exemplars of books with dedications and signatures, the activity of the women translators, and the character of the books as material objects. Of the dozens of signed books I have examined, very few show signs of male ownership. Even the ambiguous "Billy Phelps," the name of the owner of one such book, just as likely refers to a woman as a man.⁷⁷

Nevertheless, despite compelling evidence of a largely female readership, I do not mean to assert that women and girls were the only readers, especially of the earliest American translations of novels by Luise Mühlbach, E. Marlitt, E. Werner, and Wilhelmine von Hillern in the 1860s and 1870s. Some readers can of course always enjoy novels targeted at the opposite sex. As late as 1900, "Nelle" presented a copy of *The Old Mam'selle's Secret* to "Uncle Jay" for Christmas.[78] Indeed, both men and women borrowed German women's fiction in translation from the Muncie Public Library (1891–1902).[79] The books themselves were reviewed and advertised in periodicals that provided reading material for both men and women and even in periodicals such as the *Medical Age*, whose target audience was most certainly male. While journals aimed principally at men might have included reviews of these books to suggest to their male readers what books to buy for women, the reviews themselves are not overtly framed in terms of a gendered readership, though such ideas may be implicit, for example, in remarks about the sentimentality of the content. In the case of the historical novels of Luise Mühlbach, it is certain that both men and women read these books. As I note in chapter 7, one of Mühlbach's translators sent her work to Ulysses S. Grant, Robert E. Lee, and Andrew Johnson, assuming the interest of prominent men in them. Mary Chesnut records in her diary her husband General Chesnut's reading of Mühlbach's *Joseph II and His Court*.[80] Still, in 1873 the *New York Herald* characterized Mühlbach's readership back in Germany as "tender-hearted" women.[81]

"A Matter of Taste," from Edith Wyatt's collection of Chicago stories from 1901, provides a vivid snapshot of reading predilection along the fault line of gender and ethnicity, expressed specifically in terms of some of the German books at the center of my investigation and anticipating the argument I will make throughout about the special emotional appeal to American women of this set of novels from Germany. In "A Matter of Taste" an Anglo-American brother-sister pair view one another's taste in reading with incomprehension. The pretentious Henry Norris reads foreign literature about the Italian Renaissance aloud to his bored sister Elsie, who in such moments feels that life could not be more vacuous. Elsie, who, the narrator ironically notes with a dig at the snobbish Henry, "had no Standard," longs instead for *The Old Mam'selle's Secret*.[82] In her preference for Marlitt, Elsie shares the taste of her German friend who lives nearby, the sentimental and musical Ottilie Bhaer, who is reading Marlitt in the original German: *Das Geheimnis der alten Mam'sell* and *Die zweite Frau*. In Henry's view Ottilie too has no Standard. Henry and Elsie must quietly reconcile themselves to their differences, realizing that "in a various world every one has need of a great deal of patience."[83]

The affinity between American and German women's reading so gently portrayed in Wyatt's short story raises one final question concerning foreignness that must be addressed up front, namely, whether this set of German novels supplied readers with something that fiction migrating to America from France, Spain, Italy, and other non-English-speaking European countries could not or at least did not. A review of two lists of fiction popular in America strongly suggests that this set of German novels in translation did stand apart from other foreign fiction. In 1876 the *Publishers' Weekly* assembled a list of 204 novels deemed by American publishers as the most salable.[84] Most of the novels included are English and American. Of the nine German novels named, seven are domestic fiction by women. The twelve French novels on the list comprise works by five male authors—Eugène Sue, Alexandre Dumas (père), Victor Hugo, Jules Verne, and Alain-René Lesage (*Gil Blas*)—and two women—the by-then standard author Germaine de Staël and George Sand. The only other foreign works to appear are Andersen's fairytales (Denmark) and *Don Quixote*, both staples of international reading. The only foreign novels in translation ranking higher than the German *Old Mam'selle's Secret* (No. 23) and *The Second Wife* (No. 27) are Dumas's *Count of Monte Cristo* (No. 13) and Hugo's *Les Miserables* (No. 20). This list appeared ten years into the period under scrutiny here and thus could not take full account of the book publishing landscape that eventually developed. A second, late-century list of popular literature gives a better sense of what was to come.

Munro's popular Seaside Library of more than two thousand works, including mainly American and British novels, provides a compelling snapshot of the European literature that Americans liked. Novels by Wilhelmine Heimburg, Fanny Lewald, Marlitt, Mühlbach, and Werner make up the majority of the German books on the list (Goethe is represented only by the play *Faust*).[85] A review of French authors included in the Seaside Library—Dumas, Verne, Balzac, Hugo, Sue, Gaboriau, Gautier, Aimard, Feuillet, Daudet, Cherbuliez, Droz, du Boisgobey, and Ohnet—reveals that 1) in contrast to the German authors, they are all men, both standard and newly popular; 2) their novels for the most part operate in genres different from the domestic fiction by German women included on the list—science fiction, adventure, historical novel, the "mystery literature" of Sue, detective novel—and 3) on the whole, they offer much racier stuff. We find only a small handful of additional foreign authors in translation, all but one of them staples of late-century international reading and all of them men. These books include works by Cervantes and Andersen as well as the Norwegian author Bjørnstjerne Bjørnson, the Italian Alessandro Manzoni's *The*

Betrothed, two novels by the prolific Polish novelist Józef Ignacy Kraszewski, and surprisingly a couple of novels by the Dutch (and rather obscure) Carl Vosmaer. Other publishers' lists from the late nineteenth century present a similar picture. If there was French or other foreign fiction resembling the popular fiction by German women, it did not make it to the United States in translation in a highly visible way.

I REMAIN ATTACHED to texts and accord them considerable space in this study. Yet I have informed and constructed my central avenues of investigation with attention to Robert Darnton's "communications circuit" and thus to the broad context in which books are produced and read.[86] Darnton's schema conceives of the life cycle of the printed book in terms of the convergence of cultural, social, and economic pressures and networks, that is, as a fraught passage from the author to the publisher, the printer, the shippers, the booksellers, and the readers, each step of which influences the others, including the author's future production. Translation expands the cycle of production and circulation. I am therefore mindful of the broader context of translating, reading, and publishing and think about the book not only as carrying and shaping texts but also as an object subject to economies of materials, production, and consumption and vice versa.[87] In other words, in contributing to the history of reading in nineteenth-century America and of cultural transfer via that reading, I look at my objects of study both as commoditized books *and* as texts requiring interpretation and offer a braided analysis informed by the combined approaches of book history and literary criticism and theory. In so doing, I pursue many of the strategies proposed by Darnton in 1986 for a history of reading, that is, the making of meaning from reading. I study assumptions about reading by examining advertisements and marketing ploys. I examine physical evidence of historical reading, for example, inscriptions within novels that indicate how sentimental bonds were formed via books and reading. I employ textual criticism and reception theory to analyze the books and the translator's adaptations. I evaluate autobiographical accounts of reading and translating. I look at the book as a physical object, at covers, title pages, formats, and illustrations. I consider the numbers of translations of individual books and their availability in public libraries. I also survey reviews as a component of the literary system in which the books are read, and I situate the reading of these books within its social historical context.[88] I have also relied on the rich scholarship in women and gender studies, which has redirected scholarly attention to the marginalized and the popular and encouraged us to think more complexly about what may, on the surface of it, seem obvious or simple. I have generally avoided hypothesizing a monolithic "woman reader" and instead made visible that this set of books was open to different readings (and misreading) in translation. I have been mindful, too, of the fact that they were read differently as tastes changed.[89] But, as I shall argue, these novels did acquire a recognizable profile in America and appealed to and cultivated readers, largely women and girls, who developed a liking for them.

My study consists of three parts. The first section, to which this introduction belongs, along with chapter 2, introduces the principal popular German women authors who were translated in Gilded Age America, the social and economic conditions of women writers in the German territories—and later the empire—in that period, and the role of the liberal family magazine *Die Gartenlaube* in providing opportunity for these women writers and shaping their fiction and ultimately American reading of it. In this first section I supply information that contributes preliminarily to "distant reading" of the American publication and translation of approximately one hundred German novels in America and provide a characterization of these novels in the aggregate as domestic fiction.[90]

The central section, chapters 3–6, examines thirty-three representative novels. These chapters combine close reading of texts in translation with descriptive analysis of books as industrial products and material objects to parse American reception, namely, what the novels offered that attracted and satisfied readers and what they could in turn take away from their reading as specific to German national culture. Chapter 3 focuses on three novels by the perennially popular E. Marlitt and their penetration of reading culture in the United States. *Gold Elsie* and *The Old Mam'selle's Secret* helped initiate the vogue of German novels by women and shaped American expectations of these imports. I examine them both as pleasurable reading that combines the titillation of secrets and delayed gratification with "wholesome" messages concerning the practice of virtue and the expression of female subjectivity within domesticity. These novels conform to international, generic expectations of domestic fiction and romance even as they are steeped in German cultural information, having been written originally for a venue supporting German unification and the consolidation of German national identity. A third novel by Marlitt, *In the Schillingscourt*, relies on American characters and stereotypes rooted in Confederate Nationalism and myths of the Lost Cause to construct a German national imaginary. Its entry into American culture presents a rich occasion for considering mutual intelligibility, misapprehension, appropriation, and assimilation. Although it reproduces patterns familiar from the two earlier novels, it also exhibits deviations in the romance plot that captured Americans' attention.

Chapter 4 examines German novels as American reading from the perspective of the happy ending, an international signature of romance novels and of nearly all of the German novels by women in my dataset. The chapter uncovers and analyzes variations in plotting ritual death and recovery to a state of freedom that characterize these German novels and that appealed to American readers by offering them the vicarious experience of a multiplicity of female subjectivities and female-determined male subjectivities while cautiously expanding the boundaries of home in a place called Germany. I combine analysis of texts with examination of exemplars of books and the history of the book publication of each translated text.

In chapter 5 I identify and describe a significant subset that, paraphrasing Stanley Cavell, I have labeled the novel of remarriage. Deviating from the codes of romance that prescribe unmarried protagonists, these novels feature married—or sometimes betrothed—couples, tracing their breakup and reconciliation as a paean to marriage calibrated to female happiness and agency. The restored marriages project matrimony as emotionally satisfying while also economically beneficial and critical to the stability of the social order. Both men and women achieve maturity over the course of marital strife, the female characters playing a critical role in the reeducation of both sexes and the management of domestic prosperity and felicity. Close reading and book-historical analysis of ten examples, combined with examination of specific exemplars (covers, format, and inscriptions), demonstrate the variations within the genre and their American appeal.

Constructions of masculinity and German ethnicity figure centrally in chapter 6. The chapter examines how domesticated men make of German history family history and how in turn national history makes domesticated men both in Mühlbach's historical romances, set in the seventeenth and eighteenth centuries, and in novels by Heimburg and Werner featuring critical historical events of the 1840s, 1860s, and 1870s. Here I raise anew the question of the legibility of the national context of origin and examine the pleasures afforded postbellum Americans by reading fictions of family crises and national tensions that find satisfying resolution as a result of women's interventions.

The final section, chapters 7–9, focuses on cultural agents and the making of meaning and consists of three case studies of American translators (and their publishers) who together were responsible for nearly seventy widely circulating translations of German women's fiction: Ann Mary Coleman, Annis

Lee Wister, and Mary Stuart Smith. Here I reconstruct their cultural labor, their public life in print, and the importance of translation to their lives and sense of self and family. In each case a well-educated daughter of a prominent father found her way to translation as a socially acceptable positioning between domesticity and public life that allowed her to profit from her education and culture. Economic necessity in the wake of the American Civil War pushed the two southerners, Coleman and Smith, to translate but in the end did not entirely define their labors. After the Civil War and the death of her famous father, Senator J. J. Crittenden, Coleman, who, unlike her father, was a southern sympathizer, used her translations to remake connections and regain access to men of power and social circles. Through translation outside of academia with publishing companies that sprang up as the American book trade industrialized and cultivated mass audiences, Smith, a university wife, daughter, and granddaughter, realized ambition that was not encouraged at the all-male University of Virginia on whose Lawn she was born, lived, and died. In the north, the well-situated and publicity-shy Wister, daughter of a famous abolitionist minister, found in translated popular fiction an outlet for her considerable drive and intellect, even as her brother Horace Howard Furness edited Shakespeare and her brother Frank made a name for himself as one of Philadelphia's leading architects. Ultimately her labor gave birth to a vogue of German novels, and she became perhaps the best-known translator in Gilded Age America.

These translators were also readers. Their translations constitute exemplary instances of making meaning from reading and bear eloquent testimony to the American consumption of popular literature by German women. Coleman, Wister, and Smith had views about the books they selected, views that played a role in determining what German fiction reached Americans and how it was read. Analysis of these views provides a parting, illuminating glance at the assimilation of German novels by women into the North American imaginary as women expanded the boundaries of domesticity.

CHAPTER 2

German Women Writers at Home and Abroad

---·⊛·---

THE NORTH AMERICAN APPETITE for entertaining German "romances" was well supplied in the last four decades of the nineteenth century, for despite virulent and enduring prejudice in Germany against women and their artistic endeavors, German women writers of popular fiction had begun to flourish, fostered by changing political, social, and economic conditions. By the end of the nineteenth century, the industrialization of publishing and the emergence of mass markets had made possible the phenomenon of the self-supporting woman writer in the German-speaking world.[1] From 1865 to 1879 women's magazines, family magazines, and *belles lettres* experienced a 202.8% growth as a result of an increase in overall reading and women's reading and writing in particular.[2]

The popular family magazine *Die Gartenlaube* cheerfully maintained in 1876 that in Germany prose fiction was unquestionably the "natural" territory of "female production." "It is to be feared," the author asserted, "that if all the notable authors of today were assembled it wouldn't be possible to come up with even one gentleman for each lady."[3] A quarter of a century later, in 1902, Rudolf von Gottschall, who, unlike many German male authors of such national histories, devoted considerable space to women's writing, acknowledged women's significant production of novels as a part of Germany's "national literature." Yet while Gottschall offered a more appreciative assessment than most of his male contemporaries, he shared some of the common assumptions and prejudices of his times. He observed, for example, in condescending tones that the novel of contemporary life was suitable terrain for "women's more passive and reproductive talent."[4]

In America *Lippincott's Magazine* also recognized the growing prominence of women in German fiction writing, observing in 1873 that in Germany the novel had been chiefly cultivated with success by women "whose delineations have gained a popularity in America only less than that which they enjoy at home—in part because the life which they depict has closer internal analogies to our own than to that of England or of France." These depictions themselves appealed, moreover, because they were "suffused with a romantic glow which has long since faded from those of the thoroughly realistic art now dominant in the two latter countries."[5] The magazine might have added here that Americans were accustomed to reading and enjoying novels by women; women had written nearly three-fourths of the American novels published in the previous year.[6]

Four women writers, who number among the most frequently translated German authors of any kind in the nineteenth century, figure prominently in my account of translation and transnational reading. They include three popular authors who established their reputations with fiction serialized in *Die Gartenlaube:* E. Werner, whom Henry A. Pochmann identifies as ranking ninth among all German authors translated into English in the nineteenth century, E. Marlitt, who ranks fifteenth, and W. Heimburg, who ranks twenty-third. Luise Mühlbach, the tenth most frequently translated German author in this period in Pochmann's tally, also merits attention, her "historical romances" embodying an important related genre of popular fiction that in allegedly writing German history laid claim to a certain pretension as well. A fifth author, Wilhelmine von Hillern, likewise deserves a closer look up front. Hillern's novels crossed boundaries with respect to their contents, venues of publication, and reception. In Pochmann's groupings of translated German authors according to genre, Werner, Mühlbach, Marlitt, and Heimburg occupy four of the five top spots under the rubric "lesser fiction and prose writers."[7] Hillern follows in eighth place. Ahead of Werner and Mühlbach in the general rankings is a mix of highbrow and popular male authors: Goethe, Schiller, the Grimm Brothers, Richard Wagner, three juvenile authors (Christoph von Schmid, and Johann David Wyss and Johann Rudolf Wyss, the author and reviser, respectively, of *The Swiss Family Robinson*), Baron de la Motte Fouqué, whose story of the water sprite *Undine* was a perennial favorite, and the explorer-scientist Alexander von Humboldt, who, as Kirsten Belgum has observed, was an international figure who came to be adopted as an *American* national icon.[8]

The novels of eleven additional authors also figure in this study: those of Marie Bernhard (1852–1937), Nataly von Eschstruth (1860–1939), Claire von Glümer (1825–1906), E. Hartner (pseud. of Emma Eva Henriette von Twardowska [1845–89]), E. Juncker (pseud. of Else [Kobert] Schmieden

[1841–96]), Fanny Lewald (1811–89), Ursula Zöge von Manteuffel (pseud. of Frau von Trebra-Lindenau, 1850–1910), Golo Raimund (pseud. of Bertha [Heyn] Frederich [1825–82]), Moritz von Reichenbach (pseud. of Valeska von Reiswitz, Gräfin von Bethusy-Huc [1848–1926]), Hedwig Harnisch Schobert (1858–1919),[9] and Julie Adeline Volckhausen (1823–93). In four cases represented by a single novel, they were translated, marketed, and read in America alongside Marlitt, Werner, Heimburg, Mühlbach, and Hillern. The works of these less-translated authors resemble those of Marlitt, Werner, and Heimburg, testifying to the emergence of a German genre in America and to strategic mining by American publishers and translators of German publications for novels likely to please the American palate that publishers and translators had cultivated with the more successful German women authors. One final author, whose works are included in my tallies, joined this identifiable group late in the century: Ossip Schubin (pseud. of Aloisia Kirschner [1854–34]). Although an Austrian by birth, Kirschner published her novels in imperial Germany, and they arrived in America, translated by, among others, Annis Lee Wister and packaged much like the others.

Born for the most part between 1810 and 1855, these seventeen authors belonged to two generations that benefited from the bourgeoning book trade in Germany, a historical moment that enabled greater numbers of both men and women to enter print culture. Far from securing a place in the canon of writers deemed important by literary scholars, however, most of these seventeen writers are wedged in time and in literary historical scholarship uncomfortably between such now recovered, quasi-canonical older women authors with intellectual pretension as Dorothea Schlegel (1764–1839), Rachel Varnhagen (1771–1833), and Bettina von Arnim (1775–1859) and such protofeminist and feminist authors of a slightly younger generation as Gabriele Reuter (1859–1941) and Helene Böhlau (1856–1940). In 1911 the *Encyclopaedia Britannica* identified Reuter and Böhlau as the authors of "some of the best fiction of the most recent period," yet at that time none of their important works had been rendered into English.[10] Most of the novels of Marlitt, Werner, Heimburg, and Mühlbach, by contrast, had been translated and repeatedly reprinted and were still being read in America in the new century.

Clara Mundt / Luise Mühlbach (1814–73)

In May 1873 Luise Mühlbach, who was by then well known in the United States for her historical fiction, promised to serve as a foreign correspondent to the *New York Herald* on the occasion of the World Exhibition in Vienna.

The *Herald* reminded its readers of Mühlbach's importance in Germany and hence of her suitability to her present task, effusing, "Where is the boudoir in that land of philosophy and music where some tender-hearted woman has not shed tears over the loves of Frederick and Joseph? Where is the young school girl who has not dreamed of some hero with 'flaming eyes' and all that perfection of manly beauty with which every lover is endowed by Luise Mühlbach?" In feminizing history, the *Herald* noted approvingly, Mühlbach had made it more accessible.[11] While Mühlbach herself tended to speak merely of her readership and not women readers per se, the *Herald* accurately identified the tendency of her novels to foreground romance and reasonably supposed that women—as readers of fiction—made up a significant percentage of her readers on both sides of the Atlantic.[12]

Mühlbach was a prolific writer, ever more driven in later life by the need to support two daughters, her mother-in-law, and her own liberal spending habits. In his bibliography of her works, Brent O. Peterson lists more than sixty separate items, many of whose parts and volumes each amount to full-length novels.[13] A contemporary remarked that she once filled an entire bookshelf of the lending libraries with twelve volumes in a single year, and the American poet and translator Bayard Taylor maintained in 1869 that her works to that date amounted to "more than sixty volumes."[14] Even Otto Heller conceded her "considerable talent," but then criticized her "ruinously facile pen" that catered to "the shallow taste for historical anecdote."[15]

Born Clara Müller to a prominent family in the town of Neubrandenburg in Mecklenburg, Mühlbach began corresponding in her twenties with the then-infamous "Young German" Theodor Mundt (1808–61), whose works, along with those of four other authors, had been banned in the German territories in 1835 as immoral and blasphemous. When the couple married in 1839, Mühlbach had already published three novels. Encouraged by Mundt, she proceeded in the 1840s to write several more social novels that addressed political issues, including the status of women. This literary production belonged to Mühlbach's "kecke Jahre" (feisty years), as Renate Möhrmann aptly termed this period.[16] While, as Peterson has argued, these social novels are not as unambiguously progressive as they may appear to be at first glance, they number among the important early instances of German women's fiction that addresses the status of women.[17] Indeed, a younger contemporary characterized Mühlbach in the pre-1848 years as one of the most zealous and passionate German women acolytes of George Sand.[18] None of these social novels was translated in North America.

After the failed revolution of 1848, Mühlbach shifted her focus largely to the past, thus finding the vein of writing that corresponded to contemporary tastes and her own talent. She enjoyed her first big success in 1853 with *Friedrich der Große und sein Hof* (1853) and went on to publish scores of novels dealing with German history (including Austria) as well as a handful of novels on English, French, and Russian history. After unification and the founding of the German empire in 1871 and a trip to Egypt, she tried her hand at more exotic material, writing two novels set in Egypt, *Mohammed Ali und sein Haus* (1872) and *Mohammed Ali's Nachfolger* (1872). Research of German lending libraries reveals Mühlbach to be "the single most popular German author of the period 1849–88." Ahead of her were otherwise foreign authors in translation—Alexandre Dumas, Eugène Sue, G. P. R. James, and Paul de Kock. In the period 1889–1914, Mühlbach moved up to second place in Germany just behind Dumas.[19]

In the 1850s, soon after their publication in the German territories, Mühlbach's historical novels began appearing in German-language newspapers in the United States.[20] The first American translation of a Mühlbach novel appeared in 1864 in the midst of the Civil War in Mobile, Alabama, as *Joseph II and His Court*. Two years later, the New York publisher D. Appleton launched a series of Mühlbach translations, starting with *Frederick the Great and His Court*. In 1867, in an unusual gesture for the time, Appleton paid Mühlbach an honorarium of 1,000 thalers to acknowledge her achievements.[21] If, in voluntarily remunerating Mühlbach, Appleton seems generous in view of the practices of the times, the firm had no cause to regret its largesse. The combined sales of Mühlbach's historical novels in the end "reached the millions."[22] Meanwhile, in that same year, O. Janke, the Berlin publisher of Mühlbach's historical novels in the 1850s reprimanded American publishers for pirating German intellectual property, threatening to report on every such future transgression. Singling out Appleton, he claimed that the American firm was boasting of publishing the most important German authors at prices lower than the German originals and yet had never contacted the publishers or the authors of these works.[23] Perhaps this complaint prompted the remuneration.

The American liking for Mühlbach's novels is well documented. *Putnam's Magazine*, for one, remarked on their unmatched allure for postbellum Americans.[24] As Lieselotte Kurth-Voigt and William H. McClain point out, the National Union Catalogue lists "some five hundred American editions and impressions" of Mühlbach's historical novels.[25] My independently gathered data corroborates that finding (see Appendix E). According to the *Literary World*, in 1873 the Lawrence Public Library in Massachusetts listed Mühlbach's fiction as thirty-sixth in popularity among all authors checked out of the library over a year's time.[26] A year later, in 1874, the Lawrence

Public Library again supplied telling data. Within a single month the works of Mrs. Southworth, a best-selling American novelist, accounted for twenty-two of every thousand volumes borrowed; those of Dickens, the next most frequently borrowed, fifteen; Louisa May Alcott, seven; the Brontë sisters, two; and Thackeray and Trollope, four each. Mühlbach's novels, by comparison, accounted for three per thousand, which put Mühlbach in the top half of the list.[27]

In 1898 Appleton set a monument to the thirty-odd years in which Mühlbach had been avidly read in translation with a twenty-volume reprint collection titled *Historical Romances of Louisa Mühlbach*, a set that includes mainly novels about the history of the German-speaking world and of Prussia in particular. Mühlbach's novels are still widely available in American university libraries, their availability suggesting that they were once understood to have cultural value transcending their status as mere popular reading. They claimed from the start, after all, to recount history. Continued interest in Mühlbach prompted the Marion Company in 1915 to reprint the twenty "historical romances" originally published by Appleton. In 1927 Americans could still read about three of Mühlbach's novels—*Henry the Eighth and His Court, Berlin and Sans-Souci*, and *Marie Antoinette and Her Son*—in volume 12 of Rossiter Johnson's "world's great stories prepared in brief," that is, side by side with works by such American authors as London, Longfellow, and Melville (*Typee* and *Moby Dick*), and international writers such as Lewis (*The Monk*), Loti, Manzoni, Martineau, Marryat, Meredith, and Mérimée as well as novels by two German women, Lewald and Marlitt. In number of works represented, only Marryat and Meredith match Mühlbach.[28] As late as 1932, Baker and Packman listed eleven of the Appleton translations in their *Guide to the Best Fiction*, inaccurately describing them as a "patient and methodical amplification of the bare historical record, designed to illustrate any given period according to the letter and spirit of historical fact."[29]

Evaluations of Mühlbach's novels were mixed on both sides of the Atlantic. Even as this fiction found enthusiastic readers in Germany in the 1850s, literary pundits withheld approval. On the American side, Bayard Taylor, who considered himself an expert on German literature and a good judge of literary quality, asserted in 1869 that Mühlbach's romances were popular among the "'semi-intelligent' classes of readers in Germany" and that they could have no "permanent place in the literature of the country."[30] His male counterparts in Germany were unlikely to dispute that assessment. In 1860 the German critic Robert Prutz had ridiculed these novels as a "factory industry," although he conceded that readers liked them. Mühlbach, writing with both eyes on the market, plied her trade with a "grandiose lack of inhibition" and a "sublime disregard for literary criticism and good taste," he objected.[31]

Identifying her books as "historische Memoirenromane" (historical memoir-novels) and "romanhafte Historien" (novelistic histories), Rudolf von Gottschall later recognized that over the course of writing so many novels Mühlbach achieved a better style and gradually exchanged the audience of "silly little working girls" for whom she wrote in the beginning for a more refined circle of readers.[32] He identified the cycle of Frederick the Great novels, some of the same works that introduced Mühlbach to the American English-speaking public, as the turning point in her career. Still, he was not willing to grant her novels depth. Lacking a genuine historical perspective, they merely satisfied readers' wish for entertainment that focused on "the petty idiosyncrasies of great men," thus mediating a feeling of closeness to these historical figures.[33] This last point merits attention, for it suggests the highly personal ways in which readers engaged with the historical figures in such fiction. Precisely such engagement constitutes an important piece in the story of the sojourn of Mühlbach's novels in America. We shall return to this aspect of Mühlbach's work in chapter 6.

Despite its condescending tone, a review of *Berlin und Sanssouci oder Friedrich der Große und seine Freunde* (1854) in the *Deutsches Museum* usefully identifies key aspects that made possible the author's popularity in both Germany and America. After opening with disparaging remarks about "Schriftstellernden" (women trying to be writers), the reviewer scolds Mühlbach for writing sensation literature, nastily quipping that while literary criticism could not prevent her from publishing novels, Mühlbach in turn could not force critics to take note of her books.[34] When at the midpoint of the essay he finally addresses the novel at hand, his tone changes. While continuing to enumerate flaws, he admits that the enchanting subject matter riveted his attention and made it impossible for him to stop reading. He sees this novel as wholesome in contrast to what he has described as her recent sensation fiction; readers not only will be entertained but will also be able to confess to reading it without blushing.[35] This particular history, in his view, has curbed the wantonness of Mühlbach's writing.[36]

Precisely the combination of absorbing, reasonably wholesome entertainment with allegedly sound historical fact lay at the heart of Mühlbach's popularity in the United States, her books constituting, in the formulation of McClain and Kurth-Voigt, "gehobene Unterhaltungsliteratur" (elevated entertaining literature).[37] It made the novels acceptable reading for men, women, and even older girls, despite the fact that Mühlbach spiced her stories with illicit, occasionally even adulterous, romances. The *New York Times,* believing the novel written by a "Herr Muhlbach," enthusiastically endorsed *Frederick the Great and His Court* as "one of the best historical novels lately published."[38] The family magazine *Hours at Home* noted that Mühlbach's works "are full of interest and less objectionable than the highly wrought and sensational novel."[39]

This is not to say that American critics were always friendly; some were decidedly hostile and questioned the taste of her readers.[40] Furthermore, some did not find these historical novels wholesome in the least. Whereas a review of *Frederick the Great and His Court* in the *Catholic World* noted their freedom "from the false sensationalism which furnishes the spice of the lower school of modern fiction," the same journal later decried their low and "unwholesome" moral tone that is "pagan, not Christian."[41] The *New Englander* disapprovingly pronounced Mühlbach's novels "of a highly sensational order."[42]

These works baffled American reviewers who were looking to categorize them; indeed, discussion of them in print revolved largely around their generic affiliation and their relationship to history. History lent them a prestige not accorded to fiction per se. Some reviewers characterized Mühlbach as having laboriously researched her subject matter. At the same time, they remarked that in attempting to be true to the historical record, the works could not be called novels at all but rather were "ingenious compilations from historical sources, with the gaps in continuity skillfully filled."[43] Many reviewers were disquieted by the hybridity of Mühlbach's novels, their combination of fact and fiction. *Harper's Magazine* termed Mühlbach's *Queen Hortense* "only a history with a little imaginative filling," asserting that Mühlbach wrote "novels without imagination and history without facts."[44] A perplexed reviewer for the *Catholic World* complained, "unless one is exceedingly familiar with the real history of the times, one never knows whether he is reading history or only romance." The reviewer feared, moreover, that most people would read them as history and "thus imbibe many erroneous views of real persons and events."[45] Yet some reviews identified their appeal as precisely the combination of history and romance: *Hours at Home* pronounced them "exciting and entertaining far beyond the ordinary stereotyped novel," since they had "thrown the dark veil of romance over the dry records of history."[46] Sensitive to the confusion expressed in these reviews, *Appleton's Journal* published an article by John Esten Cooke in 1874 that aspired to explain Mühlbach's novel "system" and show how it deviated from that of Scott, Thackeray, Bulwer-Lytton, Dumas, Ainsworth, James, and others. Unlike these authors,

Cooke asserted, Mühlbach did not employ history "as the canvas and framework of their groups." Instead, she went to history "for the actual figures, making her books *history dramatized.*"[47]

Whereas critical American reviews of Mühlbach worry over historical inaccuracies or fault what they perceive as a lack of narrative talent, I have found only one that mentions "national convictions and patriotic impulses" in these novels, obliquely suggesting that Mühlbach's novels mediate a vision of an emergent Germany at once exciting and skewed.[48] Precisely this critical question of patriotic intention will concern us when we return to Mühlbach in chapter 6.

The mixed reviews of Mühlbach suggest deviation in the criteria and purposes of reviewing and display decidedly different attitudes toward literature that is read for pleasure. While the *Catholic World* concluded that popularity is "a pretty good indication of their merit," this same popularity prompted a harsh response in the *New Englander.* Here the reviewer judged these "widely read" novels—widely read even among "people who cannot be charged with a want of cultivation"—as "ineffably stupid, fantastic, interminable books."[49] Such critical reviews of course provide only a partial picture of American reception, since they do not tell us much about leisure-time reading itself.

While American reviewers equivocated on the value of entertainment in general, two reviews of Mühlbach from the 1860s doubted the ability of Germans in general to write "light literature." The *New York Times,* although commending Mühlbach, remarked, "The very mental characteristics which unfit [Germans] for properly appreciating what is strictly termed 'light literature' prepare them to enjoy the historical novel."[50] The *Round Table* likewise stereotyped German writers' shortcomings in the area of "light literature," maintaining,

> Were it true that the popular taste of a nation is reflected in its light literature, we should have cause to think but poorly of the readers among whom Louisa Mühlbach's interminable so-called historical novels find favor; but in Germany the novel does not suffice for the intellectual wants of the great body of her people, and save in *Wilhelm Meister,* and some noteworthy productions of Freytag and Auerbach, the attempts at this species of fiction have not been attended with success.[51]

German novels, American pundits claimed in the 1860s, are ponderous and serious. Yet at this very moment in 1868, J. P. Lippincott and the translator Annis Lee Wister were on the verge of changing this perception among novel readers with translations of two novels by E. Marlitt. Although some reviewers clung to stereotypes of German fiction writing as labored and dry as dust, Americans who read Marlitt in translation learned instead to expect German novels to be lively, entertaining, and optimistic.

Die Gartenlaube as Venue for German Women's Writing

In 1853 the liberal German publicist Ernst Keil founded *Die Gartenlaube*, a new kind of unifying publication for a politically fragmented Germany, a family magazine that provided something for everyone. With its rapidly burgeoning sales, *Die Gartenlaube* became a quintessential mass-market phenomenon in the German territories.

Die Gartenlaube offered articles on a variety of subjects of contemporary interest at home in Germany and abroad, including hygiene and medicine, the arts, technology, politics, poetry, short biographies, historical sketches, and serialized fiction. As Kirsten Belgum outlines, although claiming not to be political, the magazine from the beginning had a central political aim: it sought to popularize and solidify the idea of "nation" in the critical years of German unification.[52] And while *Die Gartenlaube* was not narrow or jingoistic in its outlook, it did cultivate and cater to an audience hungry for information about Germany and its place in the world, a place that changed rapidly after 1871. Keil intended the magazine to be a "thoroughly German magazine": its contributions were German originals from German authors, its illustrations were by German artists (not reprints from images in foreign magazines), and it treated German life and aspirations.[53] When in 1894, for example, *Die Gartenlaube* reported that the popular E. Werner was spending the winter in Egypt, where she was writing her next novel, it also hastened to assure readers that the characters in her new work were German; Egypt provided only the backdrop of the story.[54]

Growing from its first printing of 5,000 in 1853 to its peak of 382,000 in 1875, *Die Gartenlaube* reached many more readers than these numbers indicate. It was available in reading rooms, lending libraries, and the homes of middle-class families. Each copy therefore reached at least five readers, historians of the book trade estimate.[55] It circulated in the New World as well as the Old, read in America by ethnic Germans as well as Anglophone Americans who had learned German in school or from tutors at home. The translator Mary Stuart Smith, for one, subscribed to the magazine, which she combed over several decades for prospects for translation.[56] In 1873 the *Chicago Tribune* reported that, of the great number of German newspapers and periodicals subscribed to and read in Chicago, *Die Gartenlaube,* "a literary paper of rare excellence, . . . considered [by many] the best in the world, . . . takes the lead. . . . Something over 2,000 copies of this paper are circulating in this city," the *Tribune* noted. "Many Americans, understanding the German language, subscribe for [*sic*] it."[57] The article particularly remarked on the "excellent novels" of E. Marlitt that appeared therein.

While *Die Gartenlaube* was ambivalent on the subject of women's roles and rights—and became more conservative toward the end of the century—the magazine gave not only Marlitt but also a host of German women the opportunity to earn their living as writers and provided the platform for its most appealing authors to become internationally famous. Serialized fiction by the women to whom *Die Gartenlaube* had given opportunities in turn contributed significantly to the appeal and sales of the magazine. These authors and the magazine and its editor thus found themselves in a mutually beneficial and productive relationship. Secondarily and inadvertently in the broader, international publishing context, *Die Gartenlaube* provided opportunities for female translators as they too acceded to cultural activity and agency. It proved a reliable source of appealing fiction that Gilded Age American translators and publishers mined with hardly a second thought as to the ethics of doing so.

Eugenie John / E. Marlitt (1825–87)

The serialized fiction of Eugenie John was unquestionably a critical factor in the success of *Die Gartenlaube* at home and abroad. John, who initially concealed her gender under the pseudonym E. Marlitt, became not only one of the best-selling authors in Germany in the last third of the century but also an international success. Between 1865, when her first published story, *Zwölf Apostel,* was serialized, and 1871, when *Das Haideprinzeßchen,* her fourth full-length novel and sixth contribution to the periodical, began appearing in installments, subscriptions to *Die Gartenlaube* grew from ca. 150,000 to ca. 310,000.[58] Reporting in 1868 on the success of *Goldelse* (serialized 1866; book 1867), *Die Gartenlaube* gleefully noted that after only eleven months the novel had been reprinted three times.[59] By this time it was also well known that Marlitt was a woman.[60]

Marlitt's German contemporaries were keenly aware of her popularity and talent; and although she was not without detractors during her lifetime, some established male authors acknowledged her gifts as a storyteller.[61] Upon the publication of her third novel, *Die Reichsgräfin Gisela,* in 1869,

Gottschall expressed admiration for her international success—even on "the shores of the Mississippi"—wherever Germans might be reading *Die Gartenlaube*. In an attempt to explain her popularity, he praised her descriptive powers and her style. He also identified as a decisive factor what he called the "Volksthümlichkeit" (popular national quality) of her material, for example, elements of German legends and fairy tales in her plots. Yet he also noted evidence of her international reading in her inclusion of familiar titillating elements from Charlotte Brontë's *Jane Eyre* and Victor Hugo's *Notre-Dame de Paris*. Gottschall approvingly pointed to Marlitt's strong liberal messages. If several decades later German critics, among them one Otto Heller, felt that Marlitt's were battles that had long since been won, in 1870 they still rang true with readers.[62] Marlitt long remained a favorite with women readers. In 1931 in her autobiography, the anarchist Emma Goldman, for example, recalled her consumptive, tender-hearted German teacher in Königsberg with whom she had read Marlitt and wept.[63]

As Hans Arens argues, Gottschall also fostered long-enduring misapprehensions of Marlitt when he characterized her novels in terms of fairy tales, in particular their endings as "Aschenbrödels Braut- und Himmelfahrt" (Cinderella's honeymoon and ascent to heaven).[64] While, as I argue below, the happy ending was critical to the international reception of her novels, Marlitt's happy endings do not unambiguously project an intact world.[65] Nineteenth-century readers could relish the happy ending yet remain disturbed by some of the characters, situations, and problems in these books. The American Agnes Hamilton, for one, was forced through her reading of *The Old Mam'selle's Secret* to associate with "the nastiest people whom I should not speak to in real life."[66] Marlitt also does not generally traffic in rags-to-riches tales, Cinderella stories, in which women of low social rank marry aristocrats, or, as in Mulock's best-selling *John Halifax Gentleman*, men rise from abject poverty to prosperity and prominence. Some of Marlitt's heroines are themselves aristocrats or heiresses who must learn tolerance. Plots depict marriages of extreme difference as unviable, and in every case the texts emphasize the importance of the education and sterling character of both husband and wife.[67]

After her death and from the turn of the new century on, Marlitt became an easy target for critics of many stripes who saw embodied in her fiction the taste and mores of a generation that they were eager to displace, even if advice books continued to recommend her books to "young girls" into the new century.[68] In 1905, for example, the Austrian feminist Rosa Mayreder pilloried such popular reading, pointing an accusing finger in particular at the literature favored by family magazines. Although she did not name Marlitt, as the best-known writer for *Die Gartenlaube* Marlitt would have immediately come to mind. Two years later, Ernst von Wolzogen likewise excoriated the bad taste of contemporary readers of family magazines, whom he characterized as silly girls, women, and old people. He expressed disappointment that *Die Gartenlaube* had lost sight of its original national liberal mission as a result of the bad literature serialized there.[69] Forgetting that Marlitt in particular had participated in that mission, he grumbled that she and others put their indelible stamp on *Die Gartenlaube* and that subsequently all the editors of family magazines took these novels as their touchstone since they were certain to satisfy their customers.[70] In the new century even *Die Gartenlaube* began to speak of Marlitt's fiction as characterizing a past phase of the magazine and of the nation as well.[71] Yet her work continued to be republished on both sides of the Atlantic.

Marlitt wrote ten novels, the last of these completed after her death by W. Heimburg in 1888, and three shorter pieces. Her books were translated into not only English but also French, Danish, Dutch, Swedish, Norwegian, Italian, Spanish, and Polish; most of this translation took place without the permission or even knowledge of the author and publisher.[72] While her international success brought her more adulation than material gain, her German earnings were enough to enable her to live comfortably and to support her family. Her publisher, Keil, famously built her a villa in her hometown, Arnstadt, to express his gratitude.

Marlitt's novels were widely read in the United States and circulated in both German and English translation. In 1871 an article on the New York Mercantile Library described the "animated scene" on Saturdays as the clerks struggled to serve the many customers. Among the popular recent publications mentioned is Marlitt's third translated novel, *The Countess Gisela*: the library had fifty copies of it ready to meet customer demand.[73] The first two full-length Marlitt novels appeared in the United States in 1868. According to Morgan's data, seven titles appeared in the 1860s in the United States, nineteen in the 1870s, twenty-four in the 1880s, and nine in the 1890s.[74] My own tallies indicate more vigorous publication even than what Morgan records. Indeed, Marlitt's works were translated three times more frequently than Mühlbach's many novels, each of which was only translated once for book publication (compare Appendices C and D). Furthermore, the total number of translations, editions, and reprint editions of Marlitt novels in the United States places her second after the American Mühlbach factory, even though Marlitt had furnished less than half as many original texts to begin with (see Appendix E).[75] My ever-expanding database records more than 250 American editions and reprint editions of Marlitt's ten novels.

The American reception of Marlitt was cordial from the start. The very first translation published in book form in America, *The Old Mam'selle's Secret*, was reprinted at least twenty-two times over thirty-three years by J. B. Lippincott alone; I have documented 101 unique American issues of the novel in three different translations and suspect that there are still more unique issues to be found. In 1868 the *New York Times* welcomed *The Old Mam'selle's Secret* to America with a review recommending it for a "pleasant idle hour's reading."[76] Four years later *The Nation* confirmed that *The Little Moorland Princess*, the fourth Marlitt novel in translation, was "as entertaining as the first one," and *Southern Farm and Home Magazine* maintained that the "highest praise" it could give this "really charming tale" was to pronounce it "fully equal if not superior to Marlitt's former works."[77] Marlitt's popularity endured. In 1876 a reviewer deemed *At the Councillor's*, Marlitt's sixth novel in American translation, "one of the best German novels we have recently read," maintaining that Marlitt's novels were the sort that readers read through "from title page to the end."[78] Marlitt's books, the *American Socialist* averred, were "healthy"; they taught that "purity and uprightness of personal character [were] of prime consequence, and of more value than rank or riches."[79] These reviews offer only a small sample of the enthusiasm that met these Marlitt translations across a spectrum of American periodicals.

When Marlitt died in 1887 with one novel unfinished, *Die Gartenlaube* lamented the loss of an author who had known so well how to fascinate readers.[80] Two issues later, the magazine made certain with a biographical sketch that it kept Marlitt fans on the hook, also reporting that the remaining episodes of Marlitt's *Das Eulenhaus* were forthcoming and that it had designated a new author to complete the novel as Marlitt would have wished.[81] Predictably, *Das Eulenhaus* appeared in two American translations as well—*The Owl-House* (Munro) and *The Owl's Nest* (Lippincott)—even as American newspapers and magazines mourned the passing of a woman who could be counted as "one of the most popular of modern German novelists" whose novels were "never dull and never gross."[82] Mary Stuart Smith's commemorative sketch, "a fresh-plucked spring of Virginia ivy," recalled the author's contribution to the "wealth of innocent and healthful fiction" and the "loving admiration in which E. Marlitt is held by thousands of Americans."[83]

Marlitt enjoyed a robust afterlife in America that endured at least two decades into the new century. In 1876 *Publishers' Weekly* conducted a contest for the book trade asking which novels were the most "salable" (setting aside Bulwer-Lytton, Dickens, Eliot, Scott, and Thackeray). Marlitt's *Old Mam'selle's Secret* ranked twenty-third, and all five of her then-translated novels (three of them in the top fifty) made this international list of 204 novels headed by

John Halifax Gentleman.⁸⁴ These five Marlitt novels were, moreover, still circulating decades later.

An examination of thirteen late nineteenth and early twentieth-century American library catalogues reveals that all of Marlitt's novels on the 1876 list (indeed, translations of all of Marlitt's novels) were available in all of these libraries some twenty to thirty years later (see Appendix B for a list of the catalogues consulted). Some of the remaining 195 once-salable novels on the 1876 list did not prove as enduring. While predictably Mullock's *John Halifax Gentleman* and Brontë's *Jane Eyre* are present in these thirteen libraries, novels in the top sixty on the list by such once-deemed-most-salable American, Canadian, Irish, and English women writers as Mrs. Alexander (Annie French Hector), Mary Jane Holmes, M. C. Hay, May Agnes Fleming, Ouida, Mary Elizabeth Braddon, and Eleanor Frances Poynter are, by contrast, present in seven or fewer of the same thirteen libraries. Even the once perennially popular *East Lynne* turns up in only nine of these libraries. Borrowing records from the Muncie Public Library, 1891–1902, furthermore reveal Marlitt, represented by twenty-three books (some novels were held in multiple copies), to be the tenth most widely circulating author in the entire library.⁸⁵

Heller might have objected to the inclusion in 1908/1927 of digests of *The Old Mam'selle's Secret* and *The Little Moorland Princess* in volume twelve of the twenty-volume *Author's Digest: The World's Great Stories in Brief*, especially when Goethe was represented by only two works.⁸⁶ Surely still more irritating to Heller would have been the reference in the biographical sketch to *The Old Mam'selle's Secret* as Marlitt's "masterpiece," a designation reserved by contemporary Germanists for male cultural production.⁸⁷

Bertha Behrens / Wilhelmine Heimburg (1848–1912)

It fell to thirty-seven-year-old Bertha Behrens to complete *Das Eulenhaus* in 1888. Behrens, who also initially hid her gender under the pseudonym W. Heimburg, had made her *Gartenlaube* debut ten years earlier, in 1878, with her second novel, *Lumpenmüllers Lieschen*, which was to become her most enduring work.⁸⁸ Her first full-length novel, *Aus dem Leben meiner alten Freundin* (1878), had been serialized the year before in a regional newspaper.⁸⁹

A notice that appeared in *Die Gartenlaube* during the serialization of *Lumpenmüllers Lieschen* indicates that the author's sex was already known, thus suggesting that the ambiguous initial was by then a gesture so well known as to reveal the sex of the author rather than conceal it.⁹⁰ Once published in the magazine, Heimburg quickly met with success. By 1884 *Die Gar-*

tenlaube cited her as one of its favorite authors, and in 1891 Adolf Hinrichsen named her "one of the most popular women writers, especially admired by women."[91] Like Marlitt, she attained international fame and could be read in English, Dutch, Swedish, French, Czech, and Finnish. Heimburg published in *Die Gartenlaube* until her death, her last novel, *Lore Lotte,* appearing there posthumously in 1913.

In her study of Heimburg, Urzsula Bonter cites a telling vignette that an envious Theodor Fontane (1819–98), one of Germany's most prominent realists, included in a letter to his wife in 1885. Fontane, a longtime journalist, had turned novelist seven years earlier and published six novels in the interim. His novella *Unterm Birnbaum* (never translated into English) would shortly appear in *Die Gartenlaube.* In 1885 he had not yet produced his best and most enduring works and was far from attaining the stature that he enjoys in German letters today. In this letter he ruefully describes how an older married couple speaks enthusiastically of having read a novel by Heimburg: when it was serialized in *Die Gartenlaube,* they read it aloud to one another; then the wife read it a second time; now she plans to read it a third time.[92]

The repetitive reading that becomes visible in this vignette evidences a reader enthusiasm different from the "extensive reading" of mere consumption; instead, it suggests savoring and enduring enjoyment of a book that has become familiar. As will become visible over the course of this study, the American packaging of this popular fiction in translation also encouraged American readers to think of it as worthy of a second read and a permanent spot on the bookshelf. It was not understood simply as reading to be consumed and tossed aside.

American firms began publishing translations of Heimburg's novels in 1881, perhaps cued by *Lizzie of the Mill,* the British translation of *Lumpenmüllers Lieschen,* which appeared in London in 1880, two years after the novel's serialization. Praising Heimburg as standing "in the front rank of Germany's best writers," Smith claimed in 1898 that her translation of the very same novel as *Lieschen, a Tale of an Old Castle* for serialization in the *New York Tribune* in 1881–82 introduced American readers to Heimburg.[93]

The Heimburg vogue in America followed hard upon the publication of Marlitt's *Eulenhaus* in various translations in America in 1888, the association with the perennially popular author lending Heimburg greater name recognition. In 1889 *Book Chat* praised Heimburg as not merely Marlitt's successor but as possessing "a strong originality of her own" and as resembling Marlitt only "in her felicitous drawing of the cozy atmosphere of home so peculiar to the best German literature, and in her unfailing success in awakening the interest of her readers."⁹⁴ However, after a spate of translations in the late 1880s and early 1890s, the number of new translations dropped precipitously at the turn of the twentieth century, even though Heimburg herself continued to publish in the first decade of the new century and even though her works were, as Smith noted, newly available in Germany, collected in twenty volumes in three series.⁹⁵

There can be no question of Heimburg's success with American readers. Morgan lists twenty-one titles of translations published in America in the 1880s and twenty-one in the 1890s.⁹⁶ These translations are of close to twenty original German texts. According to my independently gathered data, sixteen novels and book collections of novellas by Heimburg place her third behind Mühlbach and Werner in number of works translated, second behind Werner in total number of translations, and fourth in total number of publications (see Appendices C, D, and E). Heimburg's fiction was, as these numbers indicate, multiply translated and reprinted; *Herzenskrisen*, for example, appeared in America in four translations under four different titles.

American reviews were mixed. They variously describe these novels with such terms as "wholesome and mildly entertaining," "exquisite love story," "pleasing tale," or as doing "no harm" or as at least "a shade less hackneyed than the general run of German fiction."⁹⁷ The *Nassau Literary Magazine* even found them realistic: Heimburg "puts his [sic] people in natural situations and makes them talk in a natural way."⁹⁸ Of *A Penniless Girl*, the *Literary World* maintained, charm is "not wanting in this story," for "When a German novel is at all good, it is generally very good."⁹⁹ Other reviews took a more peevish view. Reviewing *Misjudged*, the *Literary World* pointed to the novel's targeted appeal to a mass market.¹⁰⁰ A cranky reviewer writing for the same magazine dismissed *A Fatal Misunderstanding* as belonging "to that comfortless order of modern Teutonic fiction in which all life and action are regulated by the strictly sentimental," where "common sense plays no part in the behavior of anybody."¹⁰¹ Nevertheless, *Publishers' Weekly* identified *A Penniless Girl*, Wister's translation of *Ein armes Mädchen*, as "among the most notable" translations of foreign novels for the year 1884 and, likewise, in 1891 listed two new Heimburg translations as "among the more notable issues" in translations from the German in 1890—Heimburg is one of eleven German authors mentioned in this summary article.¹⁰² Heller, however, did not deign to mention her by name in his 1905 essay, perhaps because he saw her merely as one of the "swarm of busy imitators who learned the trick [from Marlitt] though they missed the grace."¹⁰³

Bonter argues for a reevaluation of Heimburg, whose reputation as an inferior imitator of Marlitt, in her view, grows largely out of the fact that she completed Marlitt's *Eulenhaus*.¹⁰⁴ She maintains that Heimburg struck out in a direction different from Marlitt's and that she, unlike Marlitt, by no means uniformly depicted an intact world with happy endings. While Heimburg's novels assuredly have a stamp of their own—of this more below—Bonter somewhat mischaracterizes Marlitt's novels to make her point. As some American reviews of Marlitt indicate, Marlitt's world was both disturbing and satisfying to readers. As we shall see in chapter 4, both Marlitt's and Heimburg's success in America depended on the happy ending, but not the depiction of a world without sadness, loss, or conflict.

Elisabeth Bürstenbinder / E. Werner (1838–1918)

Daughter of a wealthy Berlin merchant, Elisabeth Bürstenbinder made her debut in *Die Gartenlaube* in 1870 after publishing two insignificant stories in a south German magazine. As had Marlitt, she hid her gender under the initial E. Although *Die Gartenlaube* still coyly referred to Werner as "der Verfasser" (the male author) in 1872, her true identity and the secret of her sex did not long remain concealed in Germany.¹⁰⁵ By 1873 she was out, as it were. *Die Gartenlaube* reported that she had had to make her identity public since in certain circles a woman was impersonating her.¹⁰⁶ In America, by contrast, she was still known in some quarters as late as 1879 as "Ernest Werner."¹⁰⁷ In 1876, in an article titled "Eine Heldin der Feder" (Heroine of the Pen), a title that plays off her 1871 novel, *Ein Held der Feder* (Hero of the Pen), *Die Gartenlaube* stood fully behind her as a woman author, featuring a large picture of her and praising women authors in general.¹⁰⁸ In Werner, the editor recognized, *Die Gartenlaube* had another winner.

Werner would eventually publish approximately thirty novels and novellas, many of them serialized first in *Die Gartenlaube* and many of them translated into other European languages including Swedish, Danish, Norwegian, Icelandic, Spanish, Italian, Hungarian, Finnish, Czech, Russian, and Polish. Beginning in 1872 with Lippincott's publication of *At the Altar*, over half of these works were translated in North America as well, sometimes multiple times (see Appendices C and D). Morgan identifies three critical decades for American translations of Werner: the 1870s with twenty-eight items, the 1880s with forty-two, and the 1890s with nineteen.¹⁰⁹ According to my independently gathered data, Werner ranks second after Mühlbach among these seventeen women authors in number of works translated, but first in total number of translations, well ahead of Mühlbach (see Appendices C and D). Available in multiple editions and reprint editions, she occupies position number three after Mühlbach and Marlitt (see Appendix E). In its summary article for the year 1883, *Publishers' Weekly* names Werner's *Banned and Blessed* alongside Emile Zola's *Au Bonheur des Dames* among the "chief translations in fiction."[110]

When Theodor Fontane, the same journalist turned novelist whose letter testifies to Heimburg's popularity, offered an acerbic critique of German bourgeois sentiment in his novel *Frau Jenny Treibel* (1892), he supplied Jenny Treibel, the central character, with the maiden name Bürstenbinder, that is, Werner's real name. One wonders whether he thereby took revenge on *Die Gartenlaube* and its popular women authors. In the novel the prosaic name Bürstenbinder (broom binder) reveals the pretentious nouveau riche Jenny's humble origins and ruthlessly pragmatic nature. Her avarice belies her outward sentimentality and jars with the poetic world that she tries to create in her opulent Berlin villa. Bourgeois sentiment, in Fontane's scathing portrait, provides a saccharine veneer for a heartless class driven by the love of money.

Heller, however, nearly had kind words for Werner. Werner, a writer who could "lay claim to a high degree of skill . . . without being in any sense" a good writer, wielded "a good and steady pen at the business," he asserted. She surpassed Marlitt, her model, "thanks to a greater breadth of horizon, warmth of conviction, and a certain trenchant critical faculty. Instead of limiting herself to the conventional assortment of heroes, she showed a kindly attachment for misfit individuals; this even betrayed her occasionally into representing an unmitigated crank as a hero."[111] As I outline below, a signature of Werner's works is an interest in men and masculinity as it is supported and complemented by women and femininity. Even as Werner's fiction inhabits the territory of women's domestic fiction, it offers empathetic possibilities for male readers. Heller at least was susceptible to it.

Wilhelmine von Hillern (1836–1916)

The only child of the prolific, popular, and sometimes scorned nineteenth-century German playwright Charlotte Birch-Pfeiffer (1800–1868), Hillern turned to fiction writing after a brief career on the stage and her marriage in 1857 into the lower nobility, a marriage solemnized in haste with her much older admirer Hermann von Hillern (1817–82) when she became pregnant.[112] Armed with the experience of broad reading; contact with writers, musicians, and other makers of culture; an education overseen by her university-educated father and private tutors; and familiarity with the theater of entertainment, Hillern, as Rudolf von Gottschall conceded, knew how to tell a story.¹¹³ Beginning in the mid-1860s with the novel *Ein Doppelleben* (1865), which contains a fulsome dedication to her parents, she published over the course of approximately thirty years at least fourteen novels and novellas and several plays.

Hillern serialized her work in *Die Gartenlaube* and in Janke's *Deutsche Roman-Zeitung,* but also in the more pretentious journal *Die Deutsche Rundschau;*¹¹⁴ in Germany her books thus crossed emergent cultural boundaries. It is misleading to pigeonhole her, as does Lillie V. Hathaway as, like Marlitt, Werner, and Heimburg, one of the "'Gartenlaube' ladies."¹¹⁵

Eight arresting novels and novellas translated into English brought Hillern renown in America. Pochmann lists twenty-five titles stemming from these eight original German texts, all published in the United States from 1865 to 1899.¹¹⁶ Especially the novella *Höher als die Kirche* gained long-lasting currency in America, although admittedly in a niche market. It was translated four times into English. More importantly, no fewer than eleven different editors prepared it for the purpose of instructing German in the United States. The first American school edition alone, S. Willard Clary's edition of 1891, went through at least twelve subsequent editions, the last of which appeared in 1911. Eleonore C. Nippert's 1928 edition for second-year German instruction was republished and reedited as late as 1939 on the eve of the Second World War.¹¹⁷

In 1873 *Lippincott's Magazine* described Hillern as having a "large circle of readers on both sides of the Atlantic," her *Arzt der Seele* having "established her claim to a high place among the writers of her class."¹¹⁸ Inasmuch as Lippincott had published translations of her first three novels, such praise in the magazine perhaps merely served the interests of its publisher. Nevertheless, there is ample evidence for widespread reading of Hillern's work in translation in America, including, in addition to the above-mentioned *Höher als die Kirche,* especially the novels *Ein Arzt der Seele* (1869) and *Die Geier-Wally* (1875), both of which were available in multiple translations that were subsequently reprinted. Although sixth in number of works translated, Hillern ranks fifth among her fellow German women novelists in number of American publications (see Appendices C and E).

Putnam's *The Best Reading: Hints on the Selection of Books* particularly recommended Hillern's *Arzt der Seele*—in Annis Lee Wister's translation *Only a Girl*—as among the best novels of the day, relying on "the opinions of the best critics, and the judgment of the better class of readers" and designating it as belonging to category "b," that is, specifically as one of the "books that come under the designation of good novels, and which can be recommended to the readers of fiction."¹¹⁹ Hillern told stories that interested

Americans. *Only a Girl*, for example, depicted social expectations that circumscribe women's intellectual aspirations. Operating in the German genre of the village tale, *Die Geier-Wally* (translated for Appleton as *Geier-Wally: A Tale of the Tyrol*) recounted a bitter struggle between a father and daughter, which the daughter eventually wins. *Aus eigener Kraft* (1870; translated as *By His Own Might*) followed the fortunes of a physically disabled protagonist. Hillern had thus ventured with her writing into controversial territory. *Appleton's Journal*, however, expressed some dissatisfaction with Hillern's female protagonists who, the reviewer noted, tended to be a "most gushing spirit" or a "wayward creature to be tamed by love."[120] In chapter 4 we will take a closer look at one such wayward creature in *Only a Girl*.

German Popular Fiction by Women as Domestic Fiction

The German term "Familienroman" (family novel) is but one of many nineteenth-century designations for the novels by German women that Americans liked and read in the Gilded Age. American reviewers variously labeled them "romance," "light reading," "German sentimental novel," "historical romance," or "wholesome reading."[121] These American labels evoke the flavor of these novels and suggest the manner in which the books were marketed and the ways their publishers expected them to be read, but these designations are not particularly useful to situating them in literary history in the aggregate. For this purpose, Nancy Armstrong's characterization of "domestic fiction" proves more helpful.

In *Desire and Domestic Fiction: A Political History of the Novel*, Armstrong brings into focus the mindset, values, assumptions, and class allegiances within which novels classified as domestic fiction operate. "Domestic fiction" flags the function of the family in these works as the site of identity formation, conflict, culture, and politics, indeed, as the place where history is made. The designation "domestic fiction" in my study of German women's novels in America includes a range of subgenres—from the historical romances of Mühlbach to the claustrophobic family stories of Heimburg. All of these works, despite a variety of generic affinities, offer German versions of Armstrong's domestic woman and domesticated man. As Armstrong asserts of domestic fiction, in these novels the "individual's value" is represented "in terms of . . . essential qualities of mind" and "subtle nuances of behavior."[122] While I am well aware that Mühlbach's novels were largely understood in their own time as historical romances, I will argue in chapter 6 that even they can be characterized in terms of domestic fiction and that they had a similar appeal for some American readers.

In the German context, the emphasis on the power of the individual to effect change flags the midcentury liberal mindset from which the set of novels to be examined here first emerged and the national liberal context in which its earliest representatives appeared, even when the overall political message in many of them was muddy and even reactionary, especially as the century advanced. In this fiction, liberalism tends to be linked to a double vision of a national Germany conceived in the terms of the region and in turn the region conceived as the nation.[123] Although before 1871 its proponents strenuously advocated on behalf of national unity, German liberalism proved more comfortably situated in an imaginary that reflected the values of the middle classes in the scattered German home towns than it came to be in the Reich, especially after the definitive defeat of both the National Liberals and left liberals in the Reichstag elections of 1878.

The persistence of the regional setting of the so-called home town and the outlying estates of the landed aristocracy in these novels projects a Germany that eludes the ills of modernity associated with the urbanization of the last third of the nineteenth century.[124] Social tensions remain largely those between an aristocracy, privileged by birth and custom, and the middle classes, defined by virtue, initiative, ingenuity, duty, and hard work. The laboring classes, while sometimes acknowledged, are depicted in largely sentimental and paternalistic terms. The family itself, sometimes as a metaphor for the German nation, tends to function as the primary site of conflict, even when the novels allude to larger national and international issues.

In such fiction, female subjectivity is critical to overcoming social conflict and achieving social stability. Examining largely eighteenth-century British literature, Armstrong argues for seeing in domestic fiction an overt contestation of "the reigning notion of kinship relations that attached most power and privilege to certain family lines."[125] This fiction makes gender and remakes the social order, and in Armstrong's words, "individuates wherever there [is] a collective body, to attach psychological motives to what [has] been the openly political behavior of contending groups, and to evaluate these according to a set of moral norms that [exalt] the domestic woman over and above her aristocratic counterpart."[126] Such fiction persisted in Germany where the privilege of birth endured. German fiction, however, does not uniformly depict a moral middle class triumphing over its aristocratic counterpart. Rather, aristocratic characters are often imbued with middle-class values and aspirations and defend these against the villainy of other aristocrats. In the moral sense, the middle classes have always already triumphed in these works.

What, then, was the character of this translated domestic fiction by German women, and why did American readers like it? What picture of Germany did it mediate in the nationalist era in which Germany unified, industrialized, modernized, militarized, and colonized, and the United States in essence did the same? Moreover, how German was it once it had been rendered by American translators, packaged and marketed by American publishers, and widely read by Americans in a variety of editions as entertaining fiction? Part 2 undertakes close readings of texts; examination of books as the product of industry, marketing, and circulation; and scrutiny of preserved exemplars in pursuit of answers to these questions.

PART TWO

German Texts as American Books

CHAPTER 3

"Family Likenesses"

Marlitt's Texts as American Books

———⚜———

IN 1871 *The Nation* remarked on striking national affinities, a "strong family likeness," in a set of German novels, recently translated by Annis Lee Wister, half of which were by E. Marlitt.[1] Pursuing this domestic metaphor still further, the reviewer remarked on the translator's choice of material:

> By the time one has followed the four or five little Germans in whom Mrs. Wister has interested herself through their childhood of repression and outrage into their youth of noble aspirations after all sorts of freedom, and their very innocent and pretty love-making, and has seen how uniformly hypocritical and cruel are the religious people with whom they come in contact and how necessary it seems to the peace of mind of their creators that the disgraceful mysteries which usually hang around their birth should be carefully cleared away, so that notwithstanding suspicious eloquence about the natural equality of all men, they should be in reality well placed in all respects as their neighbors, it is impossible not to feel as if one had got almost as near to the sentiments of Mrs. Wister as to those of Miss Marlitt, or Miss Von Hillern, or Ad. von Volckhausen. She has almost as certainly identified herself with a peculiar kind of thought and literature as if she had been producing original works.[2]

Further characterizing this distinct set of German novels as "amusing summer reading" suitable for American readers, *The Nation* touched upon two critical aspects of the sojourn of German popular fiction in America, thus adumbrating the double focus of this chapter: on the one hand the domestic, and on the other the national.³ A closer look at three novels by E. Marlitt will bring into view some of these family likenesses as they surfaced in domestic fiction inflected by a German national imaginary. In each case close readings of the text combined with an examination of its American publication and consumption will illuminate the domestication of a foreign work in a new national context and lay the groundwork for a more comprehensive view of the library of books translated from the German and their appeal in the United States.

LIPPINCOTT'S PUBLICATION of Annis Lee Wister's translations of both *Das Geheimnis der alten Mam'sell* and *Goldelse* in 1868 marked the start of the translation enterprise that made both Marlitt's and Wister's names famous in the United States among novel readers and that helped sell these same readers on German women writers' domestic fiction in general. Both of these novels were translated into English three times in North America and appeared with many publishers. Both garnered long-term success with American readers and were reprinted into the twentieth century. They offered romance plots that contained a dose of social criticism and titillating secrets. Their mysteries catered to readers' wish for entertainment; the solving of them in turn called upon readers' sense of virtue and justice, exposing bigotry and inappropriately wielded social and economic power. These mysteries inhered in the very walls of the dwellings of bourgeois and aristocratic families: in *Gold Elsie* in an interior, hidden chapel in a rundown castle in Thuringia; in *The Old Mam'selle's Secret* in the foundation and a hidden attic apartment of a merchant's home in a German home town.

Desire on the Home Ground:
Gold Elsie

Gold Elsie exemplifies Marlitt's signature creation of an appealing simulacrum of women's agency within the family. It opens in the capital city B. where Elizabeth Ferber makes her way through crowded streets to give music lessons.⁴ The capital is, however, not at the center of this narrative and soon drops off the horizon when the Ferber family settles in a crumbling castle in the region of Thuringia, where Elizabeth's father has taken a position as a forester's clerk. The spirited young woman must find her bearings in a community threatened by moral turpitude, social injustice, religious intolerance, and aristocratic pride. As is not uncommon in Marlitt's plots, a household in disarray because of the autocratic rule of a woman with the wrong values plays a central role. The narrator describes the petty tyrannies and bigotries of the domestic sphere in excruciating detail, as Elizabeth, who is also known by the sobriquet Gold Elsie, becomes the target of the venomous bigot and snob Baroness von Lessen.

With a plot advocating virtue and insisting on social justice that is also, as Kirsten Belgum has argued, pleasurably structured around female desire, *Gold Elsie,* Marlitt's first full-length novel, and second to be translated in North America, sets the tone for the ensuing vogue of translated German fiction.[5] In a striking scene, Elizabeth, who once declared that she could not imagine "how . . . any one [could] love a stranger better than father and mother" (100), experiences a sexual awakening beneath the cool eye of the male protagonist. A gifted pianist, Elizabeth performs with the full knowledge and enjoyment of her talent. Yet this performance feels different: "something blended with the tones that she could not herself comprehend; she could not possibly pursue and analyze it, for it breathed almost imperceptibly across the waves of sound. It seemed as though joy and woe no longer moved side by side, but melted together into one" (124). Nineteenth-century American readers looking for romance in their "wholesome" reading ought to have been able to recognize the erotic undertones of this euphemistic language.[6]

The novel offers an array of delights for readers looking for virtuous yet erotic fare that privileges a female protagonist. As readers vicariously experience Elizabeth's sexual awakening, they also discern that this young woman unconsciously wields power over a much older and more experienced man, the thirty-seven-year-old Baron von Walde, by virtue of her charm, talent, virtue, intellect, and beauty.[7] The narrative signals the baron's desire for the heroine through his unexplained moodiness and unmotivated gruffness toward her. While Elizabeth mistakes these signs, the text encourages readers to relish the hero's growing yet unspoken attraction to her as well as hers to him; indeed, the pleasure of reading Marlitt's novels in general depends on readers having a clearer sense of the heroine's feelings for the male protagonist and her effect on him than does the heroine herself. The plot is designed so as to make readers feel worry and frustration when the two characters repeatedly fail to come together.

Gold Elsie embeds the happy union of hero and heroine in a social context and thus provides a richly satisfactory conclusion. In addition to emplotting the fulfillment of the heroine's desire, Marlitt censures the noxious privileges of birth by foregrounding the selfish sexual power that immoral aristocratic men exercise over women of all ranks. The story's chief villain, the aristocratic Emil von Hollfeld, tries to cheat the invalid Helene von Walde of her money by mercilessly exploiting her tender feelings for him. Furthermore, he takes advantage of the serving girl Bertha and then deserts her, leaving her to descend into madness. Finally, he twice tries to ravish the bourgeois Elizabeth.

As if the social meaning of Hollfeld's villainous sexuality were not manifest, Marlitt added the backstory of the nobleman Jost von Gnadewitz, who two hundred years earlier eloped with a gypsy and subsequently kept her prisoner in his castle where she pined for her lost freedom. Shortly after being baptized, she died giving birth to Jost's son; the Ferbers learn that they are descended from this very son. Although the narrator somewhat downplays the gypsy origins, their significance persists: rejecting their newfound nobility and thus the cruel ancestor who imprisoned the object of his desire, the Ferbers maintain a love of freedom and self-pride that, the text intimates, they have inherited from their exotic female ancestor.

As if to repair the social inequality that licenses men to treat women as they please, Marlitt refrains from killing off the jealous Bertha for her attempt to murder Elizabeth. Instead, mad Bertha recovers and emigrates to America with a man from her own social class who loves her. It is no coincidence that Marlitt's homicidal madwoman bears the same name as Charlotte Brontë's mad Bertha Mason in *Jane Eyre* (1847). Marlitt, however, treats her character more gently, blaming not her for her insanity but instead the male roué.[8]

The conclusion of the novel both communicates Marlitt's central message of triumph of virtue over "servility, malice and hypocrisy" (138) (and particularly as these vices characterize the aristocracy) and enacts the fulfillment of desire, symbolized euphemistically by the baby Elizabeth holds in her arms on the final page. Elizabeth has achieved her heart's desire; Baroness von Lessen and her deceitful son have been banished; Herr von Walde has lost his melancholy air; the castle has been remodeled and restored; and the region has relinquished its gloomy secrets of obsessive passion and social injustice to be restored to its better self.[9] Elizabeth, adored by her husband, is "happy in the fullest sense of the word" (344).

Elizabeth's happiness has been achieved not without some adventure and freedom. Yet the novel also limits women's sphere of action and thus delivers safe reading. An exciting scene, for example, in which Elizabeth physically prevents a gamekeeper from murdering Herr von Walde immediately reins in the heroine again. Just after she has pulled back the arm of the would-be assassin "with all the strength of which she was capable" (188), her "feminine" nature reasserts itself and she trembles violently, a blissful smile on her face now that she has saved her beloved. Selfless love—as the refined affective sphere in which women allegedly wield power and authority—reclaims its right to define women's agency. Elizabeth remains strong in loving but weak in acting. Nevertheless, within this narrow range, the text pleasantly insists that women have choices and a degree of independence.

Invoking and calling into question the well-worn image of oak and ivy, Elizabeth declared in the first English translation in 1868 and continued to do so upon each American reading on into the twentieth century: "I never could endure the trite image of the ivy and the oak, and shall most certainly not illustrate it in my own person" (62). The heroine in translation—perhaps like her American readers—meant to assert her independence and thus participate actively in the making of her miniaturized world. In Marlitt's world she could do so, even make mistakes, and yet never forego her happy ending.

In 1868, *The Nation* enthusiastically confirmed that there was something special about Elizabeth Ferber and Felicitas in *The Old Mam'selle's Secret*: these newly translated novels delivered German heroines who differed from the German women Americans thought they knew:

> The typical German woman, fair and rotund who "mends the pap's hose" and plays for him the part of a dutiful and overworked upper servant, and is fitly rewarded therefor by accompanying him to the family club and the festive beer-garden, has no recognized existence in Miss Marlitt's ideal world. Her heroines settle themselves firmly on the rock of their own individuality and being unusually well provided with the weapons of personal beauty, innocence, and genuine love for truth, "moral elevation and spiritual growth," do most sturdy battle with the aristocratic prejudices of their lovers. They come out victorious of course, and the heroes . . . get in the end most loving and obedient wives.[10]

Original and spirited, Marlitt's early heroines actively triumph, as the reviewer recognized, yet do not overtly violate the codes of domesticity. They, moreover, set the tone for the German domestic fiction that was to be imported and avidly read in America in the Gilded Age.

In focusing on a domestic world in a German region shaped by middle-class values, one ruled by the heart, *Gold Elsie,* like all of Marlitt's novels, depicts social hierarchy less as it was actually lived than as it was *felt*. Feeling can gloss over historical and geographical particularity. If readers can find an empathetic point of entry into the novel's imagined social world, that world need not be keyed to the specifics of their own social reality for them to enjoy the fiction. Indeed, the slight alienation produced by the foreign setting potentially facilitates the suspension of disbelief and makes the stories in a sense real. American readers quickly felt their way into Marlitt's Germany, bristling at the social injustice of a system that privileged the unworthy over the worthy and thrilling to the love story. From the start, Americans, as did *The Nation*, took "so much pleasure in reading [*Gold Elsie*]."[11]

Nineteenth-century American readers could of course also recognize the international generic conventions of romance that influenced this novel's formal and thematic structure and guaranteed a happy ending. Knowledge of that outcome did not, however, necessarily diminish suspense. As the narrative repeatedly presented new obstacles, readers must have been eager to learn how the longed-for resolution would be reached and the broken society restored. Nor did the inevitable happy ending disappoint their belief that Marlitt's novels had something to tell them about the human condition and, in particular, that of women. In 1876 a review of Marlitt's *At the Councillor's; or, a Nameless History* insisted that while many German novels were mired in the merely sentimental, Marlitt's novel informed readers about the complexities of the human heart. Marlitt's novel "does not give the first place to mere sentiment," the reviewer maintained, "but enters deeply into a story of the human heart, and an exposition of its passions."[12]

In the end Marlitt's "wholesome" romance plot with its happy ending helped smooth the way for the entry of Marlitt's subsequent novels and a host of German novels to come. *Gold Elsie* offered the empathetic and pleasurable reading that came to be linked in the minds of American novel readers to German origins, possessing that "peculiar tinge of romance which is the characteristic of German sentiment."[13]

Evidence for the popularity of *Gold Elsie* in America over four decades is legion. I have been able to confirm twelve reprint Lippincott editions from 1869 to 1901, but in fact as early as 1879, only eleven years after the translation first appeared, Lippincott advertised an "eleventh edition."[14] If there was truth in advertising, then, there were likely double the number of reprint editions I have confirmed. Lippincott, however, by no means presided exclusively over American reading of *Gold Elsie*.

In June 1887, after *Gold Elsie* had sold steadily for nearly twenty years with Lippincott for $1.50, a second translation appeared in George Munro's Seaside Library and cost twenty cents.[15] Upon receiving the request from Munro to translate it, Mary Stuart Smith enthusiastically pronounced the novel "one of E. Marlitt's first and best stories."[16] She noted, too, that she could buy the novel in German "at any newsstand for a few cents," since Munro had reprinted it in the original German six years earlier in 1881 in his Deutsche Library.[17] In that same year an unattributed third translation appeared with Lovell; it also cost twenty cents. While Lippincott continued to reprint Wister's translation (and protected its rights to it) and Smith and son's translation enjoyed the wide circulation of Munro's cheap editions, this third translation experienced circulation of another sort as part of the rapidly expanding practice of reprinting and rebinding.[18] After 1887 popular American editions of the unattributed translation proliferated, including editions with A. L. Burt; the Syndicate Trading Company; Clarke, Given and Hooper; W. B. Conkey; Crowell; Mershon; R. F. Fenno; Hurst; New York Publishing Company; Donohue, Henneberry & Company; M. A. Donohue and Company; Laird and Lee; Lovell, Coryell and Company; William L. Allison; Grosset and Dunlap; E. A. Weeks and Company; F. M. Lupton; H. M. Caldwell; and Chatterton-Peck Company. Sometimes these publishers shared the same plates, merely supplying new title pages, as did A. L. Burt, Hurst, and Lupton, for example.[19]

Catalogues of American public libraries corroborate the availability of *Gold Elsie* for borrowing as well. The New York Public Library still holds both a Lippincott edition (1882) and an undated one by E. A. Weeks. All of the late nineteenth- and early twentieth-century catalogues I have consulted list English translations of *Goldelse* in their holdings, sometimes including them under "English prose fiction," as does, for instance, the Boston Public Library.[20]

Gold Elsie was read in the United States into the new century, but some publishers began to target a younger audience by the turn of the new century. The cover of Chatterton-Peck's undated edition, for example, features a young woman dressed in the style of the early 1900s (see Figure 3.1).[21] Her skirt, which stops just short of covering her ankles, corresponds to Saidee E. Kennedy's description of the appropriate skirt length for a teenaged girl from 1907: "But Adelaide is now fifteen, / A maiden fair and sweet; / Again her frocks almost conceal / Her dainty slippered feet."[22] Advertisements for books included in the back of the book also imply a teen audience. We will return frequently to the slide of adult reading into adolescent reading, for the overt appeal to younger readers characterizes the marketing of many of these German women's novels after 1900, as it does, for example, that of such classic British novels as *Jane Eyre* or *Oliver Twist* as well.

The Mad German in the Attic:
The Old Mam'selle's Secret

The families depicted in these approximately one hundred novels exhibit a national inflection particular to the historical moment and imbricated with

Figure 3.1 E. Marlitt, *Gold Elsie* (New York: Chatterton-Peck, n.d.). Author's copy.

class affiliation and female subjectivity. We will explore the German national imaginary mediated in these novels throughout, especially in chapter 6, when we turn to novels that intertwine family stories with historical events. The legibility of this German national imaginary in nineteenth-century North America after this fiction had been translated, marketed, and widely read, however, inevitably varied. While "after the German" did suggest German content, it also became an advertising label that guaranteed a certain kind of pleasurable read.

Originally written for *Die Gartenlaube*, where they projected a domesticated version of a German national imaginary for a German audience, Marlitt's novels became a sought-after German product on an international market; in their American iterations they reveal a great deal about the acculturation of this national product in a new reading context. These novels constitute a mix of national markers interlaced with familiar romance plots and an idea of Germany rooted in its regions and home towns and infused with middle-class values. *Gold Elsie*, for example, displays its German origins in Beethoven's bust upon Elsie's piano, the montane setting of a specifically identified Thuringia, the unpronounceable German name "Gnadewitz" and other obviously German names, the aristocratic "von" in surnames, and the preservation of the courtesy titles "Herr," "Fräulein," and "Frau." The profession of the forester likewise flags the German origins of the story, the forester being a stock figure of German fiction and the woods and its management a specifically German preoccupation. Yet to an outsider Germany is not particularly visible in *Gold Elsie*, especially compared with such other novels as Heimburg's *Lore von Tollen* and Werner's patriotic *Heimatklang*, where a set of easily recognizable tropes is assembled or a picture of the beloved Prussian Queen Louise graces the family parlor. Elizabeth's family history is, moreover, not overtly rooted in a specifically German past except insofar as it suggests the abuses of feudalism, abuses that were not particular to Germany. *The Old Mam'selle's Secret*, however, makes a more overt appeal to a German national community and demonstrates how visibly the German national project can inhere in popular domestic fiction that is not jingoistic in tone. American readers' long embrace of this markedly German book indicates that when delivered in pleasurable, digestible, indeed familiar form, the national culture of others can be relished in translation.

If Germans early on revered Marlitt as the "Verfasserin der 'Gold-Else'" (author of *Gold Elsie*), her first popular success in Germany, Americans more likely associated Marlitt with *The Old Mam'selle's Secret*, a "novel of unusual merit and of great charm."[23] This popular novel harbored a mystery apparently more interesting even than the hidden mausoleum in the old castle in

Gold Elsie, indeed, a secret more fascinating to Americans than any that Marlitt would embed in her eight succeeding full-length novels.

On April 1, 1868, the *American Literary Gazette and Publisher's Circle* announced *The Old Mam'selle's Secret* as "just published."[24] Given that the conclusion of the novel appeared in *Die Gartenlaube* in early fall 1867 and that the book version was not published until 1868 in Germany, Wister must have translated directly from the pages of the magazine.[25] Her rendering shows signs of haste, above all in the chapter divisions: she overlooked the chapter break for chapter 12 and thus conjoined chapters 11 and 12 to produce a novel consisting of twenty-seven chapters rather than Marlitt's twenty-eight. The two later translations remedied the oversight, but Lippincott let it stand.

While Wister would eventually publish forty-two translations, twenty-nine of them novels by German women, *The Old Mam'selle's Secret* constituted her greatest success and became the book with which she was most frequently identified in advertising. The novel in fact accompanied her to her grave. Noting that she was famous for her translations, her obituary in the *New York Times* named only *The Old Mam'selle's Secret.* A more extensive obituary in the *Philadelphia Inquirer* judged the novel "probably the greatest of her translations from the standpoint of the sale attained."[26]

Americans—from such prominent figures as Mark Twain to thirteen-year-old Agnes Hamilton of Fort Wayne, Indiana—read *The Old Mam'selle's Secret.* Agnes wrote to her twelve-year-old cousin Alice Hamilton in 1881 that of the four novels by Marlitt she had read, "the nicest are 'Old Mam'sell' [*sic*] Secret' and 'The Second Wife,'" both of which she found "equally splendid." Fourteen years later, a grown-up Agnes reported that she still enjoyed reading the novel and that she could not wait to get hold of the copy a friend was reading and "read it through from the beginning to the end and not for the first time."[27] Twain, for his part, pronounced it an "excellent German novel" in his essay "The Awful German Language" and, as Horst Kruse has argued, may have borrowed from it when writing *The Mysterious Stranger.*[28]

Lippincott's Magazine praised the depiction of the characters: Cordula, the old mam'selle, was a "masterpiece of tender and suggestive delineation," and, furthermore, the portrait of Johannes as a practicing doctor was convincing. "This is high praise," the reviewer emphasized, "because here even Thackeray has had but a partial success."[29] Lippincott, furthermore, advertised *The Old Mam'selle's Secret* with a quotation from the *Columbus Journal* of Columbus, Ohio, that effusively endorsed Marlitt's novel as commensurate with works by Baroness Tautphoeus, George Eliot, and Reade.[30]

The Old Mam'selle's Secret was not a mere flash in the pan. It achieved long-term recognition in America as numbering among the best reads available in English. When in 1893 the American Library Association assembled a catalog of five thousand volumes for a popular library exhibited at the Chicago World's Fair, the 1892 edition of Wister's translation of The Old Mam'selle's Secret appeared on this list under both Wister's name and Marlitt's.[31] As mentioned above, Rossiter Johnson offered a plot summary of the novel in his Authors Digest (1908).[32] In 1902 Charles Dudley Warner likewise included a plot summary of The Old Mam'selle's Secret in his thirty-one-volume Library of the World's Best Literature, Ancient and Modern, along with commentary remarking, "the English version by Mrs. A. L. Wister is regarded as even superior to the original."[33] As we shall explore in greater depth in chapter 8, this notion of the superiority of the translation to the original long constituted a commonplace of Lippincott's marketing and Americans' understanding of Wister's work as translator and thus figured significantly in the acculturation of the book.

If Wister's translation of Marlitt's Das Geheimnis der alten Mamsell had made of this German novel an American fact, the Carnegie Library of Pittsburgh confirmed this transformation by cataloging Wister's translation of The Old Mam'selle's Secret, along with other such translations from the German, under "English fiction."[34] Of Marlitt's novels, the library deemed it the one worthy of the special attention of a brief plot summary in its catalogue. The Catalogue of English Prose Fiction and Juvenile Books in the Chicago Public Library likewise listed the book both under "John, E. [E. Marlitt])" and "Wister, Annis L., Translations," without remarking that the designation "English Prose Fiction" was to be taken with advisement.[35]

The numbers of editions, translations, and reprints testify to wide circulation and continued sales of Marlitt's novel. Lippincott reprinted Wister's translation at least twenty times between 1868 and 1911.[36] Over this forty-three-year period, the firm advertised it both for individual purchase and as an item in a boxed set. The book was also often promoted in the front and back matter of other novels published by Lippincott—American novels, English novels, novels translated from the German—and frequently named on the title page of other Wister translations. Insofar as the edition is indicated, contemporary library catalogues most frequently list Wister's translation in their holdings.

The Old Mam'selle's Secret remained strongly associated with Wister and Lippincott, but that association could not forestall competition. In 1882 George Munro published Mary Stuart Smith's new English translation of The

Old Mam'selle's Secret in his popular Seaside Library. Four years later Munro released Smith's translation in yet another edition, in a Seaside Pocket Edition that cost a mere twenty cents.[37] Munro had good reason in the early 1880s to believe that it was worth a small investment to publish a new translation. The novel had, after all, been ranked in 1876 as the twenty-third "most salable novel" in the United States, just ahead of Charlotte M. Yonge's *Heir of Redclyffe* in the prize competition initiated by *Publishers' Weekly*.[38]

A notice for Lovell's edition of the mysterious E. H.'s new translation appeared in 1887 in *Publishers' Weekly* right next to that for Munro's Seaside Edition of Smith's translation.[39] In July 1887 Lippincott responded to this stepped-up competition by publishing a cheap paperback edition of *The Old Mam'selle's Secret* in its Series of Select Novels at twenty-five cents a copy.[40] At the time, Lippincott's novels otherwise tended to cost $1.25 to $1.50.

While Munro and Lippincott retained their rights to Smith's and Wister's translations, respectively, new editions and reprint editions of E. H.'s translation proliferated well into the new century. F. M. Lupton, for example, published it both in the moderately priced Stratford Series and in the cheap Bijou Series. Lupton was but one in a raft of new and aggressive publishers that included the novel in series meant to address the American novel mania across budgets and social classes: Excelsior Publishing; Donohue, Henneberry and Company; M. A. Donohue and Company; William L. Allison Company; Hurst and Company; Porter and Coates (all of the preceding used the same plates for their editions); The International Book Company; Estes and Lauriat; W. B. Conkey; Lovell, Coryell and Company (these last three publishers shared the same plates); Home Book Company; G. M. Hill; Mershon (the last three named shared the same plates); E. A. Weeks and Company (Dartmouth Edition); H. M. Caldwell Company; Clarke, Given and Hooper; Empire Publishing Company; Mutual Book Company (The Bon Ton Library); and Werner. A. L. Burt also published E. H.'s translation, falsely attributing it to Mary Stuart Smith. Much later, in the 1920s, Sears and Company made E. H.'s rendering available in the American Home Classics series. In varieties of editions, E. H.'s translation in the end outstripped both Wister's and Smith's.

The editions of E. H.'s rendering came in several sizes and with an array of covers. The covers stand out for their ornamentation, especially in comparison with the poor quality of the paper and the reprinting (clearly from much used plates). A Hurst edition may serve as an example. Although the book is badly printed on cheap paper, it boasts an appealing cloth cover stamped with an elaborate art nouveau design on the front (see Figure 3.2). The design is repeated, stamped in gold and red, on the spine.[41]

The inclusion of E. H.'s translation in the 1920s in the American Home Classics series speaks volumes about the status *The Old Mam'selle's Secret* had achieved over nearly sixty years of American reading. As a classic for the American home, it was absorbed into American reading culture; it came to be a novel that everybody knew or was supposed to know. In this series Marlitt's novel stood on American bookshelves alongside English-language works—by Longfellow, Hawthorne, Dickens, Tennyson, Eliot, Stevenson, Kipling, Ouida, Doyle, and Jessie Fothergill—as well as works written originally in French—novels by Dumas, Balzac, and Daudet—and other favorites of nineteenth-century American readers and publishers.

The making of a film version of *The Old Mam'selle's Secret* in 1912 likewise testifies to the novel's long-term popularity and absorption into American culture. While the filmmakers altered the happy ending to make the heroine rich as well as virtuous, the film, as did all such short films in this period, relied on the audience's previous knowledge of the novel for its coherence and likely its box office appeal as well.[42]

How, then, could *The Old Mam'selle's Secret*, as an assimilated fact of American reading, mediate a legible, if attenuated, idea of Germany for American readers? To answer this question, we turn now to the text itself and the story it tells of an imagined Germany. In 1867, four years before German unification and the founding of the Second German Empire under Prussian hegemony, Marlitt tailored her novel to German conditions in the regions and home towns and to German middle-class ideas about the cultural nation, writing it to fit the aims of a family magazine determined to cultivate German readers with programmatically German products. Yet from the start Marlitt's text, like *Gold Elsie*, also showed signs of the author's international reading and specifically her familiarity with *Jane Eyre*.[43] The resonance with and deviations from *Jane Eyre* may have helped make the novel's Germanness visible.

Early on, Rudolf von Gottschall remarked on the resemblance of the forceful character of Marlitt's heroine to that of Brontë's Jane. He failed, however, to mention the most striking similarity of all between the two novels, namely, the "mad woman in the attic" or rather, Marlitt's German antithesis to Brontë's mad woman.[44] Unlike Brontë's Bertha Mason, Marlitt's Aunt Cordula, who lives a life invisible to the rest of the family and initially unknown to the heroine, is not a raving monster from the colonial West Indies who threatens to kill the virtuous heroine at the center of empire. Instead, she is the heroine's teacher and deliverer, and the guardian of German culture in a house ruled by bigotry and false piety in the lower stories. While Brontë called her Bertha "the foul German spectre—the Vampyre,"[45] Marlitt made

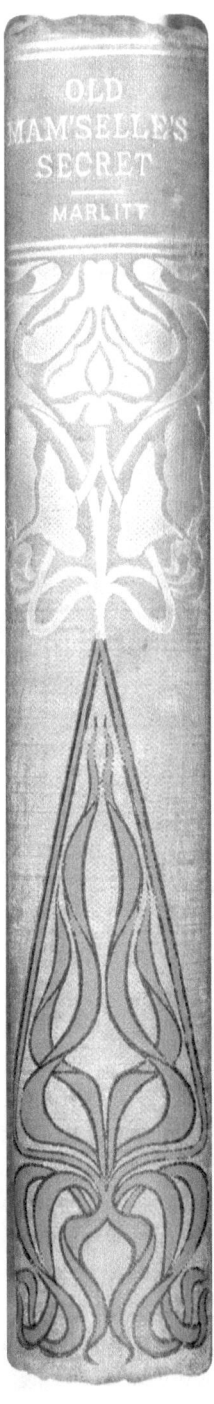

Figure 3.2 Front Cover and Spine, E. Marlitt, *The Old Mam'selle's Secret* (New York: Hurst & Company, n.d.). Author's copy.

Cordula, like her name, the hidden heart of German culture in need of preservation and restoration. Cordula, whom social prejudice and malfeasance have denied a happy ending, holds the key to the family's dishonorable past, a past rooted in German history. This past needs to be uncovered for the sake of the happy ending of the younger generation, the wedding of hero and heroine, and the redemption of the erring family.

The tale unfolds in Thuringia, where an accidental death at a traveling carnival show leaves four-year-old Felicitas motherless. The soft-hearted patrician Herr Hellwig takes in the girl against his bigoted wife's wishes and educates her as if she were his own daughter. When Hellwig unexpectedly dies, his wife, who abhors Felicitas, seizes the opportunity to alter arrangements. She gives Felicitas a new first name, curtails her education, relegates her to the servants' quarters, and raises her for a life of servitude. Despite Frau Hellwig's best efforts to erase her identity, break her spirit, keep her ignorant, and ruin her chances in life, Felicitas prevails, enabled by the old mam'selle.

Cordula, Herr Hellwig's well-to-do aunt, whom Frau Hellwig also hates, lives hidden in the upper story of the back wing of the mansion. Hellwig banished her to this part of the house years earlier on account of his wife's incessant complaints about Cordula's playing of profane music on the Sabbath. In this concealed apartment, surrounded by marble busts of great German men, books, and ivy, Cordula reads, plays the piano, treasures her autograph collection of letters and manuscripts of important composers (Handel, Gluck, Haydn, Mozart, and Bach), cultivates a garden on an inner balcony, tends to her birds, and extends charity to the needy.

Shortly after Hellwig's death, Felicitas makes her way to these attic quarters via the roof of the house when she hears the strains of a Mozart overture emerging from them. Cordula, who is well acquainted with Frau Hellwig's cruelty, takes Felicitas under her wing, becoming her secret teacher and instructing her in literature, French, music, and a form of Christianity that is joyful, loving, and tolerant, in contrast to the narrow-minded religion practiced by the Hellwigs on the lower floors. Cordula, a creation of popular culture, embodies German national high culture and the idea of aesthetic education, as well as virtue and sentiment. When Frau Hellwig's son Johannes returns home after years of studying and practicing medicine in Bonn, he finds a nearly grown Felicitas whose knowledge, proud manner, and refined bearing contrast markedly with the humble and ignorant servitude to which Frau Hellwig, with his misguided approval, had condemned her.

It soon becomes clear that Johannes, who initially treats Felicitas in the stern manner taught him by his mother, is attracted to the beautiful young woman. The growing sexual tension between the two provides titillating reading. Johannes, who is convinced that the heroine's low origins make her an inappropriate match for him, struggles against his feelings for her; Felicitas, for her part, obtusely misunderstands his every gesture of reconciliation and refuses to acknowledge her own attraction to him. Readers schooled in romance conventions, however, can quickly discern their feelings. Inevitably there is a rival for Johannes's affections, but, although Cousin Adele is Frau Hellwig's choice for her son, Adele does not possess the power to charm him and is, moreover, unmasked as a selfish hypocrite and heartless mother.

Felicitas plans to live with Cordula upon attaining her majority, but the latter dies unexpectedly before revealing her secrets and before signing a new will bequeathing her fortune to her protégé. In a shocking scene, the odious Frau Hellwig rifles through Cordula's belongings in search of the family silver. Blinded to the wealth inhering in high culture by her abhorrence of all profane music and literature, Frau Hellwig burns Cordula's collection of manuscripts and autographs, including an original composition signed by Johann Sebastian Bach.

The posthumous revelation of Cordula's many secrets requires a stern reckoning in the Hellwig household. Cordula loved the humble Oscar von Hirschsprung, an impoverished student descended from the once noble Hirschsprung family. The patrician Hellwigs vehemently opposed an alliance with this shoemaker's son. Meanwhile, Cordula's discovery in the foundations of the Hellwigs' house of a chest containing papers and money belonging to the former owners, the Hirschsprungs, and left behind during the turmoil of the Thirty Years' War, led not to the restitution of the treasure and the happy ending Cordula desired but instead to a crime. The bourgeois Hellwigs pocketed the money knowing full well that Oscar and his father were likely the rightful heirs to this fortune. When Cordula threatened to reveal the cover-up, her father collapsed and died. Overcome with guilt, she ceased to oppose her family and was eventually banished to a hidden life in the upper story.

With her will, however, she determined to make amends to the Hirschsprungs and to help atone for the Hellwigs' crime. She therefore bequeathed the Bach manuscript, an antique bracelet, and 30,000 thalers to that same "old noble Thuringian stock" in memory of her beloved Oscar.[46] As a result of Frau Hellwig's hasty destruction of the manuscript, the Hellwigs owe an enormous debt to Cordula's estate. They also owe the Hirschsprung family compensation for their ancestors' crime.

Even before this revelation, however, a pair of bracelets, each engraved with three lines of medieval love poetry, provides a clue to the crime and in turn marks its link to a specifically German history and culture. Together, the bracelets constitute a stanza from the twenty-eighth song of Ulrich von Liechtenstein's thirteenth-century *Frauendienst*. Thus the family secret is associated with recently recovered national cultural history—the German philologist Karl Lachmann had republished Ulrich's works in 1841. All three American translations reproduce the original Middle High German text, providing a highly visible national historical tag. The original Middle High German avers that where two lovers are united in mutual and constant love, God has brought them together for a "wunneclichez leben."[47] The "wunneclichez leben," which Wister translated as "bliss," serves as a thirteenth-century valorization of true love, loyalty, and the happy ending; in the nineteenth century it also confirmed the status of all three as the ancient property of the Germans.

Readers become suspicious about the rightful ownership of the bracelets when the narrative draws attention to the fact that nasty Cousin Adele is wearing one of them. Adele holds captive precisely the lines that promise the happy ending, lines reading in Wister's translation, "That this love is always new, / God to these two hearts has given / Bliss indeed, for love is heaven" (112). The old mam'selle, on the other hand, possesses the bracelet stating the conditions for this happiness—loyalty and mutual love: "Where'er love with love requited / Dwells in two hearts fond and true, / And where both are so united" (112). Marlitt ultimately unites Felicitas and Johannes in a marriage in which Felicitas, armed with an education from the German heart, Cordula, will find fulfillment, indeed, the realization of her own name—Felicitas—in loving and assisting her husband in his medical practice and, of course, in mothering their children.

While the novel worries throughout over Felicitas's low social status as the daughter of traveling "players," the final unraveling of the mystery reveals her to be the daughter of an aristocratic mother from the same Hirschsprung family as Cordula's beloved Oscar: Meta von Hirschsprung was disowned by her family when she fell in love with the Polish juggler Orlowsky. Thus Felicitas possesses nobility of spirit as a result of her good character, her education, and self-fashioning, but also nobility of origin. Johannes also proves himself by upholding the family honor in making good on the debt and by learning greater tolerance and charity. On the final page, the novel even admits the possibility of the redemption of Frau Hellwig, whom the reader has learned to love to hate. Here Frau Hellwig is viewed knitting baby clothes that might be intended for Johannes and Felicitas's new baby, and the narrator remarks, "And perhaps the love of her grandchildren may prove this unforeboded, tender spot, from which a mild warmth may stream to dissolve Madame's icy nature" (312).

Marlitt set the novel in her own hometown, Arnstadt, Thuringia, and based the story of Felicitas's mother on a local incident. She furthermore modeled the Hellwigs' house on one kitty-corner from the house where she herself was born and wove Arnstadt's strong connection to Johann Sebastian Bach, from 1703 to 1707 the organist of Boniface Church, into her tale. When she dated Cordula's manuscript 1707, she commemorated the year in which Bach left Arnstadt. For a nineteenth-century German reader, this story took place in a setting easily recognizable as a version of a German regional town, one like any number of such towns in preunification Germany and one like that in which many Germans lived. But *The Old Mam'selle's Secret* did not merely describe German realities. It also told Germans what their culture should and could be. Cordula was the guardian of a national culture that was to be preserved and honored. Frau Hellwig, her nemesis, represented a different cultural strain, however, an old-fashioned, straight-laced, egocentric piety unsuited to modern sensibilities and impervious to social misery. This kind of religiosity, as the novel asserts, has suppressed good and true German culture, which must be recovered for the sake of present happiness and future health.

A House Divided:
In the Schillingscourt in America[48]

In 1879 a German-Spanish-American cotton princess appeared in *Die Gartenlaube* (nos. 14–39) to play the heroine in Marlitt's newest serialized novel, *Im Schillingshof*. As an American of mixed origins from a southern slave state, Mercedes de Valmaseda was to aid the reconstruction of the German family and, by extension, the German nation. By the end of that same year, just weeks after the serialization had concluded, she had also put in a double appearance on the American book market. On the one hand, *In the Schillingscourt* could be purchased for $1.50 in Wister's translation with Lippincott; on the other, Munro offered Emily R. Steinestel's translation with the same title and priced at twenty-five cents as volume 14 of the Royal Series. Here it appeared alongside such favorite British novels as Hardy's *The Mayor of Casterbridge*, Thackeray's *The History of Henry Esmond*, Scott's *Ivanhoe*, Wood's *East Lynne*, and Mulock's *John Halifax Gentleman*.[49] The *Literary World* welcomed the appearance of Wister's *Schillingscourt* as a "good specimen of the best class of German novels."[50] Inasmuch as *In the Schillingscourt* overtly constructs a German-American nexus, it may fittingly conclude this first probe into the transformations that took place in German novels as they crossed the Atlantic to become facts of American culture.

By 1879 Marlitt had become a staple of American reading, and both Lippincott and Munro had good reason to believe that a new Marlitt novel would sell. *Im Schillingshof* did not appear in book form in Germany until 1880. The American publishing date—1879—indicates therefore that the two publishers were in a hurry to put this virtually guaranteed success on the American market before some other publisher in their respective price class scooped them. Wister and Steinestel must have translated directly from the pages of *Die Gartenlaube,* preparing for a quick turnaround in the United States as soon as the serialization concluded in Germany.[51]

Writing eight years after the founding of the German empire and in the American post-Reconstruction era, Marlitt set *In the Schillingscourt* in the 1860s, the decade in which both the United States and Germany (re)constructed their respective nations. The central plot begins in 1860 with an emigration to America and concludes in 1871, the year of German unification, with a marriage. Although the text offers little description of the wars that occurred on both sides of the Atlantic, they figure in the romance plot.

The novel centers on neighbors whose once-cordial relations are strained: the wealthy bourgeois Wolframs and the impoverished aristocratic von Schillings. The graceful Italianate Schillingscourt, the Schillings' home, serves as both a locus of action and the figuration of the novels' content and message. Erected and designed by a Benedictine monk after his sojourn in Italy, it originally belonged to a rambling property that was subsequently divided.[52] While the parsimonious, bourgeois Wolframs preserved the adjoining monastery in its squat ugliness, the aristocratic Schillings modernized and beautified their foreign-looking mansion. Yet moral failing has put both properties in disarray. On the Wolfram side, deception and mean-spiritedness reign. On the Schilling side, Arnold, a promising artist, has at his father's behest entered into a marriage of convenience with the wealthy Clementine to save the heavily mortgaged Schillingscourt from financial ruin. Yet Clementine's narrow-mindedness, hypocritical piety, and lack of an aesthetic sense have ruined the Schillingscourt in a different sense, creating an atmosphere antithetical to Arnold's artistic sensibilities and generosity of spirit. The suicide of the Schillings' faithful servant, Adam, when unjustly accused by old Baron von Schilling of spying for neighbor Wolfram, serves as one among many symptoms of the rotten state of things in both houses. The eventual physical restoration of the Schillingscourt under the supervision of the American cotton princess signals redemption, expressing in the very décor of the home a progressive spirit, love of art, and familial harmony. Like the opening sentence and the title of the book, the last word of the novel—Schillingscourt—underlines the real and symbolic importance to family and nation of a property shaped by foreign architecture and built on German soil.

While the Schillings struggle with profound unhappiness, the nastiness of the Wolfram family on the other side of the wall occasions exile to America. Years before the novel opens, Major Lucian divorced his wife, Wolfram's sister, and left for the slave state South Carolina, where he married a Spanish American woman and fathered a daughter, Mercedes. Felix, his son from his first marriage, follows him many years later when the birth of a son to his uncle Wolfram diminishes his financial prospects and when his engagement to Lucile Fournier, the daughter of a Berlin dancer, causes his mother to disinherit him.

While South Carolina initially offers Felix a safe haven and new opportunity, the year is 1860, and Major Lucian's days as a wealthy plantation owner are numbered. During the American Civil War, Felix succumbs to wounds sustained defending his property and family, but not before begging his wealthy half-sister to accompany the now-destitute Lucile with their two children, José and Paula, back to his German homeland to unite them with their grandmother. It has required just over one-fourth of the novel to establish the background for the love story that now develops against the backdrop of the recently divided United States and the emergent German nation.

South Carolina, the Americans' point of departure, variously serves Marlitt's script. Her novel leans heavily on the idea of the American South as racially and ethnically mixed, skin color figuring significantly in the characterizations of Mercedes and her two former slaves. Thus the narrator ironically notes how the "white marble faces" of the caryatids of the columns of the Schillingscourt look with astonishment upon the "negress" Deborah (W 130).

Black Deborah's quickly sketched portrait strikingly resembles the "mammy" stereotype that gained currency in American anti–Uncle Tom novels in the 1850s and 1860s and later served postbellum apologetics for the Old South.[53] Deborah smiles good-humoredly with her fat cheeks and thick red lips (W 130). "Her wooly head crowned with a turban of many colours" (W 146), she waddles through the front garden.[54] Although Marlitt later employs the term "Wollhaar" (M 157; woolly hair [my translation]) to describe Deborah, the German text here and elsewhere describes Deborah simply as "krausköpfig" (M 139; curly-headed [my translation]). Wister, however, conformed to American racialized language, uniformly translating "curly-headed" here and elsewhere as "woolly" (W 130). Steinestel first employed the racially coded "kinky-headed" and later "woolly head."[55] Marlitt's text also emphasizes the skin color of the American servant when it contrasts her blackness to the full-blooded European Paula, who is dressed in white, "looking like a white dove clinging about the negress" (W 130). Wister replaced the original German "weißer Falter" (M 139; white butterfly [my translation]) with "white dove," pushing the sentimental language a bit harder. Translating more freely, Steinestel highlighted skin color instead of clothing: "pressed her little white face close to the black cheek" (S 91). In this passage Marlitt, aided by her translators, thus reproduced an image of African American women that had currency in the United States for many decades. But it is not only Deborah who is black in this novel; blackness links her to her "black" mistress.

Jack, a second former slave, is also viewed against these white columns. Wister's free translation emphasizes Jack's blackness even more than the original. Jack, who in the original comes from the shores of the Senegal River and has the shining ebony skin of the "negro race" (M 157 [my translation]), becomes "a stalwart man with a shining skin as black as ebony" (W 146). Attuned to the moralizing aesthetics of the original, Wister omitted the historical details of race and geographical origin.

Upon her first appearance, the black-eyed and black-haired German-Spanish-American Mercedes, who stands beside little José, is also figured as a black maternal figure and thus completes the portrait of American southerners as black. She wears the black of mourning, without a trace of a lighter color, the text emphasizes, "like an image of night" (W 130). Her blackness also contrasts with the white caryatids. The text sustains her otherness with the hue of her skin as well, which, although not black, resembles "nothing but the clearest, lightest shade of amber" (W 137). Especially in the racialized context of American reading, yellow skin—as the hue associated with biracial children of European and African descent—could cement her association with her former slaves. Her black and yellow coloring and her affiliation with black African Americans in any case obfuscate her German heritage, emphasizing instead her status as an intruding outsider. She is, in Lucile's derisive terms, a "sallow gypsy, haughty plantation princess" (W 218). In other words, in her appearance, ethnicity, and origins in an economic system that produced a "new feudalism," she is unlike any proper German woman.

By making her heroine a defeated southerner of mixed ethnic origins and a former slaveholder, Marlitt in 1879 shifted the long-standing interest in exotic women in her fiction squarely to the center. Here Mercedes's otherness, once established, proves an asset, enabling the heroine to play a critical role in restoring the denizens of the divided property to their better selves. However, making a former slaveholder the moral center of her novel required effort, and the effort sometimes shows.

The text by no means approves of slavery. The unlovable imperiousness of Mercedes, "a princess born to command a host of slaves" (W 132), earns the narrator's disapproval, yet the novel avoids investigating the particulars of life in the Old South, the plantation system, and the slavery that supported it. The Schillings do not even mention slavery when South Carolina is to provide Felix and Lucile a safe haven in 1860. Slavery becomes a bone of contention only when Mercedes herself arrives with her former slaves. However, even then, for reasons that will shortly become clear, the novel finds ways of mitigating its criticism and of imagining within the economy of the Old South the cultivation of a benevolent affective bonding.

Besides Arnold, only Clementine directly confronts Mercedes with her slaveholding. Yet since the text so clearly repudiates Clementine for her own sins, her opinion scarcely matters. For her part, Mercedes argues for a more generous view of the American South by condemning the self-righteousness of prejudiced Germans who regard the crushing defeat of the South as just punishment for the wrongs of slavery. In a confrontational scene with Arnold, she asserts that the North exploited the "idol humanity" to break the power of the South. She insists, in Wister's translation, that the South virtuously fought for "culture over the rude masses" (W 161).

While such rationalizations echo apologetics for the Old South and thus can be seen as historically appropriate to Mercedes's character, elsewhere in the novel mention of slavery modulates into other issues that pertain to the mutual attraction between Mercedes and Arnold and thus abandons any serious interest in the American context. When Arnold declares, for example, "I have little fancy for the part of a slave" (W 213), he no longer expresses a principled objection to slavery but instead his fear of succumbing to the charms of a strong woman.

While uninterested in interrogating the inhumane system that generated slavery, *In the Schillingscourt* invests in the relationship of Mercedes to Deborah and Jack. The novel does not depict her behavior toward her servants as blameless, yet it validates her intimate and affective unbreakable bond to them. As the narrator uncritically reports, when she offered them their freedom, they chose to stay with her, trusting in her enduring care for them. When the Schillings' servants try to pump them for information, they refuse to talk. Deborah, who deeply loves the Lucian children, falls ill when José is terrorized by Wolfram's son. And when she does, Mercedes personally cares for her, "allowing no hand save her own to administer the medicine, to smooth the pillow of her 'faithful old servant'" (W 202). Together mistress and former slaves present a picture of solidarity and harmony. The loyal Deborah and Jack contrast vividly with the unruly German servants of the Schillingscourt. While Mercedes and her servants have come to Germany united in the noble purpose of restoring the Lucian children to their grandmother, the servants at the Schillingscourt are out of control, rude, and disloyal as a result of the discord between Arnold and Clementine. Viewed against the disarray in the two German households, the harmonious relationship of the American Mercedes and her former slaves reads positively.

In its affirmation of this relationship, the text employs a vocabulary that echoes revisionist apologetics for the Old South in post-Reconstruction America. If Civil War southerners had explained their social world, as Drew Gilpin Faust maintains, with "concepts like harmony, reciprocity, duty, and dependence, alongside metaphors of family and of organic unity," then Marlitt appears to have had an ear for precisely this social imaginary.[56] The Lost Cause belief that "the South had been on the verge of creating a civilization far superior to the one that existed in the North" resonates in the nobility of Mercedes's character. In this myth of the Old South, plantation owners "administered their plantations in an enlightened and progressive manner, in the process producing happy, smiling darkies who ... were content with their servitude."[57] Slaves allegedly preferred a beneficent master to the harsh world of free men and thus stayed with their masters even after being freed. Mutual, unshakable loyalty shaped relationships in a system supposedly based on love between master and slave. While Marlitt probably did not understand the particular American situation and certainly maintained no sustained interest in political and social conditions in the United States, her novel depends precisely on ideas associated with Confederate Nationalism and the Lost Cause movement that were circulating in America. Elements of the Lost Cause serve purposes in this text that relate both to the romance plot and the specific situation of German nation formation in the 1870s.

In her portrayal of Mercedes and her servants, Marlitt had tapped into elements of a myth that potentially played well in the American South and the American North, too. As Kenneth W. Goings explains, after the Civil War American northerners all too easily welcomed the idea of a benign and symbiotic relationship of southern whites and blacks in support of a noble civilization. The idea of love between masters and slaves fostered a much-desired redemptive "fantasy of wholeness." Indeed, Goings maintains, the American North wanted and needed to believe that race relations were improving in the South so that the United States at last "could all be one big, happy national family."[58] Despite having just fought a civil war that ended slavery, many northerners were therefore all too ready to gloss over the inhumanity of the slave system.[59]

Even as she deployed it, however, Marlitt ultimately presented this fantasy in a somewhat different light. The novel portrays a mistress—not a master— and her slaves, thereby disrupting the paternalistic gender hierarchy of the Old South and foregrounding the woman who was to carry the load of affect in the social order of southern planters.[60] Furthermore, since Mercedes is not exactly cast as white to begin with, her relationship to Jack and Deborah does not perfectly coincide with the racialized "myth of the Gothic 'Old South/New South,'" where white people had black servants and "where all the servants or slaves were 'happy' to be working for the [white] master."[61] Instead, by coding the mistress as, like her servants, of color, the text elides racial difference in service of an American wholeness that contrasts positively with the fissured German families. By creating affective bonds among the American migrants and then transplanting such relationships in German soil, the text asserts the redemptive power of what Kirsten Belgum has termed "virtuous love."[62] In the end, textually colored Mercedes becomes the heart of a new community in a German province that in turn is incorporated into the new nation. The characters who comment offensively on the color of her skin—Lucile and Clementine—are expurgated from the affective community of the morally redeemed and physically restored Schillingscourt. In 1879, in the aftermath of the victory over France and the ensuing anti-Catholic *Kulturkampf,* Lucile with her French heritage and Clementine as a fanatic Catholic figure as undesirables in the German national community. The Americans, by contrast, not only belong to this German family but also help reconstruct it.

Mercedes, who has come to Germany to do her duty—not to find her roots—dislikes the frigid climate and the coldness of the people, especially Arnold, whom she deems a "cold-blooded German" (W 144). Through the encounter with Germany in the form of Thuringia and the Germans in the person of Arnold, however, she eventually overcomes her distaste. The happy ending may even appear, as Todd Kontje argues, to depend on her ability to assimilate.[63] By the end of the novel Mercedes plays Bach, Beethoven, and Schubert; appreciates the modest charm of German nature; and has, in keeping with German bourgeois mores, generally taken on a softer, more feminine aspect, one that disassociates her from her past as a fierce defender of her property during the Civil War. Even her sallow face has a new "freshness and bloom" (W 380). The Germans, for their part, have adopted her. On the final page Arnold presents her to his father's portrait as "Lucian's daughter," that is, the daughter of a German.

Nevertheless, by also recalling the grave moral failing of the patriarch who demanded an inappropriate sacrifice of his only son, this same final page confounds an easy reading of this story as merely one in which a foreign woman submits to a superior German man. On the contrary: the American cotton princess has actively remade the German man and restored the German community. She has affirmed the true worth of the unloved, divorced Frau Lucian, helped rehabilitate her, and united her with her grandchildren.

As a result of this reconciliation, the Wolframs' ugly home, the locus of greed, has been torn down, leaving only the beautiful Schillingscourt standing. The presence of the Americans has further led to the discovery of a secret passage between the two properties that has cleared the reputation of the servant Adam, thus helping Arnold make amends to Adam's daughter. Finally, Mercedes has enabled Arnold to regain his integrity by divorcing Clementine. This last development has coincided, furthermore, with the rescue of the Schillingscourt itself, which in Clementine's clutches was in danger of becoming the property of the Catholic Church.

As in *The Old Mam'selle's Secret*, Marlitt relies on a work of German art to bring her plot to a happy resolution, here finally allowing the foreign Mercedes to work her magic as she defends Arnold's historical painting of persecuted French Huguenots from Clementine's attack. Clementine abhors Arnold's masterful painting as blasphemy and attempts to rip it to shreds. Mercedes, by contrast, immediately recognizes its brilliance, sensing as well that the painting of Huguenot noblewomen attacked in their own home by the Catholic queen's men reflects her own past when she valiantly protected southern secessionists hidden in her home. She feels almost as if the light from the picture were flooding her own head. The text thereby hints that the painting has been inspired as much by Mercedes's American history as by French history. This sympathetic association of the seventeenth-century French civil wars between Catholics and Protestants with the American Civil War once more invokes the alleged nobility of the plantation owners of the Old South, and Mercedes herself heroically embodies the high-minded principles depicted in the painting when she risks her life to wrest Clementine's knife from her.

As a result of witnessing the attack and seeing the beautiful American dripping with blood, the artist Arnold at last perceives the coincidence of the beautiful and the good in Mercedes, recognizing her as an agent of virtue. Only then can he admit his love for her and only then, moreover, does he perceive his own moral depravity at having entered a marriage of convenience. On the path of rehabilitation, he departs, "unwilling to draw breath in *German* air so long as the chain that had bound two people together in a miserable marriage was still unsevered" (W 371). Marlitt's task is, however, not yet complete as the novel needs to forge the link between romance, redeemed manhood, and German nation building.

In the final chapter, the Franco-Prussian War breaks out. Invoking the ancient Roman view of the fierceness of Germanic tribes that often figured in nineteenth-century German nationalist discourse, the text recounts how the "germanische Zorn" (*furor teutonicus*, M 416) drives an exiled Arnold onto the battlefield. All three American translations tone down the fierceness of the original German, missing the historical allusion: Wister translates it as "national ardour" (W 373); Steinestel, as "German patriotism," omitting the quotation marks (S 239); and Hettie E. Miller, as "German zeal."[64] Nevertheless, even in the tamest rendering the point cannot be missed: combat on behalf of the fatherland completes Arnold's rehabilitation.

The German original accompanies Arnold's return to Germany with fulsome and erotic images: "die Friedensbotschaft und der junge Lenz, innig umschlungen, jubelnd über die deutsche Erde hin" (M 417). In German Marlitt can exploit the feminine gender of "Friedensbotschaft" (tidings of peace) and the masculine gender of "Lenz" (spring) to speak factually and allegorically simultaneously. On one level, the text merely reports that the news of peace and the spring arrive simultaneously and sweep across the land; yet the allegorical language pictures the message of peace as a woman locked in an ardent embrace with a man, the spring. Wister did not even attempt to reproduce the erotic image when she translated the phrase as "The news of peace came with the spring-tide, and the joy of reawakening nature was reflected in German hearts everywhere" (W 373). Steinestel merely hinted at a sexual embrace: "The joyous news came with the glowing spring-time, and all nature vibrated in jubilant sympathy" (S 239). Miller in turn tried to convey a chaste love match: "the message of peace and spring, hand-in-hand, entered the land, awakening glad echoes" (HM 471). As in the case of *"furor teutonicus,"* the translations somewhat dampen the national zeal of the original, straitening the German contents to wholesomeness.

The central concern of the novel with German nation and German family nevertheless remains visible, and both the German family and the German nation, as Marlitt characterizes them, potentially appeal to an audience favoring domestic fiction. Indeed, the patriotic fervor in the final chapter of the original does not change the fact that the novel generally exhibits little of the offensive jingoism that dominated German public life in this period, investing instead in an attractive idea of nation rooted in family harmony in the home town.[65] Marlitt's exogamous family, the mix of North and South, of the Old and New Worlds, that upheld internationally shared moral and aesthetic values likewise had the potential to gratify international audiences and apparently did so in America.

Some Americans liked the novel from the start; *Arthur's Illustrated Home Magazine* enthusiastically praised the novel as "among the few books which, on taking up, cannot be laid down again until finished."[66] Wister's translation for Lippincott appeared in at least six subsequent reprint editions; Munro, Lovell, and A. L. Burt all published new editions of Steinestel's translation;

and 1895 saw the publication of Hettie E. Miller's translation of the book for E. A. Weeks and Company, followed by a second edition with Weeks in 1903.[67] Miller's new translation included unattributed and poor reproductions of the illustrations by Wilhelm Claudius that appeared in the new edition of *Im Schillingscourt* in the German collected works of Marlitt's novels from the late 1880s. In 1911 Donohue and Company's reprint edition of Weeks's illustrated edition was still circulating at Christmastime.[68] In 1901, moreover, *In the Schillingscourt* numbered among three hundred titles advertised in the *Minneapolis Journal* as "choice readable, entertaining; substantially bound in art cloth" available at the discount price of fifteen cents.[69] Apparently, it, like *Pride and Prejudice, Silas Marner, Jane Eyre, Black Beauty, The Count of Monte Cristo*, and others included on this international list, still had the power to captivate American readers. It was one of ten books translated from the German to make the list, five of them by Marlitt, including also *Gold Elsie, The Second Wife, The Princess of the Moor*, and *The Old Mam'selle's Secret*.

Upon the first appearance of Marlitt's seventh novel in American translation, however, some reviewers felt that the novel did not completely conform to the conventions of wholesome romance. American readers were of course familiar with international conventions of romance, in W. D. Howell's words, stories of "the everlasting young man and young woman."[70] They knew them from reading Austen and Brontë, but also in variations in popular novels by, for example, Charlotte Yonge, Ouida, E.D.E.N. Southworth, and other American women authors of domestic fiction, those christened "literary domestics" by Mary Kelley.[71] By 1879 they were also quite familiar with the brand that Marlitt and her German avatars offered. *The Nation* described the beloved formula: "the grave and stern hero maintains an agreeable and lively game of fencing with the haughty heroine till it is finished on the last page by a happy marriage."[72]

Cognizant of romance conventions, the *Milwaukee Sentinel* felt that *In the Schillingscourt* exhibited disturbing deviations from the norm: instead of allowing the young and unmarried to occupy center stage, Marlitt's latest novel featured married people as its protagonists, and the plot scandalously depended instead on the love of a married man for a beautiful widow who was a guest in his house. "A divorce is obtained with less concern than a pair of gloves," the reviewer objected. "Undoubtedly the innocent girlish heroine of old-time romances is insipid to mature minds, but it is possible to represent a woman of character, possessed of a heart well worth the winning, without placing her in an atmosphere of lax marriage ties, easily-obtained divorces, and slightly-reverenced betrothal vows."[73]

But the novel occasioned discomfort not only on moral grounds. This same reviewer identified a forced quality in this new novel. "Simplicity has given place to conscious effort, and, also, distinction to confusion," the *Milwaukee Sentinel* complained. "There is consequently a lack of compactness, looseness in the weaving of the thread of incidents."[74] The reviewer perceived a novel designed to accommodate mixed purposes, yet another deviation from the norms of romance. These mixed purposes in fact characterize Marlitt's oeuvre generally, but apparently in this case the *Milwaukee Sentinel* found her ambitious intention to infuse romance with greater social significance at once forced and too transparent. *In the Schillingscourt* does not in fact drive the plot with romance and mystery in the streamlined and suspenseful manner of *The Old Mam'selle's Secret* and *Gold Elsie*, thus allowing other themes more space. Nor does the exotic and sometimes off-putting Mercedes herself easily gain reader empathy in the manner of her literary forbears.

Identifying deviations from generic norms that made this book less enjoyable than others of its ilk, *The Nation* also maintained that romance could not gracefully bear the load of broader social or political vision: "pure romance," the reviewer asserted, was being contaminated here by social issues that made it "more unreal and far less agreeable."[75] This objection implies that the special charm of this set of German romances lay in the possibility they offered of suspending disbelief. In other words, the social context evoked therein normally did not force American readers to think hard about American realities even when it bore a pleasurable relationship to them; the social context of the original was normally sufficiently alien so as to defer the recognition that the happiness and harmony achieved therein was merely fabricated. Were then the distasteful "discussions of all sorts" in this novel the connections to the American South or the exoticizing of Americans as uniformly of color? This review, like all the other American reviews I have found, never mentions the American characters and leaves us wondering.

For some American readers, on the other hand, the racial stereotyping, the southern themes, and the echoes of the discourses of the Lost Cause, even if resignified in the foreign context of the novel, may in the end have been comfortably familiar. Alderman Library at the University of Virginia offers tantalizing circumstantial evidence of southern liking for the novel: the library holds not one but four different popular editions of the novel, donated—as a plate within each book testifies—by four different women, one of them Mrs. Charles Kent, the daughter of the above-mentioned Mary Stuart Smith.[76] Did these women especially enjoy the portrait of a beautiful southern woman to whom the text accords significant moral agency?

While this question, too, must remain unanswered, an exemplar of Lippincott's 1898 edition of *Schillingscourt* does testify eloquently to the enduring sentimental significance of the novel for more than two decades after it was first published in America. The book is signed on the front flyleaf "Emmie A. Matt June 1, 1901."[77] Slightly paraphrasing a poem by the American orator Robert G. Ingersoll (1833–99), Emmie wrote on the back flyleaf: "Love is the only bow / on Life's dark cloud / —Love is the builder of / Every hope. With Love / Earth is heaven, and / We are God" and signed it "Emm." Emmie had misremembered one of Ingersoll's lines or perhaps deliberately emended it when she replaced "home" with "hope." This substitution suggests that the values Emmie saw affirmed therein had not so much to do with keeping house as satisfying deeply felt wishes within the domestic story; a novel about Americans in Germany that ended with a transatlantic marriage addressed Emmie's hope for the power of love. As Emmie's inscription suggests, German novels in translation could become "wellsprings of personal meaning" for their readers.[78]

ALL OF MARLITT'S NOVELS contain the sort of discussions that *The Nation* disliked in *In the Schillingscourt* and thus violated nineteenth-century conventions even as they established new ones for popular German literature in translation. Yet they routinely delivered the happy ending founded in heterosexual desire, one that was not only expected, since it was internationally generic of romance, but also virtually guaranteed in the 1870s, 1880s, and 1890s by certain German women authors' names, by Wister's imprimatur, or simply by the designation "after the German." In chapter 4 we will take a closer look at the German art of the happy ending and its cachet with American readers.

CHAPTER 4

The German Art of the Happy Ending

Embellishing and Expanding the Boundaries of Home

Why is it that so few of such exquisite hours of enjoyment are allotted to poor mortals? Earth would be too blissful a place, I imagine.¹

I N THE PRESENT DAY, North Americans probably do not anticipate a happy ending when they pick up a German novel. The older canonical works they may have read in college courses tend toward tragedy, melancholy, or at best ambivalence—*Elective Affinities*, *A Village Romeo and Juliet*, *The Metamorphosis*, *Death in Venice*, *Woyzeck*, and *The Earthquake in Chile*, for example, end in death, murder, or suicide or, in the case of *Earthquake*, in multiple homicide. Post-1945 literature—for obvious reasons—seldom ends well either. In Patrick Süskind's best-selling *Perfume* (1985), set in the eighteenth century, the distasteful central character is torn to shreds by a frenzied mob. Bernhard Schlink's *The Reader* (1995; trans. 1997), an Oprah's Book Club selection in 1999, concerns an illiterate Holocaust perpetrator who does not find redemption. While countering some clichés, W. G. Sebald's brooding fiction (*Emigrants*, 1996; *Rings of Saturn*, 1999; *Vertigo*, 1999; *Austerlitz*, 2001), which Scott Denham describes as narrated with "gentle irony and quiet comic voice," maintains the association of German literature and culture with "the specifically German catastrophe of modernity that is murder, exile, loss, and grief."²

This view of German literature as pessimistic and tragic belongs to the cultural frame of the twentieth and twenty-first centuries; we misapprehend the past when we conclude by reading backward through two world wars and through select works from the nineteenth century that nineteenth-century American readers harbored the same image of German fiction and culture. Translated popular literature by German women—as in the case of Marlitt's novels—typically told nineteenth-century Americans an optimistic story of virtue rewarded, obstacles overcome, and deep happiness founded in intimate heterosexual bonding and the social renewal associated with it, that is, happiness in marriage as the "closest union that can exist between two mortals."[3] And although some reviewers scorned this "German bliss," American novel readers bought it. As the *Literary World* enthusiastically remarked of one such German novel, "The story has also the merit, and a great merit it is, of ending well, and leaving the reader with a pleasant taste in his mouth."[4] If such conclusions constitute, in Janice A. Radway's formulation, myths "in the guise of the truly possible,"[5] then these German versions projected bliss in marriage and family as within reach.

SUCH HAPPY ENDINGS of course signal the reliance of this popular German fiction on the conventions of the international romance novel. Therefore, before we examine these endings and the novels that delivered them, some brief generic considerations are useful. As Radway demonstrates in her study of twentieth-century readers, romance readers consider such conclusions essential to their enjoyment and would not read romance novels without them. Defining the romance novel as a "work of prose fiction that tells the story of the courtship and betrothal of one or more heroines," Pamela Regis concurs. The happy ending figures in her descriptive taxonomy of the genre as a "narrative essential."[6] Moreover, she argues, this vital concluding union of hero and heroine marks the achievement of a state of freedom and thus a "moment of rejoicing for the reader" (33).

Regis, who is interested in how this intensely satisfying conclusion is typically reached, identifies eight narrative events that characterize the romance genre and produce the requisite ending. Three of them prove particularly helpful for parsing the bliss achieved in our set of German novels and its appeal to American readers: (1) the embedding of romance within a defined social situation, (2) the erection within that society of barriers to the union of the heroine and hero, and (3) the jeopardizing of the happy ending by "ritual death," that is, a moment when "the hoped-for resolution seems absolutely impossible, when it seems that the barrier will remain" (31–33, 35). While these nineteenth-century German novels ultimately deviate in many respects from Regis's elaborated model, these three elements joined to the happy ending strikingly recur in the examples to be examined in this chapter.

The German setting provided American readers with an additional twist on such romance elements: imagined as the locus of romance and even decorous adventure, a fictive Germany erected barriers to happiness, yet without fail proved to house freedom and agency, steeped in virtue and sentiment.

Withholding the Happy Ending:
The Clergyman's Daughter

With few exceptions, the novels by the seventeen authors in our dataset deliver a happy ending; the rare deviation in effect confirms the norm. Wilhelmine Heimburg's *Aus dem Leben meiner alten Freundin* (1878; *The Story of a Clergyman's Daughter,* 1889) provides a case in point. Its focus on frustrated emotional fulfillment affirms the desirability of the happy ending signified by marriage. The novel opens with a discussion between the narrator and her husband as to whether Margaret, an obscure spinster, has a story to tell.[7] Determined to uncover her elderly neighbor's past, the frame narrator befriends her, eventually becoming her confidante and persuading her to tell her story. The novel concludes with the frame narrator having made her case: were it not for bad luck, Margaret would have married and entered history.

By withholding the happy ending, *Clergyman's Daughter* intensifies longing for it. After building hopes that Margaret will after many trials be united with her true love, the novel eliminates him with a fall from a horse. Heartbroken, Margaret never weds and lives a life that she herself describes as insignificant. The contrived unhappy ending seems designed to make the reader suffer vicariously; the narrative fortifies the power of love, marriage, and family by *not* gratifying the wish for fulfillment that has sustained interest in Margaret's plot strand. *Clergyman's Daughter* ultimately reinforces the romantic paradigm and by no means discounts the wish for blissful union as misguided daydreaming. Rather, it projects marriage as a desirable norm.

Aus dem Leben meiner alten Freundin appeared belatedly under two different titles in North America: the afore-mentioned *The Story of a Clergyman's Daughter* (Munro, 1889) and *The Pastor's Daughter* (Worthington, 1890). American readers, who by the time *Clergyman's Daughter* was rendered were accustomed to other fare from Germany, including Heimburg's previously translated novels, thus probably read it wishing for a happy ending. The packaging of Donohue Brothers' early twentieth-century reprint edition of Davis's translation for the Snug Corner Series suggests as much. The standard cover for this series depicts a young woman with bobbed hair sitting in a tree, a book on her lap and a satisfied smile on her face. Perhaps, in the end, the book did offer fulfillment as this cover suggests it does: despite withholding the marriage, the novel ends in harmony when the narrator visits Margaret's grave and hears the bells ringing for evening prayer: "they sounded like peace and reunion!"[8]

Heimburg changed narrative strategies after publishing *Clergyman's Daughter* in 1878 to the point of forcing happy endings on her weepy, long-suffering heroines. In *Lucie's Mistake, Her Only Brother,* and *Cloister Wendhusen,* for example, the female protagonists appear all too ready to give up on the possibility of marrying the men they love. It may be, as Urszula Bonter claims, that Heimburg labored under the immediate influence of Marlitt's happy endings, but romance qua genre exerted pressure on its own accord, and for decades Heimburg's novels, too, concluded happily in matrimony.[9]

Der Stärkere (1909), which does not end well, was never translated into English. Nor were *Antons Erben* (1898), where after much suffering the estranged couple is finally reunited, and *Wie auch wir vergeben* (1907), in which twenty years pass before the lovers can marry.[10] If, as Bonter speculates, Heimburg, freed at last from Marlitt's influence, later turned to writing more pessimistic, naturalistic novels, this turn was not welcome in America. While these darker novels went untranslated, in the early twentieth century Heimburg's happy-ending novels were still being reprinted and read. And even when *Beetzen Manor,* which ends in the heroine's emotional exhaustion and death, did reach America during the peak years of Heimburg's popularity, its unhappy ending was not always registered as such. The *Bostonian* cheerfully characterized it as containing "attractive incidents of love, humor, and ideal happiness" with a "healthful and cleanly" moral.[11] *Publishers' Weekly* also implied a happy ending, describing the heroine as "a lovely womanly character" who "in time becomes a help to every one about her."[12] In the end this book did not gain traction in the United States. Unlike most of Heimburg's fiction, it was never reprinted; its truncated publication history suggests that it did not deliver what American readers sought in Heimburg's and other popular works by German women, namely, joy in the ending.

Circumventing Incest and Creating Family:
Her Only Brother

The Heimburg novels that Americans avidly read depict heroines whose trials conclude happily with a marriage or reconciliation with the man of their choice. They rely for their effect on harrowing depictions of German families in which human foible, bad character, outright villainy, and economic distress present nearly insuperable obstacles to romantic union.

Egocentric, unfeeling brothers frequently become the central cause of the suffering of Heimburg's heroines, and thus the family seldom presents a safe haven. A Heimburg reader can become so accustomed to these bad brothers as to be surprised when a brother exhibits good character. Jaundiced readers might even find themselves idly wondering how the narrative will dispatch the offending brother without undermining nineteenth-century family values. In the 1890s both Gabriele Reuter in *Aus guter Familie* (1895) and Helene Böhlau in *Halbtier!* (1899) deployed the plot element of the bad brother to do just that: undermine the bourgeois family. However, neither of these socially critical, protofeminist works, which end in mental illness and suicide, respectively, was translated into English in its own time. Meanwhile, *Lore von Tollen* and *Cloister Wendhusen*, with their bad brothers, who fortunately cannot in the end impede the heroine's happiness, appeared in the United States in new illustrated editions in the 1890s.

Ihr einziger Bruder (1882; *Her Only Brother*) is Heimburg's most harrowing bad-brother plot and also her most telling happy resolution of sibling conflict. With the exception of the first five chapters and the conclusion, the plot unfolds as recounted in a manuscript that is being read thirty years after the principal events by a young couple, Klaus and Marie. Here, too, Heimburg deploys a spinster narrator, this time to recount a romance that restores an entire family.

The narrator, Aunt Rosamond, proves a manipulative storyteller abetted by physical disability. Her lameness prevents her from navigating space, and she repeatedly describes herself as impaired as she tries ineffectually to aid her loved ones. It also figures her status as outsider in affairs of the heart and the economy of marriage. One American reviewer saw her as playing the role of a Greek chorus, telling "the reader what he is to think of the others and their doings."[13] Yet, although she minutely records events, Rosamond only dimly senses the truth in human affairs, catching on just a little too late to be of use—certainly well after the reader does.

Part of the pleasant horror of reading this novel consists in the fact that its austere heroine, Anna Maria von Hegewitz, has, like Jane Austen's Anne Elliot in *Persuasion*, made the mistake of turning down the suit of the love of her life. For pages thereafter the novel offers little prospect of a second chance and a happy ending. Unlike Austen's Anne, Heimburg's Anna Maria has not rejected Edwin Stürmer because of poor advice, but because of her sense of duty to her brother, Klaus, who when their mother died had sacrificed his marriage plans to care for his young sister. Now grown up, Anna Maria regards it as her duty to compensate him by tending to his every need. She finds she is sorely mistaken in her sense of duty, however, when Klaus falls in love with the much younger Susanne.

Unwilling to sacrifice his happiness a second time, Klaus refuses to recognize Susanne's flaws and marries her. His bride's signature "silvery laughter" puts readers on notice that this marriage will not be a good one. The portrait of the heartbreakingly enchanting but amoral Susanne, who with her caprices effortlessly wins all hearts, seems especially designed to torment readers inclined to obedience and duty and, moreover, to enlist their sympathy for the austerely beautiful, loyal, oppressed, and repressed Anna Maria.

Anna Maria, who cannot hide her disapproval, soon finds that she has no place in her brother's home. Her sacrifice now superfluous, she begins to think again of Edwin. But she has not yet drunk the full draught of her suffering, for Edwin also has fallen in love with Susanne. At precisely the moment when Anna Maria, encouraged by Rosamond, believes he is coming to renew his suit, she learns of his love for Susanne. Although the text provides many hints that Anna Maria and Rosamond have misread Edwin, the moment of enlightenment as to the true state of his feelings is excruciating.

If, as Regis asserts, ritual death is a requisite element of romance, then Heimburg has supplied this death in spades in *Her Only Brother*. In addition to Edwin's love for Susanne, an incipient mismatch in taste and character also surfaces to impede the union of Edwin and Anna Maria. Upon his return, years after Anna Maria rejected his suit, Edwin decorates his home in exotic fashion; Rosamond cannot imagine her niece "resting, in sweet indolence, on those cushions."[14] Edwin, moreover, disapproves when the virtuous Anna Maria gives a speech at the harvest festival on the family's estate to fill in for her negligent brother. Scowling at the mannish role she plays, Edwin has no eye for this occasion as a fulfillment of duty. With her femininity under erasure and with the competition of Susanne's hyperfemininity, Anna Maria appears to have no chance for happiness. Yet the pressure of genre permits readers to hope.

Fortunes turn so as to punish Klaus, while preserving sibling love, and to unite Anna Maria and Edwin. When Klaus falls ill, Anna Maria loyally nurses him. He dies with his sister at his side, whereas the shallow Susanne is too frightened to enter the sickroom. Meanwhile, when Edwin beholds Anna Maria in the role of devoted sister, nurse, and surrogate mother to Klaus and Susanne's child, his love for her is rekindled. Anna Maria, in turn, in the pattern Regis describes, becomes free to reveal both the motherly self behind her austere exterior and her love for Edwin.

When Susanne thereafter departs for warmer climates, she leaves her son, Klaus, in her sister-in-law's care. Anna Maria considers him her "wedding present" from her only brother. The final pages make clearer that the newlyweds who have been reading Rosamond's manuscript are Anna Maria's nephew and foster son, Klaus, and Edwin and Anna Maria's older daughter, Marie. The incestuous ring of the marriage of cousins, whose names echo those of the sibling pair of the older generation and who were raised by the same parents, can hardly be missed. Yet the text registers nothing but extreme happiness in its parting celebration of endogamy and restored family. After sacrificing the foolish and disloyal brother whose memory is nevertheless kindly preserved, the text permits the sister's love fulfillment in motherhood and, in an attenuated sense, even sexual expression, in cousin marriage in the next generation.

Thirty years later, mother and father are living a version of the conclusion to many a Grimm's fairy tale: "und wenn sie nicht gestorben sind, so leben sie noch heute" (and if they haven't died, then they are still living today). Anna Maria speaks the final lines of the novel, dictating what should be written of her at the conclusion of Rosamond's manuscript: "She was the happiest of wives, the most beloved of mothers!" (319). Although the novel is set in the pastoral milieu of an aristocratic country estate, in its establishment of a family in which duty and desire harmonize and in which Anna Maria is settled into her prescribed role as wife and mother, the narrative recounts a founding myth of the nineteenth-century bourgeois family, one in which cousin marriage repairs the fissures created by a brother's exogamous desire.

American publishers calculated that their readers would like this story. Within four years (1889–92) *Ihr einziger Bruder*, this "exquisite love story," appeared in three English translations and in at least eight editions alternately titled *Her Only Brother*—translated by Jean W. Wylie for Crowell in 1888 and under the same title by E. V. Conder for Munro in 1890—and *A Sister's Love*—translated by Margaret P. Waterman for Worthington in 1890.[15] In choosing the title *A Sister's Love*, Waterman and Worthington must have speculated that for American audiences the greater appeal of the story lay not in the valorization of the brother and his prerogatives but in the power of the sister to love that brother. An unfriendly review described the novel as steadying "the nerves, like a mild narcotic," but the *Daily Picayune* found it a "sweet and wholesome story" in a "pleasant translation." Worthington touted reading pleasure: the novel fastened "the reader's attention from beginning to end."[16]

Was this founding myth of the bourgeois family recognizable as a *German* happy ending? Griswold, who listed it under the title *Her Only Brother* and devoted three columns to it, must have thought so.[17] The text does overtly indicate a German world. The opening lines set the story on an estate near the Lüneburg heath. The Hegewitz ancestral home is a "real, old-fashioned

German house; for there were dim corridors and deep niches, great vaulted rooms and large alcoves, little staircases with steep steps worn by many feet, and curious low vaulted doors" (4).

The German element additionally resonates in Heimburg's inclusion of German poems and rhymes. Heimburg selected lesser-known poems that anchor her story in its North German setting. In the German text, a poem by the North German Klaus Groth appears in its original dialect version, for example. Likewise, near the end of the novel, children's voices are heard singing a begging song in dialect and also the dialect rhyme for St. Martin's Day—"Martens, Martens Vögelken / Mit Din vergoldet Flögeken."[18] When Susanne performs in the Hegewitz manor, she asks whether she should sing in German or Italian, and all cry out for German.

Waterman translated all of the poems into English, and as a result their dialect flavor is lost. Nevertheless, the English translation signals that the poems are to be taken as specific to this (admittedly thinly evoked culture). Waterman did, however, preserve a few linguistic signs such as Fräulein, Herr, and Frau as well as retain the telling names of the characters. Stürmer's name (Stormer; reminiscent of the eighteenth-century Sturm und Drang), for example, boasts the signature German umlaut.

Most obviously marking this tale of duty and love as German are the contrasting portraits of Anna Maria von Hegewitz and Susanne Mattoni, each name telegraphing ethnic origin. Heimburg does not present Anna Maria uncritically, but the austere heroine quickly captures readers' sympathy and interest as the "picture of a typical North German woman, tall, fair, slender, and clear-sighted, serene, and calm" (104). The charm of the beautiful, blonde Anna Maria is quiet, restrained, and inward; she does not shine forth in all her ethnic virtue as a "North German woman" until she displays the womanly qualities of mothering and nursing. By contrast, Susanne Mattoni, the daughter of Klaus's tutor and a woman of uncertain origins, bears an Italian name that seals her status as other. Her dark eyes and hair and her restlessness mark her as the opposite of the North German Anna Maria. Susanne, as all that is not German, the wrong wife for Klaus the elder and the wrong mother for Klaus the younger, not only marries an Englishman but also emigrates to and dies in America. Hybrid, international, and mobile, she highlights Anna Maria's rootedness in the German family and its land.

Blackwood's Magazine, as quoted by Griswold, referred to the "venerable abode on the storm-beaten shores of the Baltic" and maintained that the characters "enlist our sympathies by their good old-fashioned german [sic] kindliness and simplicity of manners."[19] Taking Heimburg for a man, *The Critic* wrote of the author's skill in rendering "country scenes and interiors, so we can almost believe we, too, hav [sic] vegetated in a Märkisch house." The reviewer recognized the Germany of the novel, moreover, as exhibiting "the country life of the nobles, and the strong family affection which we find in the numerous novels translated by Mrs. Wister,"[20] or in other words, as mediating the same view of Germany as does the larger set of women's novels under consideration here.

Making a Good German Match:
Lucie's Mistake and Lora von Tollen

In *Herzenskrisen* (1887; *Die Gartenlaube*, nos. 1–17), a second novel involving the misguided rejection of a worthy suitor, Heimburg allowed her orphaned heroine only a narrow range of action, locating her mistake not in her German-coded sororal love and sense of duty but rather in her inexperience, her misguided wish for travel and adventure, and the bad influence of a charismatic aristocratic woman friend, Hortense.[21] Lucie, who has never experienced the world beyond the confines of her sister's home, is surprised to receive a proposal of marriage from Dr. Alfred Adler, whom she hardly knows. Her economic circumstances push her to accept. Trouble arises during their engagement in two forms. First, Frau Adler, the mother-in-law, dislikes Lucie from the start because she has other plans for her son, and the busy Alfred fails to intervene. Second, when her childhood friend, the erratic Hortense, tries to commit suicide, Lucie saves her life. Upon befriending Hortense anew, Lucie is unable to resist her invitation to become her traveling companion.

Friendship with Hortense comes with enormous consequences for Lucie's emotional and financial well-being. First of all, she must break her engagement to the good doctor—American readers must have seen immediately that this is Lucie's biggest mistake, even if they sympathized with her wish to travel. Through her travels with Hortense, Lucie becomes more sophisticated, but as time passes, she realizes not only that she has neglected her own sister, nieces, and nephews but also that she might be fond of Alfred after all. Worst of all, she has made herself dependent on a woman who could drop her as soon as she herself decides to marry. Unlike the bonds of marriage, the bonds of friendship are volatile, the text warns.

In the end Hortense does marry to the temporary endangerment of friendship. Meanwhile, both Lucie and Alfred regret their broken engagement. The novel offers little hope that this decision can be reversed until Lucie tends to her sick niece. Experienced Heimburg readers must summon hope the moment it becomes clear that Alfred will have the opportunity to observe Lucie in a maternal role. While the novel slowly brings Lucie around to recognizing the mistake she made in turning down the security offered by a doctor's love, Alfred himself recognizes that the inexperienced Lucie might be forgiven for making poor choices. He even acknowledges that he himself bears a little of the blame for pressing his suit so hard with her and then leaving her to the harsh regime of his mother. At the conclusion of the novel the newly married couple toasts the new year with their guests, Hortense and her husband. Once both women are married, both marriage and friendship can be affirmed.

American publishers must have thought they had a winner in *Herzenskrisen*. Within the space of three years it was translated in the United States under four different titles—*Friendship's Test* (Ogilvie; 1889), *My Heart's Darling* (Munro; 1889), *Lucie's Mistake* (Worthington; 1890), and *Hortense* (Rand; 1891)—helping fuel a small boom in Heimburg translations in these years. Did *Lucie's Mistake*, however, signal to American readers that it originated in a foreign culture or that it mediated information about such a culture?

The *Literary World* thought so. The "pictures of German family life in the Oberförster's home, at Frau Steuerräthin's, and at the Baron's," the reviewer declared, "are vivid."[22] Heimburg's modest literary achievement in this novel is in fact to locate a romance plot, complete with ritual death, in a differentiated and stratified social world. While Lucie appears to act in this social imaginary as an individual who can make mistakes and yet ultimately choose to be reconciled with her fiancé, the novel (even in translation) also overtly flags this setting as German, thereby suggesting that Lucie is a national type. The forester brother-in-law, Hortense's country estate, the names of the characters, and place names all telegraph German origins. One scene takes place in the Zwinger museum in Dresden before Raphael's *Sistine Madonna*—an Italian painting, to be sure, but a German tourist destination. Furthermore, when Lucie's beaming face reveals that her fortunes have been reversed, a French governess makes explicit that there is something particularly German about the heroine, exclaiming, "How extraordinary you German women are!"[23] More important, the text locates its affirmation of the middle-class marriage that Lucie and Alfred contract in the very décor of a German home in a painted windowpane.

Painted glass in the form of a diptych depicts a newly married sixteenth-century couple, Werner and Barbara Grundmann, in patrician dress. An accompanying verse expresses the view of marriage that allegedly prevailed when this one was contracted. Davis, the translator for Worthington, chose to leave the quaint motto in German, thus presenting it as conveying a particularly German sentiment: "Wo *Er* ist fest und treu gesinnt / Und *Sie* mit Demut dem hause [sic] dient, / Und Gotteswort wird recht geehrt, / Da ist ein reiches Glück beschert. / Lübeck anno domini 1536" (Where *he* is steadfast and true / And *she* serves the house in humility / And properly honors God's word, / There rich happiness is granted [my translation]).[24] Alfred envies the long-dead Werner and regrets that no such happiness is possible in his day, yet Barbara reminds him of Lucie. His reaction to this German artifact confirms that all will end well after all and, moreover, that their happiness will epitomize a long-standing German ideal of conjugal bliss.

If *Lucie's Mistake* resembles *Her Only Brother* in the heroine's rejection of a suitor whom she actually loves, Heimburg's *Lore von Tollen* (1889; *Die Gartenlaube*, nos. 1–19) returns to the bad-brother plot coupled with a family's impoverishment. Immediately available in the United States in two different translations—J. W. Davis's *Lora: The Major's Daughter* with Worthington (1889) and *Lenore von Tollen* with Munro (1890)—Heimburg's *Lora* recounts how both a bad brother and a bad sister jeopardize the heroine's marriage to her true love, the schoolteacher Dr. Schönberg.[25]

As opposed to the lightly sketched German milieu in *Lucie's Mistake* and *Her Only Brother*, the setting of *Lore von Tollen* is more fully rendered as a German one, indeed, one founded in the specific social conditions of the German home towns. American reviews picked up immediately on this German flavoring. The *Catholic World* pronounced the novel "a natural unaffected and purely domestic story of a sort on which our german [sic] kinsmen seem to have a patent," and the *Literary World* noted of the heroine, "There is a Teutonic simplicity about her which makes her a fascinating heroin [sic]." The *Athenäum* likewise praised Heimburg for succeeding "in presenting an attractive heroin of a thoroly german type [sic]."[26]

The opening lines of *Lora* situate the story in an aristocratic Prussian military family, not only by referring to the mother of the family as "Frau Majorin von Tollen," in Davis's translation, but also by noting how the autumn sun "played about the point of an infantry helmet," thus alluding to the headgear internationally coded as German.[27] We soon learn that we are in the small town of Westenberg situated not far from Hamburg in the direction of Berlin. Provincial Westenberg also harrowingly provides the setting for Heimburg's *Um fremde Schuld* (1895), translated in North America as *For Another's Fault*. In imaginary Westenberg one hears a faint German echo of Thomas Hardy's imaginary English Wessex.

In her room Lora has a portrait of the Prussian queen Louise of sainted memory, along with a second memento of the German Wars of Liberation, a writing desk that belonged to the popular Prince Louis Ferdinand when he was quartered in Donnerstadt for maneuvers. Lora's father, furthermore, is confined to a wheelchair as a result of his wounds in a war from which he returned victorious a decade earlier—presumably the Franco-Prussian War. The aristocratic von Tollen family thus has deep roots in the Prussian military and in Prussian history. Their poverty has, however, banished them from the center of that history to the more affordable home town.

In addition to the Prussian military types, several other characters enter the picture as quintessentially German. With her side curls and girlish occupation of making dolls, Lora's Aunt Melitta, for example, emerges from a German Biedermeier painting. Dr. Ernest Schönberg also bears German markers. The son of a pastor, this German teacher is writing a book called "The Reformation in the old Mark" (268).

Heimburg likewise depicts the many obstacles to happiness as rooted in German social conditions: aristocratic prejudice against alliances with the middle classes; spoiled, incorrigible, and unrepentant aristocratic sons who are expected to pursue a career in the military; the relative helplessness of impoverished aristocrats; the subjection of sisters to the whims of brothers; and the limited choices of daughters in straitened economic circumstances. Despite this oppressive social reality, her ne'er-do-well brother's emigration to America, a coerced and short-lived marriage of convenience to the vulgar Adalbert Becher, and her disloyal sister Katie's death, Lora is rewarded for her patient virtue with a happy marriage to Ernest. In the final chapter the aristocratic Lora and the middle-class Ernest, after taking tea in the parsonage with Ernest's mother, Aunt Melitta, and Frau von Tollen, are sitting in their cozy parlor with its quintessentially German olive-green porcelain stove, recalling their honeymoon in Italy. Their bliss signals the defeat of the aristocracy and its prejudices as well as a triumph over the nouveaux riches who wish to join that caste.

Were it not for the final marriages—the happy endings—Heimburg's novels could have told American readers that the grim social reality depicted in them constituted the quintessentially German. Yet the happy ending, however contrived, signaled the contrary. As in Marlitt's novels, no matter how populated with bigots and villains the German home town may be, it nevertheless comes across as a stage on which even the most sorely challenged virtue is ultimately rewarded. The novels thus present a simulacrum of a social world in which women are able not only to admit to their heart's desire but also to express their feelings and win the object of that desire. Heimburg, like Marlitt, does not assert that all is right with the world but proposes that in spite of everything, happiness is attainable in this German imaginary.

Ritual Death in the Theater:
Hulda, A Noble Name, Violetta

Although German happy endings are frequently founded in marriages between the bourgeoisie and the nobility, these romances do not as a rule favor extreme misalliances; they are not improbable stories in which a housemaid marries a baron. They do, however, experiment with some risky matches. Indeed, if social barriers presented the most daunting obstacle to the happy ending, some German women writers sought variations on the theme in the figure of the actress. Burdened by her public performances with the stigma of sexual availability and embodying the unsteady and roving lifestyle anathema to the German bourgeoisie, the actress could quickly introduce complications into domestic fiction. She could, moreover, be configured variously—sometimes as the heroine and sometimes as a threat to the social order. Sometimes she could be accepted and redeemed, and sometimes she had to be eliminated.

In Marlitt's *Schillingscourt*, the marriage of Felix and Lucile must be rushed to prevent the latter from dancing on stage; one public performance is tantamount to social death. When the widowed Lucile decides after all that she wants to dance, the narrative dispatches her with a fatal illness. Felicitas's aristocratic mother in *The Old Mam'selle's Secret*, who foolishly eloped with a "player," is violently eliminated at the outset of the novel in the very performance that figures her humiliation. Susanne in *Her Only Brother* is triply burdened with the stigma of the actress. Not only was her mother an opera singer, but she herself performs. To make clear how monstrously her marriage menaces the aristocratic von Hegewitz family line, the novel assigns a constant companion and evil genius to her, one Isabella Pfannenschmidt, an ugly, aged former actress. While the text eliminates Susanne, it does not prevent her biological son from ascending to his rightful place as the heir of the estate and the father of future generations. Anna Maria's mothering—as did Cordula's mothering of Felicitas in *The Old Mam'selle's Secret* and Frau Lucian's of her grandson, José, in *Schillingscourt*—and his marriage to his own cousin wash away the stain of his biological mother. In fact, after registering the horror of the taint of the actress, these German novels tend to be optimistic in their handling of this thematic. Even if the actress remains an outsider, her offspring find acceptance in a German society that proves elastic and forgiving.

Three novels in which actresses play a central role merit attention here, especially since all three numbered among Wister's selections and as a result were for decades widely available for borrowing or for purchase singly or in sets: Fanny Lewald's *Hulda; or the Deliverer* (1874; translation of *Die Erlöserin* [1873]), Claire von Glümer's *A Noble Name; or, Dönninghausen* ([copyright 1882] 1883; translation of *Dönninghausen* [1881]), and Ursula Zöge von Manteuffel's *Violetta* (1886; translation of *Violette Fouquet* [*Deutsche Roman-Zeitung* 2 [1885]), a novel whose title invokes the heroine of Giuseppe Verdi's *La Traviata* (1853), the French courtesan Violetta Valéry. Each novel flirts with the idea of social death brought about by public performance, and in each the initiative and virtue of the heroine revive her from the nether realm. Two conclude with the marriage of an actress and an aristocrat and ostensibly accomplish the improbable social stretch that the German fiction under scrutiny here generally avoids, thus projecting a renewed social order that reclaims the actress. The third, in which the heroine marries her childhood playmate, involves reconciliation with an aristocratic grandfather and in this manner also projects a new and elastic social order.

These three German authors, especially Lewald, wrote prolifically. Yet with the exception of these three novels, their works were barely available in translation in the United States. *Violetta* is the only one of the many novels and stories by Manteuffel to be translated in North America; *A Noble Name* is one of only two works by Glümer, and *Hulda* is the second of only a small handful of Lewald's more than thirty novels and numerous stories, written from 1842 to 1888, to appear in American translation. Wister, who rendered all three and was known for carefully selecting books Americans would like, must have judged the thematic of social redemption to be particularly attractive to her potential readers.

By 1874, when Wister translated Lewald's *Die Erlöserin* as *Hulda,* she and Lippincott had in effect established a series, five selections of which were novels by Marlitt, and Wister had acquired a reputation for choosing "wholesome" and entertaining literature with a German flair that invariably ended well. Lewald's story of a country clergyman's daughter who becomes an actress fit the emergent profile even if the actress thematic might have initially suggested that it would not.

According to a family legend based in local superstition, the Falkenhorst family awaits "the love of some fair young creature, born of the people" who will marry the family scion and thus redeem him from the curse of the "little people."[28] Descended from the Teutonic knights who colonized the Baltic, this German family retains its arrogant hegemony over the local Lithuanian population in pre-1848 Europe. The legend stems from an idea that conquerors can be redeemed only by those whom they subjugated and thus constitutes a fantasy of social justice and change, which the author, writing post-1848, of course knew was in Europe's future.

Although born a serf, the orphaned Lithuanian Simonena married a pastor. Hulda, their daughter, eventually marries a baron, thus completing an ascent over two generations from the most abject to the ruling class. Setting her story on the Baltic, Lewald supplied it with local color in the form of Lithuanian songs and dress. In her initial contact with the baronial family, Hulda serves as a translator, rendering the local Lithuanian subculture into German for the baronial family to admire. At the same time, she herself embodies this culture in an aesthetically pleasing, assimilated, and domesticated form. But when Baron Emanuel confesses his love for her, both families and their friends and retainers oppose the misalliance.

The death of Hulda's mother bifurcates the plot, separating the lovers for two hundred pages. The dutiful Hulda remains with her widowed father, but when he dies, she decides to become an actress. Meanwhile, Emanuel winters in Italy as is his custom. Lewald exploits their separation in a quasi-realistic vein to make probable the marriage of social unequals. Indeed, Lewald, whose fiction generally rejects improbable fantasies of marriage, narrowed the social gap between Hulda and Emanuel over the course of the novel to accomplish her happy ending. Wister supported this realistic vein by titling *Die Erlöserin* (The Female Redeemer) *Hulda; or the Deliverer*, shifting emphasis from the fantastic-sounding redeemer role to the woman, Hulda, and thereby muting the Christian fairy-tale quality of the original and paving the way for Americans to absorb the more socially grounded features of the plot.

The long middle section that treats the lovers' estrangement and Hulda's ritual death is centrally important to the novel. It betrays its German origins in its debt to Goethe, exhibiting the influence, on the one hand, of his *Wilhelm Meister's Apprenticeship* in its treatment of Hulda's three-year career on the stage as formative for her later social role and, on the other, of his *Elective Affinities* in its slower pace, philosophizing, and interest in marriage. In Italy, Emanuel discusses marriage and the nature of happiness with the intelligent, aristocratic Konradine. Convinced finally that companionate marriage with a social equal can bring happiness, he becomes engaged to his interlocutor. The return of the newly widowed prince, her former fiancé, thwarts this plan, and the text reaffirms passionate love as the foundation of marriage.

The meanwhile-orphaned Hulda faces the need to earn a living and determines that becoming an actress is preferable to being a governess or marrying the new pastor. Armed with talent, charm, and beauty, she soon plays female leads in a repertoire that includes the German classics: Lessing's *Emilia Galotti*; Goethe's *Faust, Clavigo,* and *Iphigenia*; and Schiller's *Kabale und Liebe* and *Wallenstein*. Lewald does not deign to mention the entertaining and now-forgotten plays that dominated the nineteenth-century German stage. The German theater therefore appears to offer the opportunity for the most culturally pretentious of performances and for deep education in the classics. It also presents a virtuous woman with pitfalls. While rumors circulate that she is the natural daughter of a famous actress, Hulda lives a chaste life, uncomprehending of the politics of the theater and finding herself unjustly maligned. At this juncture, Emanuel's plot returns him to the Baltic to reconnect with Hulda. As it turns out, the theater has prepared Hulda for marriage to an aristocrat by completing her aesthetic education.

Raised in a family where "there was an unconscious worship of culture and beauty" (9), Hulda has a rudimentary aesthetic education. Her upbringing enables her initially to perceive and be attracted to Emanuel's portrait (before she has seen the man), just as he, the refined aristocrat, is attracted to her beauty. Since sitting for the portrait, Emanuel has been disfigured by smallpox, yet the sensitive Hulda perceives his inner beauty and loves him despite his scarred face. While her early education facilitates the fairy-tale match, it is not sufficient to seal it.

In the world of novels, joining the "play-actors" could portend tragedy for the heroine. Lewald takes a different tack with the theater, using it instead as Hulda's finishing school. Here Hulda acquires the poise and bearing of the aristocracy by means of her embodiment, as an actress, of German high culture. As a result of conscientiously "[personifying] the creations of great poets," Hulda developed her understanding; "her strength of character increased, and she continued eagerly to pursue all the means of self-culture of which she could avail herself" (297, 335). On the final page, Emanuel's niece notes approvingly that Hulda "wears that spray of diamonds and enameled cornflowers on her breast just as if she had always been used to it!" (394). With the quintessential combination of duty, love, and aesthetic education, Hulda profits from a situation that in other fiction of the age would have destroyed her. Like Felicitas in *The Old Mam'selle's Secret*, Hulda earns her happy ending through immersion in German culture, ultimately turning in a convincing performance of her role as the wife of a baron.

In uniting Hulda, the redeemer, and a baron named Emanuel, Lewald valorized marriage as the salvation of both man and woman. While Hulda thereby overcomes her lowly social status, marriage redeems Emanuel from the inherited guilt of the colonizers; indeed, marriage to a commoner means freedom from the past since he must forfeit his right to the entailed family estate. His children will instead inherit properties that he has acquired through hard work and business acumen; they will enjoy the refined lifestyle of landed gentry coupled with bourgeois virtue and talent. With the name of the central character, *Hulda,* as the title of the translation, moreover, Lewald and Wister cryptically marked the novel's allegiance to domesticity. Hulda, the daughter born late in a happy marriage, bears the name for the goddess of domesticity in Germanic folk mythology.

The ten-page plot summary of the novel included in Rossiter Johnson's international *Authors Digest* devotes little space to Hulda's time in the theater, thereby suggesting that it was easy to overlook Lewald's use of the stage, in the tradition of Goethe's *Wilhelm Meister,* as a form of *Bildung.*[29] This plot summary also obscures Lewald's reliance on German high culture to make a fairy-tale ending possible. But for those who probed a bit deeper, the message could not be missed. Hulda's stint as an actress offered such readers a pleasant fantasy of an education that occurs outside of familial supervision and of an occupation that puts "the whole world of Germany at [one's] feet" (389) and yet does not preclude domestic felicity, the proper domain of a Hulda.

American readers found the book entertaining. Even if an early review in *The Nation* was lukewarm,[30] the translation went through at least ten subsequent editions. When in 1876 *Publishers' Weekly* posed the "prize question in fiction" concerning the then "most salable novel," *Hulda* appeared on an international list of forty-seven novels that had received two votes each, novels by such notable authors as Mark Twain (listed as Samuel Clemens), Hans Christian Andersen, Wilkie Collins, Longfellow, Miss Mulock, Charles Reade, Trollope, Charlotte Yonge, and Mrs. Southworth. Griswold added it to his list of German novels, and it was widely available in American public libraries, including twelve of the catalogues listed in Appendix B.

While *Hulda* acknowledges the precariousness of the actress's life and hints that going on the boards will irrevocably separate Hulda from Emanuel, the theater ultimately facilitates the happy ending. Manteuffel and Glümer, by contrast, construct plots that do not examine the potentially redemptive aspects of theater performance. Instead, both *Violetta* and *A Noble Name* deploy social prejudice against actresses, singers, and dancers as a hindrance to marriage and akin to social death.

In the backstory of *A Noble Name,* when an aristocratic woman eloped with an actor, her family disowned her. Her daughter, Johanna, must find a way to be reconciled with her stern grandfather, save her stepsister from bad influence and public performance, and recognize whom she truly loves and where she belongs. In *Violetta* the recently widowed General von Treffenbach marries the eponymous heroine's mother, Beatrice, a famous opera singer. This misalliance requires him to resign his military commission and leads to his ruin when his frivolous and selfish wife runs through his money and deserts him to return to the stage in America. Violetta atones for her mother's wrongs by caring for her impoverished and aging stepfather. For the sake of the happy ending, she must also redeem herself in the eyes of her stepbrother, Magnus. Both novels see to it that their heroines remain suitable marriage partners despite the taint of the theater. Their eligibility inheres in their virtue, loyalty, sense of duty, and hard work.

Each novel traffics in the stereotype of the vain, ruthless, and sexually available performer: *A Noble Name* reproduces it in the untalented Helena and in Carlo Batti, the circus impresario, and his circle; *Violetta* does so in the beautiful Beatrice. The crisis for each daughter of a player-parent, one that potentially leads to public performance, arises, however, as a result of economic necessity as it did in *Hulda*. Each work makes clear the difficulty of earning a living in an unforgiving world in which women's opportunities are limited. Like *Hulda,* these texts also view acting as a profession that requires talent and not simply as dubious and dishonorable. Manteuffel's Violetta has talent but does not want it; Glümer's Johanna has none and cannot hope to succeed on the stage like her father. Johanna is, however, an excellent horsewoman with the skill to perform in an equestrian circus act. In the end she resists the pressure to perform, for, as the novel makes clear, acting is one thing; circus performance is anathema.

Glümer's novel provides an interesting twist when Johanna avoids social ruin by becoming a writer. The heroine thereby draws on the artistic sensibility that had once caused her to wish to become an actor like her father. Fiction writing is less risky than public performance of any kind, for she can conceal her identity under a pseudonym. Having followed that impulse, Johanna learns "to rejoice . . . in her work for its own sake, in her gradual improvement and success, and the result which she achieved," sustained by Goethe's exhortation "Go to work and help yourself for the present, and hope and trust in God for the future."[31] Her initial desire to go on the stage, she realizes, was only "a misconception of [her] task," and in a gesture of stewardship, she explains that she must cultivate "the one talent entrusted to [her]" (330–31). To underline the importance of such creative work, Glümer brings Grandfather Dönninghausen to Johanna at her writing table for the reconciliation; Johanna will not return to him unless she can bring her work with her. The novel concludes on the baron's eightieth birthday. Johanna is married to her faithful childhood friend, who is shortly to become a university professor of medicine. The couple plan a quiet domestic life devoted to their work. In the final line of the novel, Grandfather Dönninghausen pronounces the "half-blood" aristocrat Johanna "the best Dönninghausen that ever lived," though Johanna never actually bore that noble name (360).

In Glümer's telling, noble character, defined in terms of duty, loyalty, sentiment, and work, blots out the taint of public performance, and artistry endures.

Wister's name guaranteed the circulation of *A Noble Name* from the start; the novel remained available for borrowing or purchase over several decades, having been reprinted at least four times. The *Independent* noted its similarities to others on Wister's list, pronouncing it a "particularly interesting, healthful, well-constructed one." "No young novel reader will be the worse for reading it," the reviewer declared, pointing to the heroine's nobility of character.[32] The same journal remarked two years later that by translating *A Noble Name* along with other German novels Wister had "signally widened the acquaintance of many readers of only our language with some delightfully spirited German studies of domestic life."[33] While the message of the story could be read universally, this review recognized and welcomed German particularity in the work.

In *Violetta* Manteuffel erects obstacles to her theater-tainted heroine's happiness by characterizing Magnus, her aristocratic stepbrother, as a man whose ideals of womanhood were formed by his long-suffering mother and his pious childhood sweetheart. Manteuffel must make Violetta acceptable to Magnus's high standards of womanhood and also make Magnus himself bend a little.

To secure the heroine's happy ending, the text makes clear from the start that she does not want to perform in public. Refusing to be the object of men's gazes, the talented Violetta shrinks from dancing on stage. When her mother tries to force her debut, Violetta deliberately falls from her perch in the elaborate stage scenery, thus cutting short her dancing career. Since she has not completed a performance, Magnus can see in her the possibility for redemption. Yet when her charm, beauty, and virtue begin to attract him, he flees to Brazil; he cannot imagine a woman of Violetta's dubious origins presiding over his mother's estate.

Meanwhile, a destitute General von Treffenbach must rely on Violetta for financial support. Possessing a voice equal to her mother's but abhorring the stage, Violetta embarks on a successful opera career. The tubercular fate of the diva seems imminent when the heroine appears weak and coughing. But tragedy is not the genre in which this novel operates. In the end Magnus marries Violetta despite her protests of her unworthiness. As in Lewald's and Glümer's works, the text concludes with an affirmation of the heroine's virtue, which trumps social origin and occupation, posing the rhetorical question "whether any Treffenbach who ever lived, or who ever can live, was or can be worthy a [sic] Violetta Fouquet."[34]

Advertisements for *Violetta* quoted the *New York Tribune* and the *Boston Home Journal:* Violetta was a "happy conception," the *Tribune* declared, and the *Home Journal* pointed out that Wister's name on the title page as the "translator of a German story" had come to guarantee that the book was of "high merit and fascinating interest."³⁵ This praise received an enthusiastic second in several reviews, including one from *The Chautauquan,* which declared, "a translation from a popular German work by Mrs. A. L. Wister is always welcome."³⁶ *The Critic* found *Violetta* the best among "Mrs. Wister's graceful translations of pretty German stories" and touted it as providing the reader with exciting entertainment: "it has not a dull page, nor a superfluous paragraph, nor an uninteresting character in it."³⁷ The *Literary World* remarked on it as an informative picture of contemporary Germany, noting that there was "plenty of high German life" in it and that "one may make reputable acquaintance with types and forms of present society under the Emperor William which are not without interest."³⁸ *The Critic,* in contrast, took care to point out that it gave "a noble view of life" and thus served to edify.³⁹ These reviews operate with a largely flattering idea of generic German fiction, one encouraged by Lippincott in advertisements for Wister's series of German translations, an idea that understands this literature as essentially optimistic and diverting. Marketed as a "charming summer novel" with situations "full of interest" and dialogue that was "bright and vigorous," *Violetta* took its place beside a host of similar fiction including *Hulda* and *A Noble Name.*⁴⁰

If in *Daisy Miller* (1879) and *The Portrait of a Lady* (1881) Henry James introduced naïve American heroines in conflict with, even victimized by, European society and thus portrayed Europe as sophisticated, alien, and dangerous to American women, these three novels featured Germany in a different light. Here German regions provided the capacious stage on which virtuous and dutiful heroines, "happy conceptions," could overcome the threat of social death. In all three, creative work and talent are essential to the happy ending and do not diminish femininity. What is more, all three female protagonists enjoy unconventional latitude of action before inevitably and blissfully settling into marriage.

The Woman Question and the Pressure of the Happy Ending:
*Only a Girl*⁴¹

Lewald, Glümer, and Manteuffel portrayed virtuous, dutiful, and talented women who earn a living in the arts out of necessity and nevertheless marry desirable partners who secure their respectable social standing. Glümer even allowed her heroine a creative life as a novelist after her marriage. Wilhelmine von Hillern, by contrast, created an odd heroine who wants to pursue scientific research and whose happy ending seems imperiled throughout by her inability to conform to nineteenth-century codes of femininity. On the surface, Hillern's *Arzt der Seele* delivers a culturally conservative message that limits women's endeavors, one based on essentialist arguments that appear to reach full flower in the novel's concluding chapter, in which the heroine marries and gives birth to a daughter.

Nineteenth-century American cultural pundits who read the novel in the original German heard this conservative message, maintaining that the novel was no friend of women's rights.[42] Reviewers of the American translation who praised the "purity" of the book's tone and "the sound moral lesson it teaches" or pronounced the novel "timely" and "forcible" may have likewise alluded obliquely to that message.[43] Certainly, charges of conservatism and antifeminism are, at first glance, difficult to dispute. Yet, upon examination, fissures become visible that undercut the surface message, especially when the novel is read in English translation and at a remove from the realities of its German origins. The novel in fact permits a variety of readings. As we shall see upon close examination of the happy ending, a more progressive one was available even to nineteenth-century American readers.

Although he identifies Hillern's novel as an influence on George Eliot's *Middlemarch*, E. A. McCobb has few kind words for it, mistakenly asserting that it fell quickly into oblivion.[44] In point of fact, the book found willing readers in Germany and in America, in English, for at least forty years. *Arzt der Seele* first appeared in Prussia in two versions in 1869: as a serialized novel in the *Deutsche Roman-Zeitung* and as a four-volume book. The following year Lippincott published Wister's rendering of the serialized version. It was her fourth translation of popular novels by German women, and of these, it was her first by any woman besides Marlitt.[45] If Wister and Lippincott anticipated continued success with Wister's *Only a Girl*, they calculated correctly.

On May 7, 1870, the *New York Times* advertised *Only a Girl: or A Physician for the Soul* as "Just ready. A book for the times."[46] Subsequently, Lippincott reprinted the book at least nine times up to and including 1898. Over the course of these three decades the book was regularly and aggressively advertised under Wister's name for purchase individually or in a set along with Wister's other "popular translations from the German." Lists of nineteenth-century library holdings and other contemporary sources testify to the wide availability of the book in English. In 1893, for example, the U.S. Bureau of Education recommended Wister's *Only a Girl* as one among "5000 volumes for a popular library" in a catalogue assembled by the American Library Association for the Columbian Exposition.[47] All thirteen catalogues in Appendix B indicate the availability of Wister's translation *Only a Girl*. In 1896 the novel merited an entry in the *Library of the World's Best Literature*.[48] One additional and heavily plagiarized translation, to which we will return below, also circulated in North America.

What, then, did this popular novel from Germany, "full of German quaintness,"[49] have to say for more than forty years to American readers who expected happy endings from their popular German books and who, upon its first publication just a year after the appearance of John Stuart Mill's *The Subjection of Women* in England, were moving into a period of engagement with the woman question? In 1874 an American review of Marlitt's *The Second Wife* indicated that novel readers were prepared to entertain the possibility that women could be both intellectual and loving. They liked the portrayal in Marlitt's novel of the "highest ideal of womanhood and the most intelligent ideas as to feminine culture," ideas according to which "a woman may cultivate her intellect without prejudice to her heart . . . write and paint and study science without neglecting those softer duties that attach to her sex."[50] *Only a Girl* sets out to accomplish something like what this reviewer praised in *The Second Wife*, but while Hillern's Ernestine marries as she must to satisfy readers, the journey proves very difficult. She sacrifices to reach her happy ending, whereas, as we shall see in chapter 5, Marlitt's Juliane agilely slips into hers.

Only a Girl opens with an arresting portrait of a neglected and abused eight-year-old. Hans Christian Andersen's fairy tales serve throughout as points of reference for her story—her loneliness and neglect, her introversion and individualism, her radical estrangement from society, and her inarticulate longing for love. With allusions to "The Ugly Duckling," "The Little Mermaid," "The Snow Queen," and other tales by the internationally known Andersen, Hillern tips her hand as to her wish to convey the redemptive power of love. The text holds out the hope that the ugly duckling will transform into a swan, but the question remains as to what this swan can be in the confining social world evoked in this novel.

As a child Ernestine von Hartwich is painfully aware that her father despises her as "only a girl," yet she does not know how to be a girl, for she has had no mother to teach her. Beginning with a depiction of her visit to a children's party where her oddness makes Ernestine the object of the aggression of parents and children alike, Hillern charts a thorny course for her heroine. The novel vacillates between critically assessing what it means to be a woman in this society and urging that women live within its norms for the sake of their happiness. It sharpens the question as to whether Ernestine will marry through the plot device of a will dictating that if she dies childless her uncle Leuthold will inherit her fortune. Meaning to render her both unmarriageable and undesirous of marriage, Leuthold raises her as an atheist and aspiring physiologist. In her gender-deviant behavior, a nearly grown-up Ernestine proves troubling and divisive to the local peasants, the landed gentry, and the all-male university.

Even as it portrays society's horror of Ernestine, eliciting more sympathy with her than with her tormenters, the text stacks the deck against her. When she falls ill, poor health is attributed to her scientific pursuits, since they are, after all, contrary to woman's nature. The text implies that the obsessive and ambitious scientific study stunts Ernestine's emotional growth, causing her to repress her feelings and renounce conjugal bliss and sexual fulfillment. She hears the "voice of nature," but her uncle Leuthold urges her to ignore it by seeking the "warm throb of life" in vivisection at the dissecting table.[51] His plan to keep Ernestine from marrying would succeed were it not for Johannes Möllner, who from the start sees in her the swan she will become in her white wedding gown at the end of the book.

Although it ultimately shelters a newly devout Ernestine in matrimony, the novel devotes substantial space to unsettling readers. For more than 540 pages it explores questions of religion and science, emancipation of the flesh, women's social roles, women's admission to the university, and their ability to do science. Even as Johannes pursues Ernestine, the text pushes readers to engage with these questions, make contact with an expanded intellectual world, and imagine extended, if frightening, possibilities. *Only a Girl* also puts unappealing models of femininity on display for critical scrutiny, and in featuring a series of unflattering portraits of women as they have developed in this conservative social world, it hardly suggests that the heroine should reproduce these negative examples. Rather, it encourages sympathy with a beautiful and intelligent, though odd, heroine and asserts that those who find "an expression of thoughtfulness" "strange and gloomy" are "common people"; those in the comfortable educated classes by contrast ought to find the combination of intelligence and beauty alluring (161). Although thwarting Ernestine's wish for university study, the text debunks stereotypes of intelligent women as unattractive and barren, ultimately depositing the requisite baby in Ernestine's arms.[52]

As in the case of *Gold Elsie*, Hillern's happy ending, though clichéd, spared contemporary women readers the potentially frightening consequences of pursuing the issues the novel raises; it hoped instead for the possibility of a felicitous compromise that enabled women to take part in the intellectual labor of the day, to experiment and make mistakes, and still to experience emotional and sexual fulfillment in the safe harbor of marriage.

To reach its happy ending in marriage, the text does not argue for barring *all* women from university study. Instead, it convincingly airs the possibility of that study. In reproducing the deliberations of the professors of medicine and philosophy at the local university, it recreates the exclusive, masculine "academic citizenship" of the German universities of the day and subjects it to critical scrutiny. Those supporting Ernestine's admission easily deflate the contentions of those against it. As one character powerfully asserts, science is objective and gender blind; it welcomes everyone ready to labor on its behalf. The rehearsing of the arguments in favor of women's study compellingly familiarizes readers with them.[53] The text asks in effect why a female genius cannot be admitted to the university when so many stupid men are and then proceeds to demonstrate that some male scientists are not only stupid but also corrupt and deserving of ostracism from the scientific community.

Ernestine herself is eloquent on the subject of women's pursuit of science and the history of that pursuit. She maintains that the learned Dorothea Rodde, who died in 1824, would not have been so quickly forgotten had she been a man, noting, moreover, that the history of extraordinary ability in women ought not to be less interesting than the natural history of the ape. Displaying knowledge of contemporary physiology, she again asserts women's equality by discrediting then-current arguments about brain weight and, in particular, by demonstrating how brain weight as an indicator of intelligence would deny the intelligence of some brilliant men (308–9). The shocked and offended reaction of all assembled to her razor-sharp reasoning by no means invites readers to side with social norms against her. Instead, readers conditioned to empathize with the central female figure in popular novels can easily feel sympathy for the outspoken and socially inept Ernestine.

Those against Ernestine's university study, however, carry the day when Johannes Möllner sides with them, assuming a paternalistic role in protecting her womanhood against her scholarly ambition and drive. Were it not for the dogged and ultimately rewarded efforts of Johannes, to whom all of the characters defer, the text would exhibit more progressive leanings. Even so, Johannes does not always come off well. While he acknowledges the heroine's ability to "look beyond the individual to the universal" and by implication her worthiness to practice science, he himself unapologetically acts out of individual (and not universal) interests; he votes against her study because he wants to marry her. Alert readers can readily see the inconsistency, especially since the novel has just deflated the illogical arguments the male professors have launched against Ernestine's university study. In fact, in 1877 the *National Quarterly Review* did recognize this inconsistency and railed against Johannes's perfidy, even contending provocatively that Ernestine's uncle was a more appealing figure since he allowed the heroine a scientific education.[54]

In posing the woman question in terms of women's active involvement in scientific study and research, Hillern entertained a then nearly unthinkable extreme that protofeminist novelists of the period seldom broached.[55] In nineteenth-century novels, women's impulses to freedom tend instead to reside in the practice of the arts—painting, or writing novels, or even acting—and not science. After all, Arthur Schopenhauer had asserted in his much-cited essay "Über die Weiber" that women lacked the power to reason as well as a sense for and receptivity to music, poetry, and art. Protofeminists thus had much to refute even when they entertained the possibility of women's achievement in the arts. By taking up the dominant and masculinized academic discipline of the age, Hillern, who had been an actress and was now writing novels, made women's pursuit of *artistic* endeavors seem by comparison uncontroversial.

Hillern's woman scientist had to marry in the end; the market success of the novel at home and abroad depended on it. Wister, for one, would not have translated this novel if it had lacked the happy ending of marriage and family. The thirty-nine German novels and novellas by women and men that she rendered for the American market all end with marriage or remarriage; the happy ending belonged, as it were, to her brand. How, then, does a novel that so vividly weighs the possibility of women's pursuit of science, a pursuit that virtually barred women from marriage, reach the expected happy ending without simply becoming a simpering apology for the status quo? The solution, though conforming, exhibits unconventional features that suggest that Hillern was not prepared merely to confine her heroine in marital bliss.

First, the novel by no means idealizes marriage as a universal good. McCobb rightly observes, "even though the heroine is being propelled towards marital bliss, the most interesting, albeit brief, glimpses of marriage are those implying domestic tension."[56] Unflattering portraits of bad marriages are legion. Ernestine's Aunt Bertha and Uncle Leuthold are hideously mismatched, Leuthold having wedded this innkeeper's daughter for her money. The adulterous Herbert's marriage is still more distasteful, and the text vividly depicts the sufferings of his sickly wife. Angelika and the conservative professor Moritz love one another, but Moritz's possessiveness and self-importance do not win reader approbation for their marital life. If readers rejoice in the union of Ernestine and Johannes, then they must see it as a myth of conjugal bliss against the odds. Contrasting with the flawed marriages that otherwise dot the fictive landscape, this match pairs a superior man with a superior woman who is nearly his intellectual equal, not merely his dim but virtuous counterpart. With this exceptional couple, Hillern took a tiny step toward imagining greater parity in marriage.

The heroine's choice and sacrifice, furthermore, enable the marriage. Johannes procures for Ernestine an offer of a position as teacher of natural science in St. Petersburg. There she can pursue her scientific studies at the university and earn a living. On the other hand, she can choose Johannes, renouncing "brilliant prospects" and a "great future" for his sake (536). Having provided options, Johannes again makes his wishes known, and these prevail. Yet the stodgy professor has not only acknowledged Ernestine's scientific aptitude but finally admitted that some women should be admitted to study (albeit in Russia). Most importantly, he recognizes that to give up science means sacrifice, an act of the will. To renounce a career in science is thus portrayed neither as a simple matter of deflection from error and thus submission to discipline from without nor as a mere subsiding into nature; rather, it requires self-discipline. Ernestine, who once fumed at the story of the learned Rodde, who upon marriage "arrested her scientific development in the bud," knows what matrimony could mean for herself (305).

But Ernestine is no longer alone in her understanding of the depth of her impending loss. If, as Radway claims, romance permits identification with the heroine "at the moment of her greatest success, that is, when she secures the attention and recognition of her culture's most powerful and essential representative, a man," thus functioning as "a sign of a woman's attainment of legitimacy and personhood," then in this case that recognition resides in the acknowledgment by Johannes that to marry requires of Ernestine a conscious decision and active sacrifice.[57] Indeed, in exercising her will, she proves the hypothesis of her treatise, "Reflex Motion in its Relation to Free Agency," that reflexive reactions can be ruled by the will. Here she recounted having trained herself not to scream at the sound of a gunshot through force of will. Now she exercises that faculty in order to marry. By design or not, Hillern's novel links the threat of violence inhering in a gunshot with the threat of damage in marriage, proposing in each case that women can learn to exercise reason and discipline themselves to reach an outcome that they themselves determine.

A number of details of the final scenario of the concluding chapter also demand reconsideration. Here Hillern reinserts the science that Ernestine supposedly set aside to marry, thus imagining that marriage in the end is not a matter of either-or. The heroine continues to pursue science, "invaluable to

Johannes as a scientific companion and assistant. He could as ill spare her at his desk or in his laboratory as at the head of his household" (542). Likewise, the birth of a daughter, as an element of the happy ending, provides a layer of ambiguity. It especially does so if readers recall the first chapter in which the confused Ernestine reports that her mother "died because I was not a boy" (44). Wouldn't the grown-up Ernestine want a boy? Indeed, within the economy of nineteenth-century fiction, as in *Gold Elsie,* for example, the birth of a boy figures the vigor of the union, the viability of the family, and the mother's vicarious agency. Ernestine never actually expresses her wishes—preference for a boy is merely attributed to her by another character—and the text instead bestows a girl on the singular couple, implying that a daughter might function like a son. If Ernestine happily welcomes a daughter into the world, meaning to train her "to be what a true woman should be" so that she will one day say to "one whom she loves . . . 'Thank God that I am a woman, and that I am yours'" (543), she will do so to help that daughter lay claim to the promise of love and marriage. Nevertheless, the text never indicates that the happy parents will force their daughter to eschew intellectual pursuits. She will, after all, learn science from her father *and* her mother. In other words, Hillern's novel supplies the safe ending that readers desired, but the daughter carries new possibility into the future.

In the conservative moment of closure, moreover, readers need not forget what has gone before. Rather, they may be able to recall the possibilities and the turmoil that preceded the novel's end. Furthermore, as Natalie Davis famously observed of unruly women and festive rituals of inversion in early modern France, the parading of gender-deviant behavior can reinforce the status quo yet also undermine it. Temporary airing of the possibility of the exceptional woman was, in Davis's words, "also a resource for feminist reflection on women's capacities" and "enriched the fantasy of a few real women."[58] Intentionally or not, Hillern likewise enriched the fantasy of a few real women with her novel.

The two English translations, one British and one American, provide further clues to the ways the novel could be read across cultures in the nineteenth century, read both conservatively and cautiously progressively. In the final chapter Moritz, to whom readers have learned not to attribute insight, exclaims, "Wie es der Johannes nur angefangen haben muß, den Querkopf zurecht zu setzen?" (How ever did Johannes go about setting that oddball/hardheaded person aright? [my translation]). Wister's translation reads, however, "Johannes must have been puzzled indeed to know how to train that *scatterbrain*" (541; my italics).[59] When Ernestine is understood as a "scatterbrain" rather than a "Querkopf" (stubborn person, oddball), Johannes's task becomes something altogether different. "Querkopf" in either of its meanings implies the need for Ernestine to submit when Johannes imposes a rigorous regimen on her against her will. "Scatterbrain," on the other hand, indicates that Ernestine must learn to exercise her will, not to suppress it. She must exercise self-discipline to collect herself and tend to her own desires even if under male tutelage. Neither scenario passes muster in the present day, but they do diverge somewhat in their ideas about what enables happiness.

Wister's translation also downplays the housewifely attributes that the undomestic heroine, who once confused salad oil with heating oil, must acquire for the sake of her happy ending. As a married woman, Wister's freely translated Ernestine is a "jewel of a woman . . . who fulfils every duty, even those that she once considered so dull and commonplace!" (542). Hillern's Ernestine is by contrast a "Prachtweib" (splendid woman) who has become a wonderful "Hausfrau" (housewife): "Was uns Andern alle Mühe und alle Zeit in Anspruch nimmt, das macht sie spielend nebenher, als etwas ganz Selbstverständliches, Untergeordnetes, worüber gar kein Wort weiter zu verliren [sic] ist—und macht es besser als wir Alle" (237; Those things that cost the rest of us all kinds of effort and time she does easily alongside other things as though taking care of them were a matter of course and secondary and not worth wasting words on; and she does it better than all of us [my translation]). While Hillern's "housewife" strives to be the best at everything (even things of secondary importance), Wister's "jewel" merely fulfills her obligations, duties she perhaps still finds "dull and commonplace." The final lines of the novel, which Ernestine speaks "gratefully" to Johannes, invoke the suffering and sacrifice that have brought her to marriage and family: "your medicines were very bitter," she tells him, "but they were my salvation" (544). The word "bitter"—the same word in both English and German—jars, casting doubt on the perfect happiness of the ending and thus the ostensibly conservative message.

Wister's translation retains the word "bitter" and the closing paragraph in Ernestine's voice. *Ernestine, a Novel* (1879, American edition 1881 [reprinted 1902]), translated by the British Anglican priest Sabine Baring-Gould, ends differently. While Baring-Gould otherwise plagiarizes Wister verbatim in the final chapter, he omits the last four paragraphs. He must have noticed the potentially disruptive effects of "bitter" and determined to eliminate them, thus keeping Ernestine from alluding to the pain of conforming in the moment of closure and preventing her from having the final word on her own destiny. In his version Johannes speaks for her, concluding piously: "She is reconciled at last to the destiny of her sex."[60] Seven of the thirteen libraries listed in Appendix B held Wister's translation only. Patrons of the remaining six, however, could have read either Wister's or Baring-Gould's translation. Depending upon which translation they picked up, they would have heard a significantly different message on the final page of the novel.

The first half of the title of Wister's translation, *Only a Girl; or A Physician for the Soul*, likewise favors a cautiously progressive reading of Hillern's novel. By placing the title of the first chapter of the German original in front of the original book title, *Arzt der Seele*, Wister shifted attention from Johannes, the "physician of the soul," to the social cause of Ernestine's suffering, thus encouraging a sympathetic reading of her furious struggles. The unfairness of her fate signaled in the title, the fact that she is mistreated, misunderstood, impoverished, and forced to make a hard choice because she is "only a girl" may in the end have helped extend the afterlife of this novel in nineteenth-century America. The novel did not so much answer the woman question as raise it—and with considerable pathos and knowledge of the opposition it faced.

A copy of the 1887 reprint edition of *Only a Girl* once owned by Amanda A. Durff is bound in a red cloth cover adorned with a rose branch on which a winged cherub perches. Beneath it, Wister's embossed signature can be read: "Translated by Mrs. A. L. Wister." In a steadily selling series of translations from the German that included Marlitt's novels; the romances *Hulda, Violetta, Banned and Blessed, A Noble Name*; and many more, books whose flowery covers overtly appealed to popular taste and female readers, Hillern's novel was still voicing the question of women's intellectual pursuits. By 1891, however, when Amanda carefully entered her name in the book, women were beginning to be admitted to graduate study in the United States. Indeed, a generation of American women was coming to maturity that, as Sicherman points out in her study of women's reading in the Gilded Age, "individually and collectively left an unparalleled record of public achievement—as physicians and scientists, social workers and educators." These women "maneuvered their way from overprotected childhoods marked by extreme gender stereotyping to lives of adventure."[61] With new possibilities for careers, most of which meant that they would have to forego marriage, Amanda and her American sisters—including the 128 female borrowers of the book in Muncie, Indiana (1891–1902)—perhaps had more reason to worry than had their mothers whether the needs of the heart and the mind could be reconciled and whether they might be forced to choose.[62] They perhaps also had renewed cause to take flight to ostensibly safe reading about a privileged class in a distant time in a far-off land to circle warily around the question instead of confronting it head on.

Men's Happily Ever After:
At the Altar and *Banned and Blessed*

Both Regis and Radway characterize the romance novel as featuring female protagonists. Not all of these novels by German women do so, yet they share the other narrative elements outlined above. Hillern's *Aus eigener Kraft*, translated for Lippincott as *By His Own Might* (1872), for example, recounts the trials of a man who overcomes physical disability to become a doctor and marry the woman he loves. Julie Adeline Volckhausen's *Das Kind aus dem Ebräergang* (1870), translated as *Why Did He Not Die? or, The Child From the Ebräergang* (1871), features the abused natural son of a prominent Hamburg citizen, telling the story of his disappearance, ritual death, and subsequent resurrection as a famous painter who wins the object of his affection. E. Werner's popular novels, in particular, tend to shift attention to the male half of the blissful couple, gradually unveiling the attractiveness of unusual and initially unprepossessing men and recounting their emergence from isolation and passivity. *Am Altar* and *Gebannt und erlöst* exemplify this focus on the hero within the patterns of the romance novel. In linking male redemption and success to a woman's love, they make a strong appeal to female readers; at the same time, their emphasis on the hero provides more action and a broader canvas upon which to imagine the expression of subjectivity.

Am Altar (1871; *Die Gartenlaube*, nos. 1–17), published in 1872 by Lippincott as *At the Altar*, was the first of Werner's novels to reach Americans in English.[63] On September 12, 1872, not long after the serialization ended in Germany, *The Nation* listed the American translation among "recent novels."[64] Subsequently, the translation appeared in new American reprint editions and in two additional translations with London publishers. Finally, *At the Altar* turned up in 1895 in the pocket edition of Munro's Seaside Library, its appearance there testifying to its enduring appeal.

At the Altar shares many of the elements of Marlitt's novels: the regional setting, the social milieu of the middle class and landed aristocracy, class tensions, a lively and appealing young heroine, past transgressions that need to be atoned, family conflict, critical portraits of the aristocracy, and anti-Catholicism. It also features a happy ending founded in the union of man and wife—in the words of Werner's narrator—"the holiest and sweetest ties that unite mankind on earth, . . . wife, and home, and family."[65] This conclusion is, however, reached with especial difficulty, since the protagonist is a monk. Thus in a surprise twist, the altar of the title refers not to a wedding but to monastic vows, a sacred obligation presenting an insurmountable hindrance to the marriage that readers expected to conclude such a novel.

At the Altar exhibits striking signs of postunification imperial Germany in its concern with tensions between Protestant northern Germany and Catholic southern Germany and in its critical portrait of the Catholic Church and its authorities. Bismarck's anti-Catholic *Kulturkampf* had begun in 1871 and lasted until 1878. When Werner wrote the novel, the May Laws of 1873, which sharply curtailed the power of the Catholic Church, had yet to be passed in the German parliament but were nevertheless on the horizon. While in 1870–71 Germans had rejoiced in the unity forged between the North German Confederation and the South German provinces to do battle against the French, in the aftermath of the founding of the Reich the cultural, religious, and political differences between North and South and long-standing regional loyalties were coming into view.

The snobbish Rhaneks, descended from old South German nobility, have many secrets that must be revealed to end the sufferings of the male protagonist, Bruno. In his youth Ottfried von Rhanek, the youngest of three brothers, married a Protestant middle-class girl in a Protestant ceremony without his parents' consent. When the eldest Rhanek son died, Ottfried inherited the estate, because the middle brother had meanwhile become a priest. When Ottfried confessed that he had married a Protestant to his brother, the priest, the latter pronounced the marriage a sin and persuaded him to abandon his wife and their son, Bruno.

Upon his ex-wife's death, Ottfried secretly reclaimed Bruno and, at his brother the priest's urging, consecrated him to the church to atone for the unlawful marriage. At the same time he contracted a marriage of convenience with a Catholic of his social rank that produced one son, Ottfried Junior. Unaware that they are half brothers, Bruno and Ottfried detest one another, and both are attracted to middle-class Lucie, the sister of a North German who has recently settled in the area. Lucie dislikes Ottfried from the start, but Bruno, the monk, is hardly an appropriate match.

Chaffing against the sacred bonds forced upon him, Bruno preaches liberationist theology to the peasants, endangering the very foundations of the Catholic Church. The narrator hints that the Church may imprison and kill him. Meanwhile, Bruno struggles with his feelings for Lucie. In a titillating scene in a mountain chapel, the sexually unavailable monk and Lucie address one another by their Christian names, but Bruno remains mindful of the vow that denies him "what the ministers of your Church are allowed to possess." The Catholic altar stands between them and they have only the choice "between renunciation and crime" (235–36).

When, however, Bruno later discovers that his uncle, the priest, is plotting his death and also learns of his own origins and baptism as a Protestant, he feels licensed to leave the church. Now he must ask Lucie if she is willing to enter a marriage facilitated by a broken vow. The anti-Catholicism of the novel allays all pangs of conscience: marriage trumps celibacy, and a coerced vow of celibacy need not be kept. *At the Altar* ends as Bruno hastens "to meet the new future, his young wife at his side," the "blue misty distance before him" as a caroling lark rises above him (343). If, as Regis claims, the romance typically concludes by projecting an idea of freedom in a renewed social order, then this conclusion fits the prototype. Moreover, it reflects the historical moment in which it originates when it figures newfound freedom and a renewed social order housed within Protestantism.

American reviews readily picked up on the "Protestant tone" of this "not uninteresting" novel.[66] They saw the book as possessing a "German character" preserved by the translation, and the unlikely plot and happy ending did not deter them from reading the novel as a portrait of contemporary Germany. The *New York Times* piously remarked that, although exaggerated in detail and prejudiced against Catholicism, this "very entertaining novel . . . may be taken as a vigorous exposition of what South Germany has been under the rule of the Roman Catholic clergy; how far for purely clerical ends individual happiness has been interfered with; and how far, for the same object, right feeling and right action have been put aside."[67]

Eleven years later, Werner returned to a South German Alpine setting where the machinations of a Catholic priest again impede the happiness of the central couple and endanger the gullible villagers. Serialized in 1883 (*Die Gartenlaube*, nos. 1–29), *Gebannt und erlöst* was multiply translated in North America. Well known by 1883, Werner had over the intervening decade caught on with American readers; nine of her works had appeared in English translation as books, some of them in multiple renderings and editions. The year 1883 alone saw the publication of four new translations of four different novels by Werner. Lippincott promoted Wister's translation *Banned and Blessed* (1883) with a quotation from the *Boston Courier* as "by far the strongest of [Werner's] stories" whose novels are "always readable and to the highest degree entertaining."[68] *Publishers' Weekly* listed *Banned and Blessed* along with twelve additional works, including novels by Daudet, Zola, and five male German authors, as "the chief translations in fiction" of 1883.[69] In short, the publishers expected the book to be read and it was.

Banned and Blessed plots the redemption of three men, relying on the recently widowed Anna to help bring it about. Raimund von Werdenfels must regain her love; his cousin and ward, Paul, must transfer his love for her to her younger sister; and Gregor Wilmut the priest, her cousin and former guardian, must renounce his love for her. The narrative ties Raimund's redemption and the union of Raimund and Anna to the establishment of a new order in the rural setting, one that promises the peasants a better life and expels the priest and the noxious influence of the Church. Set in the countryside on the estates of the aristocracy and in the neighboring villages and featuring alliances of male aristocrats and bourgeois women, *Banned and Blessed* reproduces the social conditions that tend to characterize the German novels by women translated for Americans.

Gregor, who had long fought his attraction to his ward, Anna, arranged her marriage to a rich aristocrat fifty years her senior. The widowed Anna returns to become a disturbing presence in the Alpine countryside where her first love, the aristocratic Raimund, has become a brooding recluse on account of quarrels with his father over his love for the then-bourgeois Anna, the villagers' suspicions of his culpability in an unsolved case of arson and homicide, and the loss of Anna, who, encouraged by Gregor, shares these suspicions. Anna's return awakens Raimund from his lethargy, and he prepares to work on behalf of the village, even though the peasants deeply resent him. His rehabilitation is to be accomplished through a flood control project.

Long ago Raimund's autocratic father erected a floodwall to protect the manor house and the surrounding lands but ignored the safety of the village. To compensate for his father's crass irresponsibility, Raimund determines to build a dam at his own expense. However, since Gregor has persuaded the villagers to ask for government assistance instead, Raimund fails to gain their cooperation and the dam is not built. The spring thaw brings about the catastrophe adumbrated by the novel's first mention of the village's vulnerability, providing Raimund with the opportunity to redeem himself. To save the village, he breaches the old floodwall, diverting the waters toward his castle, park, and fertile fields. Moreover, imperiling his own life, he rescues the child of the man he is rumored to have murdered.

This sacrifice changes the lay of the land. No longer a reclusive dreamer, Raimund enters "life and the world with [Anna] beside [him]" and now has the grateful villagers "well in hand" in a relationship of mutual trust.[70] Like *At the Altar*, the novel concludes with a flowery assertion that the happy couple and the community have achieved freedom from the past: "The old ban . . . had vanished like the clouds and mist of those stormy spring days, and a free and blessed life was dawning" (390).

The optimism of the happy ending of *Banned and Blessed* stands out in sharp relief when compared with the tragic conclusion of a now-canonical German novella from the same decade: Theodor Storm's *Der Schimmelreiter* (1888). Storm, who also occasionally published in *Die Gartenlaube*, had likely read Werner's novel or at least knew of it. The two works share several motifs including a male protagonist who must prove his manhood; a water control project; bad relations between the protagonist, who occupies a position of authority, and his community; affirmation of marriage; a male nemesis who spreads falsehoods; sacrifice; atonement; and a devastating flood. Storm's novella, famous for its triple narrative frame; atmospheric evocation of regional peasant culture; descriptions of the conception, financing, and building of a dike; and its ambiguous presentation of the aloof Hauke Haien not only offers a thick account of the hero's psychological development and his fraught relations with the village but also ends with his sacrificial suicide by drowning and the total destruction of his family. His legacy consists of a ghost story that would have been anathema to his rationalist sensibilities and of the dike itself, which remains standing one hundred years later.

Hauke has been called a "Gründertyp," that is, a male type that emerged in postunification Germany, the ruthless individualist determined to profit through speculation and technology. Critics, however, remain divided as to whether the novella affirms or rejects this type, interpretation having been complicated by the conflicting evidence of the multiple narrative frames. Is Hauke a genius defeated by the stupidity of the backward villagers, or is he an arrogant loner lacking in self-knowledge and feeling? The work supplies evidence for both readings, projecting complexity into human relations and actions. Affirming her male protagonist's accession to leadership through work, sacrifice, righteousness, far-sightedness, and sheer force of will, Werner, by contrast, offers a less ambiguous view, one in keeping with the "habitual tone of confidence in human mastery" of nature that characterized the liberal optimism of the age.[71] Suffering only material loss, Raimund faces a future in which he will be able to exercise his will and talent for promoting communal good, sustained by a happy marriage to a woman he loves.

Storm's vivid evocation of regional German culture and the building of a dike presents thorny problems for the translator who is confronted with dialect, local customs, technical terminology, and the local offices and regulations governing maintenance of dikes. The work was not rendered into English until the eve of the First World War, when it appeared in two ill-timed projects: Kuno Francke's *The German Classics of the Nineteenth and Twentieth Centuries* in 1913–14, which paraded German literary achievement, attempting to counter popular American conceptions of German life and culture, and a 1917 anthology of canonical nineteenth-century German writers—Storm, Goethe, Fontane, and Keller—titled simply *German Fiction*.[72] In 1917 American women sending their sons and grandsons off to war to whip the Kaiser therefore more likely knew Werner's Germany as the setting of individualist happiness than Storm's Germany as the locus of tragedy.

Like Werner's *Banned and Blessed* and unlike now-canonical works of realism, the "German domestic love-story" with its strong family resemblances once so "agreeable and familiar" to American readers avoids tragedy, uniting duty with the attainment of the object of desire.[73] It erects ostensibly insurmountable barriers and then determinedly removes them to emplot union.

Reading for the Happy Ending: Realism, Contingency, and Myth

The virtually guaranteed happy ending of these German novels by women powerfully encouraged nineteenth-century American consumption of them. While it may be tempting to condescend to American liking for these imported happy endings, there are good reasons not to do so. Reading pleasure can signify deep human need rooted in specific historical conditions. Yet while literary criticism has validated aesthetic pleasure with respect to high comedy with its happy endings, it has often dismissed the pleasures of reading popular fiction, particularly romance novels, on political grounds. Romance allegedly provides a reductive view of the human condition, promotes false consciousness, and elides the contingency that shapes reality. As Alison Light observes, the discussion of romance has been criticized from the Left as a form of oppression under capitalism; in this line of thinking romance "is a form of oppressive ideology, which works to keep women in their socially and sexually subordinate place."[74] Light maintains that discussions of romance ought instead to consider that "literature is a source of pleasure, passion, *and* entertainment" and that pleasure must not be seen as "explain[ing] away politics" (372).

In Light's view, romance grants women "uncomplicated access to a subjectivity which is unified and coherent *and* still operating within the field of pleasure" (391). The need for such access as indicated by the repeated reading of romance can be seen as symptomatic of the difficulty of fulfilling the demands and promises of femininity in real life. Advocating a more complex and less judgmental understanding of the consumption of popular literature, Light models an approach to studying it that recognizes active seeking on the part of readers and that suggests, furthermore, that reading for happy endings, while likely not politically progressive, can have transgressive effects in the context of readers' realities, that is, realities that withhold what the novels deliver (392).

In her work on the romance novel from the 1980s, Radway, somewhat in the leftist vein that Light means to supersede, points out the false consciousness that, she believes, the structures of romance produce. Romance, she asserts, leaves male authority intact and reintegrates women into patriarchal society (RR 217). Thus romantic fiction may deflect and circumscribe "real protest . . . by supplying vicariously certain needs that, if presented as demands in the real world, might otherwise lead to the re-ordering of heterosexual relationships" (RR 217). At the same time she insists, as does Light, that we should not assume that "commodified objects exert such pressure and influence on their consumers that [consumers] have no power as individuals to resist or alter the ways in which those objects mean or can be used" (RR 221). Radway emphasizes, moreover, that we should not assume that these objects "bear all of their significances on the surface" (RR 221). Both Light and Radway thus underscore the value of the closer and more careful reading of these novels undertaken in this chapter and support the hypothesis that nineteenth-century Americans consumed German happy endings for reasons that are not trivial per se.

Radway also importantly identifies the proximity of romance novels to realism and thus the possibility that the fantasy of romance bears upon readers' reality. While readers do not expect the world of the romance novel to be theirs, they nevertheless understand it to inform and instruct them about a "real" world, indicating that "they also believe that the universe of the romantic fantasy is somehow congruent, if not continuous, with the one they inhabit" (RR 186). Romance readers, Radway argues, cleave to the fiction that romance works like history. They *pretend* that they do not know that events are lining up to produce an inevitable happy ending, even if they would not have read the book in the first place had they not been assured of that conclusion. Radway points out that romance appears to offer the mimetic fiction of novels: each time one begins reading, one accompanies new characters on a new journey "whose final destination is unknown at the moment of embarkation. Thus the act of reading a romance that is constructed like a novel is fraught with the excitement of open-ended potential and simultaneously marked by the threat of the unknown" (RR 199). Romance writers thereby "supply a myth in the guise of the truly possible" (RR 207).

"Myth in the guise of the truly possible" aptly describes most of the German novels by women that emigrated from Germany to America to deliver a happy ending. While some of these plots are improbable, they are not impossible, especially not under the terms that the narratives establish to begin with.[75] Moreover, they take place in a pleasantly congruent but foreign Germany; American realism need not apply. Nineteenth-century readers could consider—at least while under the spell of reading—that what was clearly impossible in America as they daily lived it just might not be in far-off Germany.

Dozens of German novels in English translation ritually made visible a myth of community founded in virtue and sentiment and anchored in marriage. They offered Americans variations of scenarios in which it was possible to make mistakes, take risks, express emotion without embarrassment, experience a degree of freedom, and still reach a safe port in a marriage characterized by mutual obligation and desire, one in which women retained and exerted influence. The books thereby invited American readers to imagine Germany as a place where some of their fondest hopes for the enduring power of feminine virtue and domestic sentiment could be blissfully realized—if arbitrarily and temporarily—even as the fictive heroes and heroines mapped out scenarios of action that expanded the boundaries of home.

IN 1900 "Miss Nellie Rank" presented Nataly von Eschstruth's *The Erl Queen* to "Miss Ethel Roby." Ethel, it appears, carried the book with her into her married life, carefully placing a book plate in it and signing herself "Mrs. Percy H. Bell."[76] As *Peterson's Magazine* noted in 1892, the book made "an acceptable birthday gift," and as Rothschild and Company advertised in the *Chicago Tribune* in 1895, it made a good Christmas present.[77] Five years later, Nellie must have thought so, too.

The Erl Queen opens with a fairy tale in which a prince searches for the meaning of love. Reality replicates the fairy tale when Norbert de Sangouleme meets the young Ruth von Altingen and falls in love with her only to be disappointed when she rejects his marriage proposal. After many misunderstandings, however, the couple marries and has a son. Thus in the late nineteenth century the book provided American readers with yet another version of the happy conclusion of the German domestic romances that in the preceding decades had become standard reading. Upon the appearance of the translation in 1892, *The Critic* pointed out that "like most German novels, this one is full of fancy and sentiment."[78]

This novel itself disingenuously illustrates the immaturity of a minor character, Ännchen, through her liking for novels that end well: she looks "at the last page first, and if nothing is said of an engagement or a wedding, [she throws] the book aside" (79). Even if *The Erl Queen*, with its allusion to Goethe's famous ballad "Der Erlkönig," laid claim to a more profound treatment of love than that in the novels Ännchen prefers, this novel would have pleased her, and the author surely knew it. Beginning at least as early as 1895, *The Erl Queen* was marketed in America, alongside novels by Heimburg, explicitly to girls, suggesting that American publishers and booksellers recognized that many of this latter-day generation of German novels did not have the power of their predecessors from the previous three decades to fascinate adults.[79] Yet, as Nellie's gift to Ethel testifies, American reading of German happy endings continued into the new century and into many an American marriage.

CHAPTER 5

Enduring Domesticity

German Novels of Remarriage

W HEN AN AMERICAN REVIEWER of *In the Schillingscourt* objected to a book in which a "divorce is obtained with less concern than a pair of gloves," he made it clear that readers expected romance plots to be built around an unmarried heroine and hero who marry.[1] As we observed in chapter 4, Regis also sees plotting toward marriage as a central feature of romance: romance is courtship of the unmarried. Likewise, when the Austrian feminist Rosa Mayreder criticized women's popular reading, she asserted that these novels were all based in courtship and that marriage itself was left unexamined.[2]

In point of fact, a subset of the domestic fiction by German women that reached American readers comprises what, borrowing loosely from Stanley Cavell, we might call novels of remarriage. These stories of remarriage, in which femininity matters deeply, allowed for the possibility of reconciliation and acknowledgment where life experience likely offered none. While in *Schillingscourt* marriages of convenience are shown to be immoral and unhealthy and are replaced by second marriages to new, desiring partners, in novels of remarriage men and women who are already bound to one another—either betrothed or married—discover or recover their love for one another. Despite troubled social conditions, all is well that ends well. Marriage is redeemed as an arrangement that tends to both emotional and economic needs, and in the process, these novels of remarriage map gendered subject positions. These works are comedies insofar as they conclude happily with the community restored. However, with the exception of Werner's stock comic subplots concerning marriage of eccentric secondary characters, they offered little for nineteenth-century readers to laugh about.

Upon the 1882 publication of Heimburg's *Lottie of the Mill* (translation of *Lumpenmüllers Lieschen*), a reviewer identified the book as characterizing a specifically German deviation from the romance genre: "The minor German novelists are fond of taking for a theme the love which develops after betrothal or marriage, and Heimburg is no exception. Lottie is betrothed to the Baron before he loves her, which is certainly a new departure from the romance which always considers a *misalliance* to be a love match."[3] In other words, these German novels characteristically explore the possibility of mutual love when social arrangements are imposed, not when they are breached.

In 1882 a host of American translations substantiated the reviewer's observation: Moritz von Reichenbach's (Valeska von Bethusy-Huc's) *The Eichhofs* (1881); E. Juncker's (Else [Kobert] Schmieden's) *Margarethe; or, Life-Problems* (1878); Werner's *Good Luck!* (1874/75) and *Broken Chains* (1875); Golo Raimund's (Bertha Heyn Frederich's) *From Hand to Hand* (1882); and Marlitt's *The Second Wife* (1874), a novel that had enjoyed significant and enduring sales in America since its publication and that reviewers sometimes used as a touchstone when reviewing German novels.[4] Heimburg herself would thereafter write three additional novels of remarriage that appeared in American translation: the variously translated *Herzenskrisen*, discussed in chapter 4; *Gertrude's Marriage* (1889); and *An Insignificant Woman* (1891; alternately titled *Misjudged*). In most but not all of these plots, an engagement or a marriage contracted in response to social economic pressure transforms into a union based in mutual desire and acknowledgment. What is officially imposed becomes emotionally confirmed in a form of remarriage that constitutes the text's happy ending.

Before we scrutinize this subset of German novels, a look at the film genre that Cavell termed the "comedy of remarriage" will be useful for identifying powerful narrative patterns that occur in these popular German novels. In his examination of a set of Hollywood movies of the 1930s and early 1940s, Cavell distinguishes the "comedy of remarriage" from two types of comedy classified by Northrup Frye: Old Comedy and New Comedy. While Old Comedy involves a young man's "efforts to overcome obstacles posed by an older man . . . to his winning the young woman of his choice," New Comedy focuses on the heroine, "who may hold the key to the successful conclusion of the plot, who may be disguised as a boy, and who may undergo something like death and restoration."[5] The Hollywood "comedy of remarriage" exhibits an affinity to New Comedy in its emphasis on the heroine, but it differs from both New and Old Comedy in making its heroine a married woman. It flirts with divorce and emplots the *re*-union of the central pair, getting them "*back together, together again*" (2).

These American film comedies, Cavell proposes, project an idea of marriage that deviates from popular fictions in which the married are "forever stuck in an orbit around the foci of desire and contempt" with no real past. The genre of remarriage is, by contrast, concerned with acknowledgment and genuine forgiveness, "a reconciliation so profound as to require the metamorphosis of death and revival" and a "new perspective on existence" (19). Cavell sees in these Hollywood films a response to struggles earlier in the twentieth century for a new social and political status for women and maintains that they imagine a new "consciousness of women" that seeks reciprocity, a "demand for acknowledgment" in a Utopian longing for "mutual freedom" (17–18). Over the course of his analysis of seven examples of the Hollywood comedy of remarriage, Cavell derives additional elements that characterize the genre, including a retreat to the green spaces of pastoral, the recovery of a shared history, and the founding of love in the innocence of childhood. Some of these elements figure in German novels of remarriage and, where pertinent, will be adduced in our examination of these works.

First a caveat: I do not mean to argue that these nineteenth-century German novels constitute antecedents of American films or to assert that they are comedies in the common usage of the word. Rather, I borrow here from Cavell to bring into focus features of a set of novels that likewise originated in a period in which the status of women began to be questioned and that also investigate marriage as the joining of the social economic with desire. While in their emphatic affirmation of marriage these works reserve particular roles for women within domesticity and are thus conservative, they also concern themselves with desire, acknowledgment, and an idea of women's agency within marriage, even if only in a limited sense. Elise L. Lathrop's translation of Heimburg's *Lumpenmüllers Lieschen* highlights that agency with the title *A Maiden's Choice*. In no sense resembling the original German, the American title voices a key element of the plot; it emphasizes an idea of free choice that results in the woman's acknowledgment by her husband-to-be within an already contracted marriage. In their idea of a romantic marriage in which spouses are mutually attracted to one another within the framework of real social economic necessity, these novels offered Gilded Age American readers, to paraphrase Cavell, a vision that those readers knew at bottom could not be inhabited in the world in which they lived (18).

The Second Wife as a Novel of Remarriage

In 1878, four years after the publication of Wister's translation of Marlitt's *Die zweite Frau*, the *American Socialist* belatedly observed that with this novel Marlitt provided a welcome contrast to tales ending "with marriage and not enlightening us as to how the enamored pair, after having labored so assiduously to get together, have endured the close and unromantic contact of matrimony."[6] Seeing in *The Second Wife* the moral message that "love may be won by sterling integrity and simple honesty," the reviewer went on to espouse a fierce eugenics of marriage. In this view of wedlock, children of superior intelligence and character emerge from couples who are not only healthy of body but "united by a chaste, continent and self-denying love," as opposed to those who marry because they desire to possess one another. The novel had also been praised four years earlier by *Godey's Lady's Book* as advocating the "dignity of labor and the advancement of women."[7] Touting Marlitt's novel as deserving to "rank with the best work of modern continental novelists—even with that of Tourgenieff [sic] himself," the *Literary World* saw the female protagonist as embodying the "highest ideal of womanhood and the most intelligent ideas as to feminine culture." In this kind of feminine culture a woman could "cultivate her intellect without prejudice to her heart."[8] While it may be difficult in our day to recover the mindset that gave rise to these enthusiastic assessments, *The Second Wife* does provide an electric moment of female empowerment through science: the heroine Liana discovers the forgery on which the novel's mystery turns by examining a document with her microscope!

Ruth-Ellen Boetcher Joeres outlines how this novel both sustains and transgresses ideas of class and gender that prevailed in 1870s Germany. Citing Tania Modleski's response to Fredric Jameson's "Reification and Utopia," she makes a plea for popular literature as not mere repetition of the same but as exhibiting subtleties and nuances in its handling of class and gender.[9] Joeres also points out that, although Marlitt's characters are designated as aristocrats, the values and worldviews affirmed in these novels correspond to those of the German middle classes. Within that worldview, marriage reigns supreme as the guarantor of those values and the guardian of property. The highly successful *Second Wife* demands renewed scrutiny in our context, especially since it helped establish the novel of remarriage, a subgenre that became recognizable in late nineteenth-century America, as "made in Germany."

The Second Wife does not fail to deliver what readers might expect of a novel thus titled. The Protestant Liana must occupy the blue salon that is still redolent with the ineradicable perfume of Raoul von Mainau's Catholic first wife, his own first cousin. Raoul's uncle and former father-in-law, the Hofmarschall, advised by a Jesuit priest, rules the household, and Leo, the son, whom Liana as the second wife is to mother, promises to be an incorrigible brat. The marriage has been contracted under odd circumstances, engineered in part by Liana's snobbish and impecunious aristocratic mother because of the material advantages it brings. The restless Raoul wants a mother for his son and a wife who knows her place and can also serve as a means of taking revenge on the duchess who long ago abandoned him for a marriage of convenience. The newly widowed duchess looms larger than the first wife as the embodiment of a past when a younger Raoul had loved passionately, as opposed to the oppressive present, when he maintains a fragile façade of aloof cynicism. A marriage could hardly begin less propitiously (or in a more contrived manner). Raoul plans to leave on a journey to the East as soon as his new wife establishes herself, and he is assured that she will run his household to his liking.

Raoul and Liana have no physical contact beyond playing the part of a harmonious couple in public for decorum's sake, which requires that she rest her fingertips on his arm.[10] Readers seeking romance may thrill to the light touch even of fingertips with hope for more. Liana otherwise does her duty, quickly taking charge of Leo, who magically responds to her combination of mothering and pedagogy. When the Hofmarschall taunts Liana with a letter from her mother asking for money and ridicules Liana's botanizing and her art, which she has sold in the past, Liana begins to think of returning to her home.

Following an incident in which he accidentally strikes Liana, Raoul enters her boudoir for the first time. He not only pronounces her luxuriant hair magnificent—as Joeres notes, Liana's red-gold hair signifies a sexuality that is otherwise masked (245)—he remarks on the improvements that she has wrought in a room that he could not abide when his first wife inhabited it. But in precisely the scene in which Raoul begins to betray signs of his attraction to his unloved second wife, her resolve to separate from him becomes firm—and so begins Marlitt's signature choreography of fencing but mutually attracted protagonists. At roughly the midpoint of the novel, Raoul reads a letter from Liana to her sister in which she analyzes his faults as one would "an unfortunate butterfly on a pin beneath a magnifying glass" (167). Upon this unpleasant and embarrassing enumeration of the husband's flaws, the marriage might seem to be over, but the pages that remain to be read signal that it is not.

Liana's intellect, her ability both to mother and detect and thus to unravel the mysteries haunting Schönwerth castle, which the irresponsible male protagonist has chosen not to probe, plays a critical role. When Raoul finally confesses his love to Liana, he castigates himself for his blindness. And despite the concluding lines of the novel, in which he insists that he has arranged everything to suit his future happiness, readers should be able to see that Liana's wisdom and insight prevail in the marriage, that is, Raoul's idea of happiness has come to conform with hers and not vice versa. Indeed, Marlitt has over many pages carefully delivered the protagonist up to Liana. When Liana cries out affirmatively to his plea for her to stay and thus is in effect betrothed for the second time, the assent can occur only because she knows that Raoul has at last acknowledged her and that desire and virtue are finally in harmony. She will no longer play the part of the submissive and unloved wife, mother, and glorified governess but will instead shape the contours and modes of being of this restored marriage. Within the trajectory of the novel, the profound reconciliation that Cavell sees as the signature of the "comedy of remarriage" has thus taken place. Its profundity is revealed in the terms of popular literature by the solving of the mystery that has made the house the site and shelter of multiple crimes.

Marlitt's text extravagantly figures the rampant male sexuality of the Mainau family in the "valley of Cashmere," a garden on their estate filled with exotic plants and animals, where, in a bamboo hut, lies paralyzed the Hindu woman who is said to have been a bayadere and the mistress of Gisbert, one of the three Mainau brothers from the previous generation. While, upon its construction, the zoolike compound had been a testimony to a man's consuming love for an exotic woman, it has become a festering sore on the estate. Once known for his wildness, Gisbert, who created the valley, had doted on the Indian woman. In his declining months, however, he, under the noxious influence of his brother (the Hofmarschall) and the priest, disavowed her as faithless. Thirteen years later, her son, Gabriel, who is presumed to be neither Gisbert's legitimate son nor even his natural son, is systematically brutalized while being prepared to become a monk against his inclination. As Joeres remarks, the woman lying mute and paralyzed in the bamboo hut vaguely recalls the mad Bertha Mason of *Jane Eyre*. The affinity lies, among other things, in her marginalized status as a colonial Other, her suffering, and her containment in a stigmatized space. While Bertha screams insanely, Joeres notes, this woman is entirely mute (241–42). In the end Liana must speak for her. As in *The Old Mam'selle's Secret* and *Gold Elsie*, Marlitt derived inspiration from Brontë's novel when she created a woman-centered tale in which men's misdeeds are unmasked and the sexual-social order is rearranged to favor women who are motherly and intellectual—and sexual.

As Liana's detection eventually reveals, the Indian woman was legally married to Gisbert; she never practiced a dishonorable profession and never betrayed her husband. Gabriel is the legitimate heir to a third of the Schönwerth estate. Behind the cruel treatment of the once beloved woman is the Hofmarschall, the second brother, who, because he coveted this woman and was spurned, tormented her while preserving his pious courtier's exterior. Furthermore, when he in a rage of sexual frustration attempted to strangle her, he paralyzed her. Her subsequent muteness worked to his advantage. Meanwhile, his coconspirator, the Jesuit priest, who can justify his mistreatment of the woman and her son by the fact that she is not a Christian, also proves to be ruled by sensuality. The priest repeatedly attempts to force his attentions on Liana, and in his frustration at being rebuffed, he ultimately tries to drown her, thus nearly reenacting the crime of the Hofmarschall.

Raoul, the son of the third brother, whom Marlitt portrays as, like Brontë's Mr. Rochester, darkly appealing, himself has a profligate past, one that is, among other things, memorialized in a woman's blue slipper that he keeps under glass. It marks the triumph of sentimental love over libertinism when he empties his room of the trophies of his past conquests and hangs a picture of his son on the wall. With Liana's help, he finally takes responsible charge of his estate, expiates the crimes committed within its confines, and properly husbands its resources.

As in *Gold Elsie,* male sexuality both repels and attracts, is destructive and productive. When his sexuality is finally channeled and expressed in a sentimental marriage to an intellectually and morally superior woman, the male hero reaches his full maturity as the master of an estate and as a father, in this case, a father to a biological son and an adopted son who is also his own cousin. The now uxorious hero believes he has arranged everything according to his lights, but, as mentioned above, readers must recognize that this marriage conforms to his wife's ideals, ideals that in turn coincide with ideals of marriage treasured on both sides of the Atlantic.

And what of Liana's sexuality? When the priest warns Liana that she cannot expect her freshly reaffirmed marriage to last more than a year, she retorts, "One single year! But a year of delight!" thus speaking in the register of the passion of the short-lived marriage of the Indian woman and Gisbert (283). Joeres sees the final chapter as eclipsing the sexuality otherwise signaled by Liana's red-gold hair and reads the final line in which Raoul claims that he has manipulated everything to suit himself as favoring and reconfirming Liana's "representational function as wife and mother" (Joeres 246). Yet even if we accept Raoul's words at face value, we ought not to underestimate readers' ability to recall Liana's attraction to Raoul and her passionate affirmation of marriage as "delight." Readers need not forget that Liana is the agent of her own happy ending, a marriage in which she will not enjoy merely a year of bliss but can expect an entire lifetime of it.

Die zweite Frau ran serially, nos. 1–21, in *Die Gartenlaube* from January until May 1874; in early July, not long after its conclusion in Germany, the *Christian Union* announced Wister's translation of *The Second Wife* as among "the latest novels in our hands."[11] As she had done repeatedly, Wister translated Marlitt right off the pages of *Die Gartenlaube*. Annie Wood's translation appeared in London in the following year, and by 1880 Munro had published Wood's translation in his Seaside Library and again in 1887 in the Seaside Library pocket edition. From the mid-1880s onward, editions proliferated, including those by William L. Allison; F. M. Lupton; E. A. Weeks; the Federal Book Company; Donohue, Henneberry and Company; A. L. Burt; Mershon; George M. Hill; and Hurst and Company. Meanwhile, in London, Ward and Lock published a new translation of the book titled *The Second Wife. A Romance of Castle Schönwerth* (1881) while Lippincott reprinted *The Second Wife* at least through 1902. Its enduring success prompted a fourth translation of it in 1891 as *A Brave Woman* with Worthington. The new title suggests the reason for the long-term appeal of Marlitt's novel. When the teacher Miss Florence J. Pepin presented *A Brave Woman* to her pupil Paulina S. Schwarz for Christmas in 1896, she must have thought the book still had something to say to budding womanhood.[12]

Americans liked this book. Praising it as absorbing reading with a moral tone, *Godey's Lady's Book* declared, "We are pleased to see the better class of foreign literature introduced to American readers." The magazine found it "exceedingly entertaining as a story, and most unexceptionable in point of morals."[13] The *Literary World* enthusiastically named the book "one of the very best novels of the year," opening its review of *The Second Wife* with a declaration of joy in reading it: "We rarely encounter a novel that we can read with so much pleasure."[14]

The favorable judgment of the first reviews was born out two years later in 1876. According to *Publishers' Weekly*, when publishers were asked the "Prize Question in Fiction" as to the most salable novel in the trade, *The Second Wife* ranked twenty-seventh with nineteen votes, four steps below *The Old Mam'selle's Secret* and tied with Charlotte Yonge's beloved *Heir of Redclyffe*. *Jane Eyre* occupied second place on this same list.

As we have seen, there is no doubt of Brontë's long-lasting influence on Marlitt's writing. A closer look at *Jane Eyre* and *The Second Wife* reveals commonalities beyond mere sensationalism that must have appealed to Americans and helped secure a place for both novels on this list. These include the strong heroine who acquires everything she desires on her own terms and the protagonist whose masculinity is both created and tamed by the heroine.[15]

In 1881 Agnes Hamilton told her cousin Alice that *The Second Wife* was splendid. The Hamilton girls associated reading "with freedom and possibility" and enjoyed "plots of adventure and social responsibility," Barbara Sichermann maintains.[16] The novels they preferred, "—even those that end with an impending marriage—provided models of socially conscious and independent womanhood."[17] For all its sensational elements, elements that now seem painfully contrived, Marlitt's novel of remarriage could fit this bill for nineteenth-century readers. In any case, in 1899, twenty-five years after it first appeared in the United States, Buck and Annie must have believed that *The Second Wife* would make a fine present for their mother. On the flyleaf of an edition of the novel published by Donohue, Henneberry and Company, they wrote, "A Happy birthday to Mamma / from Buck + Annie / Nov 21–99."[18]

Producing the Right Kind of Masculinity:
Good Luck!

Werner's *Glück auf!* appeared in 1873 (*Die Gartenlaube,* nos. 1–23), one year before *Die zweite Frau.* In May 1874, one year after the completion of its serialization, it was available for purchase in the United States from Osgood in Frances A. Shaw's translation, *Good Luck!*[19] It remained in print until at least 1912, when A. L. Burt reprinted a translation of the novel for its Cornell Series. Available for borrowing in lending libraries and for purchase in various formats in prices ranging from ten cents to $1.25, the novel was read over nearly forty years in at least four different English renderings and at least twenty editions and reprint editions. In the American context, advertisements encouraged readers to associate Werner with this early work by touting her later novels as "by the author of *Good Luck!*" The novel offered Americans the good and wholesome read they sought, publishers claimed; in 1877, for example, Estes and Lauriat advertised it as "Healthy Light Literature. Which should be in every Library."[20]

Together with *The Second Wife, Good Luck!* led a German invasion of novels of remarriage in which coerced economic unions transform into love matches and end with what amounts to a renewal of marriage vows. *Good Luck!* opens with a wedding of an indifferent bride and the groom. A bourgeois captain of industry has engineered this marriage by bankrupting the aristocratic Baron Windeg. Marriage to Windeg's daughter, he hopes, will gain his son entrance into the aristocracy and seal his own success. The bride, Baroness Eugenia Maria Ana von Windeg, is given to aristocratic arrogance, despite her family's poverty and her degraded status as bartered object. The groom, Arthur Berkow, for his part, appears to be merely the compliant tool of his father's machinations. The marriage seems doomed from the start. Once Arthur learns that it was coerced and not merely a business arrangement between equals, he refuses to remain his father's dupe and promises Eugenia her freedom as soon as decorum allows, that is, after one year. Thus begins the breakup.

Yet even as the unhappy couple lives estranged, their marriage unconsummated, they are drawn to one another. In a scene that occurs in variations in most of Werner's novels, Eugenia and Arthur have an intimate conversation in the forest after their carriage breaks down. Nature serves as the green space where the evils of social convention and a misguided education fall away and a possibility of reinventing themselves as a couple emerges. Brightening, Arthur tells his wife that he knows "his" woods and it becomes clear that his salvation lies in finding his way back to his "early, sunny boyhood years," which were "the only ones worth living" (119). Eugenia's happiness, too, had ended with her childhood, for her entrance into society had been accompanied by humiliation and despair. As they stand beneath a fir tree in a downpour, Eugenie notices her husband's "very handsome eyes" (122) and recognizes that his languor results from the terrible education imposed on him by his father. In temporarily recovering the innocence of childhood in the pastoral space of the forest, they discover their mutual attraction.

Even if the reader has not suspected it previously, it becomes hard to miss at this juncture that this couple will ultimately be reunited with Arthur confirming the power of two words that "have helped [him] to victory: my *wife* and my *child!*" (418). More than 250 pages will, however, be required to bring about the insight needed to accomplish the thaw between husband and wife. As a favorable review in the *Literary World* observed, the charm of the story (and the pleasure of reading it) resides "in the gradual approximation of husband and wife, the slow crumbling of the barrier which separates them, under the influence of the noble qualities in each."[21]

Even so, readers doubtlessly fastened onto differing aspects of the book. The three variations in the titles of the English translations themselves suggest alternate readings: *Good Luck!* (1874); *Good Luck, or, Success and How He Won it* (1876); and *She Fell in Love with Her Husband* (1892). If nineteenth-century Americans understood "good luck" as the special greeting of German miners (*Glück auf!*), which they could have known had they read Heinrich Heine's *Harzreise* as it was translated by C. G. Leland in 1855, then the title highlighted for them the social economic setting of the novel.²² If they did not—and despite Leland's Heine translation, most American readers probably did not—the title told them little about the book's content. Shaw, however, provided a footnote on the first page of her translation explaining the title's significance. The second version of the title, *Good Luck, or, Success and How He Won It*, by contrast, promised readers a male-centered story of achievement. The third rendering suggested a different plot altogether: instead of a tale of male success, *She Fell in Love with Her Husband* implied a female-focused account of emotion and inner struggle. The novel offers both but privileges the achievement of masculinity as it is linked to the exploitation of science and technology. Conjugal love and femininity are in turn critical to realizing this masculine ideal and indeed to imagining it to begin with.

Eugenia's eventual recognition and acknowledgment of her husband's true worth and her subsequent emotional and erotic attachment to him model for readers an appropriate response to the male protagonist. The narrator makes clear that, in falling passionately in love with the man foisted upon her in a marriage of convenience, Eugenia has acquired good health. The newfound manly vigor of her once languorous husband has revived her, too: "The old pallor and marble-like coldness had vanished from [her rosy face], which was now beaming with happiness" (417). In these concluding pages, Eugenia and Arthur are living a "real romance which is not yet ended" (413). The book frames this romance with a paean to nature and science befitting the industrial age that had been newly invigorated in the German territories by the founding of the empire. The final lines describing the conquest of nature by means of the technology of mining are distinctly erotic and at the same time give voice to a fantasy of sexual fulfillment: "Science had forced those barriers and had wrested from the clefts and abysses of the earth those treasures so long imprisoned in deepest night," the narrator effuses. "And now they had been borne upward to the light of day, unfettered by that ancient magic word of the mountains, *Glück auf!*" (419).

While the erotic connotations of this particular passage may not be visible to every reader's eye, Werner's text overtly links the plot of remarriage to the male protagonist's role as heir to a mining industry to cement the connection of the erotic and the industrial. When his tyrannical father is killed in a mining accident—slaughtered by the industry he built on the backs of his suffering workmen—Arthur, who has previously shown no talent for or interest in heading the company, takes charge. He must contend with a formidable opponent, the demagogic Ulrich Hartmann, an experienced miner of gigantic physical proportions. Werner portrays this worker in 1873, in the decade after the founding of Ferdinand Lassalle's General Union of German

Workers (1863) and the Social Democratic Workers' Party of August Bebel (1869), as all muscle and passion with little ability to reason.[23] In addition to his uncompromising views on labor, Ulrich has conceived a hopeless and overweening passion for Eugenia. Despite his transgressive acts and passions, the text redeems him but also conveniently eliminates him, when he nobly sacrifices himself for Arthur when they try to avert an even greater mining disaster.

The portrait of labor embodied by Ulrich versus management incorporated by Arthur in the miners' strike that takes place in the novel is largely one-sided.[24] Unreasonable in their ambitions, the striking workers refuse to listen to the cool-headed and well-meaning Arthur, and they verge on losing everything since Arthur plans to close down the mines rather than give in to their excessive demands. Arthur, in turn, expects the workers to wait for him to make their lives better on his terms as he tries to implement better business and industrial practices. The novel features dramatic scenes in which Arthur must face an angry mob alone. In the end, a mining disaster leads management and labor to forget their differences and join forces—"Ulrich Hartmann with his iron body and Arthur Berkow with his iron will" (391).

This joint effort prefigures the harmonious conclusion of the industrial plot in which the pragmatic and well-intentioned Arthur has established practices that benefit the workers and also increase profits. But as it turns out, the brawny and violent Ulrich represented only a minority of the workers to begin with. The text praises the majority of the miners: except for Ulrich and a few of his followers, the good workers remain calm in the moment of crisis. By waiting and granting Arthur "time and permission to proceed in the way he thought best" (405), they ultimately enable him to do for them even more than he originally promised.[25]

Werner's Arthur is diminutive compared with the worker Ulrich, yet he represents a new superior male type of the industrial age: the man of iron will armed with reason, the man who for all his outward sangfroid is nevertheless susceptible to the heroine's charms. Even as she creates this paragon of a new masculinity, Werner keeps him securely contained by the feminine. We recall the presence of this type in *Banned and Blessed* as well, a novel that, given its story of the reconciliation of once-betrothed lovers, itself offers a variation of the plot of remarriage. In both *Good Luck!* and *Banned and Blessed,* the new man that Werner creates for family reading in imperial Germany requires education and instruction to realize his potential, and that education and instruction tend to reside in Werner's feminine imaginary. In the summary statement in the final chapter of *Good Luck!* the narrator speaks of Arthur's learning to have "confidence in himself" with "his wife at his side." He gains courage from his new understanding that "he had a whole future, a life's happiness for her and himself to win" (402). It appears, moreover, that the happiness of his workers derives from his own, a happiness that originates and resides in his achieving reunion with his lawful wife.

In 1893 *Die Gartenlaube* began advertising a new illustrated series of Werner's collected novels, characterizing her works so as to appeal to a new generation of German buyers and readers.[26] The advertisements asserted that in contrast to Marlitt, who read female hearts, Werner's exciting and suspenseful novels entered the noisy world of struggling and achieving. Werner, the advertisements claimed, captured the roaring winds of the times yet also portrayed the struggle in women's hearts.[27] The advertisements thus alluded to the tendency of Werner's novels to focus on male protagonists' accession to their manly place in the social and political order. Yet this attention to male characters rendered the novels no less appealing to a nineteenth-century female readership. They addressed women readers by attaching the struggles of the protagonist to his love for a heroine who was typically painted in vivid colors.

In focusing on men and the achievement of proper masculinity, what the *Literary World* formulated in its review of *Good Luck!* as "the highest qualities of manhood,"[28] not as mere accessories to the happiness of female characters but as the principal task of the narrative and its female protagonist, Werner's novels highlight what is implicit in all of these German examples of domestic fiction. Within an economy that privileges heterosexual marriage, women's happiness is critically tied to producing the right kind of masculinity in their husbands. Werner's appeal in *Good Luck!* consisted, then, in offering nineteenth-century readers the pleasant fantasy that it mattered whether "she fell in love with her husband."

Family Matters Frozen in Time:
Lumpenmüllers Lieschen

Four years later *Die Gartenlaube* published yet another variation of a novel of remarriage in which the plotting of reconciliation returned to the husband's need to acknowledge his wife as a precondition to his achieving manhood and becoming the master of his inherited estate. Wilhelmine Heimburg's *Lumpenmüllers Lieschen*, which first appeared in *Die Gartenlaube* in 1878, nos. 40–52, was published in at least three different North American translations: Mary Stuart Smith's serialized *Lieschen, A Tale of an Old Castle* (1881–82), which in 1889 appeared as a book in Munro's Seaside Library as *A Tale* of an Old Castle;[29] Katharine S. Dickey's *Lottie of the Mill* (1882) with Lippincott; and Elise L. Lathrop's *A Maiden's Choice* with Worthington (1891).[30] It was also translated in Great Britain in 1880 as *Lizzie of the Mill* by the prolific Christina Tyrrell. R. F. Fenno must have thought Heimburg's novel worth a double risk. In 1896 the publisher advertised Smith's *A Tale of an Old Castle* in its Lenox and Summer Series; in 1899 it brought out a new edition of Lathrop's *A Maiden's Choice*.[31] The illustrations accompanying Worthington's and Fenno's editions of *A Maiden's Choice* are poor reproductions of the illustrations provided in 1891 by R. Wehle for volume two of Heimburg's ten-volume illustrated *Romane und Novellen*.[32] The poor quality of the illustrations in the American editions suggests unauthorized printing.[33]

Mary Stuart Smith thought *Lieschen* "perhaps the very prettiest story" she had ever translated.[34] *The Critic* likewise pronounced the novel a "very pretty German story" and a "pleasant little German story" in two different articles in 1882.[35] As one of a "number of novels and romances . . . admirably adapted for whiling away the slumberous days of summer," American translations of *Lieschen* register in contemporary reviews as both profoundly feminine and German. *Godey's Lady's Book* waxed enthusiastic, describing this "clean, natural story of German life" as "a delicate mingling of pathos and humor, stamping it, all in all, as a work of exceeding power."[36] *Peterson's Magazine* remarked that this "remarkably good story" was available in a Worthington series characterized by a "dainty and attractive fashion."[37]

An exemplar of Fenno's illustrated edition of *A Maiden's Choice* (1899) bears witness to the "dainty" appeal of an illustrated edition at reasonable prices within a female gift economy, dedicated as it is to "Ada B. Parker from Mrs. Bartholomew."[38] The spine and the front cover boast a crudely rendered design of hearts and flowers, stamped white, red, and green on blue (see Figure 5.1). While this book may now appear childish, *Publishers' Weekly* remarked in 1891 that this title numbered among a half dozen books that Worthington was publishing for "older readers" (as opposed to its stock of juvenile literature).[39]

When in 1882 a more critical reviewer for *The Critic* spoke condescendingly of the last page of Dickey's *Lottie of the Mill* as "appropriately full of quivering moonbeams, roses, white dresses, and all the melody of spring," he showed himself impervious to the very power that *Godey's Lady's Book* praised in the story.[40] In short, the insistence of the novel that even a marriage contracted for economic reasons could result in passionate love between spouses made a strong appeal to those readers who needed to believe in the institution. A review of *Defiant Hearts*, another Heimburg novel from sixteen years later, underlined the divergence of taste and enjoyment between

Figure 5.1 W. Heimburg, *A Maiden's Choice* (New York: R. F. Fenno & Company, 1899). Author's copy.

the readers of such novels and the reviewer's own. Acknowledging that this "typical German novel of the sentimental order" was better than "most of its class," the reviewer characterized *Defiant Hearts* as presenting a "state of society familiar to Americans chiefly through novels, in which the necessity of a definite amount of money as a primary consideration in marriage is frankly acknowledged, in which the narrow interests of women lower the general tone, and where differences in rank lead to arrogance on the one side and undue humility on the other." The reviewer, however, thought the novel "well fitted for popularity in circulating libraries" and thus condescended to readers who wanted precisely those novels that addressed their "narrow interests."[41] Whatever the opinion of critics, American readers, publishers, translators, and libraries kept versions of Heimburg's *Lumpenmüllers Lieschen* in circulation into the new century.

Set in an unspecified rural Germany, *Lieschen* explores relations between an impoverished aristocratic family, the von Derenbergs, in the decaying castle on the hill and the wealthy family that owns the paper mill in the village. Social conditions in the countryside appear suspended in time. Although a factory might herald modernity, the narrator points out that the mill has operated there for generations.[42] Even the visit of the shallow, aristocratic Blanche to the castle fails to provide opportunity to specify the novel to a historical period. Her beautiful clothes are noted on several occasions, but in terms too vague to connect them to a specific fashion trend.

It suited one American reviewer of *A Maiden's Choice*, the fourth English translation of *Lieschen*, to identify this peculiar combination of frozen time and loosening social barriers as German. *The Critic* pointed in 1892 to the "social conditions so different from ours" that test the hero and heroine "by the amount of social sacrifice they are willing to make for each other."[43] Insisting that the English novel no longer concerned itself with such matters and that the American novel—presumably by virtue of its origins in a democratic society—never had "any legitimate right to found a plot on such a point of view," the reviewer asserted that "the feeling of rank and class and fortune is still a very vital consideration in Germany." A decade earlier *The Critic* had in the review quoted above labeled the handling of misalliance in this novel peculiarly German.[44]

While class resonated differently in America, the reviewer's point seems disingenuous. Americans were well aware of class and by 1892 could have read, for example, *The Rise of Silas Lapham* (1885) for a treatment (albeit benign) of class difference. Of course they had yet to read Edith Wharton's more harrowing, best-selling *House of Mirth* (1905) and *The Custom of the Country* (1913) or Booth Tarkington's *Alice Adams* (1921), novels that explore the excruciating and finely drawn lines of social class in precisely the country that "never had any legitimate right to found a plot on such a point of view." But in fact *Lieschen* is not predicated on an idea of Germany as a land fissured by class, but rather as one in which sentiment and family affinity suspend social difference.

The story opens with an account of the childhood trio, consisting of a sibling pair, Nelly and Army, and Lieschen as they play in the decaying Derenberg castle. Nelly and Army are children of the castle on the hill; Lieschen is the rich paper mill owner's daughter from the village below. Army is ready to depart for military school where, as befits his noble rank, he will become an officer. Later, upon obtaining his officer's epaulettes, he must confront the harshness of his family's impoverishment, and his grandmother urges him to court his cousin Blanche, who is expected to inherit the family fortune. His growing concern with rank and wealth, under his grandmother's noxious tutelage, leads to estrangement from Lieschen, who adores him and to whom he was once emotionally attached. As he departs for military school, however, Army notices that Lieschen is now charmingly grown up, and responding to his appreciative gaze, she blushes. Thereafter, for nearly two hundred pages, he is blind to his childhood friend whom he believes beneath him, even as he is dazzled by red-haired Blanche.

Although *Lieschen* concludes by suspending class prejudice and removing barriers to marriage between an aristocrat and a bourgeois woman, the text, from the start, configures these obstacles as largely arbitrary and imagined since the three children once happily played together on an equal footing that prefigured the marriage of Lieschen and Army. Class prejudice is harbored and fostered by the Derenbergs' grandmother and not in the end by the grandchildren. While the grandmother's age signals that such impediments belong to the past, her Italian nationality makes clear their cultural inappropriateness. As the narrator stresses, this Italian woman has no sympathy for the German sentimentality that bridges class divisions. The text figures this lack of sympathy in, among other things, her dislike of the German Christmas tree, the emblem of the most sacred emotional and intimate of German holidays, one that in nationalist literature of the time embodied German culture.[45] It turns out, moreover, that even in the backstory—a love story from two generations past—this same outsider was at fault: had it not been for the scheming of the bigoted Italian, a marriage between the mill and the castle would have been solemnized decades earlier. In the end, the novel expels the grandmother from the affective community reaffirmed by the marriage of childhood playmates. She becomes the traveling companion of the newly rich Blanche, thus commencing an unstable and suspect life of wandering through the watering holes of Europe.

When Army's cousin and fiancée, Blanche, inherits the money on which the Derenbergs' future seems to depend, she terminates their engagement. A desperate Army suddenly recalls Lieschen and his own childhood, "when the little girl had so often charmingly consoled the wild boy, when, in childish play, he lost patience, and in his defiant, boyish rage had shed hot tears" (226). On Christmas Eve the impoverished Army asks the wealthy Lieschen to marry him. Eventually forced to recognize that Army does not love her, the enamored Lieschen nevertheless consents to a companionate marriage. Army must pretend to love her for the sake of her family, yet he comes to love her on account of her "pure heart," her "lovely womanliness," and the possibility that she will restore his peace of mind (328).

The novel provides multiple explanations for Army's change of heart. While Lieschen's feminine virtues are critical, the story founds mutual attraction in the innocence of childhood and in family history with deep roots in the local. In their childhood, before the confusions of sexuality that attracted Army to Blanche and before social barriers imposed by the grandmother separated them, Army and Lieschen were fast friends. In the opening depiction of childish play Army is shown as not only attached to Lieschen and his sister, Nelly, but also to the portrait of Agnes Mechthilde, Freifrau von Derenberg, a long-dead ancestor whom his grandmother facetiously calls his "first love" (27). While Agnes's portrait figures Army's primal attachment to Lieschen, Army is slow to recognize it. Indeed, since his cousin Blanche has Agnes's hair, he sees her as the embodiment of his "first love," while failing to notice another more powerful family resemblance, namely, that Lieschen has Agnes's eyes (328).

Once he is able to see past Agnes's red hair, he recognizes the resemblance between her eyes and Lieschen's: "the red luxuriant hair disappeared in the dull light—only the two dark, sad eyes looked unchangeably out of the pale face at the young man, so steeped in misery, so timidly, as if they sought a lost happiness" (338). Once this recognition occurs, the remaining pages can be devoted to recovering the happiness and unity that Lieschen and Army knew as children as the basis of an adult marriage founded in mutual desire. The final chapter burgeons with the coyly erotic imagery of spring as the two are reunited in the moonlight of a May evening to the song of nightingales.

The rediscovery of Lieschen in the eyes of his ancestor also carries a political meaning implied more than explained in this novel of remarriage. In not merely imagining a marriage between a bourgeois woman and an aristocratic man in the present, but also suggesting through family resemblance a long-standing affiliation between the mill and the castle in this rural setting, *Lieschen* shares in the national liberal ethos of *Die Ahnen* (The Ancestors; 1872–80), the ambitious six-volume novel by the German best-selling author Gustav Freytag. Here Freytag seeks to demonstrate with a thousand years of history that the modern-day, middle-class Königs—the telos of German national history—are descended from real kings (Germanic chieftains) via centuries of intermarriage among petty nobility, free peasants, and townspeople.[46] In Freytag's telling, in the German regions class barriers were repeatedly breached to produce a middle class synonymous with the nation.

Less clearly supporting bourgeois ascendency per se than *Die Ahnen*, *Lieschen* concludes with the prospect of restoring the aristocratic Derenbergs to something of their former splendor. Army learns how to manage his estate, but, more importantly, the Derenbergs are to be reinvigorated with bourgeois money and bourgeois cheerfulness and good health, and—of course—a woman's love. Heimburg's novel thus offered the American reader a "very pretty" and "pleasant story" in an alien landscape dominated by an old castle with solid roots in middle-class family values.

The Reconciliation of Art and Life:
Broken Chains and *Misjudged*

If Lieschen receives acknowledgment from Army as a result of her self-sacrifice and his recovered knowledge of the love that he felt for her as a boy, the heroine of Werner's *Gesprengte Fesseln* must gain her spouse's recognition more actively by transforming herself. Werner's *Gesprengte Fesseln* was serialized in *Die Gartenlaube* in 1874, nos. 23–40, and appeared a year later in the United States as *Broken Chains* in Frances A. Shaw's translation for Osgood.[47] A second translation by Bertha Ness, *Riven Bonds*, was published in England in 1877.

Reinhold Almbach, the nephew of a stern merchant, has been coerced by his uncle into marrying his cousin Ella in the expectation that he will become a partner in the Almbach firm in the northern port city of H (Hamburg). Although Ella and Reinhold have a child, Reinhold does not even know the color of Ella's eyes. As the narrator remarks, Ella is so meek and nondescript that people frequently overlook her presence altogether. She wears unbecoming clothes and scarcely opens her mouth or raises her eyes. Everyone accepts the family line that Ella is limited. Only the narrator's mention of her blue eyes and her luxurious blonde braids, which are covered by a cap—hair functioning here as in *The Second Wife* as a signifier of energy and sexuality—offers hope that there is an interesting woman behind her insipid exterior. The fact of the child—itself a signifier of sexuality despite the sentimental discourses surrounding children—makes a distinctly unpleasant impression: one must imagine sexual intercourse without desire (or in our day, marital rape), given Ella's listlessness. Nevertheless, the child conceived without love will help restore the marriage.[48]

A musical genius, Reinhold appears to be modeled on an idealized Richard Wagner. As the composer of operas, he chafes at the confines of his marriage and the merchant world. The Italian diva Beatrice and the Bohemian life she promises him prove irresistible, and Reinhold abandons his wife and his work as a merchant to follow Beatrice to Italy, where he becomes a famous composer. Before leaving he fulminates against marriage as an institution and against Ella as its embodiment. Ella, he believes, "cannot rise above the kitchen and the domestic sphere."[49] He disingenuously chastises her for not granting him a year of freedom to pursue his art. It should have been enough for her, he rants, to devote herself during his absence to their child and the "insipid prose of domestic life" (41). Ella will not agree to this preposterous proposal of separation, yet even when he leaves for Italy with Beatrice, Reinhold does not officially divorce his wife, since he hopes to retain access to his child.

Years later Reinhold, now famous and called Rinaldo, is living in Italy; Beatrice, his mistress, still fascinates him but also makes him miserable. Celebrity exhausts him, and in composing the Italianate music that has brought him fame, he has lost his national mooring. At some level he misses his homeland. Reinhold has tried to make contact with his son, but Ella has rebuffed his every attempt. When an unidentified German beauty turns up in Italy, readers can easily guess that this woman is Ella. Stylishly dressed, charming, and educated as the result of a transformation she has wrought for the sake of her son, she is now able not only to understand Reinhold's music but also to recognize the burden her ignorance once placed on her gifted husband.

The ever-nationalistic Werner sets up a confrontational scene between German Ella dressed in white lace and Italian Beatrice dressed in black velvet, from which Ella, as the champion of home, marriage, family, and Germany, emerges morally triumphant. When Beatrice kidnaps Ella and Reinhold's child, husband and wife join forces to stop her. Beatrice commits suicide, trying in vain to murder the child as well. In love and reconciled, Ella and Reinhold return to northern Germany.

His wild oats sown in Italy and home again in the German north, Reinhold acquires, with Ella's help, "calm, reliant self-possession that was an advantage to the man as well as to the artist" (131) and learns the important lesson of self-conquest. His music, which was previously limited by the fetters of foreign influence, attains a new "freedom and clearness of artistic composition" (129). In a pattern shared by many of Werner's novels, proper femininity enables the achievement of proper masculinity. In the end Reinhold gladly submits to the bonds of endogamous marriage and parenthood, realizing that his happiness consists therein. Thus Werner asserts that a man's artistic genius can be fully realized within marriage and family once both partners have fully matured.

Fifteen years after Werner's *Broken Chains* first appeared, Heimburg also constructed a plot around a marriage troubled by the mismatch of art and life in *Eine unbedeutende Frau* (1891). Serialized in *Die Gartenlaube* (nos. 1–21), this novel hit the American market in 1891 in three North American translations: Smith's *An Insignificant Woman: A Story of Artist Life* with Bonner; Mary E. Almy's *Misjudged* with Rand, McNally; and Mrs. J. W. Davis's *Misjudged* with Worthington. Minnie Klamm's copy of Davis's translation, dated December 25, 1911, testifies to at least twenty subsequent years of American reading.[50]

Reviews of the novel were mixed. A slightly condescending *Literary World* saw it as typical of the "German sentimental novel" so enjoyed in America: we "leave the hero and heroine in a perfect bower of German bliss."[51] *The Critic* claimed it gave a bad name to the "Teutonic races" that should be punished as a "national libel."[52] Yet *The Congregationalist*, barring all irony, pronounced the author, whom it thought to be a man, "a skillful and entertaining delineator of German Life."[53] The publisher Bonner, in turn, had a good sense of the audience for *An Insignificant Woman* and advertised it as a "vindication of woman": "every woman who lives for her children, her husband, and her home will find her heart mirrored in the pages of this fascinating story," declared an advertisement in the *New York Times*.[54] The Chicago publisher M. A. Donohue and Company must have thought the story good for summer reading and made it available as *Misjudged* in the Snug Corner Series. On the cover a young lady with long braids perches on a rocky shore, a parasol in one hand, a book in the other, and gazes at the sea (see Figure 5.2). At Christmas 1903, "Fanny" presented "Irma" a copy of this edition, presumably believing that it promised Irma a good read.[55]

In *Misjudged* the artist Leo Jussnitz is married to Antje, the beautiful and rich but shy and modest daughter of the owner of a foundry located in the Harz Mountains. Jussnitz has used Antje's fortune to live lavishly and to pursue his painting, but he has shown little gratitude or consideration for her, viewing her money as his to spend as he likes—and the besotted Antje has

Figure 5.2 W. Heimburg, *Misjudged* (Chicago: M. A. Donohue & Co., n.d.). Author's copy.

encouraged him to think just that. Leo has never recognized his good fortune in having a wife who loves him deeply, and the naïve Antje has in turn never grasped that Leo married her for her money. After a year of marriage he is bored with a wife whom he considers intellectually inferior. He flirts with other women and pays no attention to his namesake, his daughter, Leonie. Painfully aware of her husband's disregard, Antje wonders why he values her so little and how she can gain his attention and affection for herself and Leonie. Leo's chance meeting with the naïve and aspiring painter Hildegard nearly leads to adultery.

Unaware that Leo is married, the ambitious Hildegard agrees to sit for a painting in an atelier that he has rented in Dresden to escape his domestic life in the suburbs. Obliviously flirting with disaster, Leo justifies his physical and emotional estrangement from Antje with his art. To add to Antje's suffering, when Leo's circle brings the slippery relationship between Leo and Hildegard into the public eye, Leo insists that his wife take Hildegard under her wing to quell gossip. Ever the obedient wife, Antje assents. If readers cringe at Antje's readiness to suffer in her wifely role, they are rewarded for reading on, for in the end Antje triumphs.

Leo, who as it turns out is a mediocre painter, continues his solipsistic downward spiral. His disastrous speculation with what little remains of Antje's fortune and the reading of his mother-in-law's will, which denies him access to the remaining family assets, prove a tipping point. Antje now emerges from the shadows and takes charge of the family foundry, as no one could have predicted she would or could. Believing that Leo still loves Hildegard, she plans to divorce him. Her talent for managing a household proves transferable to running a business, and she quickly proves herself in her new role. Leo meanwhile despairs and for the second time tries to kill himself. He once again proves a bad shot (and the text thereby casts still more doubt on his shredded masculinity). Antje nurses him back to health, but the text does not deliver a sickbed reconciliation: a male character whose masculinity has been so undermined can hardly be a worthy partner for the virtuous Antje.

Instead, Heimburg engineers a rehabilitation of her hapless hero that exceeds expectation. Recognizing his mediocrity as a painter, Leo returns to his true métier and medium. As readers now learn, Leo had early excelled as a sculptor, and his medium was bronze. His abandonment of his true artistic calling lies at the root of his moral and artistic failings. The restoration of his masculinity through three-dimensional work with metal cannot be missed; painting seems a soft and feminine calling by comparison. But while the text labors on behalf of Leo's masculinity, this masculinity is circumscribed by Antje's domesticity. Antje's old Dutch nursemaid sums up the trajectory of the narrative when she enumerates the undesirable characteristics that Leonie shares with her father, declaring that the child must be tamed: "we won't give in to her; she has to mind" (317).

Readers, who by now must be entirely of the opinion that the irresponsible Leo must learn to mind, discover that he is ready to be managed by his wife when a heavy package arrives. The bronze sculpture therein conveys an unmistakable message:

> Wonderful alike in composition and modeling was this ideal figure of a man bending forward: he was standing on the summit of a great rock which he seemed to have just reached; his foot was already hanging over the precipice, and the next moment he would plunge over into the abyss, which his eyes, looking upward, did not perceive. There was a chain about his waist, and the other end of the chain was wound round a beautiful woman's figure; she in chaste garments of antique fashion was leaning against the rock, her hand holding a spindle, the symbol of womanliness and domesticity, the slender foot firmly placed against a stone on the ground, but her eyes were fixed on the man. There was a wonderful expression of love and anxiety in the features of this young woman.
>
> Below on the pedestal were engraved these words: "Well for the husband bound by such a chain! From Misery and death it draws him home again." (352–53)

The artistic object crystallizes a reconciliation based in recognition and appreciation of Antje's old-fashioned domesticity and devotion. An attentive reader might notice, however, that gratifying though the sculpture may be, the spindle in the woman's hand evokes the dutiful housewife Antje once was rather than the businesswoman she has become.

Upon receipt of the sculpture, Antje, who now wants Leo to come home, summons her business connections and industrial resources in order to create, alongside the family iron foundry, a bronze foundry that will support Leo's sculpting.[56] If Adolph Menzel's famous painting *Iron Rolling Mill* (1872–75) had celebrated the new industrial age in Germany, this novel seeks to aestheticize industry, revamping the iron works with the bronze foundry for art's sake. In the final chapter Antje is running the business to everyone's satisfaction and Leo is finally inhabiting a real "work-room" (358), unlike the sexually charged Dresden atelier. Strangers from far and wide journey to the obscure location in the Harz to visit the bronze foundry with its celebrated artistic products. In this pastoral setting where art is linked to the industry, commerce, and consumerism of modern times while the family is safe from the dangers of those times, a now content and fully domesticated Leo concludes the novel, entirely to Antje's liking, by thanking God for the "chains" of marriage (302).

The closing reconciliation of art on the one hand and life, family, and industry on the other, within heterosexual remarriage in *Broken Chains* and *Misjudged*, bears little resemblance to the problematic as German Nobel Prize winner Thomas Mann articulated it in the following decade in *Buddenbrooks* (1901), "Tristan" (1902), and "Tonio Kröger" (1903). Mann by contrast posited the opposition of bourgeois life and its attendant concerns of marriage, family, business, and industry to the homoerotically coded practice and connoisseurship of art as nearly irreconcilable, bridgeable only with irony. Mann's Germany was, however, one that American readers had yet to experience, indeed, one that nineteenth-century American Heimburg readers probably never knew. *Buddenbrooks* was first published in English in the United States in 1924, "Tristan" in book form in 1924, and "Tonio Kröger" in volume 19 of Kuno Francke's unwieldy *The German Classics of the Nineteenth and Twentieth Centuries* (1913–14) and thereafter not until 1929 in the more accessible, affordable, and long-enduring Knopf anthology, that is, two reading generations after *Eine unbedeutende Frau* put in its first appearance in America.[57]

The Recovery of Desire and Trust:
Gertrude's Marriage and *Margarethe*

Both Heimburg's *Gertrude's Marriage* (1885, trans. 1889) and E. Juncker's *Margarethe; or Life-Problems* (1878) examine marriages freely entered into by unequal partners who love one another and thus constitute variations on the novel of remarriage. These variations come closer to the customary understanding of misalliance, but they differ from many popular novels of the age in examining the situation of the couples after they marry. In both works, only after husband and wife have committed to one another across social and economic barriers do they discover "life problems." Over the course of each novel, the spouses recover their mutual desire and thus a basis for conjugal bliss, a bliss that cannot be merely companionate.

In *Gertrude's Marriage* Frank Linden, whose family name bespeaks the beloved sweet-smelling tree that figures so sentimentally in German culture, must prove himself to his wealthy wife, who suspects after the fact that he has married her for her money. Although the couple seems destined to be together by their chance meeting at a baptismal font, Gertrude remains blind to his true nature until he plays the hero when his property catches fire. On the final page, Frank can aver in the language of resurrection that although his crops were destroyed by the fire, "in place of that a new life has risen out of the ashes." The book concludes with a toast to the "peace and prosperity of [their] household."[58]

Given two American translations and the existence of reprint editions, *Gertrude's Marriage* must have found an American audience. The *Literary World* pronounced the novel tedious, but it also identified elements that must have appealed to some readers when it noted that the "story itself is sentimental and has a strong flavor of the 'fatherland.'"[59] The *Catholic World* also saw *Gertrude's Marriage* as incorporating a quintessentially German quality: it was written "in the homely manner which our German brethren chiefly favor."[60]

The novel does contain details that mark its German setting—from the description of the North German town with its Renaissance-style town hall and its Roland statue on the town square (a place not unlike Bremen) to furnishings, reading habits, and the meals consumed in Gertrude's parental household, but its American appeal inhered in its perceived universality and adherence to generic convention. Worthington advertised the novel in the *Christian Union,* the *Independent,* and the *Art Amateur* as one in a boxed set of novels by Heimburg. The set made a "handsome Christmas present," the advertisement claimed. Heimburg's novels "are spirited, representing real people, their loves and sorrows, pure in tone, thoroughly elevating, told with grace and cleverness."[61]

In July 1878 an advertisement in the *Christian Union* announced *Margarethe; or Life-Problems* by E. Juncker as a "most charming story." The review included a quotation from the *New York Tribune* praising Wister, its translator, as showing "admirable taste and unusual knowledge of current German literature in the novels which she selects for translation."[62] The German original, *Lebensrätsel* (Life's Mysteries), had been serialized in the *Deutsche Roman-Zeitung* earlier in that same year. In *Margarethe* Wister found yet another popular German novel treating a hastily contracted marriage that soon becomes troubled.

Margarethe bears markers of the literary culture of its origin. It prominently signals a debt to the German classical tradition on its title page with a quotation from Goethe. Wister's renaming of *Lebensrätsel* as *Margarethe* after the novel's female protagonist underscored the character's vague affinities to Gretchen in part I of Goethe's *Faust*. The novel also resembles *The Second Wife* and other novels by Marlitt, as well as Hillern's *Only a Girl,* in its inclusion of conversations about the right kind of religion for modern times, materialism, and Darwinism. At the same time, Juncker's treatment of marriage, education, religion and hypocrisy, and political reform in this rural community also recalls George Eliot's *Middlemarch*, which had appeared four years earlier, a novel that in turn exhibits some influence of the German *Only a Girl*.[63]

The *New York Times* ridiculed the ambition and grave tone of Juncker's novel, suggesting that "we should strip to wrestle with it," and then summarized the plot so as to make it sound silly. As a romance, the reviewer maintained, *Margarethe* is "crude, lumpish and impossible."[64] The *Atlantic Monthly* likewise scoffed—with an allusion to Goethe's *Elective Affinities*—at "the tread of the German elephant" that "is in all the pages of Margarethe, where the high-souled *dramatis personae* talk skeptical philosophy, and experiment, timidly, in elective affinities."[65] Yet the *Saturday Evening Post* pronounced the story "very ingenious in plot and passionate and dramatic in situation," and the *Literary World* maintained that Wister had again made an admirable selection and described the plot as one "to gratify the reader."[66] Novel readers apparently were not put off by the "tread of the German elephant." Lippincott reprinted the book at least four times up to and including 1900, Wister renewed the copyright in 1906, and *Margarethe* appeared one final time in 1911, thirty-two years after its initial appearance in America.[67]

Margarethe tells a story of near adultery and remarriage. The much older aristocrat, Günther, Count of Randau, has unaccountably married the young and naïve Margarethe Treutler, a wealthy merchant's daughter. Despite the social misalliance, the family accepts the marriage, for they are modern and democratic in spirit. The count's sister nevertheless worries about the prospects of this marriage since, as she observes, husband and wife are mismatched in character and experience. Meanwhile, Günther's quoting of Catullus makes clear that this is a passionate marriage, and Margarethe herself avers that she does not understand marriage based in mere friendship. The marriage prospers for a time, but Günther becomes bored with his naïve young wife and begins spending time with the more mature and worldly widow Edith. Günther nearly succumbs to her blandishments and considers following her to Italy. For her part, the pious and childish Margarethe is disturbed by the intellectual and skeptical atmosphere of the Randaus' circle and feels a certain estrangement from her husband.

In a bizarre scene Margarethe, who is pregnant, is singing Mignon's song from Goethe's *Wilhelm Meister*. As she does so, she looks into a mirror, watches as Edith lays her head on Günther's shoulder, and realizes that her husband's affections have been alienated. As a result of the collapse of her naïve worldview, Margarethe miscarries at the very moment her child quickens. She is saved from death only by a transfusion with her husband's blood. The transfusion does not, however, bring about reconciliation, even if it signifies intimacy. Many pages remain to be turned before the couple can be reunited.

As in other German novels of remarriage, reconciliation ensues only after the husband becomes better suited to domesticity. Günther must acquire self-discipline and shoulder his responsibilities. Aside from repenting his faithlessness, he serves in the German Reichstag, where he becomes known for his eloquent speeches in support of the liberal cause, and he begins to husband his estate as he had not previously. His ascent to responsible manhood is further affirmed when he rescues a shepherd in a flood in full view of his wife. Margarethe now allows herself to act on her enduring attraction to him, and the couple is at long last reconciled.

While Günther was learning how to be a man, the bourgeois Margarethe was becoming more sophisticated and discerning. Although she initially excoriates those from her husband's social rank as "without religion, without fidelity, without truth," she eventually repudiates the narrow, pietistic religious views that have heretofore guided her and thus recognizes the limitations of her upbringing.[68] At the same time, she takes charge of herself as she had not when, first married, she was still her husband's "little one." Having literally grown taller, she appears at the conclusion of the novel better able to fulfill the social role of a countess and capable of acknowledging her transformed husband.

Having supplied a happy ending for the estranged couple, the novel ends on a melancholy note with the burial at sea of the son of the idealist reformer Pastor Dossow. It closes with Dossow's contemplation of the eternal, thus attempting to place the "life riddle" of conjugal love in a broader context of an idea of transcendence freed of biblical literalism and appropriate to the nineteenth century.

Growing Pains:
The Eichhofs

All of these German novels of remarriage pay close attention to masculinity as both menacing and necessary to female happiness. *The Eichhofs* (1881), however, puts men squarely in the center of an inquiry into domestic felicity and remarriage. Whereas the prolific Valeska von Bethusy-Huc, writing under the male pseudonym Moritz von Reichenbach, was widely read in imperial Germany, only *The Eichhofs* reached the English-speaking public in the United States. In 1881 Wister translated the novel, and Lippincott kept it in print into the new century, for sale individually and as one of a set of Wister's translations from the German.[69]

Wister's imprimatur coupled with Lippincott's marketing appears to have been critical to the reception of *The Eichhofs* in America.[70] Even upon its first appearance, a reviewer suggested that, although no one had previously heard of Reichenbach, the "novel-reading public seem to have implicit faith in Mrs. Wister's ability to cater to their tastes."[71] The *Literary World* similarly asserted confidence in Wister's taste and skill: "Mrs Wister always puts enough of herself into her adaptations to make them charming, whoever may be the original author," the reviewer wrote, implying that Wister's intervention was necessary to make the book palatable.[72] Nevertheless, *The Independent*, which identified the flaws of *The Eichhofs* as typical of German novels, also admitted that it was "neither better nor worse than the rest" and in fact "executed with much literary skill and finish." One of the faults of the "average German novel," this review asserted, consisted in the fact that such stories "prepare for tragedy and wind up in a comedy," that is, they end up with precisely the happy ending that played a critical role in their appeal to nineteenth-century American readers.[73] A more appreciative review of Bethusy-Huc's novel liked the book's conclusion and quoted liberally from the couple's reconciliation, characterizing the work as a "modest and moderate novel . . . in which a true and worthy husband and wife run against each other in the dark, as it were, and are led out into the light and reconciliation."[74] Certainly, *The Eichhofs* flirts with tragedy yet ends in conjugal harmony. And like the other popular German novels of remarriage, it projects models of masculinity and femininity whose achievement is hard fought but necessary to a happy marriage.[75]

Bethusy-Huc situates her remarriage plot within an exploration of multiple models of masculinity in imperial Germany. Set in the German countryside on the estates of the landed gentry, *The Eichhofs* traces in a quasi-realistic vein, within a vaguely fairy-tale structure, the fates of three aristocratic brothers whose existence is endangered for a multiplicity of reasons, one of them being the economic pressures of modern times. Bernhard, the eldest and best fixed of the three, marries Thea, a beloved young neighbor from his own social class. The couple then struggles to find a firm basis for their marriage amid social and economic trials and family conflict. A seductive and light-minded Polish aristocrat from Bernhard's past poses an additional threat, as does Bernhard's own ne'er-do-well brother, Lothar, who has fallen in love with his sister-in-law. The readiness of Bernhard and Thea to believe the worst of each other leads to estrangement, and the couple is only reconciled at the deathbed of their child, at which point acknowledgment and forgiveness occur. The narrator provides a florid apotheosis of marital love, rebirth, and reconciliation as the couple stands hand in hand before their son's coffin in a country chapel. As they quit the chapel, "forest and field [lie] before them bathed in the gold of sunset," and the couple leaves the graveyard "towards a new life in the old home."[76]

Meanwhile, plot strands involving the two younger brothers offer a complement of imagined masculinities in modern times. The second aristocratic brother, the hapless Lothar, has followed the traditional profession of the second son and is a military officer. Unlike Heimburg's *Lore von Tollen* and others, *The Eichhofs* does not feature defenseless sisters who suffer from their brothers' egotism, yet Lothar's gambling debts and his passion for his sister-in-law do wreak havoc. Lothar thus offers a variation of the bad-brother plot. His weak character makes him vulnerable to the worst faults of the military officer. In portraying the economic hardships of aristocratic men, the text also reproduces the casual (and sometimes rampant) anti-Semitism of the period. Lothar thinks of turning to Jewish moneylenders, but when a comrade marries a Jewish heiress to save himself from financial ruin, Lothar avers that he would rather blow his brains out than marry a Jew. While his friend Werner points out that he could put an end to his financial woes by simply learning to live within his income, Lothar is not man enough to discipline himself. Suicide becomes the solution for this imperfect "man of honor."

The third son, Walter, is studying law at the university, a traditional course for third sons. He actually wants to practice medicine, but his aristocratic family views medicine as déclassé. Walter, however, finds a source of encouragement in his friend Dr. Nordstedt, who overcame his humble origins to become a physician and, later, a university professor. Walter's plot follows his successful struggle to pursue his medical calling against his father's wishes. As a physician, Walter, who as an impecunious youngest son was not initially good marriage material, is transformed and rewarded with the hand of his childhood friend, the aristocratic Adela.

In narrating the lives of the three brothers, the novel rewards self-discipline, hard work, and righteousness. Along the way, it poses the question as to what makes us happy. The beautiful Julutta almost succeeds in seducing Bernhard when she muses, "Happiness can hardly ever stand the test of critical reason, but depends upon imagination, which is often folly. And what is happiness, after all? A moment, an intoxication, a dream,—and yet we all long for it" (284). Significantly, Julutta has been reading Eichendorff's *Taugenichts,* a whimsical romantic tale in which the passive hero's happiness is left to good luck alone. Bethusy-Huc, however, has no intention of rewarding passive men or those who are governed by overactive imaginations or the spell of the moment. Years later the righteous, steady, and self-sacrificing family friend Werner pronounces the moral of this fairy tale of German masculinity and remarriage: "What a wonder life is . . . But it all amounts to the fact that if you would be happy—and who would not?—you must do what is right" (322). The *Literary World* heartily approved of this conclusion, pronouncing it "a good lesson for a novel to teach, and *The Eichhofs* reaches it well."[77]

In the final chapter, the novel offers one last glimpse of the Eichhofs. If readers thought that Thea and Bernhard would simply remain frozen in their glorious sunset, Werner's brief stop at the train station on his way to conduct urgent business in Berlin recalls that even the German countryside is subject to the rapid changes of modern times and that it is connected to the historical events taking place on the rim of the bucolic horizon. Among other things, this German province—probably a reflection of Bethusy-Huc's own Silesia—is now directly connected by train to Warsaw. Werner, the good German officer and model of discipline and sacrifice, alludes to troubles with Russians and Turks and thus to the conflict that had reached a temporary resolution with the Treaty of Berlin in July 1878, shortly before Bethusy-Huc wrote her novel. The soldier-officer, who has nobly served his country by leading a "vagabond life" that has made him a stranger at home, reflects on the full life unfolding in the countryside, modeling for readers an affirmation of this world from a perspective outside it. Despite modernization, home—the true heart of Germany—can blissfully go about its business while great things happen in a far-off somewhere.

French Courage/German Romance and Fidelity:
From Hand to Hand

Von Hand zu Hand by Golo Raimund (Bertha Heyn Frederich) combines the remarriage plot with interest in ethnicity tied to the historic events of the Franco-Prussian War. Like *Margarethe*, it was first serialized in the *Deutsche Roman-Zeitung* and translated by Wister. *The Critic* announced its publication on March 11, 1882, just months after the German serialization ended, and it gained attention immediately as one "in the Wister series," remaining in print for at least twenty years.[78] In marketing *From Hand to Hand* as a Wister translation over these years, Lippincott quoted the judgment of the *Boston Saturday Evening Gazette* that the novel "may be ranked among the best of the many very admirable stories Mrs. Wister has translated."[79]

A reviewer for the *Literary World* summarized its appeal as genre fiction from Germany: "[It] has no small interest of the sort that relates to European aristocracy, steady-going love, wicked conspiracies and persecutions and a happy union of hearts and hands at the end."[80] The reviewer, who found the original story "a rather mixed and muddy work," nevertheless thought that the heroine's loveliness would win reader's sympathy and also acknowledged the appeal of a story in which virtue is rewarded.[81] Worried that the title *From Hand to Hand* might have an immoral ring to it, *The Critic* assured American readers that the vicissitudes of the heroine's life in no way "imply a lack either of strength or sweetness."[82] Thus both Wister's signature and the generic combination of romance and virtue rewarded guaranteed the novel a hearing in America.

The remarriage plot of *From Hand to Hand* centers on Erwin von Tromberg and Clemence von Herberg, whose marriage is contracted at the insistence of Clemence's father, when she is only sixteen. Marriage to Erwin is to protect her from her mother's French family, who, Herberg fears, will corrupt her should they get their hands on her. To give Clemence the time to grow up and be educated, the marriage is to be kept secret for two years and she is to be hidden from her relatives.

Little schooled in the ways of the world and reared in the absence of her French mother, the pure and simple Clemence repeatedly violates gender norms; she loves riding and shooting her revolver. While these skills later serve her well, they and her other unorthodox behaviors offend those who harbor strict ideas of gender. She herself is easily duped and too ready to listen to untruths about her husband's relationship to Nora, his former fiancée and sister-in-law. The arrival of a French cousin prompts her to flee to her husband's estate six months before the arranged date of their reunion. To her dismay, she discovers that the widowed Nora has taken up residence there, as she has every right to do as Erwin's sister-in-law.

Reunited with her husband, who regards their marriage as his second chance in life and who loves her deeply, she obtusely misconstrues his every effort to please her. Madly in love with Erwin yet misled both by her own French grandmother and the scheming Nora, she comes to believe that Erwin has betrayed her with Nora and therefore abandons him to flee to Paris. The middle section of the novel devotes many pages to the couple's misreading of one another, misreading fostered by the odd circumstances of the marriage, Clemence's youth, and the scheming of the French family aided by Nora.

The novel reaches closure two years after Clemence has left for France, where she has not only become more socially presentable but also surprisingly learned, unconsciously hoping through her efforts at self-improvement to please her estranged husband. Erwin, meanwhile, patiently tries to win her back, but he finally gives up and consents to a divorce at the very moment when France declares war on Germany. War prevents him from signing the divorce papers, and he is called to arms as the head of a regiment of Uhlans. As a uniformed Prussian soldier, the handsome Erwin embodies German masculine duty. When he is wounded on French soil, he and Clemence meet again.

An older and wiser Clemence has meanwhile recognized her folly in succumbing to the scheming of others that blinded her to Erwin's sterling character. When her wounded husband is brought to the country estate where she is staying, she determines to nurse him back to health, cost what it may. Disguised as a sister of mercy, she tends to him at night until she is turned out of the house as a traitor to France. Erwin, too, is to be shipped out, since French patriotism dictates that he become a prisoner of war. Clemence, disguised as a boy, secrets him out of the house and transports him by cover of night not to a French prison but to the German camp. Arriving there safely—after displaying masterful abilities as a driver and firing her pistol several times at Frenchmen—she commends him to the embrace of a Prussian general, who enters the narrative as a surrogate father.

Having allowed her heroine and her readers some gender-bending excitement, Raimund reinscribes Clemence in the feminine. While Erwin remains ignorant of the identity of the sister of mercy and the brave boy who saved his life, Clemence returns to the Tromberg estate, where she assumes her rightful place as Erwin's wife and begins cleaning house, as it were, securely attached to feminine spaces and attitudes. On the penultimate page, the couple in effect remarries when Clemence confesses her error and declares her wish "only to be yours,—yours forever,—try me once more, Erwin!"[83] For all the sensational aspects of the plot and the aristocratic, international setting, *From Hand to Hand* at bottom tells a simple story of mistrust in marriage encouraged by those who do not wish the couple well; the couple relearns trust, recognizes one another's virtues, and forgives one another in the signature turn of the novel of remarriage.

In the aftermath of near divorce and war, the rural Tromberg estate, however, is "still unchanged, but a different life has developed there" (372). While continuing to mature in her proper feminine role as Erwin's wife, Clemence remains a hybrid character, uniting "womanly grace with masculine force of character" (372). The French grandmother, commenting on Clemence's bravery under fire (and not her housewifely role), observes as well that her unusual character arises from "the mingling of nationalities. . . . The fidelity and the romance were German, but the courage was French" (372).

In conceding Frenchness some virtue in the final line of *From Hand to Hand,* Raimund deviates from much German popular literature of the era, for example, from Marlitt's work, which tends to locate villainy in French characters as in *Schillingscourt* and *Countess Gisela.* The fidelity and romance of Clemence's German side correspond, on the other hand, to the generic conventions in which this novel operates, that is, romance coupled with fidelity in remarriage, generic conventions that Americans learned to associate with enjoyable popular literature from Germany.

THESE GERMAN NOVELS of remarriage affirm marriage as both an economic unit and a deeply experienced and significantly formative affective bond. They depict the mistakes made by both husbands and wives and, in the particular case of wives, assert the possibility of acknowledgment, choice, and agency within marriage. Wives can choose to love their husbands or not, and husbands must become worthy of their wives by means of self-discipline (including the disciplining of their sexuality), work, management of resources and, most of all, through acknowledgment of their wives' virtues. In other words, the worthy husbands model a desirable masculinity that purports to respond to the demands of modern times and yet affirms the enduring values of marriage and life in the German villages, home towns, and country estates.

Four decades of publishing and reading in America indicate that this particular plot and this particular resolution attracted Americans to German novels. The question arises anew as to whether their perceived Germanness added to their appeal. Perceived Germanness certainly did provide the occasion for condescension on the part of some reviewers. In many of the brief notices that these books received, disdainful American reviewers relied on ill-founded stereotypes to characterize what they identified as German in them, often merely attributing what appeared to them as improbabilities or clumsy writing as deriving from some unarticulated quality held to be German. Yet the reviewers who did not care for the novels did not speak for the many readers who liked them or for the publishers who thought they could sell these books. Reviewers' ideas of Germanness, moreover, also did not necessarily correspond to what readers and publishers perceived as German about these novels.

Griswold includes all of these novels of remarriage in his *Descriptive List of Novels and Tales Dealing with Life in Germany,* as if there were something to be learned about Germany in them. Yet Germanness as a "dynamic set of circumstances" that determine the values, actions, and fates of the characters is, for the most part, visible in these novels of remarriage in translation only to the knowledgeable and discerning eye. For casual nineteenth-century American readers Germanness was probably more legible in paratextual formulations such as "after the German of," formulations that branded the novels, promising a reading experience rooted in domestic values shared by both cultures. Nevertheless, the translated novels did provide enough information for nineteenth-century American readers to perceive these settings as an "insistently acknowledged background" (if not fully realized) of the remarriages that took place in them.[84] In other words, even if these stories in the end did not obviously supply information about modern-day Germany as a complex social system, the stories clearly did not take place on American soil. American readers could thus experience the "life problems" of marriage at a stage of removal. Since the stories were foreign, readers did not necessarily expect them or their solutions to be precisely true of life as they knew it and thus did not need to demand verisimilitude of them for the sake of enjoyment and edification. Thrilling to the profound joy of acknowledgment, forgiveness, and renewal within marriage, the institution supported so ardently in the American social imaginary, they could happily inhabit alien yet familiar idealized marriages of free choice, reciprocal desire, and mutual recognition for the time it took to read a German novel.

CHAPTER 6

Feminized History

German Men in American Translation

POPULAR NOVELS by German women operated within a set of social assumptions and conventions recognized and shared by German readers of that fiction. This imaginary was, however, not always readily identifiable in translation as German per se, except insofar as American readers associated it with the patterns outlined above. "German" was most visible as genre and brand and thus not always as the product of deeply rooted and profoundly felt historical conditions. Nevertheless, as artifacts produced under a specific set of historical circumstances, the novels bore a relationship to their national origin and in the end transferred cultural information, social assumptions, and mores.

The regional settings of most of these novels, for example, reflect German particularism and the continued imagining after 1871 of culture as made in the regions rather than in a modern urban center, a regionalism that characterizes canonical work of German realism as well. Some of these novels even evoke the topography of specific German regions. Marlitt's *Little Moorland Princess,* for example, opens with a description of the Lüneburg heath; Werner sketches a German Alpine landscape in *The Alpine Fairy,* and Heimburg and Lewald the Baltic in *Her Only Brother* and *Hulda,* respectively.

Stock figures in the novels are likewise tied to particular historical circumstances. For example, the Jews who surface occasionally in these texts as helper figures—as literary agents or money lenders (demonized or not)—bear an at least tenuous relationship to perceived German realities and to ambivalence on the part of the majority culture toward the Jewish minority.

The unworthy soldier-brothers reflect both the militarism of Wilhelmine Germany and enduring middle-class allegiance to the idea of civilian volunteers, as opposed to career soldiers, in such times of national need as the Napoleonic wars and the Franco-Prussian War.

The business and industrial undertakings—successes and failures—that shape plots in such novels as Marlitt's *At the Councillor's* and Werner's *Alpine Fairy*, furthermore, reflect the boom and bust economy of imperial Germany, as the strikes in Werner's *Good Luck!* and *Clear the Track!* point to the emergent workers' movements and the strategies developed and employed to counteract them. Likewise, anti-Catholicism, anti-Pietism, and questions of religion and science that circulate in such novels as *The Second Wife, At the Altar, Only a Girl*, and *Margarethe* reflect the intellectual and religious controversies of the age. The Woman Question, as it is examined in *Only a Girl*, also preoccupied Germans. Moreover, far-off Brazil, as in Marlitt's *Countess Gisela* or Manteuffel's *Violetta*, or Africa, as in Werner's *Fata Morgana*, serve as destinations for exiled protagonists, scientific undertakings, and ambassadorial missions (as they do also in never-translated German realist works by men). These destinations are but one of many indications that popular German women writers wove a growing, if primitive, global awareness into stories of romance, love, and remarriage; as Todd Kontje has demonstrated, all of Marlitt's novels negotiate the discourses of empire and colonialism that characterized imperial Germany.[1]

American reviews, however, seldom mentioned these specific elements, even if they occasionally insisted that certain of these novels depicted German life as it really was, and even though Griswold included most of these books in his list of popular novels depicting "life in Germany." It is doubtful, moreover, that American consumers of "wholesome" and entertaining fiction read with a finely analytical historical awareness to begin with. Their critical awareness lay rather in their ability to judge the authors' skill in depicting affairs of the heart, that is, the personal, private, and yet universally legible. Some of these books, however, more insistently directed readers' attention to historical conditions and events even as they told personal stories. Heimburg's *Die Andere* (1886; The Other One [Woman]), translated in 1889 with a quotation from Tennyson as *Two Daughters of One Race*, presents a case in point.

Two Daughters of One Race offers yet another of Heimburg's excruciating accounts of family tensions in a regional setting, including a bad soldier-brother, who emigrates to America, and a selfish sister, Lotta, who captures the affections of Fritz, the narrator's true love, only to abandon him for Otto, the local prince. Readers who, confident of a happy ending, enjoyed Heimburg's harrowing depictions of family cruelty and the sufferings of good women had plenty to occupy their attention. Nevertheless, Heimburg deviated here from her pattern of narrating transhistorically.[2] Instead she relied on the Franco-Prussian War to extricate her characters from an impasse and to bring about and safeguard the private domestic bliss of the female protagonist.

In *Two Daughters* the Franco-Prussian War provides the first-person narrator with the opportunity to nurse her beloved Fritz back to health when he is wounded, and this intimacy at long last enables him to recognize her worth. The war also punishes the selfish Lotta. Since Lotta is not of sufficient rank to become a royal consort, Prince Otto divorces her upon ascending to the throne after his older brother dies in combat. His duty to his family and his home territory supersedes his private happiness. Later Lotta marries an Austrian, this new husband's nationality resonating significantly after 1871. The Austrians, who earlier in the century might have ruled a united Germany, are now excluded from imperial Germany. Lotta is thus multiply repudiated: by her first husband, by the German principality he rules, and by the German nation as constituted within the new empire. The narrator, by contrast, is securely established in the region and the Reich. In closing, she sentimentally speaks of her bliss, invoking the oak tree as the symbol of the new empire: "Then we turned to look at our children playing in the shadows of a mighty German oak. In our old-fashioned house dwell happiness and peace."[3]

In *Two Daughters* Heimburg links domestic contentment with national unity, depicting the ways in which the Franco-Prussian War was felt and the manner in which it altered the course of events even in a tiny town in an insignificant principality. Nevertheless, despite the author's mention of explicit dates and battles and the reliance of the plot on the war, only two of the seven American notices I have found mention the war and its role in the novel. But in fact the female protagonist and her husband, Fritz, ultimately encourage readers to ignore history when they themselves turn their backs on public, political life to devote themselves to their private happiness. When the little town of Rotenberg rejoices in the Frankfurt peace treaty with a banquet, Fritz, the wounded veteran, does not attend. Instead he and the narrator marry, and the newlyweds retreat to their own garden to sit under a linden tree and reflect on their personal history "and how wonderfully it had all come about" (326). Even as she instrumentalizes German history in her plot, Heimburg intimates that personal happiness exists outside history. Domestic bliss is, as in *Lieschen,* transhistorical—and as far as American readers were concerned, transnational.

WHILE THE MAJORITY of the novels in our dataset do not rely explicitly on German historical events to tell their stories, as we have seen, German history does, for example, figure centrally in *From Hand to Hand* and, to some degree, *In the Schillingscourt* and *The Old Mam'selle's Secret*. German history, however, comes to the fore most emphatically in a subset of Werner's works and in most of Luise Mühlbach's translated novels. While even here history remains more, in the words of Lilian Furst, an "insistently acknowledged background" and an "omnipresent context for the action" than a "dynamic set of circumstances," the specific sets of circumstances and conflicts that constituted German history do matter to plot and character, to the production of gender, and to the cultivation of domesticity within which individual choice and action signify.[4] The novels, moreover, affirm the German nation-state and celebrate the achievements that led to the founding of the empire as the telos of German history.

Werner's Germany:
The Achievement of Masculinity and the Course of German History

Werner's fiction emerged during the Franco-Prussian War, the founding of the Reich, and its immediate aftermath, and thus in a period of intense engagement with ideas of nation, family, and gender. *Hermann*, the title of her debut novella (1870; *Die Gartenlaube*, nos. 45–52), had patriotic connotations for Werner's German readership, since Hermann/Arminius, the Cheruskan chieftain who defeated the Roman army in 21 C.E., had regularly been celebrated in German nationalist discourse. As it turns out, the title's patriotic resonance gives a false impression of the content; the story has little to do with military conflict or current events. It does, however, conclude with the eponymous hero's achievement of manhood when he marries and enters into service to the state. In subsequent novels Werner repeatedly depicted such attainment of manhood as it affects family, property, community, and industry, and she often connected it to specific national events. Her signature favoring of male protagonists enabled a more direct engagement with the national imaginary as it was produced outside the immediate sphere of the home, though home remained of central importance.

Werner's labor on behalf of an explicitly German masculinity becomes especially visible in a subset of five novels that evoke world-historical events. Four of these turn on nineteenth-century conflicts with neighboring countries: *Held der Feder* and *Flammenzeichen* set in the Franco-Prussian War, *Heimatklang*, which takes place during the Danish-German War of 1864, and *Vineta* set in the Polish uprising of 1863. A fifth novel, *Um hohen Preis*, concerns German internal affairs. Each novel views historical events through the lens of family romance in which the protagonist's love of a woman figures significantly.

The Order of Gender and the Franco-Prussian War:
A Hero of the Pen

When *Ein Held der Feder* was serialized in 1871 (*Die Gartenlaube*, nos. 14–28), newly unified Germany was celebrating victory over France. The novel exhibits strong allegiance to those times, investing heavily in the production of gender tied to ethnicity and national unity: it recounts both how femininity and ethnicity are restored to a woman of German birth who grew up in the United States and how a German bookworm achieves masculinity in war.

Ein Held der Feder first became available in English to American readers in book form in 1875 from William F. Gill and Company as *A Hero of the Pen* in a translation by Frances A. Shaw. Three additional translations followed.[5] One of these translations, *The Quill-Driver*, was reprinted at least as late as 1900 with E. A. Weeks. In 1897 the *Chicago Tribune* carried an advertisement for Weeks's "Dartmouth Edition of select classics and modern literature," which promoted the novel side by side with works by Austen, Dickens, Eliot, Hardy, Scott, Stevenson, and Thackeray, as well as novels by Heimburg and Marlitt.[6]

Touted in advertising from 1875 as "the most brilliant novel of the season," *Hero of the Pen* recounts how headstrong Jane Forest journeys from the Mississippi to the Rhine only to find herself in a region at war with France.[7] Raised by her German parents in America and devoid of sentiment for Germany, Jane promises her dying father to return to the land of her birth in search of her lost brother. Although she plans to make an expedient marriage with the American Henry Alison, she loses her heart to the German Walter Fernow. The title of the novel alludes derisively to this professor who, Jane believes, is all talk and no action. Over the course of the novel the Americanized Jane recovers her ethnic roots as well as her femininity, and Fernow transforms from a professor into a heroic officer in the "band of brothers" that defeated the French.

Shaw recognized that Werner aspired to link her fiction to real places and historical events and that her American readers needed to be oriented to the German setting and required more specificity to believe in the American one. Whereas Werner's original opens with the line "Ein klarer Januartag lag über einer jener Städte des Mississippi" (A clear January sky lay over one of those cities of the Mississippi), Shaw wrote, "The scene of our story is a town on the Mississippi about midway in the course from Lake Itasca to the Gulf; the time is a cloudless January day of the year 1871."[8] Shaw, however, mistook the date by one year, for the Franco-Prussian War has not yet begun when the novel opens. Yet Shaw tried, with the addition of the date, to signal to American readers that the story begins in the penumbra of that war.[9]

Professor Fernow has little to recommend him. A caricature of the withdrawn, awkward, and sexless academic akin to the odd male figures in such Carl Spitzweg paintings as *The Bookworm* (1850), *The Hypochondriac* (ca. 1865), and *Newspaper Reader* (ca. 1860), "the consumptive professor," as he is termed, has little practical knowledge; nothing that is "not bound in calf" exists for him, and certainly not women (49). When Alison fears a rival in Fernow, the jaundiced Atkins, Jane's American business associate and nominal guardian, assures him that Fernow is a "precious example of a German scholar, who with his investigations, and thousand-year-old rubbish and hieroglyphics, devotes himself to the good of humanity and meantime withers up into a mummy" (48). This mention of arcane studies suggests the German romantic, a type that is rampant in the sluggish "land of poets and thinkers" and hardly to be admired by practical and energetic Americans—and certainly not by Jane.

The narrative, however, moves quickly to attach the Americanized German-born woman to the German professor. Significantly, they meet by chance along the Rhine. Thus in this novel Werner's signature encounter of hero and heroine in nature is doubly coded, both erotically and patriotically. Jane hears the "mist-voices" (25) of the Rhine, and Walter stoops to retrieve a twig with the first spring buds that Jane has carelessly crushed. Jane does not yet have the heart for German sentiment and nearly becomes angry when Fernow reproaches her for having trampled on German nature.

A sacred geographical space in nineteenth-century German nationalist discourse, the Rhine eventually works its magic on Jane. She recalls her early childhood and the songs and legends her mother taught her. The text makes explicit that her awakening feelings for the Rhine are attached to the man who stood near her when she first heard the whispers of the river. Despite her outward disdain for Fernow, at the Rhine Jane has always been able to see a vigorous man beneath the exterior of the sickly professor. As in the case of Arthur Berkow in *Good Luck!* the wrong sort of education has not only ruined Fernow's health but also driven poetry from him, even if his reaction to the trampled twig suggests otherwise. The task of the narrative is thus to restore him to health and manhood. In the pair's second encounter by the Rhine, that purpose seems nearly accomplished: in a passionate comparison of the Mississippi to the Rhine, Fernow stands "erect and tall, his face almost transfigured by an inner light. . . . The chrysalis had suddenly fallen from the pale suffering form, which . . . soared to its true place" (42). Thereafter, the Rhine returns repeatedly as a dreamscape in which Jane hears in the German version of her name on Fernow's lips the "melody of . . . her childhood" (103).

Poetry, however, does not suffice for the practical Jane, who insults Fernow with the epithet "hero of the pen" (44); nor is it enough for Germany. The transformation of the shrinking eccentric can only be completed once Professor Fernow responds to the call to arms against France and becomes Lieutenant Fernow. As part of that transition, he first rises to his poetic calling with a stirring exhortation to the German people that echoes Frederick William III's patriotic call to his people to rise up against Napoleon, and then he heeds that call himself despite his poor health. Combat reinvigorates him: "the forehead and cheeks were deeply sunburned, the blood coursed vigorously through the veins, the blonde hair . . . waved in luxuriant profusion under the helmet," and what is more, "the once smooth chin wore a heavy beard" (85). With the mention of the heavy beard, the text, in the euphemistic language of the nineteenth century, figures his transformation into a fully sexual and social male. It falls to Atkins to characterize the new German type embodied by Fernow that has emerged in wartime: "Once tear them from their commonplace ruts in which they have been wont to tread, and they go on in unaccountable ways. It is so with solitary individuals, it is so with the whole nation. They hurl the pen into a corner, and draw the sword from its scabbard, as if this had been their sole business their whole life long." Atkins predicts German dominance: "for the next hundred years we shall not forget in what hand the pen lay!" (99).

Werner describes the response to the call for total war as a mobilization of a united German manhood and womanhood on the battlefront and the home front, respectively. With the exception of gender roles, all divides—class barriers, the fissure between north and south—are bridged in the national cause. As Germany and Fernow enter full manhood, heterosexual love grounded in explicit roles for both genders is critical to the process and the new order.

The second "specimen" of German man whom Jane meets is, unbeknownst to her, her lost brother, Frederic, whom she has come to Germany to find. A giant of a man, this German male is loyal, boorish, dull witted, and effeminate in his role as Fernow's factotum. The text eventually sacrifices him in service of country and the marriage plot. Rather like the oafish and brawny Ulrich Hartmann in *Good Luck!* the dim Frederic, who has "grown up in wretched servitude" (133), represents a male type that is superfluous to the new German family. Frederic sacrifices himself for his sister at the very moment she discovers his true identity, and his death helps restore her to femininity. For years dry-eyed, she can finally weep "as a woman weeps in hopeless anguish and despair" (136). But in fact, once he is sacrificed, the new familiar and, by extension, national order, which will be supported by complementary gender roles, American money, German poetry, and German might, no longer needs him.

The strong interest of the text in masculinity does not prevent Werner from attending to her heroine; she has, moreover, not forgotten the vicarious pleasure of the female reader who might identify with Jane. The Americanized Jane, as a complement to the male hero, undergoes a transformation as a result of her encounter with the land of her birth and a newly "manned" German male. Initially she offends her German relatives with her haughtiness. Accustomed to freedom and wealth in America, she finds Germans "slavish," and "the exclusiveness of certain circles ridiculous" (30). She especially detests Fernow as the embodiment of much she dislikes about the Germans. Yet as romance readers know, a heroine's hatred for a handsome man promises narrative titillation and a romantic union. The search for her brother and thus the restoration of family, moreover, permits Jane a series of adventures, including playing the role of detective. Her quest takes her not only across the Atlantic but also behind enemy lines.

At the same time Jane faces quandaries that inscribe her in traditional roles and that address women readers' finely tuned knowledge of decorum. In response to Fernow's declaration of love, she cannot bring herself to speak of the possibility of incest but falls back instead on propriety: she is irrevocably engaged to another. When she subsequently learns that Fernow is not her brother, she continues to insist that she is bound to Alison. While her loyalty to her vow could signal her moral authority, her fealty in point of fact consists in mere adherence to social convention that supports male prerogative. As it turns out, Alison exploits that prerogative to force her against her will.

Six months after the end of the war, in a chapter that Shaw, maintaining the connection between international politics and romance, titled "The Balance of Power," Jane remains trapped by her pledge. Rather than break her word, she asks only how Alison can demand that she marry him when he knows that she loves Fernow. The balance of power does not tip in her favor until she conforms to her womanly role with gestures previously not in her repertoire, that is, when she submissively falls to her knees and begs.

Werner's story concludes with springtime on the Rhine. Jane has become Johanna, having relinquished her American ties for life in a newly united Germany. She will use her American dollars, as Atkins dolefully predicts, to support the career of her future husband, who will probably become Germany's next celebrated national poet. Readers have the satisfaction of knowing that in the German Fernow, Jane has found a partner who fully recognizes her charm and has never cared about her money. With this union of differentially gendered partners, Werner shows how gender and nationality are to be construed and enforced in the new empire. Difference as romance can of course be titillating, and the swelling springtime on the Rhine promises sexual fulfillment even as the text supports separate spheres. If Louisa May Alcott's sentimental preunification German professor, Mr. Bhaer, was too grandfatherly for some American readers who hoped for more romance for Jo March, Werner's postunification Fernow gave them a German professor-soldier-poet who could satisfy romantic dreams of war and peace.

The relatively long afterlife of Werner's *Hero of the Pen* in America may perhaps be attributed in part to its romantic enforcement of gender and nationality, insofar as it echoed America's own in that time period. In postbellum America, in June 1871, at the very moment in which *Hero of the Pen* was running in *Die Gartenlaube*, Reverend William A. Harris, president of a Methodist college for women in Virginia, preached once again to his female pupils the doctrine of separate spheres: woman "is most admirably adapted to the sphere of private life, and, above all, to the home circle," the reverend asserted. "This, it is true, is a narrow sphere; but it is, nevertheless, a high and holy one. . . . Of all the institutions of society, that which is the most important to its order and happiness is the constitution of the family, and its government."[10]

Learning to Love the Father(land):
The Sign of Flame

Twenty years later, at a watershed moment for the German empire, Werner's *Flammenzeichen* opened the 1890 volume of *Die Gartenlaube* and ran in fourteen installments for just over half a year in the then-biweekly magazine. Even as Werner wrote nostalgically of masculinity proved in the Franco-Prussian War, the erratic William II succeeded in forcing the resignation of the longtime chancellor Otto von Bismarck, who, as the historian Peter Gay formulates it, had "practically invented the German Reich" and had become a legend in his own time.[11] While a German empire without Bismarck was, on the one hand, nearly inconceivable, in his absence significant changes in foreign and domestic policy transpired immediately. In the year 1890 the empire was therefore on its way to becoming unrecognizable to the generations that had come to maturity in the first two decades of the Reich.

Although Gay barely mentions *Flammenzeichen*, his trenchant analysis of the tenor of *Die Gartenlaube* in 1890 helps situate Werner's novel historically and suggests why it resonated in America. In 1890, Gay observes, *Die Gartenlaube* gave little indication of an empire in crisis, never directly confronting the circumstances of Bismarck's departure from office or any other politically significant issue. Gay sees the absence of politics not as a confirmation that the magazine intentionally served as a prop to an increasingly aggressive German imperialism but rather as a symptom of the anxiety of the times, a sign that the empire was in the "grip of profound and pervasive anxieties." This bland, apolitical volume signaled a "regressive flight into literally childish ways of seeing the world" as a way of evading a profound "uneasiness too exigent to be managed by rational conduct" (163–64). The evasions of *Die Gartenlaube* therefore "betray not merely a self-satisfied surrender to the powers that be," Gay argues, but also "a way of coping with a deeply felt, often deeply concealed need: the need to be reassured that all was, after all, well" (164). As we shall shortly see, Gay's sense of a culture in denial aptly characterizes the modus operandi of Werner's optimistic narrative of a reconciled father and son and the overcoming of obstacles to a love match in the midst of the Franco-Prussian War.

North American presses and translators hurried to publish *Flammenzeichen* in English. Given nearly two decades of success with Werner in translation, publishers saw renewed opportunity in this latest novel. By November 1890 *Book Chat* had reviewed the first American translation, *His Word of Honor*, which must have been rendered directly from the serialization. The London publisher Bentley brought out *Beacon-Fires* the following year. Likewise, two American firms published a third and fourth translation, *The Northern Light*, appeared with Bonner, translated by D. M. Lowrey, and *Flames* appeared with Donohue, Henneberry and Company, its translator identified only as "The Adaptor."[12]

A fifth and sixth translation appeared in the United States over the following decade: *Beacon Lights* in 1899 with Munro by Mary Stuart Smith and Gessner Harrison Smith and *The Sign of Flame* (1902) by Eva F. Hart and E. van Gerpen. Smith and her son had begun translating the novel in late 1890, hoping to place it with Bonner, but they were not quick enough and were scooped by Lowrey.[13] Their manuscript lay fallow for eight years. After an unsuccessful attempt in 1897 to place it with A. L. Burt, who apparently wanted to start a new series of German books with "something fresh" and thus put the Smiths off for the time being, Smith placed it with Munro.[14] Meanwhile, A. L. Burt, having missed the opportunity to bring out the Smiths' work, published Hart and Gerpen's translation in 1902. This final rendering remained available for purchase until at least 1912. On January 20, 1912, Frederick Loeser and Company advertised *The Sign of Flame* in the *New York Times* as a featured volume of the "1500 Volumes of the Home Library for 25c. a Volume," marked down from "40c. to 45c."[15] Americans thus read *Flammenzeichen* in an array of English versions for at least twenty-two years, 1890–1912.

Street and Smith marketed its edition of *His Word of Honor* in its "Seashore and Mountain Series" as summer reading.[16] The light green binding stamped with a repeated pattern of a cluster of pink flowers with green leaves suggestively feminizes the book but may merely signal "light reading." Ella Dorman Ward Short entered her name in her copy of the work in the middle of the summer, on July 1, 1904, and presumably then settled in to enjoy a good read. If Ella read other books in the Seashore and Mountain Series, she would have found *His Word of Honor* in the company of Werner's *The Price He Paid*, as well as that of such favorite international works as R. D. Blackmore's *Lorna Doone*, and novels by S. Baring-Gould, Robert Louis Stevenson, and Charles Reade. Street and Smith promoted the book on the title page as another by E. Werner, the author of *The Price He Paid* and *She Fell in Love with Her Husband*, but did not make visible its origins in another language and culture.

In 1891 *Belford's Magazine* pronounced *The Northern Light* a novel that "stirs one's heart and holds one's interest to the very last line."[17] Smith, however, who elsewhere expressed admiration for Werner, fretted over how to render the book in English so that it did not sound bombastic.[18] There was good reason to worry in the early 1890s about bombast in a narrative of heroism and German superiority as William II aspired for a German "place in the sun." Yet, however overblown, the novel adhered to beloved patterns that Werner had established years earlier when unified Germany and *Die Gartenlaube* still bore traces of their national liberal origins.

"The Adaptor" of *Flames*, who dedicated the book "To my Mother, in recognition of the lavish affection bestowed upon me, and with true filial devotion," had passionate views about the merit of Werner's somewhat old-fashioned novel, believing it important to make the work available to Americans: "*Firstly:* To turn aside the current of the rushing stream of highly sensational, realistic, nineteenth century novels, and *Secondly:* To etch upon the reading public a lasting imprint of a good moral lesson and of a worthy hero and heroine" (5). Eschewing "the French school of absolute, lurid naturalism" and "*Tolstoism*," the Adaptor defended *Flames* as "an exact portrayal of the soldiers and officers of the world's army" and as wholesome and "worthy of circulating and penetrating into the hearths of every American home" and lauded the novel's advocation of "the right of the true Christian heart over the mind" and its condemnation of "the illegal marketing propensity of parents" (5). The last formulation points to the liberal message of the novel, according to which individuals can overcome the determinism of biological and familial inheritance. Couched in vehement yet oblique language, this praise points to what the translator understood to be the book's outlook, namely, an emphasis on the ethical and religious as opposed to the social and political. The Adaptor's preface can of course be read less charitably: in its abhorrence of the depiction of pain and also of social and political questions, it duplicates the modalities of denial that Gay detected in *Die Gartenlaube* in 1890.

In the backstory of *Flammenzeichen,* the passion of the Prussian officer Falkenried for a foreign woman with "dark demoniacal glowing eyes," whom he married against his parents' wishes, tore his family apart.[19] The blond, blue-eyed Falkenried later divorced his adulterous wife to preserve his honor, but not before the couple had produced their only child, Hartmut. Especially since Hartmut has inherited his Romanian mother's looks and passionate temperament, Falkenried fears her moral influence as well and has therefore kept Hartmut in ignorance of her whereabouts and her scandalous behavior. Moreover, to combat the biological burden of this maternal inheritance, he has disciplined his son harshly for a career in the army.

The restless seventeen-year-old chafes at restrictions imposed on him by military discipline and his strict Prussian upbringing. When his mother reappears and entices him to leave with her, he cannot resist the freedom she appears to offer and abandons military school. Although he has not yet sworn the officer's oath of allegiance, his departure is regarded as dereliction of duty. He has also shamefully broken his promises to his father. Replacing the name Falkenried with his mother's maiden name, Hartmut commences a nomadic life with his immoral mother, who, unbeknownst to him, also works as a spy.

In her portrait of Hartmut's parents, Werner deploys crass stereotypes, linking Germanness and the virtues of manhood, on the one hand, and foreignness and the deficiencies of womanhood, on the other. In following his mother and taking her name, Hartmut not only repudiates his German homeland but also endangers his manhood. The central plot is devoted to his recognition of his error and his struggle to mend his ties to his father and his country. German national history enables a happy resolution of family conflict, war constituting the venue in which honor can be restored and individuals can fulfill high ideals.

Hartmut's travels lead him back to the South German territory where he was raised. Here he meets the icy, blond North German Adelheit von Wallmoden. A young, duty-bound woman who has married an older man to help her family out of financial difficulty, Adelheit contrasts starkly with his dark, seductive mother and embodies the virtues of his father. In the end her high ideals save him from himself. When the Franco-Prussian War erupts, she uses her influence to enable him to serve as a volunteer in the German army under an assumed name. In the war Hartmut proves his mettle by undertaking a dangerous mission to warn of an impending attack, saving the day for the Germans, and rescuing his father. At the conclusion of the novel, the recently widowed Adelheit has lost her icy demeanor in response to Hartmut's new vigor. Hartmut, who is a poet, has, for his part, learned to write poems different from his passionate "Arivana," which once took the literary world by storm. The text leaves little doubt about the nature of the "different spirit" breathed by his new poetry. He has learned "to know his fatherland and his home" (371).

As an American reviewer noted, *Flammenzeichen* repeats familiar motifs and conceits that circulate throughout Werner's oeuvre. However, it is significant that in 1890, at an uneasy moment in the life of the empire, Werner returned to a great moment in the empire's story of itself, the Franco-Prussian War. Her conceit that fighting the French for the love of country makes a man of even the most abject is underlined by her signature comic side plot. In this secondary plot Willibald, the dull-witted mama's boy, also becomes a man upon donning a uniform. He throws off his domineering mother Regine's yoke and marries the woman he loves—to his mother's horror, a former actress. Even Regine recognizes that he has gained something that she had been unable to teach him; he "had never before seemed so handsome in her eyes, for his military life and discipline had given him a fine, stately bearing" (361). As Werner tells the story, the new empire restores the gender order at the expense of overweening mothers, too. Regine, having relinquished her power over her son, is now prepared to accept a proposal of marriage from the forester whom she has long held at arm's length. She promises to be "a good and true wife," in essence surrendering control to her new husband (369).

The illegible but tantalizing German title *Flammenzeichen* relates to several motifs in the novel. "Flammenzeichen" alludes to the *ignis fatuus*, the treacherous will-o'-the-wisp, that accompanies Hartmut when he succumbs to his passionate nature and his longing for freedom, most notably when he breaks his word to his father and when he nearly commits suicide. The same term signifies the healing and redemptory flames of the Franco-Prussian War.[20] The locution also concludes the novel as the beacon of the happy future awaiting the couple and Germany. The six English translations of this title provide insight into the ways the novel may have been read in nineteenth-century America.

Mary Stuart Smith was of the opinion that "the simplest term . . . Signs of Fire or Signs of Flame" was the best. Choosing in the end *Beacon Lights*, the Smiths relied on the author herself to know how best to title her work. The variations *Flames, Sign of Flame,* and *Beacon-Fires* also approximate the German original, but, unlike *Flammenzeichen,* none of these applies equally well to the multiple contexts in which "Flammenzeichen" appears in the original and instead privilege the vaguely patriotic message and happy ending. Smith's son, Harry, had suggested "Adelheit" as an alternative to Werner's opaque title, a title that could appeal to readers who were looking for female protagonists. Had they titled the translation *Adelheit,* the Smiths would have highlighted the femininity that figures centrally in this story of war and redeemed manhood.[21] Lowrey obliquely emphasized precisely this femininity in choosing the title *The Northern Light.* As Hartmut observes, the reserved heroine possesses a face like a "northern light, above a sea of ice" (133). The sixth title, *His Word of Honor,* by contrast, centers attention on Hartmut, his moral failing and his troubled relations with his father and country.

None of these choices suggests that the translators and their publishers expected readers to take up the novel as one concerning specific world-historical events; rather, they presented it as a story of an affair of the heart and of proper (manly) behavior supported by armed combat. The Franco-Prussian War served the genre and provided the therapy necessary to a desirable outcome in a family drama. Americans could read past Werner's insistent patriotism and German ethnocentrism, focusing instead on family conflict and romance. In 1890 the outcome of a war that had ended nineteen years earlier was probably not of burning interest to American novel readers.

The optimism of the novel, however, must have appealed to readers like the Adaptor. Although *Flammenzeichen* trades in the stereotypes and prejudices of its time, the hero triumphs over the forces of inheritance and bad upbringing, and this happy message was what regular Werner readers could expect from each new novel. Indeed, Werner's works display persistent faith in the power of individuals to overcome adversity, a belief that is otherwise undermined in late-century, now canonical German literature, literature that at the time found little resonance in America. A pessimistic story by Werner's German contemporary Theodor Storm provides a useful point of comparison.

Storm's "Carsten Curator" first appeared in *Westermanns Monatshefte*, thirteen years before Werner's novel ran in *Die Gartenlaube*. It did not become available in English until 1936, however, and thus could not have provided a counterimage for American Anglophone readers before that time.[22] It recounts the story of a stolid North German middle-class man who foolishly falls in love with a young and flighty Frenchwoman. Significantly, the upheaval of the Napoleonic era, the time that many late-century Germans saw as the worst in recent German history, brings the pair into contact.[23] Their son, Heinrich, bears the genetic burden of his mother's nature: he is undisciplined, unprincipled, and incapable of shouldering his manly responsibilities despite his widowed father's efforts to raise him properly. Storm narrates a deterministic tragedy; the eruption of passion in an otherwise sober man produces a defective son who destroys them both. Werner, by contrast, works in the mode of romance, happy endings, and affective individualism. Individual will and action can overcome defects of origin and past mistakes, no matter how heavily these weigh.

If Storm's tragic and deterministic work represents the nineteenth-century German literature and culture we now think we know, Werner's optimistic work was the German literature that nineteenth-century American novel readers thought they knew and, moreover, the one they wanted to know. Werner's Germany was also—if Gay's analysis is correct—the Germany that many German *Gartenlaube* readers wanted it to be. Werner made certain in 1890 with *Flammenzeichen* that a vision of Germany as the grateful canvas for affective individualism was attached to the founding of the Second Empire, a tagging that may not have registered deeply with American readers, even when they, as did the Adaptor, fully understood and relished the text's optimistic liberalism.

Cousin Marriage and Ethnic Conflict:
Vineta

Flammenzeichen resembles not only *Hero of the Pen* but also *Vineta* (*Die Gartenlaube*, nos. 27–52 [1876]). *Vineta*, set on the German-Polish border and obviously influenced by part 2 of Gustav Freytag's best-selling *Soll und Haben* (1855; Debit and Credit), recounts how Waldemar Nordeck, the product of a marriage of convenience between a middle-class German man and a Polish aristocratic woman, brings order to his property after his Polish nationalist mother has allowed it to go to wrack and ruin.[24] By May 1877 the newly founded Estes and Lauriat was advertising Frances A. Shaw's translation, *Vineta; or the Phantom City*, as a "Thrilling Novel of German and Polish Life."[25]

In keeping with the anti-Polish sentiments of Bismarck's Prussia, the novel criticizes Polish nationalism, yet it also recreates the somewhat positively coded stereotype of the gallant Polish aristocracy that will never declare the Polish cause lost, a stereotype that traces its origins in the German-speaking world to the German Left's sympathy with the Polish rebellion of 1830. The Polish uprisings of 1863–64 did not at first directly involve the Germans but took place in territories claimed by Russia. Prussia, however, eventually aided the Russians in suppressing the rebellion. The issue, as presented in the novel, concerns the use by Waldemar's mother and uncle of his estates on German territory as a staging area to abet the rebels across the border on Polish Russian territory.

Waldemar shows little sign of his mother's heritage; only the prominent blue vein on his forehead indicates the strong will they share. His Polish nationalist and strongly prejudiced Polish family greatly underestimates the unsophisticated Germanized Waldemar, scarcely realizing that he has returned to claim his inheritance and to "impress something of the 'History of Germany' upon [his] Slavonic estates."[26]

As a boy Waldemar fell in love with his Polish cousin Wanda, who mercilessly ridiculed him. Now that both are grown up there exists an unmistakable attraction between the two, despite their mutual animosity. Nature signals that they belong together when Waldemar and Wanda, whose union appears nearly impossible at this juncture, behold a mirage on the Baltic: the sunken city Vineta. In addition to foreshadowing the union of the cousins, the vision, in comprising an entire city and thus a social system, also implies a context for love fulfilled. It intimates that not only will the cousins unite but also that there will be a place for them to live.

Vineta concludes with the defeat and flight of Waldemar's Polish uncle and mother, who, undaunted, will continue to support the Polish cause. Waldemar illegally helps his uncle and future father-in-law escape, thereby obtaining his blessing for his marriage to Wanda. Following the flight of the elder Polish generation, the cousins marry and the novel thus reaches its happy conclusion. Unlike the previous generation, they will live on Waldemar's estate in German territory free from national animosity, that is, Polish national animosity.

The American actor Frank Mayo's adaptation with John G. Wilson of *Vineta* as *Nordeck* (1883; premiere May 25, 1884, Chicago) testifies not only to the currency of Werner's novel in the United States but also to an additional manner in which Americans adapted and made meaning of this German cultural material. Mayo's many performances of *Nordeck* with his itinerant acting company, over approximately ten years, left a trail of press reviews across the country from New York to San Francisco that bespeak mixed success. In his adaptation Mayo allowed himself poetic license and romance by setting his drama not in a Prussian province in the 1860s but in "German Poland near the border of Russian Poland" in the "latter part of the eighteenth century."[27] The five-act play streamlines the principal events of the novel, sharpens the ethnic conflict, portrays Waldemar's mother, uncle, and brother with even less sympathy than does Werner, and makes of a minor character, the forester Osiecki, a major villain.

By shifting emphasis from delineation of character, setting, and the developing love between Wanda and Waldemar to dramatic conflict for the stage, Mayo and Wilson rendered the events more improbable and opaque than they are in the novel. In late middle age, Mayo played the part of young Waldemar Nordeck, sporting a mustache and shoulder-length hair, fur-trimmed cape, and over-the-knee boots, with more than a hint of swashbuckling.[28] Upon the New York debut of the play in 1885, the *New York Times* remarked that it was imbued with romance and dealt "with persons removed from the sphere of everyday existence."[29] Although he doggedly tinkered with the play, Mayo never quite managed to tailor his romantically embellished rendition of Werner's domestic fiction to match the taste of American theater audiences. His finances in ruins in 1894, in part because of his misplaced faith in *Nordeck*, Mayo put renewed efforts into a new adaptation, this time of American fiction: *Pudd'nhead Wilson*. Unlike the German *Nordeck*, this play brought him reliable revenues as had, in his younger years, the American plays *Davy Crockett* and *The Streets of New York*.[30]

Returning to the German Fold:
The Spell of Home

Twice rendered into English in the United States, Werner's *Heimatklang* (1887) also expressed German national allegiance within a love story resulting in cousin marriage. Wister translated it for *Lippincott's Magazine* as *The Spell of Home*, where it appeared in February 1888 as the featured novel of the month. In 1887 Lippincott had determined to publish twelve novels per year in toto in the twelve issues of the monthly magazine to benefit authors and readers: readers would enjoy getting the novels "straight instead of mangled out of shape and recognition by the serial process, which has so long been the curse of fictitious literature."[31] Authors in turn would no longer have to write to produce artificial climaxes at the end of each installment. *The Spell of Home* appeared one year into the experiment and was expected to help procure and retain magazine subscribers. In that same year Werner's novel appeared a second time in English, this time translated by E. W. Conduit with Munro in the pocket edition of the Seaside Library, priced at twenty cents. The venue of both publications promised readers entertainment.

The wish to provide pleasurable reading prompted an additional noteworthy American edition of *Heimatklang*. In 1903 New Haven high school German teacher and future German department head at Vassar College, Marian P. Whitney, published the novel in German with Holt with an instructional apparatus for school and college German courses.[32] Whitney's preface provides evidence, first, that the novel was still being read and, second, of how and why it was read. "This is a modern novel, dealing with love and patriotism and with a touch of fighting; it is well constructed and the action moves forward without a break," Whitney asserted. Given its simple style and the absence of philosophizing and irony, the novella offered a picture of German life and thought that, while "perhaps not always realistic, correspond[ed] to the ideals of a large class of Germans." Furthermore, her reader had been tested, she claimed, and had proven "interesting and stimulating to both boys and girls."[33] She touted especially the ability of *Heimatklang* to entertain. Approved by German professors at Yale and Harvard, it would teach the "very important lesson that a German book is a thing to be read and enjoyed, not merely to be translated into English." Unlike her contemporary Otto Heller, Whitney regarded popular literature kindly if it could engender an affective relationship to German language and literature. She moreover believed—and was not entirely mistaken in this point—that *Heimatklang* could convey to Americans how many contemporary Germans thought.

Werner's *Heimatklang* does offer a fast-paced and simple plot. Set in Schleswig during the Danish-German War of 1864, one of the three wars that facilitated German unification under Prussian hegemony, it tells the story of Baron Hellmuth von Mansfeld, who must learn to love his German homeland, which at the outset of the novella is still under Danish rule. As a result of his mother's second marriage to a Danish count, Hellmuth is estranged from his German family and feels no allegiance to the German cause. His grandfather's fondest dream is for Hellmuth to marry his cousin Leonora and be restored to the family and his true heritage. While

Leonora's origins in a misalliance between aristocrat and bourgeois have left her without a dowry, Hellmuth's faulty education and development result from another kind of misalliance that has left him without a country. This international misalliance is much more troubling at this historical juncture. While in *Flammenzeichen* and *Vineta* conflicted loyalties arise from mixed biological heritage, here estrangement from one's birthright and true self results from a bad upbringing.

The plot conflates the love story—the simultaneous repulsion and attraction of the cousins—with Hellmuth's wavering attitude toward the Danish-German War. In the end the protagonist awakens to the "spell of home," confesses his love for his cousin, participates in the resistance to the Danes, and separates himself from his Danish stepfather. As a local patriot affirms, he has thereby become "a true man."[34] The novella concludes mid-war with Leonora and Hellmuth's impending marriage and with Leonora's urgent message: "Wait, and hope!"[35]

Thirty Years after 1848:
At a High Price

Of Werner's explicit historical treatments *Um hohen Preis* (*Die Gartenlaube* nos. 9–37 [1878]) was doubtlessly the most opaque to a foreign audience, yet the publication history of the book in translation indicates that it generated considerable interest in the English-speaking world. In 1879 it appeared in Great Britain translated by Christina Tyrrell as *No Surrender* and in the United States translated by Mary Stuart Smith as *At a High Price* in Estes and Lauriat's Cobweb Series. Its spine announced it as by "Ernest Werner." Smith's translation remained in print until at least 1897 in a reprint with Fenno. Tyrrell's translation circulated under two new and different titles in the United States and remained in print there as *The Price He Paid* until at least 1902, when both Street and Smith and Rand McNally republished it. Schlesinger and Mayer advertised it in the *Chicago Daily Tribune* just in time for Christmas as one on a list of twenty-five-cent "standard books for everybody" in "large type, fine laid paper, artistic cloth covers."[36]

A novel in which social-political unrest plays a critical role, *Um hohen Preis* appeared in Germany three years after the establishment of the Socialist Workers' Party (a merging of the General Union of German Workers and the Social Democratic Workers' Party) of Germany in 1875; its serialization concluded just one month before the German parliament passed the Anti-Socialist Laws banning socialist and social-democratic organizations and their activities in the German empire. Seven years after the founding of the empire, old-fashioned German national liberalism (the politics of the founder of *Die Gartenlaube*) had been soundly defeated to be replaced in positions of power by conservative parties with whom Bismarck, once allied with the National Liberal Party, established closer ties. The year 1878, the thirty-year anniversary of the failed revolution of 1848, constituted an occasion for reflection on the brutal state repression of the revolutionary activity of another era and on the first and unsuccessful attempt to forge German unity under liberal governance. For many, however, the anniversary was not so much a moment to reflect on yet another failure of liberal and left-wing causes but instead a reminder of social unrest and revolution.

The crushing of the March revolutions had led to the emigration of political radicals, many of whom, such as Carl Schurz, Friedrich Hecker, Franz Sigel, and Reinhold Solger, settled in the United States, where they supported the Union and, as did Schurz, Hecker, and Sigel, served in the Union Army. By 1878, many of these men had in the interim risen to prominence in the countries where they found asylum and where they sometimes became outspoken patriots on behalf of their adoptive country. Schurz had become Secretary of the Interior in the United States, Solger had served under Abraham Lincoln, Hecker had become involved in the German-language press and the Republican Party while farming in Illinois, and Sigel had become a newspaper editor in New York, active in Republican politics. Just beyond the German border in Zurich, another former radical, Johann Gottfried Kinkel, who had fled Prussian incarceration in 1850, was teaching archeology and art history at the Polytechnikum. Many of these men flourished in exile even as Werner wrote this novel, which seeks reconciliation, redemption, and justice and is therefore haunted by men such as these former radicals.

At a High Price opens in Switzerland, the nearby destination for exiled 1848 revolutionaries, where Dr. Rudolph Brunnow long ago sought asylum after being arrested for his radical activities. Werner never explicitly names 1848, but her German audience could easily understand her meaning. She proceeds to intertwine a love story and family drama with politics in a novel that explores the long-lasting effects of revolutionary activity on family and country. The conclusion offers an illegible picture of contemporary German politics, yet the text clearly worries over social unrest in the empire and obliquely over the German government's response to it under Bismarck's chancellorship.

The budding radical George Winterfeld has become friends with the political exile Brunnow. He also loves Gabrielle von Harder, the ward of Baron Arno von Raven. Both affiliations potentially impede his promising government career under the regime of the iron-fisted Arno. The imperious Arno has a secret, namely, that he himself is a former radical whom fortune treated differently from his coconspirators. Although he was incarcerated along with Brunnow, he was subsequently and inexplicably released. He then married the governor's daughter and ascended to the aristocracy, thereafter becoming the governor of the province. A hardworking opportunist, Arno has ruled autocratically, suppressing any sign of rebellion. His charisma has helped him maintain his power, and his tough-mindedness has benefited the province in some respects. When the novel opens, the days of his harsh regime are numbered.

The narrative takes an unexpected turn when it begins to present the flawed Arno sympathetically. Initially, he appears to be the villain of the story, resembling some of Marlitt's nefarious men in power, but he, and not young George, turns out to be the novel's central character. When seventeen-year-old Gabrielle, who is secretly engaged to George, falls passionately in love with Arno, who is at least thirty years her senior, the author's intention of gaining reader sympathy for him becomes clear.

By the conclusion of the novel, his power in shambles and exposure of his hypocrisy and radical past imminent, Arno determines that his honor can be restored only in death and therefore engineers a duel with Brunnow, his former friend and now sworn enemy. The sorely goaded Brunnow shoots to kill, while Arno, the far better shot, fires in the air. In a dramatic scene of male bonding, Arno dies in Brunnow's arms, thanking him for his honorable death and begging his forgiveness. The mild-mannered Brunnow must now be eternally tormented by the thought that he had perhaps misjudged his former friend.

Despite this affecting account of Arno's death, the text leaves little doubt that a new day has dawned to the good of this province; best of all, in Werner's liberal, gradualist vision, revolution has become unnecessary because power is now in the proper hands: "The last four years had wrought many changes . . . ," the narrator summarizes. "The once persecuted and oppressed liberal party now stood at the head of affairs, and with this complete reversal of the situation a revolution of opinion had come about in every sphere of official activity."[37] Middle-class George has under these circumstances risen in the ranks and become a more suitable partner for the aristocratic Gabrielle. In the end Gabrielle, who can never forget Arno, with whom she experienced the "pinnacle of human bliss" (306) (though this happiness lasted only a matter of hours), consents to marry George. The narrator explains that although she fell in love with Arno, she never stopped loving George. As a "true woman" she is only too ready to experience love in a self-sacrificing mode, that is, through the happiness she can give to others by disciplining herself. In case readers are not convinced of the propriety of her marrying George with the memory of Arno (and the implied longing for ecstatic sexual fulfillment) still fresh, the narrator explains, "Gabrielle felt that life and love were given back to her, but remembering the price paid, she felt too, that love, life, and happiness were dearly bought!" (307)—in the original German "um hohen Preis" (at a high price).

By ambiguously citing her own title as the last words of her novel, Werner appears once again to shift her focus, for these words no longer invoke the price that Arno paid for his success but rather Gabrielle's loss, the death of the fascinating man who was not good for her. At the same time, the impersonal formulation suggests that many have paid a price for the new order. The text thus obliquely asserts that the happiness of the younger generation has been forged on the suffering and sacrifices of the previous one. The price of purchase has been the toppling of an oppressive regime and a revisiting of and atonement for the injustices of 1848.

The variations in the English titles suggest different readings. The German *Um hohen Preis* is rendered literally in Smith's translation as *At a High Price*, retaining in the impersonal formulation the ambiguity of the original. The title of Christina Tyrrell's translation, *No Surrender*, aptly reproduces the dramatic turn the novel takes when it focuses on Arno's heroic determination to end his life and his career on his own terms. Tyrrell and her British publisher thus expressed the novel's attempt to gain readers' admiration for Arno. When the American Munro reprinted Tyrrell's translation in the Seaside Series, however, the old title was replaced by the lengthy *At a High Price, or The Price He Paid*, a title that duplicates Smith's but by virtue of the extension distinguishes itself as a new product. Only Tyrrell's name linked the Munro edition to the earlier *No Surrender*. The second part of the Munro title, *The Price He Paid*, like the English *No Surrender*, focuses attention on Arno, though less on his heroic stance than his mistake, the price paid to achieve power and influence, when he betrayed his radical friends and abandoned his political cause to collude with the conservatives. When in the 1890s Street and Smith, Lupton, and Rand McNally began publishing Tyrrell's translation without crediting her, the book was renamed *The Price He Paid*, this final title giving way to the more moralizing reading.

American reviews of the various translations are mixed, but some of them do take up the politics in Werner's "story of love and German politics curiously interwoven."[38] In 1879 *The Independent* remarked in this vein on the "strongly drawn" Baron von Raven.[39] Seventeen years later, the political aspect was still visible: the *Medical Age* found the book a "most interesting bit of fiction dealing with German politics, revolution, and love."[40] This reviewer was, however, less interested in Arno than in a minor character who belongs to Werner's signature secondary comic plot, a man who changes his pragmatic views on marriage to embrace love. In 1896 the *Literary World*, noting that *The Price He Paid* felt a little "passé and absurd," nevertheless conceded that the novel was interesting for its "glimpses" of "German life in certain official circles."[41] A review from 1891 mentioned the novel's political grounding only to hint that it was tedious.[42]

A brief look at the never-translated *Eulenpfingsten* by Wilhelm Raabe, a leading German realist, provides a sense of the incomplete picture of German literary treatment of politics that Americans had if they had access only to German fiction in translation.[43] At the same time it reveals the proximity of popular writing such as Werner's to more pretentious literary production such as Raabe's. Serialized in 1874 in *Westermanns Monatshefte* and later anthologized in book form as one of several *Krähenfelder Geschichten* in 1879, *Eulenpfingsten*, like *At a High Price,* treats the long-term effects on German families (and by extension Germany) of the brutal treatment of revolutionaries. It involves the suppression of radicals that had occurred in the German states over the course of the nineteenth century and that in the 1870s was again on the horizon. In both Werner's and Raabe's novels, state-sponsored repression and individual collusion with it have indelibly marked families and individuals.

Eulenpfingsten (literally "Owl's Pentecost"), meaning "once in a blue moon," concerns a family divided by politics and betrayal in the politically repressive 1830s. When the novel opens the Nebelung family awaits the return of Aunt Lina from New York, where she has lived for twenty years. It is Pentecost, May 22, 1858, ten years after the March revolutions and the May opening of the Frankfurt parliament. This day of reunion is, as the narrator asserts, St. Nimmerleinstag (St. Neverkin's Day), meaning something like "when pigs fly." With the novel's title and the invented saint's day, the narrator, from the start, expresses skepticism about the reconciliation and the happy ending that he recounts.

Thirty years earlier, while Alexius, Lina's older brother, was currying favor with the local prince of a tiny principality, young Lina was at home knitting socks, reading the left-wing German Jewish writer Ludwig Börne, and thinking of her true love, Fritz, the local radical. When Fritz was arrested, the Nebelungs found many of his papers with Lina, and these were used to convict him. When Lina stood up to her family on Fritz's behalf, they sent her away. Thereafter she emigrated to America, thereby sharing the fate of many male political radicals. Alexius meanwhile prosecuted Fritz, who was imprisoned and later escaped to Switzerland where, his radical edge blunted, he married, fathered three children, and became a tanner. When Lina arrives in Frankfurt, where her brother, Alexius, now lives with his daughter, Käthchen, she is not surprised to find her mean-spirited family in disarray.

In the lightly ironic, chatty, convoluted, and experimental narrative style for which the author is known, *Eulenpfingsten* recounts how Alexius by chance meets Fritz, whom he does not recognize; how he is shaken out of his complacency and prevented from simply erasing the past and pretending that all is well; and how he must finally stop quarreling with his neighbor and give his consent for his daughter to marry his neighbor's son, Elard. Lina herself exploits the opportunity of thwarted young love to interfere in family affairs and to make certain that this time a comedy and not a tragedy plays on the world stage.

The novel concludes not only with the union of Käthchen and Elard and a reconciliation of sorts of brother and sister, but also Lina's reunion with the now-married Fritz. Of that, we have only Lina's ambiguous "Oh Friedrich!" and the astonishment of Alexius and his neighbor. Meanwhile, Elard and Käthchen remain oblivious to the pain of the previous generation: "ein rosig durchleuchtet Gewölk trug sie, und Arm in Arm schwebten sie ins Paradies hinein"[44] (a rosy cloud, flooded with light, carried them and they floated arm in arm into paradise), and happily, no one attempts to call them back down onto solid ground. Even as he supplies the requisite happy ending of comedy and romance, the narrator remarks on the egotism of the lovers and uses their happy ending to obscure Lina's, Fritz's, and Alexius's stories, which remain unresolved.

In taking up the tumultuous past of nineteenth-century Germany, Raabe and Werner both suggest that its long-term effects remain, yet their texts, both of which end in romantic union, offer different ideas as to how the wounds of the past are healed through love and marriage. Raabe's narrator does not fully believe in his happy ending; Werner's text, through the perspective of a sadder but wiser Gabrielle, does, even if the "golden sunshine" is momentarily pathetically "blotted out by a tear" (307). This was the sentimental Germany loved by American novel readers and sometimes scorned by American reviewers. It was one that by 1879 they had encountered in a different dress in the historical novels of Luise Mühlbach.

Prussian Family Romance as German History:
The Historical Novels of Luise Mühlbach

For approximately half a century, in the years between the Civil War and the First World War, Americans avidly read the historical romances of Luise

Mühlbach in translation, published by D. Appleton. This historical fiction was consumed and marketed alongside the novels that have hitherto been our focus; indeed, the publication of three Mühlbach novels about Frederick the Great, translated by Ann Mary Chapman Coleman and her daughters (published 1866–67), and two novels about Prussia's Great Elector, translated by Mary Stuart Smith (published 1896–97), comes close to bracketing the entire translation enterprise under scrutiny here.

Mühlbach's novels delighted the American public with stories of the German past told through the lens of ruling families, their courts, and their romantic attachments. The immediate success of these historical novels in postbellum America suggests that they struck a chord with readers recovering from the bloody Civil War; chapter 7 considers the translator and southern sympathizer Coleman herself as just such a reader of these books. In the Prussian/German history purportedly mediated in these works, Americans could enter an alternate world of conflict and resolution, resolution brought about by the interventions of forceful individuals and sealed in royal families. As Drew Gilpin Faust observes of southern elite women's reading during the Civil War as a source of consolation, "waking excursions into the realm of books and intellect offered them a world beyond suffering, war, and death, a world in which they found an order, a meaning, and a sense of control and purpose too often lacking in their disrupted, grief-filled lives."[45]

The five volumes that opened and closed Appleton's historical series provide a representative picture of Mühlbach's fiction and the version of Germany therein. The record of consumption of them in America reveals, moreover, a long afterlife of this picture of Germany in the world of American novel readers, publishers, and booksellers. All five were written before German unification and share in the national ethos of the liberals of that era, an ethos fueled by belief in affective individualism and dependent on top-down reform. They promote a Prussian-centered view of German history whose telos was realized in 1871 with the founding of the German Reich.

By the end of the period in which they were read in America, these novels were, however, rather antiquated in genre and in worldview. The belated publication of the two Great Elector novels in the later 1890s did not create much of a stir in the literary press, even though the two volumes did expand the Appleton series of Mühlbach's historical novels from eighteen to twenty and, as part of this set, sold in several editions with multiple publishers. Indeed, old-fashioned or not, as late as 1917 Mühlbach's novels were advertised with Frederick Loeser and Company in the *New York Times:* "Muhlbach [sic] (Frederick the Great)" in four volumes available in full leather for $4.00 just in time for Christmas 1917.[46] Loeser marketed the German author as a classic side by side with Dante, Eliot, Emerson, Fielding, Flaubert, Hawthorne, Maupassant, Poe, Plato, Schiller, Turgenieff [sic], and Tarkington—to name a few of the American and international authors appearing in the cheapest group of the standard sets advertised, namely, "Standard Sets at $2 to $7.50." Mühlbach's novels likewise could be obtained for $22.00 in twenty volumes bound in half calf or in "full limp leather" for $22.50. Here the works found themselves in the good company of Balzac, Bulwer-Lytton, Dumas, Dickens, Maupassant, Hugo, Scott, Voltaire, and Wilde. Mühlbach's novels, bound in limp leather, were thus destined to find a place on the shelves of the well-heeled book buyer intent on assembling a solid home library. The volumes of a partial set of these historical novels published by the University Society and once owned by Fay B. Harder contain a carefully penned record of Fay's acquisition of them in May 1911, thus testifying to consumption of the books well into the new century and, notably, by a woman.[47]

Frederick the Great and the Disciplining of Desire

As Brent O. Peterson outlines in his study of the German historical novel, Mühlbach devoted approximately four thousand pages in fifteen volumes to her "Frederick cycle," beginning in 1853 with *Friedrich der Große und sein Hof* and concluding with the multipart *Deutschland in Sturm und Drang*, published 1867–68.[48] The three Frederick novels, translated by Mrs. Chapman Coleman and her daughters, that belonged to this cycle captured American attention. With American English-language editions and reprint editions numbering at least fifty (*Frederick the Great and His Court*), forty (*Berlin and Sans-Souci, or Frederick the Great and His Friends*), and thirty-five (*Frederick the Great and His Family*), these three novels rank in my dataset, respectively, as second and third after *The Old Mam'selle's Secret* and fifth after *Gold Elsie* among the most often reprinted. Unlike these two Marlitt novels, however, they were translated only once for book publication.

The Frederick trilogy focuses on the first half of the forty-six-year reign of Frederick the Great, opening in 1740 during the last months of the reign of Frederick William I and concluding in 1763, not long after the Third Silesian War, with Frederick aging from twenty-eight to fifty-one. The three Silesian wars, which mid-nineteenth-century German nationalists regarded as German civil wars, constitute a dimly lit backdrop for personal interactions spotlighted in the foreground. As Peterson explains, Mühlbach's Frederick novels number among many German attempts to rewrite and popularize Frederick the Great of Prussia in service of the German national project of the nineteenth century.⁴⁹ Mühlbach's three Frederick novels, however, outsold all others on both sides of the Atlantic, and as popular reading marked by "hero worship," they played a seminal role in creating and disseminating an image of Frederick sympathetic to national-liberal Germans and of a past that was being woven into Germany's unifying, and later unified, story of itself.

The naming of the Prussian ruler and nineteenth-century German national icon in the titles of the three novels in the trilogy signals a read different from that of the domestic fiction of Marlitt, Heimburg, Werner, and others. In her Frederick novels Mühlbach places Frederick the Great himself at the vortex of conflict and action and sets the works largely at the Prussian court or in the pleasure palaces of the ruling Hohenzollerns. Thus these novels do indeed contrast with those we have hitherto examined, which, even when they are informed and shaped by historical events and conditions and purport to tell the story of such events, feature invented, not historical characters and tend to be set in areas marginal to politics.

Yet for all their inclusion of historical material, the Frederick novels resisted easy generic categorization in their own time. They did not, for example, focus on the middling hero in the manner of Walter Scott's then well-known historical novels. At the same time, though professing to be historical, they included such elements from the European romance tradition as transvestism, rulers traveling incognito, exotic women, and separated but steadfast lovers. The *Catholic World* despaired of classifying them, pronouncing them "too historical for romances and too romantic for histories."⁵⁰ The *Old Guard* formulated the resistance of the books to generic convention in yet another way: Mühlbach's novels were not "historical romances," because they lacked a plot altogether. The reviewer admitted, however, that they "embody much of the very *romance of history*," aptly describing them as "exhibiting [the notable personages of history] in a sort of panoramic 'dissolving view' to the public," or, in other words, as episodic.⁵¹ Recognizing their generic ambiguity, John Esten Cooke tried, as we noted in chapter 2, to characterize Mühlbach's "system" in her historical fiction as producing "*history dramatized*."⁵²

The discomfort of contemporaries with the resistance of these books to easy classification as either history or romance encourages us to think about them differently, and in our specific context, to think about them as domestic fiction. As Nancy Armstrong characterizes it, domestic fiction depends on affective individualism and psychology and a conception of the family as the locus of the production of identity, gender, desire, and agency. As will shortly become clear, despite the historical characters, events, and settings of Mühlbach's novels, their vision and ethos cohere with this broad idea of domestic fiction. Certainly there is evidence that they were marketed in America to some of the audiences who read Marlitt, Heimburg, and Werner.[53]

Even as the Frederick novels insist on their historicity with, for example, frequent footnotes identifying sources for an utterance or an episode or notes asserting the factuality of an episode, they are situated in a family—a highly exceptional one to be sure—yet a first family that can also be read as the quintessential German family. As the Prussian king, Frederick is burdened not merely by affairs of state and foreign wars but also by family tensions. These conflicts weary him, taxing his ability to assert his will and his capacity to balance desire and duty and to manage his household and, by extension, his kingdom. Throughout the cycle, he must admonish himself, his unruly family, and his retainers to do their duty; this duty—in the case of his siblings—largely involves suppressing desire and marrying the appropriate partner. In Mühlbach's account, individuals make world history at the expense of the royal heart at the heart of the nation. Once seen in terms of family dynamics and portraits of individuals, the three Frederick novels betray a consistency that lends them the shape that their episodic (albeit chronological) structure does not. Their dramatization of historical anecdotes aside, the three works consist in the end largely of an account of the vicissitudes of the royal family and Frederick's struggle as its head to press its members into service to the nation.

Frederick the Great and His Court, the first in the trilogy, opens when Frederick is still crown prince of Prussia. The well-known painful experiences of his adolescence are behind him; he is married to Elizabeth Christine, in fulfillment of his father's command, but is living a relatively unencumbered life apart from her that allows him to devote himself to artistic and philosophical pursuits. Mühlbach exploits this moment to offer vivid and entertaining parental portraits.

In the opening pages Queen Sophia Dorothea takes advantage of the temporary incapacity of the bedridden King Frederick William I to wear the royal diamonds, play cards, and invite the court to indulge in frivolity otherwise forbidden. The king, however, recovers and restores order, commanding his rebellious wife to lie down, fully dressed, in her coffin in a spectacular public performance. The royal pair thereby reminds the entire court of their mortality, and the king puts his wife in her place.

With this episode, the text establishes that—in the extravagance of its gestures and in the sweep of the canvas upon which it writes its story—this family is like no other. Yet in its straight-laced piety in small matters such as playing cards and displaying vanity, it must have been familiar to nineteenth-century readers on both sides of the Atlantic. If readers wonder about the family events that unfold in the following pages or question Frederick's virtues and motives, they can ponder the psychological impact of the family drama signified by the episode with the two coffins. The thwarted Sophia Dorothea in any case means to exercise influence over her son once he becomes king as compensation for her long years of domestic oppression. Frederick will parry his mother's attempt to dominate him, and yet, as readers learn in *Berlin and Sans-Souci*, he reveres his mother and mourns her passing, just as any virtuous bourgeois son should. Frederick thus plays a part designed to delight the hearts of a nineteenth-century middle-class audience.

Mühlbach also works the territory of the novel of remarriage that looms so large in the German domestic fiction translated into English. Although the historical facts and the circumstances of a royal, as opposed to bourgeois or aristocratic, family set limits to her deployment of this plot, its outlines become visible in *Frederick the Great and His Court* as the text milks the well-known estrangement of Frederick the Great and Elizabeth Christine for its pathos. In Mühlbach's version of this dynastic marriage, Elizabeth loves Frederick deeply even though he disdains her. Throughout the three novels she suffers from her husband's lack of interest in her and from jealousy when other women attract him. In a sympathetic portrait of a woman who normally merits little more than a historical footnote, the novel imagines the queen's private thoughts and motivations. She is so cowed in the presence of her adored husband, whose disregard sorely wounds her, that she is barely able to speak to him on the rare occasions when he addresses her. With its affinity to the novel of remarriage, however, the first book in the trilogy provides her with some validation. As the *New York Times* remarked, "the long-suffering constancy of Queen Elizabeth is very touchingly portrayed."[54]

When Frederick finally accedes, the court wonders whether he will divorce the wife forced on him by his father and marry another. Elizabeth wants to be queen, not because it will bring her power but because she loves Frederick. When he asks her shortly before his coronation whether she is "willing to remain Queen of Prussia, and nominally wife of the king," she answers affirmatively.[55] This odd proposal of remarriage for the sake of public image does not, however, bring the couple closer together. Frederick assumes that they are both doing their duty for the benefit of their people and promises her that she will ever find in him a "true friend, a well-meaning brother" (181). Elizabeth can only weep at this declaration, and Frederick obtusely interprets her tears to serve his own intention never to consummate the marriage in continued defiance of his deceased father's tyranny. Mühlbach could have made this scene the conclusion of the Elizabeth plot but instead supplied her readers with a modicum of the emotional satisfaction that the novel of remarriage can deliver, that is, she provided Elizabeth with personal, emotional acknowledgment from her neglectful husband.

Mühlbach brings about this acknowledgment with a masked ball on the eve of Frederick's departure for the First Silesian War. First, Elizabeth appears unmasked in the role of queen, glittering with the diamonds that Frederick (unlike his father) wants his royal women to wear as a sign of their rank. Ever hoping for approval, Elizabeth has bedizened herself to please Frederick, and his affirmation of her provides public acknowledgment of her wifely status. The evening, however, also grants Elizabeth private acknowledgment.

Concealing her identity with a black domino, Elizabeth arranges an interview with the king. Meanwhile, Frederick has just rebuffed a former love interest who wishes to insinuate herself into his good graces. The woman has previously given Elizabeth cause for jealousy and embarrassment. Readers who feel sympathy for the neglected queen thus perceive that the masked ball is to deliver her several small triumphs. When Frederick then turns to Elizabeth, who appears before him heavily veiled, she expresses her desire to hear his voice once more before he goes into battle and admonishes him to guard his life on behalf of his country, people, and family. At last finding her own voice, Elizabeth tells Frederick that he is deeply loved and that she knows a woman who would "die of despair" if he should perish in combat (374). But she does not stop with this oblique declaration; she goes on to assert explicitly that his *queen* adores him. The all-wise Frederick of Mühlbach's construction recognizes his wife in the lady in black, but respecting her disguise he asks her to tell the queen that he "honors no other woman as he honors her" and that he considers her "exalted enough to be placed among the women of the olden times" (374). He will think of her on the battlefield and gratefully remember her prayers for him (375). Weeping, Elizabeth retreats to her chamber to pray with the satisfaction of knowing at least that she is in her husband's thoughts.

Insofar as she could in the case of a historical couple notorious for living apart and never consummating their marriage, Mühlbach provides the queen with acknowledgment from her husband, the highest authority in the land. From then on, Elizabeth recedes into the background, periodically called upon to play the role of the mother of the country who has a sympathetic ear for members of the royal family, courtiers, and other retainers, while her husband shows a sterner mien to the world. Her unfulfilled, enduring love for the king affirms his potential worth in the heterosexual economy, even if (in Mühlbach's version) he chooses not to participate in it for the sake of duty. We will return below to Mühlbach's handling of Frederick's own desire.

Mühlbach's reliance on domestic plots to hold her dramatized historical episodes together becomes visible also in the attention accorded the romances and state marriages of four of Frederick's siblings: Augustus William, Henry, Ulrica, and Amelia. *Frederick the Great and His Court* spotlights Henry's thwarted romance with the virtuous Laura von Pannewitz. *Berlin and Sans-Souci* turns to the sisters Ulrica and Amelia. *Frederick the Great and His Family* completes Amelia's story as well as William Augustus's and focuses especially on Henry and his marriage to Princess Wilhelmina of Hesse-Kassel.

In her unfolding of the romance between Laura and Augustus William in *Frederick the Great and His Court*, Mühlbach allows Laura to assert the primacy and unruliness of emotion: "love is not given by command, it cannot be bestowed arbitrarily" (230). Schooled in duty, the queen mother, Frederick, and in the end none other than the long-suffering Queen Elizabeth herself admonish the prince and his beloved to suppress feeling. "It is the duty of all in our station to veil our feelings with a smile," Elizabeth instructs Laura (240). Duty creates a dynamic of expression and suppression of feeling that informs all three novels.

When, hundreds of pages later in *Frederick the Great and His Family*, Louise von Schwerin is forced to wed a man whom Frederick supplies so as to prevent Prince Henry from marrying her, Mühlbach offers another twist on the arranged marriage. To revenge himself on Louise, the clueless Henry himself assents to a state marriage negotiated by Frederick only to fall in love with his wife, the woman he had once scorned as a mere political pawn. His wife, however, proudly rebuffs him, disbelieving in the mercy of the second chance.

The suit of the king of Sweden for the hand of Amelia opens *Berlin and Sans-Souci*. The Calvinist Amelia, who does not wish to marry a Lutheran and who also dreams of true love, resists the match. Believing that she is merely discouraging Sweden, she becomes an unwitting accomplice to Ulrica's cynical and successful pursuit of the Swedish crown. Ulrica is the only Hohenzollern sibling to pursue dynastic alliances through marriage as a strategic life plan. However, since she contracts this loveless marriage to serve her pride and not her country, she proves to be the only Hohenzollern sibling without a heart and hence does not come off well.

Meanwhile, Amelia falls in love with the dashing Baron von Trenck. Their love provides plot interest until the conclusion of the following novel, *Frederick the Great and His Family*. As descriptions of Amelia's courage and combativeness repeatedly make clear, in the stubbornly loyal Amelia, Mühlbach created Frederick's female counterpart. When Trenck is imprisoned, Amelia immediately begins plotting his escape, and when he is imprisoned yet again, she spends a fortune trying to secure his release.

Amelia does not merely sacrifice her fortune to aid Trenck, but also her beauty to keep her vow to marry no one but him. When Frederick tries to force her to wed the king of Denmark, she throws acid on her face and hideously reflects back to Frederick the wounds that duty inflicts on the royal family. This portrait of the conflict between the siblings blunts Mühlbach's seemingly unrelenting admiration for Frederick, instead pushing family drama to the fore. In fact, Mühlbach does not manage to justify Frederick's harshness toward the wayward Trenck and instead calls upon readers' sympathy in repeated accounts of Trenck's abjection and courage during his shockingly inhumane imprisonment and in descriptions of the physically disfigured and exhausted Amelia's single-minded determination to free him. Trenck's liberation finally comes about only because Frederick allows it out of the compassion he feels (and has allegedly always felt) for his sister. Even if the reader has otherwise accepted Frederick's insistence on suppression of feeling in favor of duty to the nation, this belated compassion casts the Prussian king in a dubious light.

The struggles of the members of the royal family with duty and desire are amplified by subplots concerning proposed marriages that breach social barriers of courtiers and other retainers. While in *Frederick the Great and His Court*, Frederick declares his hatred of misalliances, which he will not tolerate at his court, love blooms everywhere. With the many subplots that portray romance as well as marriages cynically contracted to aggrandize personal wealth and status, these novels operate in the affective world of love, marriage, and family. Even in *Frederick the Great and His Family*, where the Seven Years' War and Frederick's time in the field command readers' attention over several chapters, a love story surfaces on the battlefield. Two valiant and inseparable brothers-in-arms reveal themselves to Frederick as a man and woman who wish to marry.

Mühlbach's narrative also investigates Frederick's desire but from the start suggests that this desire weakens the king. When Frederick accedes, the impecunious courtier Pöllnitz schemes to penetrate the secrets of his heart in the hope of controlling him through his emotional attachments. Pöllnitz's machinations fail when Frederick turns his back on women and love. Nevertheless, in the following novel, *Berlin and Sans-Souci*, Mühlbach improbably invents a heterosexual romance for Frederick, based on Antoine Pesne's famous portrait of the dancer Barbarina that still hangs in Sans-Souci Palace.

Frederick is happy in this love until Barbarina destroys their romance by trying to rule him. The end of their affair terminates his risky sally into affect. A desiring monarch is a vulnerable one, as Pöllnitz recognizes, and Frederick concurs. As Peterson rightly observes, Mühlbach "relies primarily on means other than romance to make Frederick attractive to her readers."[56]

Instead, Mühlbach painfully constructs a solitary sovereign who can ultimately assert his will within his family but who must also separate himself from them emotionally to live happily ever after, as it were, with his dogs and his flute. If these novels in any sense provide the happy ending expected of romance and characteristic of the fiction that we have hitherto examined, this ending consists in the endurance of the monarch and Prussia after the three Silesian wars and in his abiding and heroic devotion to his paternalistic duty to his people, even when this duty requires his personal sacrifice or brings misfortune to family and friends. In other words, in a version of history that sees Frederick and his family in terms of the telos of Prussian ascendance and national unification, their sacrifice of personal happiness and freedom for the greater good of Prussia can be seen as a happy one. In the 1850s, when Mühlbach wrote the novels, the greater good of Prussia was becoming ever more associated in the minds of nationalists with the greater good of an imagined German nation. This was a nation that would merit sacrifice on the part of all Germans and not just the royals—this was the happy ending that nationalists yearned for and finally seemed to achieve in 1871.

The Great Elector and the Achievement of a Happy Ending

If the three Frederick novels end on a melancholy note, with the happy ending sublimated in the preservation of the nation and the monarch, Mühlbach's double-decker about the Great Elector, Frederick William, who commenced his rule exactly one hundred years before Frederick the Great, exploits historical material to return to romance and a happy ending that functions somewhat like that of the novel of remarriage but with strongly patriotic implications. *The Youth of the Great Elector* commences around 1638 in the midst of the Thirty Years' War, a war that nineteenth-century nationalists regarded, like the Silesian wars of the Frederick novels, as a kind of civil war. The second part, *The Reign of the Great Elector,* concludes approximately fourteen years later. In this period of his reign, the elector of Brandenburg is still seeking to consolidate his power and to unify the disparate territories under his rule.

Written just over ten years after the Frederick novels, this two-part account of the Great Elector is much less episodic in structure. The historical circumstance of the Great Elector's marriage to his Dutch cousin Louisa Henrietta of Orange, which produced the son who was to crown himself king in Prussia, enables a more felicitous combination of the trajectories of domestic fiction and the recounting of Prussian history than did Frederick's notorious resistance to his marriage to Elizabeth. The text also intertwines a fictional subplot—the story of the painter Gabriel Nietzel and his Jewish wife, Rebecca—with the personal and political stories of the Hohenzollerns.

As in the Frederick novels, the royals dominate in this duology. While Mühlbach once again personalizes history, the national telos of this Prussian history becomes clearer here. Furthermore, in keeping with the historical moment in which the two novels were written, the central story of the growth into manhood and of the love match of the Great Elector is firmly tied to the forging of Prussia from a disunited set of fiefdoms—in effect, ex nihilo. The Great Elector is to have the privilege "to create [his] own state" and will owe his position thereafter to "[his] own powers."[57] As in Werner's novels, hard-fought masculine maturity here plays a central role in the making of German history.

The Youth of the Great Elector opens as Electress Elizabeth Charlotte and Elector George William, like concerned middle-class parents, worry over their disobedient son. While the narrative puts this family turmoil in a larger historical context according to which the prince-elector is being manipulated by opposing forces—agents of France, on the one hand, and, on the other, of the Holy Roman Emperor in Austria—it maintains the personal focus. As his parents fear, Frederick William is in love, and as it turns out, with the wrong woman, a cousin named Ludovicka who does not have his best interests at heart. While he is in danger of being persuaded by her to contract a hasty marriage that will estrange his parents, put his inheritance in danger, and place him under the control of France, he has the good luck to encounter yet another cousin, the child Louisa Henrietta of Orange, a "fair apparition" with "such a wondrous magic, so superhuman a loveliness, that it might have been supposed that an angel from heaven had descended" (111). Frederick William is immediately captivated, despite his love for Ludovicka. The motif of the bewitching child who stirs the heart of a young man only to become his later love interest circulates in such Werner novels as *Fata Morgana* as well.

As the text makes ever clearer, Frederick William's relationship with the alluring Ludovicka is the aberration of the unruly desire of male adolescence. When Frederick William encounters the child Louisa Henrietta a second time, this time in her dairy, where, dressed in a royal version of the national costume of Dutch peasantry, she oversees the milking of a cow, he is reminded of his duty to his country. Louisa has been taught "that the Princesses of Holland must seek their greatest renown in becoming wise and prudent housewives, and understanding farming thoroughly, in order that all the rest of the women of Holland may learn from them" (132). She "should be the first housekeeper of the Dutch people" (132–33). After this sweetly quaint expression of domestic virtue, Louisa presciently invents a device for Frederick William in a mock knighting ceremony: "Be a good man," she instructs him (134). The prince-elector is not being a good man at the moment, but Louisa, a model of duty, will put him on the right path.

In the following scene at the meeting of a secret society, a mannered allegory contrasts starkly with the solidly grounded world of animal husbandry of the previous one. In the very moment in which Ludovicka nearly entices the intoxicated prince-elector to sign a marriage contract putting him under obligation to France, he hears Louisa's voice admonishing him to be a good man. He resolves to return home to fight openly for his love instead of eloping. Ludovicka wants no part of this more difficult path. Thus Frederick William must return, lovelorn, to his father, who has become a testy old man, envious of the signs of his young son's superiority.

The internal family struggle continues, fueled by Count Schwarzenberg, who is allied with the Catholic Holy Roman Emperor. When Schwarzenberg arranges for the prince-elector to be poisoned, the latter refuses to take any medicine but milk. While his call for milk—as an antidote for poison—shows his awareness that his illness stems from an assassination attempt, in the narrative economy of the novel milk is strongly associated with Louisa Henrietta, who will become the mother of the country, and with the domestic virtues of discipline, work, and duty that are helping Frederick become a good man. Upon his recovery, he reins himself in and waits out the remaining years of his father's rule, ever the dutiful but unappreciated son.

His courting of Louisa Henrietta provides the stuff of the second novel. As the elector of Brandenburg, he must contract a state marriage because "he has a whole nation to love, and he owes it to his people to give himself a wife, the throne a successor, the princely house a family."[58]

Our second look at a now grown-up Louisa Henrietta is awash in milk as Louisa goes about her tasks tending the dairy in the Hague, proving herself a stern but fair taskmaster and a skilled and thrifty manager of the domestic economy. In portraying her as a good and sensible housewife who knows the value of money, Mühlbach exalts the future mother of the first Prussian king as a female role model for a nineteenth-century German nation, styled according to bourgeois virtues. She moreover transforms the match of Frederick William and Louisa from a state marriage into a romance. Louisa has allegedly loved her cousin since she first met him and has recently resisted a state marriage on his account. Moreover, Mühlbach's Louisa sentimentally preaches "true love" as "unselfish and self-sacrificing"; love asks "no earthly possession, yet possess[ing] what is inalienable, herself, and in herself the purest enjoyment. Every desire of her nature is concentrated in the one wish, to know the object of her devotion blessed, and for this she lives, for this she would gladly die!" (138). In its use of feminine pronouns, Smith's translation retains the grammatical gender of the German word "Liebe," making doubly clear that Louisa, in her avocation of true love, fulfills the sentimental gendered conventions of domestic fiction. Frederick William for his part falls in love with Louisa, believing that in her he has "found a mother for my people, a wife for my heart" (151). What began "only as a question of policy had now become . . . an affair of the heart" (196). At their wedding he confirms the felicitous combination of duty and desire, averring that this hour "gives to my heart a wife, to my people a noble Sovereign!" (200).

To reaffirm the sentimental tenor and national import of this union, Mühlbach engineers spousal estrangement by reintroducing Ludovicka, who nearly succeeds in separating the couple. When Ludovicka proves a knowledgeable connoisseur of art and music, the electress believes herself a "poor, pitiable woman" who compares badly with her sophisticated cousin (388). In a private meeting with Ludovicka, the elector confesses that "only his hand" is wedded to his wife and not his "heart and soul" (405–6). Nevertheless, he immediately succumbs to jealousy when Ludovicka convinces him that Louisa loves another.

The "remarriage" occurs on Louisa Henrietta's new farm in Brandenburg. In this domestic setting the elector catches up with his wife as she sings a pious song to be published in a book dedicated to none other than himself. In this "hallowed moment" of reconciliation between the elector and electress, much like the novels of remarriage of Marlitt, Heimburg, and others, the elector "held his beloved wife in his arms, and she leaned on him in the blissful consciousness that on his breast was her true, her inalienable home" (415); she is content that her husband has fully acknowledged her and rejected her rival. Readers have the further satisfaction in the following chapter of seeing Ludovicka sensationally unmasked as not only a political schemer but also a sexually profligate woman who has borne many children out of wedlock.

This episode leads to a general housecleaning, as it were, that seals the elector's attainment of maturity. Having conquered his passion for Ludovicka, he also banishes Burgsdorf, a retainer loyal to him in his youth in a scene that recalls Prince Hal's repudiation of Falstaff in *Henry IV, Part 2*. When Mühlbach finished the novel in 1866, German unification was not far off. The allusion to Shakespeare's Henry plays, which conclude with the glorious defeat of France by the "band of brothers," presciently anticipated the German armies that would defeat France in 1871. Mühlbach closed *The Reign of the Great Elector* with Frederick's pious wish for God's help "so that from the little Electorate of Brandenburg may spring up a mighty and united kingdom!" (426).

The sensational fictive subplot interwoven with the sentimental, allegedly historical account likewise idealizes the good wife and conjugal fidelity. In this plot the Jewish Rebecca has married a Christian, the painter Gabriel Nietzel, but promised her father never to give up her faith. The interfaith marriage is roundly condemned, but the spouses remain loyal to one another. When the nefarious Count Schwarzenberg coerces Nietzel into poisoning the prince-elector by holding Rebecca and their child, Raphael, hostage, Rebecca determines to rescue the prince-elector to redeem her husband and to avoid the stain of crime that would brand their child. She saves Frederick William's life but loses her own when Schwarzenberg strangles her.

Meanwhile, Nietzel, who expected to meet her with their son in Italy, spends years trying to find her. Realizing at last that she has been murdered, though this fact is not confirmed until Rebecca's skeleton is found in a secret chamber in the Berlin castle, Nietzel castigates himself relentlessly, gives up his son for adoption, and lives the life of a beggar, considering penury, loneliness, and suffering his due. Twists and turns in the plot lead to his condemnation as a sorcerer, a charge that he refuses to dispute, since he wishes to atone for Rebecca's death and to die so as to be reunited with his wife "who would again receive him, purified of his sin, to her love and her blessed embrace" (354). With these words, Mühlbach's idealized Jewish heroine oddly takes on aspects of the Madonna. Certainly the names of the men in her family—her husband, Gabriel, and son, Raphael—surround her with an aura of archangels. The beautiful and courageous Jewish redeemer figure Rebecca may have been influenced by the idealized healer figure Rebecca in Walter Scott's perennially popular *Ivanhoe*.

The text graphically describes Nietzel's beheading but then transforms the public execution into an apotheosis of spousal love and fidelity: Nietzel's corpse is set on fire on a pyre, and "soon nothing was to be seen but a pillar of fire rising up bright and high, from which monstrous black clouds floated up to the sky. This pillar of fire was Gabriel Nietzel's grave. And upon the clouds his beautified spirit soared upward to heaven" (354).

The University Society, the publisher of one of the later American editions of *The Youth of the Great Elector*, had a sense of the importance of the exceptional, idealized Jewish woman to the overall sentiment of the novel and reader interest in America. The frontispiece consists of a photographic reproduction of Rembrandt's *Saskia as Flora* (1634). Rembrandt is, however, not identified as the painter, and the image is relabeled "The Jewess in her Bridal Dress," thus transforming Rembrandt's fanciful depiction of the garb of the goddess of flowers and spring into an idea of exotic Jewish dress. Although Rebecca's wedding has occurred before the novel begins, it is here accorded central importance, and in placing what is to be read as a bridal image at the front of the novel, the publisher pushed the virtuous wife Rebecca and her marriage into the foreground.[59]

Americans first read Mühlbach's Great Elector novels in English more than thirty years after they were written in preunification Germany and twenty-five years after German unification. By this time Americans had decades of reading both German domestic fiction and Mühlbach's historical novels behind them. Much that in the late 1860s might have felt new and resonant with postbellum America may by the mid-1890s have seemed quaint and derivative. Indeed, when in *The Reign of the Great Elector* Frederick William finally bids the memories of Ludovicka adieu by casting away the lady's blue slipper, which he has treasured as a souvenir of their love, readers of Marlitt's *Second Wife* might have recalled the scene in which Liana scolds Raoul for the unhealthy collection of mementos from his sexual past, in particular the "faded, light-blue satin slipper" that sets a bad example to his son.[60]

The Second Wife shares additional details with Mühlbach's novel: a character named Gabriel, the wheelchair of the Hofmarschall (recalling Elector George William's wheelchair), and the anti-Catholic sentiment. Mühlbach certainly could have influenced Marlitt, for *The Second Wife* appeared in Germany a decade after the Great Elector novels. But if alert to these common features, the American public, which had enjoyed *The Second Wife* for more than twenty years, must in the case of the Great Elector novels have thought Mühlbach derivative of Marlitt. Be that as it may, the resemblances signal the propinquity of Mühlbach's historical romances to the German domestic fiction popular in America.

By spotlighting Frederick the Great and the Great Elector, their courts and their families, and by occasionally deploying such conventions of historiography as footnotes, these five novels claim proximity to history writing. Werner by contrast narrates stories of fictive characters, to whom German history matters *personally* to their identity and maturation, the discovery and expression of desire, and the founding of family. Despite these differences, Werner's and Mühlbach's novels share the reliance on affect, family conflict, and characters that play familiar gendered roles; both authors focus on male acquisition of a sense of duty, responsibility, and authority as critical to the historical process and the national story. In Mühlbach's novels, like Werner's, male maturity and authority must be negotiated within family settings, and these settings are the feminized territory of affect. Indeed, even Frederick's courtiers aver not first and foremost their obedience and subordination but their *love* for their king. Like domestic fiction, Mühlbach's novels invest in female characters, even when male historical figures stand at their center. Women figure as objects of desire, moral and social educators, mothers, sisters, temptresses, opponents, redeemers, and inspiration to men. In its focus on men and women, Muhlbach's brand of historical fiction addresses translator Mary Stuart Smith's wish for greater emphasis on women and domestic life in history writing in general: "Eliminate from the life of any one man all those actions to which he has been prompted by the desire to please the woman who stands closest to his heart," Smith admonished, "and it were indeed strange if some of the fairest achievements of his life are not lost."[61]

The Germany that nineteenth-century American readers encountered in novels by Werner and Mühlbach reflects the German liberal bourgeois self-image as it was shaped by discipline, duty, responsibility, loyalty, work, and emotion. In this national projection the actions and private feelings of individuals who assent to complementary gender roles matter to the foundation, cohesion, and future of the whole—Prussia (understood as Germany) in Mühlbach's works, united Germany in Werner's. That this Germany—the Germany of happy endings, reconciliation, acknowledgment within marriage, emotion, and gendered virtue—was imaginary hardly needs repeating, yet it was the Germany American novel readers enjoyed. The following three-chapter section examines the labor, enterprise, and critical reading of translators and publishers that for half a century ensured the availability of this feminized German imaginary in American translation.

PART THREE

Three Americanizers
Translating, Publishing, Reading

... words will be spoken when a woman's soul is stirred, and she uses her tongue, the only weapon she feels to be peculiarly her own, with freedom; then we smile, perhaps not approvingly, but pleasantly withal; for the stroke of nature hits, we feel its force, and henceforth are at home, our sympathies being touched.[1]

I F MARY AUSTIN, reflecting on the values of her social class with a jaundiced eye, thought that the "status of being cultivated was something like the traditional preciousness of women, nothing you could cash in upon," three women translators from the generation preceding hers sought to "cash in upon" their culture.[2] As opportunistic readers, they appropriated German popular literature for their own purposes and made meaning in the process. Through active intellectual engagement with this German fiction to produce an American product, they gained a degree of cultural agency and an otherwise elusive publicity. Sometimes they made money. The activity of three women translators—Ann Mary Coleman, Annis Lee Wister, and Mary Stuart Smith—and the presses that published and marketed their translations stand at the center of this final part. Each case sheds light on how, through translation, American women could fashion themselves as cultural agents, allying themselves with the book trade. As intentional "Americanizers" they undertook labor that shaped the consumption of Germany by American readers.

IN LOUISA MAY ALCOTT'S *Little Women* Josephine March writes her family of the impoverished German professor whom she eventually marries. "Now *don't* laugh at his horrid name," she admonishes, "it isn't pronounced either Bear or Beer, as people *will* say it, but something between the two, as only Germans can give it."[3] While there may now be much to criticize in Alcott's dispatching the independent Jo by means of a marriage to an older man, in the German Professor Bhaer Alcott created a clever and felicitous match within the limitations of 1860s American fiction for a strong, somewhat eccentric female character with whom "brain developed earlier than heart."[4] Although Mr. Bhaer dissuades Jo from writing sensation stories, putting her writing career temporarily in abeyance, he supports her ambition for self-cultivation and points her toward the kind of writing that eventually brings her success. When straitened finances later serve as the pretext for returning to her vocation in the sequel *Jo's Boys* (1886), Jo produces entertaining and edifying books, while also finding a happy balance between intellectual work and domesticity in her personal life: "If all literary women had such thoughtful angels for husbands," she declares, "they would live longer and write more."[5]

While imagining this German angel for the American Jo, Alcott tripped. Although she recognized that Americans could not pronounce his German name properly, she herself unwittingly misspelled it. Reinventing it as an American idea of a German surname, she transposed the symbol for a-umlaut (ae) and the "h," which in German orthography is used to signal a lengthened vowel. As a result, her professor is named Bhaer instead of Baehr, thus looking oddly foreign to those familiar with German.

Alcott's inadvertent transposition neatly figures the appropriation of German culture that concerns us in part 3: a romance of letters allied with the book trade, a story of reading, writing, and translating that profitably altered the original while retaining, even recreating, its foreign flavor. Coleman, Wister, and Smith and their publishers took up German fiction and both consciously and unconsciously generated, in the sense of Michael Werner and Michel Espagne, creative permutations or, in Darnton's formulation, made meaning.[6]

Coleman, Wister, and Smith are both representative and exceptional. All three achieved a degree of success and public recognition through their work as translators while other women translators did not. Furthermore, all three left behind substantial historical traces in addition to the books they translated that permit a more intimate look at their lives, while other women translators did not. The preservation of their letters must be attributed in part to their exceptional families of origin—to their famous fathers and brothers and each family's sense of its own importance.

The success especially of Smith and Wister, their extraordinary capacity to translate rapidly and diligently allied with the enterprise of their respective publishers, had an impact that transcended the personal and private ambition of self and family. These translators made possible not merely the entry of German popular literature by women into American culture but also its widespread enjoyment. We turn first to the less prolific Coleman, who published only five translations but nevertheless made a lasting mark on nineteenth-century American reading by translating three books that helped launch Appleton's Mühlbach series.

CHAPTER 7

Family Matters in Postbellum America

Ann Mary Crittenden Coleman (1813–91)

COLEMAN, DAUGHTER OF the Kentucky senator John J. Crittenden, belonged to an "old and distinguished family lineage," and this entitlement shaped her life and values.[1] The second child and eldest daughter, one of the children from Crittenden's first family of five, and one of nine children altogether, she was related to Thomas Jefferson on her father's side and on her mother's to Zachary Taylor, who became the twelfth president of the United States when she was thirty-five.[2] She was accustomed from her childhood on to contact with prominent figures. Among others, Jefferson Davis was a family friend. At age eleven this precocious daughter, the most gifted and favored child of a powerful patriarch, recited an original poem for the Marquis de Lafayette when he visited Frankfort, Kentucky.[3] Even as a child, she displayed the assertiveness that characterized her as an adult. At age fourteen she had the temerity to write a letter to her father criticizing the quality of the French lessons offered by the nuns at her boarding school in Bardstown, Kentucky, and reproaching him for not writing her.[4] Two of her brothers served as generals in the Civil War: Thomas Crittenden for the Union and George Crittenden for the Confederacy. Until the defeat of the Union Army of the Cumberland at Chickamauga, she could read in the Kentucky papers praise of Thomas's skill as a "chivalric" leader and of his wisdom, prudence, and gallantry in battle.[5]

Married at seventeen to Chapman Coleman (1793–1850), a prominent Louisville businessman and U.S. marshal for the district of Kentucky who was twenty years her senior, she was accustomed as daughter, sister, and wife to negotiating a place for herself in a social system that favored men, and she well knew that this system functioned via social networks and alliances supported by women. The forming of connections figured importantly in her own life, and she called on these tirelessly to promote especially her son Chapman.

Living and translating in a moment of profound upheaval and change, the energetic Coleman cherished romantic notions of history and culture as made by wise and dashing men, even as the personal circumstance of her widowhood after a twenty-year marriage and the Civil War and its many economic and social consequences pushed her into a new age in which women were beginning to acquire greater agency and public recognition and were ever less dependent on the gallantry of men of honor. Her translations served her as she renegotiated her place and influence after the Civil War; the translations of Mühlbach's Frederick novels in particular aided her in sustaining a view of history, the family, military conflict, and paternal leadership that preserved the values and emotions that had attached her to the cause of the South during the Civil War, even against her father's wishes and her own best interests.

ON SEPTEMBER 17, 1857, Senator John J. Crittenden wrote a worried letter to his forty-four-year-old daughter Ann Mary, who in 1856, six years after the death of her husband, had left Louisville for Europe with six of her seven children in order to realize a long-cherished dream.[6] Crittenden gently teased his daughter: "I am afraid we shall have to treat you on your return, as *foreigners,* & to have you *Americanised* again by subjecting you to the process of our laws of naturalisation."[7] For some time Coleman's fascination with European royalty in general and her fondness for hobnobbing in court circles in Stuttgart in particular had given the senator cause for alarm: "Let it not be said that you are a *seeker* after Princes or palaces, or that you estimate yourself the more because you are received by them," he had admonished her on February 10, 1857. "That privilege of admission is to be valued only as a recognition of your estimation & standing *at home*."[8] While in the 1850s Coleman could blithely ignore her father's sage advice to remember her American values, the 1860s would give her reason to rethink what it meant to be an American and what it meant to her personally to migrate and mediate between cultures, foreign and domestic.

After a visit to Louisville in 1860, Coleman returned to Europe for a second extended stay. A few months later, on April 14, 1861, Confederate forces fired on Fort Sumter. In July 1861 Coleman's elder son, John Crittenden Coleman (Crittenden), died in a Confederate army camp in Florida under mysterious circumstances. Senator Crittenden, who had sought to prevent the secession of the southern states and preserve the Union with the Crittenden Compromise, did not pull punches when he later wrote Coleman on the subject of her son's death and her attachment to the South on that son's account. "Why should you love the Rebellion?" he wrote to her in April 1863, two months before his death. "Your son, you answer, 'gave his life for it.' Is it not a much truer statement of the case to say that the rebellion seduced & sacraficed [sic] your son, as it did thousands of other inexperienced & thoughtless young men."[9]

Crittenden's admonition fell on deaf ears. Coleman remained a southern sympathizer loyal to the "noble cause" of the South despite her father's further chiding about her enjoyment of the privileges of living under the Union while supporting the South.[10] Upon returning from Germany in the fall of 1861 after having survived the maritime catastrophe of the famous luxury liner the *Great Eastern*, she moved to Baltimore where she frequented circles of southern sympathizers.[11] She also delivered information on behalf of the South.[12] Such actions were tantamount to treason from the perspective of the Union, but Francis Hudson Oxx, a historian of the Crittenden family, speaks of Coleman as an "unsung heroine of the war."[13] Even after the war she persisted in her sympathy for the South and determinedly petitioned the U.S. government on behalf of imprisoned Confederate soldiers.

In 1863 Coleman agonized over bringing the twenty-year-old Chapman home from Europe. If he failed to participate in the war and "quietly stayed in Europe," she thought, it might "be forever a reproach."[14] As she well knew, whichever side he chose would cause pain to the divided Coleman family. Although she claimed not to have influenced her son, Coleman had taken sides; she accepted the rebellion and the idea of two countries.[15] In May 1863 she wrote a heartrending, if melodramatic, letter to her father:

> It seems to me, if I have one son in the Southern army & the other in the Northern, my sons will have been *born in vain!* If Chapman comes home, cold & indifferent without the courage & manliness to take an earnest part in this great question, I shall be ashamed of him! If he goes into the Federal army I shall hear always a dear young voice from the grave reproaching him & me, if he goes into the southern army my heart & my hopes will follow him & his cause. I know myself in this, it cannot be otherwise! I go with my sons. Where they die, there also would I die & there would I be buried.[16]

This passage suggests a heroic and highly subjective scripting of war in general and the cause of the South in particular, one akin to the romanticized view of history in the Mühlbach novels that Coleman and her daughters and son Chapman would translate just a few years later. Coleman's vehement support of the rebel cause in this letter in painful defiance of her father and for the sake of her dead son, Crittenden, seems overwrought, given that the ne'er-do-well Crittenden had never seen combat. Although he was said to have succumbed to a fever, his death followed hard upon his involvement in an affair of honor while he was inebriated; the intervention of a cousin had prevented a duel.[17] Crittenden by no stretch of the imagination died in the service of the glorious cause of the South.

In this letter Coleman also shows herself to be, as always, highly involved in her second son Chapman's life. In his will her husband had given his wife a free hand in raising their children, and Coleman had taken charge with determination.[18] While she never convinced her father of her views of the Confederacy—he died shortly thereafter—and while she wished that Chapman would not have to go to war at all, Chapman did sign on to the Confederate cause as she clearly wished him to.

Even as she styled herself a southern sympathizer, Coleman faced pecuniary hardship now that she was back in the United States and living in wartime Baltimore. Never one to spare expense, despite her repeated protestations that she was economizing, she now found herself in dire financial straits as a result of unwise speculation in gold, the vagaries of the wartime economy, and her own liberal spending.[19] In April 1864 she wrote from Baltimore to her son-in-law Patrick Joyes, who managed her money and real estate back in Louisville, that her affairs were "desperate." Five months later she commanded him simply to send her some money.[20] In July 1865, three months after the war ended, she reported that she was having trouble paying her property taxes.[21]

At some point during these desperate years of 1864–65, Coleman must have hit upon the scheme of translating as a means of increasing her income. Translation was in some respects an obvious choice for a woman of her intellectual gifts and social standing with years of living in Europe behind her; indeed, it may have been her only option, as her social class and family circumstances prohibited her from undertaking other forms of gainful employment and as she of course was not educated to ply a trade. With translation she could work at home with the help of three of her five daughters at a semischolarly pursuit while avoiding the risk of excess publicity. The decision to identify herself as "Mrs. Chapman Coleman" in all her published translations insists on preserving her gentility, as does the decision not to identify by name her unmarried daughters who assisted her: Eugenia (1839-1916), Judith (1845-1929), and Sally Lee (1847-1903). Her beloved father, after all, had once counseled her: "There is a certain dignity & reserve that should always mark the conduct of a married lady—Just enough of it to proclaim that she is a *wife*, that she knows what is due to her & from her."[22] As I shall outline below, in the end, having once taken the step into print culture, Coleman did not show herself to be completely averse to the publicity it brought her, reconciling it rather easily with the dignity due her.

THE PUBLISHING HOUSE Appleton dated its founding to the year 1825, when Daniel Appleton settled in New York and opened a general merchandise store whose largest section was dedicated to books. The first book with an Appleton imprint—a miniature book with religious content—appeared six years later in 1831. Like many other publishers in antebellum America, Appleton became involved in the business of reprinting standard English authors early on but also published translations of German religious and scientific works. Devotional, theological, and scientific works, along with such textbooks as Noah Webster's *Elementary Spelling Book* and such reference works as Appleton's *New American Cyclopedia*, dominated Appleton's annual list. Not until the 1850s did the firm begin to publish novels for adults with regularity. The decision in the late 1860s to publish a series of novels by Luise Mühlbach marked a new direction and an enduring success for a publishing house seeking to expand its products to include more fiction for adults (as opposed to children's literature).

As Samuel C. Chew, Gerard R. Wolfe, John Tebbel, and George E. Tylutki tell the story of the Appleton Publishing House, William Worthen Appleton, the grandson of the founder, Daniel Appleton, discovered the German writer Luise Mühlbach when he came across the translation of *Joseph II and His Court* by the schoolteacher and textbook author Adelaide de Vendel Chaudron while traveling through the states of the former Confederacy in 1865.[23] Chaudron's translation had been printed in Mobile, Alabama, in May 1864 on "wretched straw paper and bound in thick covers made of brightcolored wallpaper" and copyrighted under the Confederate government.[24] According to Wolfe, Appleton republished Chaudron's translation, which was an "instant success"; "the public soon clamored for more of Mme. Mühlbach's works."[25]

In fact, Appleton did not republish Chaudron's translation until early in 1867.[26] Before that date it was available, even after the war, from the southern publisher Goetzel. By the time Appleton did bring out *Joseph II*, the press had already published translations of two of the eighteen novels that would make up its series of Mühlbach's historical novels until the late 1890s: the Colemans' *Frederick the Great and His Court* (1866) and Amory Coffin's *The Merchant of Berlin*. Over the course of the remaining months of 1867, nine additional novels appeared. Numbers 4 and 5 in this series were two additional translations by the Colemans. If any of the novels constituted an "instant success" for Appleton, leading the firm to publish still more works by Mühlbach, then, as I shall explain, it was Coleman's first translation, ungainly though some reviewers thought it was. "Instant success," however, is a bit of an exaggeration.

We do not know how Coleman came into contact with Appleton. Coleman in any case played a larger role in the inauguration of the Appleton series than has hitherto been recognized—at the very least because her *Frederick the Great and His Court* was the first of Mühlbach's novels to appear under Appleton's imprimatur. More tellingly, correspondence from Appleton to Coleman indicates that Coleman peddled the manuscript as she would later *Charlotte Ackermann*, that is, she herself selected the novel for translation hoping for financial gain.

Alone among the four previously mentioned historians of the House of Appleton, Chew vaguely alludes to the fact that "translations of some of Madame Mühlbach's novels had already been offered to other Northern publishers but had been declined," but he then glosses over what happened next and incorrectly reports that Chaudron's *Joseph II* was reprinted in 1866, adding, also incorrectly on almost all counts: "but arrangements were made for translations of all the other novels by this author—more than twenty in all. *Frederick the Great* and *The Merchant of Berlin* were soon out, and the series was completed by 1868."[27] A closer look at publication dates, reviews, and Coleman's and Appleton's correspondence reveals that this accepted account requires revision.

A letter from Daniel Appleton to Coleman, dated May 8, 1866, refers to Coleman's "Ms which has been in our hands some time," that is, *Frederick the Great and His Court,* which Appleton is now prepared to publish. Likewise, Appleton's letter mentions that "our reader speaks very well of the translation, but in these days of high prices, it is difficult to estimate the results."[28] By June 1866 Appleton had announced the forthcoming publication of the novel.[29] The time frame established by the letter and the announcement indicates that the translation, which became a densely printed 433-page book, was probably begun in the previous year, namely, 1865. Appleton stipulated the conditions for publishing the translation: "no payments [will] be made until we have been reimbursed for our investment, or in other words until we have sold enough to secure ourselves against loss."[30] Such insistence hardly bespeaks a grand plan on the part of Appleton to capitalize on a sure thing. The *Round Table* announced the publication of the novel on September 22, 1866, following it with a review a week later.[31]

The *Round Table* observed that Chaudron's *Joseph II* "is scarcely known by American readers" and asserted, furthermore, that with *Frederick the Great and His Court* "Mr. [sic] Mühlbach has written an admirable work of the [modern type of the historical novel]."[32] Privy to inside information about the publication of the Frederick novel, the reviewer added that Chaudron had almost completed a translation of the same book "but relinquished it on learning that others had essayed the task." Given the flaws of the Colemans' translation, the *Round Table* maintained, the "merits of the novel [i.e., *Frederick the Great and His Court*] deserve the publication of the suppressed translation."[33]

A letter dated December 6, 1866, from Coleman to Patrick Joyes tells a similar story. According to Coleman, Chaudron contacted Appleton about translating "Frederick and his Family" only to learn that Appleton already had the Colemans' translation in hand. Coleman wrote her son-in-law: "I think this must have put a stop to her translation. She would not have run the same risk she did with Frederick & his Court."[34] Coleman's *Berlin and Sans-Souci* appeared by February 15, 1867, and *Frederick the Great and His Family* by April 1, 1867.[35]

How could Coleman have inserted her translations ahead of Chaudron's if, as the four historians assert, Appleton had "discovered" Chaudron's first translation in the South and decided to commission an entire series of Mühlbach novels based on the merit of Chaudron's first translation? It appears more likely that Coleman had completed her first translation independently and pitched it to Appleton with impeccable timing. Coleman had not previously published translations or writings of any kind and thus had no reputation as a translator or author that could have prompted the publishing house to contact her with a commission.[36]

Unlike Appleton, Coleman had the experience of living for several years in German-speaking Europe, where it would have been easy enough for her to come across Mühlbach's popular historical novels, in particular the three novels that she and her daughters translated. These three novels had appeared with O. Janke in Berlin shortly before she and her children arrived in Europe: *Friedrich der Große und sein Hof* (1853), *Berlin und Sanssouci oder Friedrich der Große und seine Freunde* (1854), and *Friedrich der Große und seine Geschwister* (1855). *Königin Hortense*, one of the novels that Coleman's son Chapman later translated, appeared in that same decade in 1856. During her sojourn in the German territories, Coleman could also have become familiar with Adolph Menzel's woodcut illustrations, which had been produced in the 1840s for Franz Kugler's *Geschichte Friedrichs des Grossen* (1840), or have known of the Frederick cycle that Menzel was creating on large canvas in the late 1840s and 1850s. She must in any case have had ample opportunity to discover how revered Frederick was in nineteenth-century National Liberal circles and with Prussian patriots.[37] In short, she likely needed neither Chaudron nor Appleton to introduce her to Mühlbach, especially Mühlbach's Frederick novels. Her life experience, her correspondence, the review in the *Round Table*, and the long-term success of the Frederick novels provide grounds for concluding that Coleman took an active role in promoting her translation to Appleton and that her Frederick novels provided more of a direction for the series than historians of the book trade and of the House of Appleton have acknowledged.

Coleman may even have exerted influence on subsequent publication of Mühlbach's works. In 1867, after the publication of the three Frederick translations, Appleton thanked Coleman "for the remarks made in reference to the selection of her [Mühlbach's] books for publication" and pointed out that Mühlbach's works were "not all equally good." Nevertheless, the firm planned to "publish them all, and have the greater part of them translated." *Prince Eugen* was nearly ready, the letter reported.[38] Chapman Coleman's three translations, *Goethe and Schiller, Mohammed Ali and His House,* and *Queen Hortense,* did not appear until 1868, 1869, and 1870, respectively.[39] In August 1867 Coleman still had the possibility of influencing the choice of novel as well as to secure work for her son Chapman as translator. Appleton's letter suggests that she did so.

While Chaudron had selected a novel by Mühlbach that treated the history of Austria, Coleman chose three novels that formed a coherent core focusing on the life and times of Frederick the Great, historical material that was central to current developments in Europe and the self-understanding of the Prussian-led German empire that was on the horizon in the 1860s. Together the six volumes produced by the Coleman family constituted one-third of the set of eighteen (and as of 1897, twenty) volumes of Mühlbach's historical novels, whose many editions with Appleton and other publishers testify to their popularity over five decades in America. For Chapman Coleman, who in 1867 was not yet gainfully employed, translation may have served in the immediate postbellum years largely as a stopgap.[40] For his mother, Ann Mary, translation certainly was that, but it additionally became a source of pride and the stepping stone to further literary activity, public prominence, and—perhaps most important—more connections.

Coleman was not one to hide her light under a bushel. Just as she had not been shy about promoting her children, she did not hesitate to promote her translations. Considering novels about Frederick the Great worthy reading for the statesmen and generals of the United States, she sent a copy of *Frederick the Great and His Court* to President Andrew Johnson in 1866. In that same year she sent another to General Ulysses S. Grant, who assured her that he would place this volume in his library "with the acknowledgement written on the title page."[41] In 1867 Robert E. Lee became the recipient of *Berlin and Sans-Souci*, which he acknowledged with a touch of condescension by referring to her famous father and their family ties: "I feel much flattered by your kindness, and am glad to recognize as relatives the worthy descendants of the distinguished statesman of Kentucky."[42] The gifts attempted to curry favor and secure relationships. That to Grant may have marked the beginning of Coleman's lifelong friendship with him, a friendship that culminated in her vocal support of the Grant Retirement Bill in 1885, shortly before Grant's death.[43] In 1866, in the wake of the defeat of the South and the death of her famous father, this southern sympathizer and mother of a Confederate soldier needed to establish and renew relations with the Union. The contact with Grant bore fruit: in 1869, during the first year of his presidency, the Republican Grant appointed the former Confederate and Democrat Chapman Coleman attaché to the American Legation in Berlin, an appointment that secured for him a career in foreign service and made use of the German skills that his mother had forced him to acquire more than a decade earlier.[44]

The publication and commercial success of the three translations of historical fiction may also have prompted Coleman to attempt a task still largely alien to women in the early 1870s, that is, the project of writing American history. Coleman set out to assemble a biography of sorts of her prominent father based on his correspondence and public speeches. While compiling this work, she wrote to dozens of prominent statesmen soliciting their memories of Crittenden and their correspondence with him. The undertaking of the onerous task of compilation in and of itself bespeaks energy, determination, and ambition on the part of the fifty-eight-year-old Coleman. Her work did not end with the compilation, however, since her profits from this effort depended on subscriptions as well as sales. She pursued these subscriptions with persistent determination as dozens of letters held in the John Jordan Crittenden Papers at Duke University testify.

Coleman's *The Life of J. J. Crittenden* appeared in 1871 with Lippincott, containing a dedication to her grandsons that provides a sense of her values and purpose: she had undertaken the task "that this record of a noble life may inspire them to unselfish patriotism and acts of love and kindness."[45]

She could be secure in the thought that in 1871 and the restored Union her father's patriotism would be unquestioned even if she and her children had been on the wrong side of history.

"It may not seem appropriate that the life of so great and good a man as Mr. Crittenden should be written by the feeble hand of a woman," she initially apologizes, assuming a pose of modesty in her preface. Yet shortly thereafter she asserts her own importance: she in particular must write this history, and, as editor, she has been forced to make editorial decisions.[46] She moreover included a number of letters from her father that address her personally and thereby doubly inscribed herself in history as author and player. This published undertaking visibly affirms the importance of the father-daughter relationship in Coleman's intellectual development and her sense of her own place in the world. Inasmuch as her father died in 1863, at the very moment when the two were estranged on account of the Civil War, she must have felt a compulsion—both psychological and expedient—to reattach herself publicly to him. Tellingly, the title page of *The Life of John J. Crittenden* proclaims that it is "edited by his daughter, Mrs. Chapman Coleman"; the spine reads simply "edited by His Daughter." There is no mistaking their relationship (the spine of the book avoids using her legal name, which, after all, no longer matches her father's) or the filial devotion behind the project.

As translator and author, Coleman had by the early 1870s gained entry into the cultural scene in Baltimore and Washington, DC. When in 1874 the exclusive Literary Society was founded, she immediately became a member. There she further established and cultivated contacts with scholars and statesmen, including Rutherford Hayes, James Garfield, and Carl Schurz, and had the opportunity to associate with such women writers as Frances Hodgson Burnett and best-selling author E. D. E. N. Southworth. Members were required to present intellectual work in regular rotation.[47] Not surprisingly, Coleman's presentations at least occasionally consisted of new and never-to-be-published translations from the German.[48]

The biography and the translations also merited Coleman an entry in 1872 in the first edition of Mary Tardy's *The Living Female Writer of the South*, where Tardy writes of her: "She has always been ambitious of attaining to distinction and the highest degree of excellence in everything she attempted."[49] Coleman no doubt read with satisfaction Tardy's conclusion comparing her favorably with her prominent father: just as he was "one of the most distinguished men of the country," so she was "one of the most distinguished among the brilliant women of Kentucky."[50] At age fifty-nine this precocious daughter and favorite child of a Kentucky senator had at last received public acknowledgment, recognition partially enabled by the publicity and connections afforded her by translation. Nineteen years later her obituary claimed that in her "long and brilliant life" Coleman "had an influence in official circles that few men in the State have possessed."[51]

While Coleman gained recognition, she, ever lavish in her spending, remained dissatisfied with her financial situation most of her life. Her wealthy husband, Chapman Coleman, left her with substantial property, but upon his death she also confronted financial losses, as he had not conducted his business with his own death in mind and was overextended. The widowed Coleman had seven children to support, one of whom (Eugenia) remained unmarried and her lifelong financial dependent. Coleman's letters to her son-in-law Patrick Joyes indicate that much of what she was able to rescue was in the form of real estate and rental properties. While the rental properties did provide regular income, the possession of large amounts of real estate must also have meant that she was persistently cash poor compared to her net value. It is also possible, though not easily verifiable from extant correspondence, that Coleman's son-in-law tried to curb her spending by parceling out her revenues in small amounts that did not meet her perceived needs.[52] The mere fact that in 1861 Coleman booked passage home from Europe on the *Great Eastern* luxury liner, which offered only first-class seats, gives a sense of the style to which she was accustomed. Her correspondence reveals a woman who traveled frequently, sometimes staying at hotels and resorts, and who was not readily willing to forego such luxuries. Three years before her death she was still protesting that she was economizing and yet short of money. In October 1888 she insisted that she and Eugenia needed new cloaks and that they wanted other things, too.[53] Two weeks later she wrote Patrick Joyes, again insisting on the cloaks.[54] Eight months later she informed Patrick's son Morton of her need for money, making the audacious suggestion that he not wait for the first of the month to collect her rents.[55]

For a time Appleton proved a source of much-needed revenue for Coleman. Her correspondence with the publisher from August 1867 indicates that a balance of $3,761 was due her—a sizable sum at that time and generous compensation for her translation work. Nevertheless, it did not content Coleman; in November 1867 she wrote to Patrick Joyes, worrying over her finances: "in counting up their money the girls say they have not *half enough*. We must go to work & try to make some more."[56] Less than a month later, on December 3, 1867, she reported to Joyes that she and the girls expected to have two more translations ready by the end of January, one from German and one from French. They were currently translating *Mon Village* (1867), she wrote, "a series of stories all considered written by Ponson du Terrail." This project was never published as a book. As she further reported, they expected the German book—presumably she meant their translation of Otto Müller's *Charlotte Ackermann* (1854; trans. 1871)—to do well, too; she and Eugenia planned to go hunting for a publisher.[57]

By 1871 Coleman and her daughters had managed to publish two additional translations, not with Appleton but instead with Porter and Coates in Philadelphia. Porter and Coates promoted both *Fairy Tales for Little Folks,* by Sophie Feodorovna Rostopchine, Comtesse de Ségur (1799–1874), and Müller's *Charlotte Ackermann* on their respective title pages as translated "by Mrs. Chapman Coleman and Her Daughters, (The Translators of the Mühlbach Novels.)."[58] Despite the fact that Müller (1816–94) was considered a "starkes Erzähltalent" (a strong narrative talent) in Germany,[59] *Charlotte Ackermann,* based on the life of an eighteenth-century Hamburg actress who died at seventeen, did not sell in America. The Colemans' *Fairy Tales* did not prove a success, either. Ségur's moment in the United States did not arrive until the following century, when American translations of her tales multiplied.

Four years earlier, in 1867, Coleman had become infuriated upon learning from Appleton that the fee of $1,000 that she wished to charge for a new translation was double what the publisher considered market price.[60] In 1872, in a letter to her daughter Florence, she mentioned a manuscript that Eugenia was peddling to various publishers, declaring that she and the girls would rather throw it into the fire than offer it to Appleton.[61] Whatever the circumstances, the termination of relations with Appleton was not a wise move if Coleman hoped to continue to earn money from translation. Indeed, neither Coleman nor her son published further translations after 1872. As it turned out, $500 would have been a generous offer, especially compared with the honoraria Mary Stuart Smith was to receive from George Munro in the 1880s.

It is unclear what long-term financial arrangements Coleman was able to make with Appleton, who, according to Tebbel, garnered profits in the millions from her translations.[62] A letter of December 6, 1866, indicates that she presciently suspected that it would be a mistake to sell the copyright for the translations to Appleton: "The fact of Appleton wanting this Copy Right made me think it would be a good thing to hold it."[63] Appleton had seven months earlier offered her 10% of the retail price of sales once his costs were covered and alternatively the possibility of her paying cash for the stereotype plates and Appleton's paying for paper and print, allowing her 15% of the retail price of all sales.[64] This same letter indicates that she chose the former and that even as the first revenues came in, she expected more. When in August 1867 Appleton wrote her of the balance due her of $3,761.57, he also mentioned a previous offer of $150 for the copyrights of the books translated by her.[65] At this point, at least, she still held those copyrights. Twenty-seven years later, her fulsome obituary in the *Louisville Courier Journal* asserted that the Mühlbach translations netted her more than $10,000.[66] While minor mistakes in the article suggest that this figure may also be unreliable, the three novels unquestionably sold and sold and sold.

Coleman and her daughters' work yielded approximately 1,500 densely printed pages with Appleton in less than two years' time. Coleman put her name alone on the translations, subsuming the daughters' work under an implicit idea of a family cottage industry. It is impossible to know how much of this work Coleman did herself and how much of a taskmaster she was. The manuscripts of unpublished translations that she completed later, held in the Crittenden Papers at Duke University, confirm at least that she herself could and did translate. While translation proved a boon in crisis, it did not become for Coleman a lifelong occupation as it did for Wister and Smith.

Not surprisingly, given the group effort and the speed, the Colemans' translations are uneven. Contemporaries note their nonstandard use of "shall" and "will" and compare the Frederick novels unfavorably with Chaudron's Joseph translation, which they, in contrast, praise for sounding as though it had been written originally in English. One can indeed frequently hear the original German in the Colemans' sometimes awkward English. A figure in a painting in *Berlin and Sans-Souci* is, for example, the "seducing Cinnia"—*verführend*—rather than "the seductive Cinnia."[67] Throughout the trilogy Frederick will inevitably say something "smilingly" instead of simply "smiling," or a character will say it "pleadingly" instead of just "pleading" or "making a plea." In *Frederick the Great and His Court,* Queen Elizabeth of Prussia "exclaim[s] sympathizingly" instead of merely "sympathizing" and "look[s] frowningly" at another character instead of just "frowning" or "looking with a frown" at her.[68] Moreover, the scheming courtier Pöllnitz awkwardly asks in the Colemans' translation, "What do you here, Doris Ritter?"[69] In *Berlin and Sans-Souci* the courtier Pöllnitz speaks of "quick advancement, which the king, no doubt, signalized."[70] Six formative years in Germany may well have had an impact on especially Coleman's younger daughters' English, but in fact the Coleman women had no professional experience of literary translation and no one to guide them in this task.

Yet even if the Frederick translations do not always testify to skill, and even if they are inconsistent, they are fluent enough for casual readers to enjoy; sometimes they read quite well. One reviewer even praised one of the Colemans' translations as one "which in graceful ease of style, nice perception of idiomatic equivalents and smoothness of diction, it would be difficult to rival." Overlooking the fact that the translation was the result of a collaborative effort, the reviewer went on to pronounce it to possess "that rarest merit of a translation—it does not read like one."[71] Even so, Mühlbach, who turned out her lengthy volumes at an astonishing pace, was hardly the author to be read for literary style in the first place. Her appeal lay rather in the "element of *interest*" that permeated her novels.[72] The Frederick translations assuredly delivered ample interest to postbellum American readers.

Ann Mary Coleman as Reader

While it cannot be proven that Coleman herself selected the Frederick novels to translate, circumstantial evidence suggests, as we have seen, that she did and that she can therefore be considered a primary recipient of the material that she and her daughters translated for an American audience. We may be permitted therefore to speculate briefly on the affective attachment to these stories of the monarch considered to have laid the foundation for the modern Prussian state of the well-connected and socially acute Coleman, the southern-sympathizing daughter of a U.S. senator who supported the North, and the sister of both a Union and a Confederate general.

Coleman was familiar with the intimate view of historical events from within a leading family. The small betrayals, opportunistic retainers, the tensions between Frederick and his brothers, his thwarting of his sister's love for Trenck, and the blurred loyalties that come into play when German-speaking territories go to war against one another and when centuries of dynastic intermarriage assure that key players, including Frederick himself, have relatives, godparents, and godchildren on opposite sides of conflicts—Coleman knew this family landscape well.

Coleman also shared the romance with history that characterizes Mühlbach's novels, romance that turns on the charisma, honor, heroism, wisdom, and sense of duty of a paternalistic monarch. Undemocratic yet interested in individuals, Mühlbach's dramatic renditions of the enlightened monarch Frederick resonate with myths of the gallant rebel cause of the South on behalf of an emergent "civilization far superior to the one that existed in the North."[73] Coleman's dramatic letter to her father concerning her oldest son's devotion to the cause of the South expresses her shared sense of just such a superior civilization made by gallant men—in Kenneth W. Goings's bitter formulation, the sense of those who "equated themselves with the knights of medieval England," who had allegedly "lived according to their own unique and unbreakable code of honor; had administered their plantations in an enlightened and progressive manner."[74] Even if "enlightened and progressive," these southern knights—in this romantic view of history—knew when to be autocratic and how to assert their authority in the name of what they saw as "the good." The Frederick novels, with their focus on personality and their grand sense of Frederick's nobility and dash, as well as his personal suffering and sacrifice as king, bear an affinity to Coleman's understanding of her own country's recent history as revealed in her correspondence and her biography of her father.

The well-to-do Coleman had owned slaves, yet her extant letters allude only obliquely to the issue of slavery that led the southern states to secede from the Union and form the Confederacy. She accepted the rebellion and the possibility that as a result two great countries could exist simultaneously. This war, to which she claimed to have been opposed from the start, was for her a matter of personal loyalties and family connections, living according to high-minded personal principles that conveniently overlooked the slave system. She experienced it affectively, personally, and subjectively. An emotional letter to her father from May 1863 is telling. Here she avers, "it speak[s] for the South that these men [Lincoln and Butler] live"; in other words, by not assassinating Lincoln and Butler, the South proved its morality in contrast to the example of history since "there have been secret assassins formed in all ages of the world for such men." She furthermore laments the destruction and terror wrought by the North, alluding cryptically to "the freed negroes." The letter is peppered with the verbs "feel" and "think."[75]

Her biography of her father, in essence hero worship akin to Mühlbach's adulatory portraits of Frederick, likewise contains no historical analysis, consisting as it does largely of a compilation of his correspondence or letters about him from prominent men. Although Coleman supplies some background information as a frame for the letters, she sets out here not to analyze the past, to explain historical conditions or events, but to illuminate the personality and sterling character of her father, the man who was to serve as a model for her grandsons. Introducing her father's final will and testament, for example, she explains, "I give it as evidence of Mr. Crittenden's generosity and simplicity of character."[76] History as the story of individuals of the finest character, beset by the evil-doing of those around them and circumstances not of their making, upholds a cherished notion of heroism, masculine strength, personality, and personal agency, one that the unprecedented carnage of the American Civil War should have cast into doubt.[77] Mühlbach's fictionalized account of Frederick the Great burnished anew this tarnished myth of history told in terms of personality.

Whereas Marlitt's *In the Schillingscourt*, as we observed in chapter 3, appropriated American culture and history to recount a story of German nation, an American reader, positioned as was Coleman by her family, life experience, and beliefs, could, at a stage of removal, read the Frederick novels as stories reflecting familiar situations and ideas of leaders, family, and country made pleasantly strange in German dress. While reading the Frederick novels, Coleman could side in the Silesian wars with the Prussian monarch, thus enjoying the vicarious experience of for once being on the right side of history.

The third aspect that may have appealed to Coleman and readers like her is Mühlbach's portrayal of the monarch and the functioning of monarchy. While Mühlbach's Frederick shows some interest in public opinion and is heartened by the loyalty of his subjects, public opinion in the end matters little for the decisions he makes. He appears taciturn and sovereign, following his own hidden wise agenda and in the end always besting his opponents, be they Maria Theresa of Austria or schemers in his own court. How different matters were in the political reality of the United States! In the years in which the Frederick novels first appeared, Americans were laboring under the burden of the hard-fought victory of the Union, the assassination of one president in 1865, and the near impeachment of another in 1867. Two years later, in 1869, they put a general in the highest office of the land, implicitly calling for discipline and order. Americans had to wonder anew whether their hard-fought republic, for the people and by the people, would endure.

Mühlbach's novels and the Germany they created offered a countermodel of unification for Americans to ponder or at least to relish momentarily while lost in reading: unity under the will of a powerful enlightened king with the inherited right to rule, not unity by law and the will of the people. As Germany struggled toward empire under the force and charisma of the Prussian monarchy and its retainers, the United States continued the experiment of union under a constitution. Many of America's citizens, however, remained, like Coleman, fascinated with European royalty and the idea of leadership as birthright.

The fragility of the American presidency had been on the mind of the translator's father in the years before the war. Even as Senator Crittenden chided his daughter for her misplaced love of royalty, he expressed dismay that former president Pierce was then spending "so much of his time in Europe, rambling about obscurely in a manner . . . to diminish and cheapen the dignity of an Ex-President of the United States. Europeans must think that Presidents are *cheap* with us."[78] Presidents of a republic, leaders not by blood but by the will of the people, leaders who serve only temporarily, it seems, ever ran the risk of deflation in the European political economy; in Mühlbach's novels, by contrast, elected leaders would never even have the opportunity to test their mettle, for her German Frederick was always in command.

IN CHAPTER 2 of *An Old Fashioned Girl* (serialized 1869), Louisa May Alcott stages a conversation about reading that features contemporary fiction. The virtuous Polly informs her new friends that the only thing she has read since her arrival is a historical novel by Mühlbach (by 1868 sixteen Mühlbach novels had appeared in translation in America, including the three Frederick novels; the seventeenth in the series was published in 1869). Polly likes Mühlbach's novels, she explains, because "there is history in them." On the other hand, she is, unlike her flighty acquaintances, ignorant of such popular fiction as *The Phantom Bride* and George Alfred Lawrence's *Breaking a Butterfly* (1869). Mühlbach's novels, the girls concede in response to Polly's assertion of her preference, "are well enough for improving reading," but the girls do not find them exciting; for excitement, one needs Ouida or *Guy Livingston* or Edmund Hodgson Yates's novels.

Polly's friends, who preferred lighter and more sensational fare but whose parents no doubt wished them to read wholesome novels, could in 1869 have found a safe compromise in *The Old Mam'selle's Secret* and *Gold Elsie*. Wister and Smith devoted most of their labor to the domestic fiction of Marlitt and her avatars, to pleasurable reading with moral messages and happy endings realized in German regional settings, German novels of remarriage, stories of gender made and secured in the family, where femininity appears to matter deeply and where it is assiduously cultivated and validated. A review of one of Smith's translations celebrates this German fiction, implying that it, like Alcott's Polly, is delightfully just a bit old-fashioned: "there is a charm about German romances that seldom finds its way into lighter American works of fiction. They are never harsh or pronounced in their treatment of life.... It is like a glimpse of another clime to drink in the details of a quiet and restful picture, like this, in the midst of the turmoil and hurry of modern life."[79] Chapters 8 and 9 trace the Americanization of these "German romances" by Wister and Smith for American readers who longed for virtue and sentiment and did not always find their just reward in the "turmoil and hurry of modern life."

CHAPTER 8

German Fiction Clothed in "so brilliant a garb"

Annis Lee Wister (1830–1908)

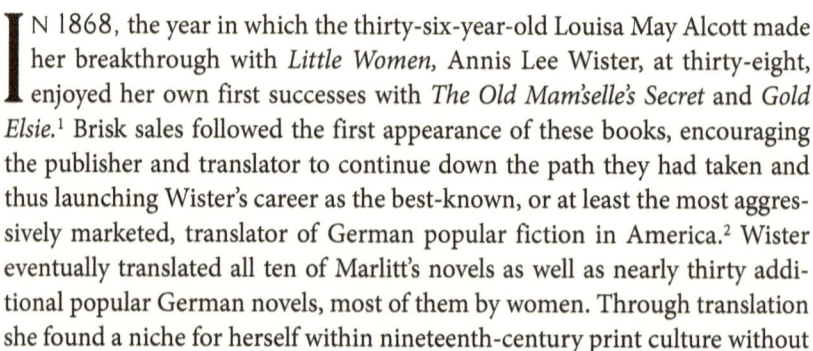

IN 1868, the year in which the thirty-six-year-old Louisa May Alcott made her breakthrough with *Little Women*, Annis Lee Wister, at thirty-eight, enjoyed her own first successes with *The Old Mam'selle's Secret* and *Gold Elsie*.[1] Brisk sales followed the first appearance of these books, encouraging the publisher and translator to continue down the path they had taken and thus launching Wister's career as the best-known, or at least the most aggressively marketed, translator of German popular fiction in America.[2] Wister eventually translated all ten of Marlitt's novels as well as nearly thirty additional popular German novels, most of them by women. Through translation she found a niche for herself within nineteenth-century print culture without excessive public exposure and without compromising her place in the social stratum of her birth and life experience.

What, then, was the shape of Wister's career? When an obituary in the *New York Times* summarized her life largely in terms of male connections, it provided only scant indication as to why her death merited notice:

> Mrs. Annis Lee Wister, widely known as a translator of German novels, died to-day at the home of Dr. Horace Howard Furness, the Shakespearean scholar, at Willingford [sic], where she had lived for several years. Mrs. Wister began writing in 1864, and in a few years her translations were being read throughout the country. In 1888 thirty volumes were published from her pen. One of her translations was "The Old Mam'selle's Secret." Mrs. Wister lived in an atmosphere of culture all her life. Her father, the Rev.

William Henry Furness, was the first pastor of the First Unitarian Church. During the agitation of the slavery question, just before the war he was known throughout the country as an abolitionist. Her husband was one of the most prominent physicians of the city and a close friend of Dr. S. Weir Mitchell. Capt. Frank Furness, the architect and Dr. Horace Howard Furness are survivors of the original family. Owen Wister is her nephew.[3]

After detailing her achievements, the reporter drifted in the obituary to her family connections and fixed on the men in the family, apparently unaware that Wister herself, not merely her husband, was a close friend of physician and novelist Silas Weir Mitchell (1829–1914). The reporter of course could not have read the gallant words of Wister's brother Horace Howard Furness (1833–1912): "[Mitchell will] reserve No. 1 for you, who, as he said to me, always write half his stories. I replied that you wrote all my work, which you do."[4] Nor presumably was he familiar with the preface to the Austrian writer Ossip Schubin's *Countess Erika's Apprenticeship*, where the author lavishes praise upon her translator as realizing her intentions and "clothing [her] ideas in so brilliant a garb."[5] While doggedly enumerating Wister's famous male relatives, the reporter lost his grip on the fact that many American novel readers could have reeled off the titles of the thirty volumes mentioned here and that the wide circulation of these books was the reason for including an obituary for Wister in the *New York Times* in the first place, not her connections to important men.

The *New York Times* had come closer to getting it right a year and a half earlier upon the publication of Wister's final translation with a notice that recalled,

> Mrs Annis Lee Wister's translations of German novels, beginning with "The Old Mam'selle's Secret" in 1864 [sic], used to be held in the highest esteem by habitual novel readers who were particular in their choice of books.... She was one of the few translators of foreign fiction in our literary history who made literary fame for herself by translating. Mrs. Wister's books were what people used to ask for in the bookshops.[6]

Yet after confessing uncertainty as to whether Wister's reputation had endured to the present day, this article too lapsed into enumerating Wister's relations to famous men.

Had Wister, however, not issued from a family of famous men, we might know her only as a dashing signature on the cover of many a German novel still found today in the obscurity of used bookstores or as a name that frequently appears online in digitized books and reprints from the nineteenth century. Her extant correspondence might, furthermore, have been discarded—in a letter to her brother she herself maintains that such correspondence ought best be destroyed[7]—had it not been directed largely to her famous brother Horace Howard Furness (and preserved in the Annenberg Rare Book Library at the University of Pennsylvania) and to Mitchell, the famous physician and author (and preserved at the College of Physicians of Philadelphia). Without her connections, Wister might never have entered the public life of print culture at all, first as the premier American translator of Marlitt and later as a de facto arbiter of American (women's) taste and mediator of German culture as she became known in the world of "light" reading for selecting the most entertaining German books to translate.

Like Alcott, who was the daughter of a utopianist and educator, Wister, as the daughter of a Unitarian abolitionist minister, grew up in a family that valued virtue as well as intellect. Her politically active and cultivated father, William Henry Furness (1802–96), whom Henry A. Pochmann identifies as belonging to the transcendentalists and among the critics and translators most "active in transmitting German authors to American readers," undoubtedly introduced her to German. As a "young girl," she had translated *Struwwelpeter*, and her father had made a present of it to one of his closest friends, that same Emerson whom Alcott adored.[8]

Despite "living in an atmosphere of culture all her life," Wister spent much of her time hovering on the edge of cultural significance and public life. As her obituary indicates, her father, her famous brothers, and her husband guaranteed her access to intellectual and social circles in Philadelphia, circles with a penchant for high culture. She, along with her wealthy sister-in-law, Kate, assisted her brother Horace Howard with his scholarly work. Her husband, Caspar, a prominent physician, belonged to the American Philosophical Society and was a fellow of the College of Physicians of Philadelphia. This company of men and a number of Philadelphia societies solemnly commemorated Caspar's passing in 1888, barely mentioning his wife.[9] Another sister-in-law, Sarah B. Wister, a well-known Philadelphia writer and crusader for social causes, was the daughter of the famous British actress Fanny Kemble, who herself was known, among other things, for her Shakespeare readings.[10] With *The Virginian*, Wister's nephew Owen fathered western fiction in 1902. These eminent connections mark the ghostly outlines of Wister's circumscribed life.

Jones Wister, a relative, remembered Annis Lee in 1921 as a "scholar and social leader and also as an untiring worker in hospitals during the Civil War."[11] His mention of her charitable activity recalls that, aside from such good works, social class and marital status virtually barred Wister from work outside the home. Translation took place at home, and yet through translation, Wister emerged from domestic obscurity and her uncompensated and unacknowledged labor on behalf of scholarly men engaged with high culture to enter the publicity of print culture and the world of sentimental, moral, and entertaining reading. And as the translator of German fiction, she became a willing and self-conscious agent of transatlantic cultural transfer.

In the years immediately following the Civil War, J. B. Lippincott strove to recoup the wartime losses of his publishing house by expanding and diversifying its products with, among other things, "gift books, deluxe editions and standard editions of favorite British authors."[12] We do not know, however, what prompted Lippincott and Wister to begin publishing and translating Marlitt in particular. The enterprising Lippincott, "the Napoleon of the book trade," appears in any case to have had his eye on the German publisher Ernst Keil and his family magazine, *Die Gartenlaube,* whose circulation had expanded rapidly beginning in 1865, at least in part because of the Marlitt serializations.[13]

In 1869, the year after the publication of *The Old Mam'selle's Secret* and *Gold Elsie,* Lippincott used Marlitt, as did Keil in Germany, to sell his own magazine. *Lippincott's Magazine* had been launched in 1868 as "a new monthly of science, literature, and education" that promised "light reading together with articles of the more thoughtful class"; like *Die Gartenlaube,* it promised to address a broad range of readers.[14] In its second year the magazine serialized two of Marlitt's shorter pieces: "Blaubart," translated by Mrs. B. Elgard as "Over Yonder," and "Die zwölf Apostel," translated as "Magdalena."[15] Wister herself, whose first Marlitt translations were selling well and whose name was becoming linked with Marlitt's, also contributed to the magazine in 1869 with a serialized translation from the German of the anonymous "Only No Love."[16] Wister's name also appeared in this volume in repeated advertisements for her first three Marlitt translations. Thus in 1869 the magazine attempted in multiple ways to fuel and capitalize on an emergent vogue of German domestic fiction in translation as American recreational reading initiated by Wister's Marlitt translations.

While Wister's first two Marlitt translations are based on Keil's book publications, some of the later ones appear either in the same year or even in the year before the respective novels were published as books in Germany. Textual evidence confirms that their serialization (and not their subsequent book publication) provided the basis for the later translations.[17] As Marlitt caught on with the American public, it became increasingly imperative for

Lippincott to bring out the translations quickly before some other publisher and some other translator claimed the territory.

From 1868 to 1891 Wister published at an astonishing rate, turning out thirty-eight of her forty-two titles. She had impressive examples of scholarly industry in her father William and her younger brother Horace Howard and no doubt herself brought considerable powers of concentration to the task. One additional life circumstance may, however, explain the long-term dedication, indeed addiction, to translating. On December 14, 1869, in the very year in which she could find on the pages of *Lippincott's Magazine* ready evidence of the success of her first three Marlitt translations, Wister lost her thirteen-year-old son, Caspar, her only biological child, "a promising boy."[18] His death notice indicates that he died of "consumption of the bowels," some form of dysentery. This untimely and painful death can only have brought his mother heart-rending grief. It is startling, therefore, that in less than a year and a half, Wister had translated and published two additional translations of full-length novels—Wilhelmine von Hillern's *Only a Girl* (announced May 7, 1870), and Julie Adeline Volckhausen's *Why Did He Not Die? or, The Child from the Ebräergang* (announced April 15, 1871)—and a collection of five fairy tales by Friedrich Wilhelm Hackländer—*Enchanted and Enchanting* (announced May 16, 1870).[19] By November 1871 the notice of the publication of a fourth translation, Marlitt's *Little Moorland Princess,* had appeared.[20] Wister then went silent for a time, only to return with three more novels published in a short period of time: Marlitt's *The Second Wife* (1874), Fanny Lewald's *Hulda; or the Deliverer* (1874), and Ernst Wichert's *The Green Gate* (1875). The publication pattern suggests translation as a welcome diversion immediately following Caspar's death only to be followed by exhaustion and, later, renewed vigor. From 1874 to 1891 Wister translated at least one novel a year (in 1885, three); in the banner years 1888 and 1889 she published four and three translations, respectively. Not until age sixty-one did she lapse into silence for sixteen years, from 1891 to 1907.

Wister's decision to wear spectacles in photographs taken of her bespeaks a wish to record her devotion to reading and study, hinting at the passionate single-mindedness necessary for her to complete so many translations at so rapid a pace (see Figure 8.1). A note from 1896 corroborates her resolute toil and devotion, characterizing her as habitually exhausting "her nervous system by intense mental application." In that same note she is prescribed the universal cure for "nervous" women of the age: "to take waters mildly alkaline & containing iron."[21] The irony of Wister's submitting herself to this nineteenth-century cure-all, the medical substitute for the improvement of women's political and social status, cannot be missed.[22] Nor can we overlook

Figure 8.1 Annis Lee Wister. From the Furness Manuscripts, Annenberg Rare Book and Manuscript Library, Van Pelt-Dietrich Library, Philadelphia.

the irony of Wister's warm friendship with Silas Weir Mitchell, the originator of the rest cure, a course of treatment that dictated that suffering women be isolated from mental activity of any kind. In a letter to Mitchell himself, written when she was abroad in Europe and ailing, Wister mournfully describes herself as "nothing but [my doctor's] puppet."[23]

Wister, however, differed from such women as Alice James and Meta Fontane, the frustrated, sick, and neglected daughters and sisters of famous men.[24] She did not simply languish in the shadow of important men; rather, she found in translation a public and creative outlet that enabled her to employ her intellectual gifts and yet retain the middle-class respectability and security conferred upon her by her prominent husband's name, her "Mrs. Wister." The status of translator spared her the anxiety of authorship and the competition of a man's world and yet brought her approbation. Endowed like her signature author, Marlitt, with an excellent voice, she refused to sing in public. Translation offered a more tolerable form of publicity, one that granted Wister the quiet gratification of circulation and recognition without requiring her physically to enter public life. In translating she could exploit and transform into a lifelong occupation the talent that she had exhibited as a girl, which had in turn been fostered in a highly educated household.

Over the decades of her translating Wister acquired fame in the world of popular reading and, among those men who knew her personally, intellectual stature. Her correspondence from the 1890s with the historian and former publisher Henry Lea (1825–1909) and Mitchell, who beginning in the 1880s tried his hand at literature, suggests that both men looked to her for intellectual exchange and affirmation, implicitly deferring to her well-established fame. A shaky hand, identifiable as Lea's, recorded her public achievement under the signature of one of her letters "Mrs. Caspar Wister / Translator & rewriter of German novels."[25] We shall return to the designation "rewriter."

Nevertheless, despite success and fame, Wister permits herself in her extant letters to express little more than ambivalence toward her translations, if she mentions them at all. In a letter to an autograph collector, she refers to her literary abilities as "so slight that I must beg you to [remove] my name from your collection."[26] Writing to a Miss Dickinson, she speaks dismissively of her books: "I am rather ashamed of them, for it seems to me that my father's daughter and my brother's sister ought to do something better." However, in that same letter, she concedes, "I become half reconciled to them when I hear such kind words as you speak to me." This time she is prepared to grant the autograph: "For my 'likeness' which you are good enough to want—there is none extant—for my autograph—it is with all my heart yours."[27] A certain pride shines through her deprecating manner here, as she disarmingly yet tellingly displaces appearance in public—her likeness—with writing—her autograph.

Wister felt that she was engaged in work less important than that of her younger brother Horace Howard, who, after all, was editing Shakespeare. The novels she translated were unlikely ever to number among the books that family friend Emerson had deemed worthy in an essay titled "The Progress of Culture" (1867). Although the *St. Louis Republic* lauded "Mrs. Wister's successful translations of the very best German authors," these novels did not have the "vital and spermatic" character that Emerson required.[28] Although read for decades, they still did not fulfill the spirit of the criterion he formulated, when he cautioned against reading popular works: "Never read any book that is not a year old."[29]

No German book that Wister translated, with the exception of Eichendorff's *Taugenichts* (*The Happy-Go-Lucky; or, Leaves from the Life of a Good for Nothing* [1888]) belongs to the present-day German canon.[30] Tellingly, in the case of this text by a male author of distinction, Wister permitted herself for once to express cautious pride in her work. Presenting a copy to Mitchell, she confessed, "I am vain enough to think that this rendering into English is the truest to the spirit of the original, which is so charming that, as you see, I do not hesitate to ask your acceptance of it in its English dress."[31]

Wister's modesty notwithstanding, some of her translations did command the attention of pundits, appearing, for example, among "the most desirable and important books" in *Hints for Home Reading* (1880), even if only on the third-ranked list of such books.[32] Wister and Lippincott were not cultivating an audience interested solely in what came to be known as highbrow or, in Emerson's terms, "spermatic"; rather, they targeted readers, largely female, who sought pleasure in fiction that also rewarded reading with moral edification and lightly served cultural and social information. As such, Wister's translations, published in affordable (but not cheap) editions, facilitated what Barbara Sicherman characterizes as "expanding access to culture that brought with it new consumers and new opportunities for self-creation."[33]

The combined efforts of translator and publisher had an impact on American popular reading that exceeded anything the modest Wister could have imagined of her "slight" literary abilities. Together they mined German print culture for entertaining and wholesome novels and transformed them into American best sellers for leisure-time reading. Its specialty in novels, strength in advertising, and eagerness to turn out new products and to recirculate old ones in new packages enabled the publishing house to encourage and profit fully from Wister's talents. Even if Wister shrank from publicity, Lippincott thrust it upon her, striving to make her name synonymous with a good read "from the German."

Marlitt's ten novels form the centerpiece of the corpus that Wister translated and Lippincott sold, marking a fortunate conjuncture of a translator's skill and energy, supply from Germany, publishing enterprise, a burgeoning industry, and reader demand. Ten novels were not, however, sufficient to keep Wister occupied and Lippincott's lists fresh over a thirty-five-year period. Having discovered Marlitt's appeal on the American market, Wister and Lippincott sought to expand the corpus of novels from the German with similar works that likewise promised to fascinate American readers.

In time Wister's imprimatur sufficed to sell any fiction she translated from the German and to guarantee it an afterlife among American readers even if only as a hanger-on in boxed sets. The *New York Times* confirmed in 1907: "We have known novel readers to make a complete list of her translations, with the intent to read them all, with anticipations of pleasure, just as they noted the titles of the various series of Trollope novels."[34] As *The Critic* asserted in 1884, "Mrs. Wister may safely be trusted not to select anything poor for translation and not to translate anything poorly."[35] Wister's selections did resemble one another, and in making these choices she helped shape American readers' perception of what German novels generally had to offer. We shall return below to these selections.

The Americanization of German Fiction

The success of this German domestic fiction in America rested not merely on its content, engaging plots, and messages, but also on the enterprise and marketing skill of the publisher. Lippincott pursued a number of strategies, touting the books not as important works of German literature that educated Americans ought to read but as American/ized products that provided access to German life and delivered a good read. How, then, did Lippincott appropriate German novels to make of them an American product calibrated to American tastes?

In the period during which Lippincott began publishing Wister's translations, the American literary world, led by, among others, the New York publisher William Henry Appleton, had begun to discuss the merits of international copyright with renewed fervor.[36] Yet up to 1891 "most works of foreign authors were ineligible for copyright protection under U.S. Law." Exceptions included foreign residents or collaborations with American citizens.[37] While legislation of 1891 recognized the principle of international law, no effective law was passed until 1909.[38] The American argument in favor of international copyright tended to center on unauthorized foreign editions of such worldwide American hits as *Uncle Tom's Cabin* (1852) or on the wish of American publishers to secure exclusive rights in America to foreign works; the idea of an obligation on the part of American publishers to compensate foreign publishers and authors for translations undertaken in America, however, remained in the background.[39]

Lippincott, for one, did not hurry to acknowledge such an obligation to the German authors whose works the firm published in translation; in 1872 *Die Gartenlaube* complained concerning *The Little Moorland Princess*, Wister's translation of Marlitt's *Haideprinzeßchen* with Lippincott, that the translation had been undertaken without the permission of the author and the publisher.[40] I have found no evidence that Lippincott ever remedied the situation, and there was certainly no legal action that the publisher Keil could take, for foreign works were considered common property in the United States. Indeed, the second general revision of the copyright code of July 8, 1870, reiterated "that copyright does *not* 'extend to prohibit' the printing, publishing, importation, or sale of works made by noncitizens."[41] *Die Gartenlaube* did not complain again in print about unauthorized translation in America, leaving the question of compensation open. Silence on the matter could mean that in the end Lippincott, as did occasionally other American publishers, voluntarily paid a token fee. Yet in the enduring absence of an international copyright law, it is equally probable that Lippincott paid the German author and publisher no compensation whatsoever for Wister's translations, although, according to *Publishers' Weekly*, by the late 1870s it was common to remunerate the foreign author if "the book prove a paying success."[42]

Lippincott, however, from the start pursued a strategy in its advertising and packaging of these books that presented them not so much as the German Marlitt's work as Wister's adaptations and thus as an *American* product. With the idea of creative American labor, the firm moved the issue of copyright to the question of protecting Wister's work and away from the rights of the original German authors. Furthermore, Lippincott apparently effectively protected its rights in America to the fruits of Wister's labor; the publishing house kept her translations in print into the new century, retaining them under the firm's label and its copyright protection. As cheap reprint editions of Marlitt and Werner, for example, proliferated under the auspices of a variety of publishers, none of these was a reprinted Wister "adaptation."

Almost from the beginning, Lippincott accorded Wister a prominence unusual for a mere translator. In 1870 *Lippincott's Magazine* listed Wister, alongside E. Marlitt, Julia Ward Howe, and Anthony Trollope, as a contributing "well-known *writer*" [my emphasis].⁴³ Altogether omitting the name of the original German author of "Only No Love," the magazine simply ran the story under Wister the translator's name. This gesture was part and parcel of Lippincott's broader strategy of displacing the German authors—even Marlitt—whom Wister translated, in favor of Wister, the American "writer." A closer look at the bindings and title pages of the books themselves makes this strategy visible.

While the spines of early editions of Wister's translations of Marlitt's novels identified the books as "From the German of E. Marlitt / Mrs. A. L. Wister" with both names in the same size print, later editions simply read "Translated by Mrs. A. L. Wister."⁴⁴ Marlitt's name had vanished from the cover, although the author is credited on the title page.⁴⁵ Similarly, in 1869 Lippincott included an advertisement on the back facing leaf of *Countess Gisela* that promoted the German author: "Recently Published. By the Author of this Volume." Three years later, however, in 1872, the firm highlighted the translator with an advertisement on the leaf facing the title page: "Popular Works after the German. By Mrs. A. L. Wister."⁴⁶

In 1879 a reviewer for *The Nation* remarked on Wister's growing fame: "Mrs. Wister's translations from the German are better known by her name than by those of their several authors, and a new translation by her is as sure of a welcome as if the merits of the original were already notorious."⁴⁷ In the absence of copyright protection against translations of the same German works by rival publishers, the prominence of Wister's name served Lippincott well as it enabled a de facto claim to the German property by virtue of superior American production. Indeed, in 1881 the *New York Times* deployed an economic metaphor to describe Wister's relationship to Marlitt's works: "Long ago Mrs. Wister laid a natural embargo on the novels of Marlitt."⁴⁸ In other words, Wister acquired the status of an adaptor with special claims on this fiction.

A year before her death, *The Dial* summarized her near-status as an author: "Mrs. Wister's translations from the German have long been recognized as contributions to English literature. Librarians and booksellers find that these romances are almost invariably called for as Mrs. Wister's books, not as E. Marlitt's or Werner's or Frau von Hillern's. This involuntary and inevitable ascription of authorship to the translator is without a parallel."⁴⁹ The notice substantiates its claim by pointing out that in the *A. L. A. Catalogue of 5000 Volumes for a Popular Library* "Mrs. Wister's name appears in its proper alphabetical place, at the head of her translations—or such of them as are included in the selected library; but no other translator is similarly honored."⁵⁰ Catalogues of public libraries likewise support this assertion of

Wister's reputation. In 1893 the state of Pennsylvania sent Wister's ten Marlitt translations to the Columbian Exposition in Chicago for the Library of the Women's Building as American book products.[51]

In 1892, after Wister had all but ceased to translate and Marlitt had been dead for five years, Lippincott offered the public a boxed set of Wister's Marlitt translations just in time for the Christmas rush. It led the advertisement with Wister's name:

> Even those (and they are legion) who have read Mrs. A. L. Wister's delightful translations through all the years of their perennial appearances have not realized what a handsome set they would make collected on the shelf, or encased in a convenient box for a Christmas-gift. For at least one portion of them this last office has now been done by the J. B. Lippincott Company, who have brought forth a new edition of the ten volumes of E. Marlitt, Englished by Mrs. Wister, in uniform binding and with abundant illustrations from the German edition. It would be hard to find, up and down the holiday counters, anything more thoroughly acceptable than such an armful of fiction to both giver and receiver, or even to the lonely buyer himself.[52]

Lippincott's repackaging of books made agreeable to the American reader by Wister's "Englishing," a process that added value to them, invited the consumer to rediscover these well-known and beloved books in an appealing new format.

Lippincott had some years earlier begun issuing a series titled "Popular Works from the German, Translated by Mrs. A. L. Wister" that included, in addition to Marlitt's novels, new editions of Wister's translations of works by E. Werner, Claire von Glümer, the Austrian writer Ossip Schubin, Wilhelmine von Hillern, W. Heimburg, and others. Data from the Public Library of Muncie, Indiana, corroborates the effectiveness of Lippincott's strategy for marketing these translations from the German under Wister's name. From November 5, 1891, to December 3, 1902, 203 borrowers at the Muncie Public Library checked out Marlitt's *The Old Mam'selle's Secret*. Numbering among the top thirty-two choices in the eclectic list of over 2,300 additional books that these borrowers read are twelve additional Wister translations. Furthermore, in the aggregate, the twenty-four Wister translations held by the library logged 2,157 transactions. These numbers rival the 2,967 transactions recorded for the forty books by Alcott in the library's holdings. Alcott was the seventh most widely circulating author in the library in that period (Marlitt—not always in Wister's translation—follows in position number ten with 1,823 transactions). Were Wister understood as an author, she would assume position eight immediately following Alcott.[53]

Lippincott tried out different bindings to embellish the set, seeking to create recognizable and distinct American products whose value surpassed their story content. One such product consists of clothbound books in duodecimo format whose embossed front covers feature Wister's signature along with a cupid perched on a flowery bough. Although the cover design is uniform, each cover is of a different color, making the individual volumes easy to spot on the shelf. Each spine displays the title, the publisher, and the designation "After the German by Mrs. A. L. Wister." Whereas Wister's name is displayed prominently on the spines and front covers, the names of the original German authors appear only on the title pages. The books are designed to ornament a home, both in size and cover. As Frank Mott remarks concerning the rise of the handy duodecimo format, buyers of cheaper books preferred "volumes they could put on their shelves" to the old quartos.[54]

Amanda A. Durff acquired eleven volumes from this series over a span of eight years (1884–92).[55] She meticulously recorded in pencil the month and year of the acquisition of each and also carefully placed inside the front cover a bookplate with her printed name and a picture of a young woman in eighteenth-century dress. As material objects these books take on a life of their own. Their covers lend them a decorative or shelf value. One can imagine them lining bookcases in Amanda's parlor or perhaps her bedroom. The meticulous care accorded them, the delicate cherishing of them, suggests that Amanda understood the objects themselves to have an inherent value.

Fifty years later *Good Housekeeping* characterized the tendency of such books to encourage their purchasers, in Janice Radway's formulation, to "invest material forms exchanged on the market with certain naturally occurring inherent properties."[56] The magazine noted that the very bindings of certain books "hint repose, the welcome quiet hour in this rushing world of ours. Moreover, books are full of suggestion. . . . They are essentially feminine, too. They hint mystery, the alluring unknown."[57] Lippincott's decision in the 1880s to clothe Wister's famous translations with hearts and flowers, the emblematic possibility of romance, anticipates *Good Housekeeping*'s notion of books as suggestive elements of interior decoration.

Even as Wister, thanks to Lippincott, began to acquire something akin to authorial status, she also acquired something akin to that of a literary critic; she became known as a critical reader on behalf of her audiences. We recall that as early as 1871 *The Nation* remarked on the "strong family likeness" among "five or six" German novels translated by Wister.[58] Subsequent translations bore out that family likeness and in the process guaranteed readers who enjoyed this kind of fiction that Wister chose novels they would like. In 1879 the *Literary World* declared that with *Castle Hohenwald* Wister "proved her eminent capacity, not as a translator only, but—rarer-gift still—as a selector. Her happy faculty of insight, like a spiritual divining-rod shows her just where and how to dig rewardfully into the mine of foreign fiction."[59] A few months later the *Literary World* repeated its belief in Wister's ability to choose good books: "We have learned to place an almost implicit confidence in the selections from German fiction presented to us by Mrs. Wister, so surely has each successive translation from her hand proved an interesting and profitable tale."[60] Seven years later a notice in *Publishers' Weekly* praised *Violetta* in a similar vein, making clear that Wister in particular understood what women wanted to read:

> It is sufficient for the lover of good novels to know that "Violetta" is translated by Mrs. A. L. Wister. Mrs. Wister selects novels for translation into the English with an educated discrimination, and in the fullness and richness of her English vocabulary has a great advantage over most other American translators of foreign stories; and long familiarity with the taste of average American womanhood enables her now to feel sure of the success of her books. They can always be relied upon for sparkling and witty illustrations of character, agreeable situations, delightful scenery, and dramatic action.[61]

Likewise, in 1879 Lippincott quoted the *New York Tribune* in advertisements for *In the Schillingscourt*, according to which "Mrs. Wister shows both admirable taste and unusual knowledge of current German literature in the novels which she selects for translation."[62] In 1890 H. C. Walsh still marveled at Wister's ability to find German literature that would appeal: "It is a wonder where Mrs. Wister finds so many clever German novels to translate, for really clever novels are rare, and the Germans furnish their quota of dull and stupid ones."[63]

Lippincott fueled—and profited from—the idea of Wister as a pundit. Nearly two decades after Wister first translated *The Old Mam'selle's Secret*, the firm continued to point out the importance of her discriminating taste. In an advertisement for *Saint Michael*, Lippincott declared in 1887: "Mrs. Wister's refined and pure taste never leads her amiss in making her selections."[64] *Godey's Lady's Book* repeated the phrase verbatim a year and a half later in its brief notice of Wister's translation of *The Owl's Nest*.[65] A review published in 1889 in *Lippincott's Magazine* agreed: "She selects her books with such admirable judgment that one is always sure of being richly repaid for the reading."[66] Having supplied the public with quality reading experiences over many years, Wister—and by implication Lippincott—could be touted simply as knowing and delivering what Americans wanted to read.

In point of fact, following the success of the first two Marlitt novels in 1868, supplying the public with "what they wanted to read," with books "full of suggestion," had presented a challenge. Marlitt wrote slowly and with long gaps between her publications; from 1869 to 1874 and 1881 to 1885 the public had to wait five and four years, respectively, for the next novel. To keep Lippincott's customers satisfied and herself occupied, Wister had to look elsewhere for equally entertaining and wholesome reading. In addition to identifying novels by other regular *Gartenlaube* contributors such as Werner, she looked to the popular *Deutsche Roman-Zeitung,* published by O. Janke, a Berlin publishing house that, like Lippincott, sought especially to profit from the publication of fiction. Here, she found six novels: *Only a Girl* (1870), *Hulda* (1874), *Margarethe* (1878), *A New Race* (1880), *From Hand to Hand* (1882), and *Violetta* (1886).

Even as she relied on promising German venues to yield fiction appealing to her American public, she tried out various authors: one novel each by E. Juncker, Claire von Glümer, E[va] Hartner (Emma von Twardowska), Wilhelmine Heimburg, Wilhelmine von Hillern, Fanny Lewald, Ursula Zöge von Manteuffel, E. Oswald (Bernhardine Schulze-Smidt), Valeska von Bethusy-Huc (a.k.a Moritz von Reichenbach), Hedwig Schobert, and two male authors, Ludwig Harder and Ludwig Ernst Wichert. Her failure to translate a second novel by any of these authors when most of them had more to offer—not even a second novel by Heimburg, who did eventually make a splash in America—suggests that Wister and Lippincott indeed brought literary discrimination, attention to reviews, and an eye to sales to bear on each subsequent selection.

None of her translations from the German found the same resonance with American readers that Marlitt did. Wister did, however, judge a few authors worthy of more than a single translation: she tried twice with Golo Raimund (Bertha Heyn Frederich), and four times each with Werner and Adolf Streckfuss, a male author. At the very end of her career in 1889 she discovered the Austrian writer Ossip Schubin (Aloisia Kirschner) whose work sold well enough in America in the 1890s to warrant translations of twelve different titles. While in Schubin's work Wister potentially identified a new set of novels to please her readers, she herself rendered only three of them, ostensibly concluding her series of translations with Schubin's *Countess Erika's Apprenticeship.* In this last work, readers were reminded again of Wister's abilities as a discriminating reader and translator. "What a rare delight it is to an author," Schubin writes in her preface, to be so admirably rendered and so perfectly understood only those can feel that have undergone the acute misery of seeing their every thought mangled, their every sentence massacred, as common translations will mangle and massacre word and thought. Therefore let every writer thank Providence, if he find an artist like Mrs. Wister willing to put herself to the trouble of following his intentions. . . . It is only natural, therefore, that, having been lucky enough to find so rare a translator, I should authorize the translation to the absolute exclusion of any other.[67]

Neither Wister nor Lippincott (with some other translator) pursued the opportunity for the future exclusive relationship intimated here. In fact, even as Wister translated the preface, she rendered words that pertained to herself as translator: "I should like to shake hands with them at parting," Schubin declares in closing her preface, "and say good-bye with the Old World saw, 'Auf Wiedersehen.'"[68]

In the end *Countess Erika's Apprenticeship* was not Wister's last word, although it appeared to be so for sixteen years. In 1907, one year before her death, she rendered one last text, Adolf Streckfuss's novella *Das einsame Haus: nach den Tagebüchern des Herrn Professor Döllnitz* (1888) as *The Lonely House; after the diaries of Herr Professor Döllnitz*. Lippincott's advertisement for this murder mystery in the *New York Times* celebrated Wister's return: "Mrs. A. L. Wister who made the names of Marlitt, Werner, and Streckfuss famous throughout America, after fifteen years has acceded to the popular demand and translated one more work—a novel by her favorite German author, Adolf Streckfuss."[69] The claim of Wister's special liking for Streckfuss is of doubtful veracity, but its purpose in an advertisement is clear. Wister's reputation as a sharp reader able to select entertaining German novels apparently endured in 1907 (or at least could be usefully recalled) and still served to sell one last book.[70]

Lippincott capitalized on the event, producing an edition with color illustrations by Charlotte Weber-Ditzler that begged to be collected. Its front cover features a house on a hill, white clouds, butterflies in the four corners of a frame, and the white outline of a dagger that telegraphs murder and mystery as Lippincott's nineteenth-century editions of Marlitt and other authors had not (see Figure 8.2). The large print and the color illustrations of some of the more sensational incidents in the novel make an appeal to a young reader or at least suggest that the book offers engrossing and undemanding reading. Below the title, the cover proclaims in large capital letters: "Translated by Mrs. A. L. Wister."

Figure 8.2 Adolf Streckfuss, *The Lonely House* (Philadelphia: J. B. Lippincott Company, 1907). Author's copy.

Thirty-nine years after her publication of *Gold Elsie* and *The Old Mam'-selle's Secret*, the seventy-seven-year-old Wister dedicated this translation, which this time she explicitly (and correctly) insisted would be her last, "to the children and grandchildren of those who so kindly welcomed the first, published a lifetime ago."[71] And as if responding to this dedication, a reviewer wrote of those who read her translation of *The Old Mam'selle's Secret* "more years ago than we are anxious to confess to." Wister had, the reviewer continued, translated "mostly masterpieces" and of course this new one was, like all the others, "charming."[72]

The word "charming" provides an important key to the status of these translations as American products. Even as Wister's translations were aggressively marketed by Lippincott under Wister's name and privately cherished by their owners over "more years than we are anxious to confess to," another transformation took place. The American reviews of Wister's translations of German novels increasingly conferred upon them the status of an American *literary* product. Laudatory reviews of Wister's translations of Marlitt noted Wister's skill in rendering the novels in an *American* idiom. A review in *Lippincott's Magazine* made the exaggerated claim that it was "impossible to detect a single Germanism in these pages," declaring, "Mrs. Wister's work is singular in the freedom and force of its English."[73] Such phrases as "attractive in style" and "force of its English" express more than praise of competency in translation; they attribute literary quality to these translations, implying that in this case something more significant than "mere" translation was occurring.[74] Some reviewers proved willing to make a still greater claim for Wister's accomplishment as a cultural mediator.

In 1888 a reviewer of *The Owl's Nest* (Wister's translation of Marlitt's *Eulenhaus*) hinted that Wister was not merely translating the tales but rewriting them, observing, "there is seldom any lack of picturesqueness in a novel which has gone through the hands of Mrs. Wister, whatever be true of the German Original."[75] Similarly, a notice from that same year in *Publishers' Weekly* regarding Wister's *Owl's Nest* underscored the notion of the translator as an adaptor: "Thus far [Wister] has steadily demonstrated the possession of that peculiar ability which understands what to translate and how to translate it."[76] Three years earlier a review of *A Penniless Girl* had explained that Wister's "secret" lay "not nearly so much in translating as adapting; gracefully putting in a light here or shadow there while the original tale has no liberty taken with it by which the author could feel aggrieved."[77] And a year before that, the *Literary World* had praised *Quicksands* as "another example of the unerring instinct with which Mrs. A. L. Wister detects the best German fiction of the day and rehabilitates it for American readers."[78]

The awkward word choice—"rehabilitates"—suggests that German fiction required American therapy. In 1891 a review of a work by another translator remarked, "That there is a large class of people who enjoy the typical German sentimental novel is amply proved by the popularity of Mrs. A. L. Wister's adaptations."[79]

While the reviews and advertisements imply that Wister rewrote the novels, she did not do so in quite the way intimated by some of her reviews. She did not alter the plots or digest the texts. Rather, quite simply, she freely (and sometimes very freely) and stylishly translated; she seized opportunities to make Marlitt's prose sparkle in English; she expressed with a single word lengthy locutions that could only sound clumsy in English or added words to make Marlitt's prose more forceful. In other words, her so-called rewriting consisted of minute work at the level of the sentence. As we saw in chapter 4 in the case of *Only a Girl*, liberties at the sentence level could matter significantly to meaning. Nevertheless, many of Wister's liberties had more to do with style; they yielded a lively, light prose that is pleasant and easy to read.

Thus, for example, at the conclusion of *The Lady with the Rubies*, Wister writes of rubies, "They must never glitter in your hair," while the original reads, "In dein Haar werden sie nie kommen" (They will never come into your hair [my translation]).[80] Where Marlitt's text proclaims, "'Dieser verderbliche Zauber muß sich meiner armen Blanka förmlich an die Fersen geheftet haben, als sie von hier wieder in die Welt hinausgegangen ist,' setzte die alte Frau mit gepreßter Stimme hinzu" (326; "This corrupting magic must have dogged my poor Blanka at every step when she left here and went out again into the world," the woman added in a tense voice [my translation]), Wister translates the sentence as "'That baleful charm must have possessed my poor Blanka, and have pursued her out into the world when she left us,' the old woman added in a low voice" (333). In the German text, "Blanka bog sich, voller Neugierde, wie es schien, aus dem Blätterrundbogen; dabei fielen zwei dicke Flechten darüber und hingen jenseits des Geländers lang herab, sodaß der Zugwind die blauen Bandschleifen an ihren Enden hin- und herwehen machte" (6; Filled with curiosity, so it appeared, Blanka leaned over from out of the curved arch of leaves; as she did so, two thick braids fell over it and hung down long on the other side of the balustrade so that the breeze caused the blue ribbons at their ends to blow back and forth [my translation]). In Wister's version, however, Blanka "leaned forward curiously, it seemed, from her leafy screen. As she did so two thick braids of hair fell far over the balustrade, so that the breeze fluttered the blue ribbons with which they were tied" (18). By taking small liberties Wister produced an English text that is at once tighter and richer.

Wister did make mistakes and also by no means avoided Germanisms—despite reviewers' exaggerated claims to the contrary. These Germanisms, intentional or not, often lend the English translation a gaiety, a pleasant touch of foreignness that can come across as an English speaker's attempt to convey Germanness rather than as a failure to render German in standard English. The American reviewers—if they were not simply mechanically reproducing received opinion about Wister—may have been reacting to this quality in their mention of the charm of the translations.

Ultimately, the making familiar of the foreign proved the key to Wister's success. Readers "learned to expect with pleasure" "German stories" when the American Wister "rehabilitated" them.[81] Praising Wister's translation of Streckfuss's *Castle Hohenwald* in 1879, *Arthur's Illustrated Home Magazine* relished Wister's ability to make the foreign palatable to American tastes: "We do not feel the oppressive atmosphere of a different country than our own, filled with institutions repugnant to our feelings. We forget that we do not see and converse with men and women of flesh and blood like ourselves, living beneath walls, and trees, and skies exactly like our own."[82]

In this regard, too, Wister's translations fit Lippincott's program. Lippincott, it appears, had a keen sense for the American reading public's appetite for Europe as long as it was presented in a digestible and not too alien form. Thus, while in *Lippincott's Magazine* Wister's sister-in-law, Sarah B. Wister, taught eager readers and would-be tourists how to visit European art museums,[83] the same magazine aggressively marketed Wister's translations. These translations offered their readers a good read in the safety of the armchair as a sentimental and much less arduous entry into German life and romance, or to put it another way: German life and romance entered the American home looking familiar.

CHAPTER 9

Germany at Twenty-Five Cents a Copy

Mary Stuart Smith (1834–1917)

"THE PLACARD 'No translations wanted,' which repels aspirants from the doorway of one of our publishing houses most noted for its success with translations, is not sufficient to convince the eager herd that translations are for the most part even harder to market than most MSS," sighed *Publishers' Weekly* in 1878,

> and the sad lady in black who calls in behalf of a friend in reduced circumstances and wishes the publisher would look at this translation of a most delightful German story is still as disappointed as ever when the not unkindly publisher, aware of the chronic subterfuge, tells her the honest truth. There are a good many of the sad ladies in black in these sad days; for writing and still more translating, will always be a last resort for the victims of hard times, and it is the general testimony that publishers have never been more flooded with MSS. than during these past seasons of general distress. The publisher's desk is no easy position for a man of kindly heart.[1]

The author thus presented a sorry picture of an industry dominated by pragmatic (though tender-hearted) male publishers and served by female occasional laborers whose wages were volatile. Still, he went on to admit, Lippincott and Wister had formed a felicitous partnership, and Wister's name had become a "valuable trade-mark," immediately stamping a work as a "marketable book."[2]

Wister had truly done well. By 1878 she had published fifteen translations and had many more ahead of her. In his own interests, Lippincott supported her work, providing a reliable outlet for it, vigorously advertising it under her name, and gaining for her recognition denied to most translators. It did not matter, moreover, if Lippincott paid her poorly—and there is no proof that he did—since unlike the "sad woman in black," she did not translate out of economic necessity to begin with.

By contrast, after the Civil War, the southerner Mary Stuart Smith, the mother of eight surviving children and wife of a professor of natural philosophy, needed money badly. As of 1878 Smith had struggled for around ten years to gain a foothold in the market for novels in translation and had yet to see one of her translations appear in book form. *At a High Price* became her first the following year. Subsequently, over twenty-one years, she published thirty translations as books with an array of publishers. Her last translation in book form appeared in 1900—this time a translation from French, namely, Alexandre Dumas's *Monsieur de Chauvelin's Will*. While she rendered some of the same novels and authors as Wister, she never gained an equally secure footing in the publishing world and seldom had the satisfaction of reading a laudatory review in a prominent print venue. Her publishers did not use her name to guarantee readers an American quality production. While Wister relied on Lippincott, Smith had to seek opportunity, peddle her manuscripts to multiple publishers, work quickly—sometimes to meet publishers' deadlines and sometimes to best competitors—and haggle over honoraria. When publishers did accept her work, she emphatically laid claim to it. Unlike the genteel Coleman and Wister, she often forewent her "Mrs.," thus cultivating a public persona that was neither visibly circumscribed nor elevated by her marital status. Eventually, she built a reputation as a translator sufficient for her to receive work "unsought."[3]

A tiny grave marker nearly sunken from sight in Philadelphia's Laurel Hill Cemetery commemorates the publicity-shy Wister. Contrasting starkly with Wister's minuscule stone, Smith's large and communicative tombstone at the University of Virginia lists among other things her work as a translator. Smith had learned to put herself forward. Although a "victim of hard times," she provided a spirited counterimage to *Publishers' Weekly*'s sad lady in black. Her energetic and obsessive translation over three decades reveals motives that, while not divorced from profit, were mixed.

BY THE CONCLUSION of the Civil War, few students remained at the University of Virginia. Faculty salaries, dependent on student tuition, had plummeted, and professors had been cast into penury.[4] In 1867 the thirty-three-year-old Smith, university wife, daughter, and granddaughter, found opportunity amid this misery and began translating Mühlbach's *Der große*

Kurfürst und seine Zeit for Appleton. Despite the demands of running a house on a university campus and tending to a large family and a professorial husband suffering from chronic dyspepsia, she determined to increase the family's income with her pen through journalism, creative writing, and translation, largely of German popular fiction by women. She had, after all, been educated at home in classical and modern foreign languages and possessed uncommon energy and intelligence. She was confident she could turn some of this learning into cash; and, although she seldom owned up to it, at bottom she knew that applying her talents to improving family finances would also expand the boundaries of domesticity for her. Twenty years later, however, she still felt compelled to justify her work: "the opposition to my being literary continues at home and often unnerves me," she wrote her son. Coupling an idea of stewardship and cultivation of talent that is to benefit her family, she continued, "I well know that results are beneficial to the family and *necessary* if I am to give an account of the talents committed to my charge."[5] If Goethe's individualistic self-cultivation resonated with her, then she doggedly submerged it in domestic altruism.

For three and a half decades Smith, described by contemporaries as "frail" and as bearing a likeness to Murillo's Madonna in Dresden "with one of [her] first children in [her] arms," was nearly always working on a translation project.[6] Now forgotten, she has nevertheless left historical traces. A stained glass window designed by her son Duncan and installed ca. 1921 in the chapel of the University of Virginia commemorates her—the sentimental Smith would no doubt be pleased by the many weddings celebrated in this nostalgic spot. Her tombstone in the university graveyard commemorates her work and familial devotion: "As daughter, sister, mother she excelled. As correspondent, author, translator, and teacher, she left no moment idle." Most important, dozens of her letters have been preserved in the fifty-five boxes of the Tucker-Harrison-Smith family papers at the University of Virginia and provide an intimate look at the life of a woman who translated for more than thirty years "interrupted as usual."[7]

Smith was born and died on the Lawn of Thomas Jefferson's university, an institution that did not admit women until 1972 but that, like many such universities, trades in its historic and historicist architecture coupling nostalgia with the purveyance of knowledge. Brown College on Monroe Hill, the residential campus opened in 1986, boasts twelve portals, named for nineteenth-century professors, as a tribute to the university's (all male) past. These portals include three named for Smith's husband, father, and grandfather—Smith, Harrison, and Tucker, respectively.[8] While the university honored its male professors and forgot their families, who also lived on the Lawn and supported university life, the American publishing industry proved porous to women's intellectual activity long before the university officially did. Smith's book publications outnumber those of her professorial husband, father, and grandfather combined. While Wister's Marlitt translations, representing the state of Pennsylvania, found a place of honor in the Women's Building at the World Exposition in Chicago in 1893, Smith, empowered by her literary activity, arrived in person, speech in hand, to represent the state of Virginia.[9]

Translation belonged to a broadly based strategy to turn a profit from her pen. Smith tried her hand at writing a cookbook, a collection of household hints, historical fiction, a Sunday school book, and book reviews. She compiled a song book, contributed to *Harper's Cook Book Encyclopaedia,* and wrote dozens of occasional pieces for newspapers and magazines including Harper's *Bazar* and Munro's *New York Fashion Bazar.*[10] Yet her translations of novels, most of them by German women, took up the greatest space on her shelf and perhaps also in her mental life. Initially, Smith characterized translation as a duty, often speaking of it with the imperative "must." "I only feel urged to exert every power and energy while I have strength for the benefit of our little family," she wrote her husband in 1871. "If I try and fail I do not feel disheartened but comforted by the consciousness of having at least made the effort."[11] But however modestly and altruistically she began, however modestly and altruistically she presented herself, her letters testify to obsession with that "slow, laboring, artistic and yet thankless task of translating."[12]

In 1887, after she had labored for two decades, she characterized translation as a "quiet[,] interesting occupation, better than teaching perverse pupils for instance," but added, "I dread the engrossment of mind."[13] Dread it she may have, for she knew the long hours and sheer determination required to complete such projects. Yet as a woman of drive and talent, she also sought out that engrossment along with its reward of honoraria and publicity.

A letter from 1896 to her son Tucker provides a picture of how determinedly she translated even as she balanced the challenges of doing so with the tasks of mothering her children and running a large household. She recalled rendering *The Great Elector:*

> You were only two years old . . . and you used to sit at the table by my side for hours holding the pen in your hand, as grave as a judge, all the while evidently believing yourself to be sharing my labors. I had to think it so sweet and smart of you. Long years afterwards, Elise too used to insist upon "translating," and when I gave her pencil and paper would look at me, in disgust, and say "But, Grandma where's the book."[14]

Literary translation was a way of life in the Smith home, an occupation pursued by the matriarch, who while doing so became uncommunicative, a sight so familiar that a young grandchild knew the objects that had to be assembled to perform the task and could not be fooled by pencil and paper alone.[15]

In 1896, still feeling compelled to justify her absorbing occupation to her husband, she continued to speak of her intellectual work as undertaken for the sake of her family. "I feel lost without regular work in which there is hope of helping the family," she wrote him. But then she admitted what it meant for her to be intellectually engaged over decades, voicing a cautious affinity to contemporary women's movements: "Spoiled you see, by the aspirations or habits of modern womanhood, I should be comforted if I had a few good, useful works to read and *review* . . . of course I do what I can to help here, but I am used to having something *besides* domestic things to attend to."[16] In expressing the wish to have something "besides domestic things to attend to," sixty-two-year-old Smith, stolid southern Methodist though she was, pushed against the doctrine of separate spheres that in her day had preached that her place was in the home. Yet, for her, "home" had always been literally on a university campus. In the Virginia system of pavilions, home was the locus of university classes for young men taught by older men; it was where students boarded. Despite the prohibitions on women's admission to the university, the interior spaces of her home itself had thus not exactly constituted a separate sphere. Smith was deeply interested in the affairs of the university and the behavior of its male students. She owed her own education in foreign languages to her father and to foreign tutors who were also university students.[17]

In the speech she delivered at the Congress of Women at the World's Columbian Exposition, a nearly sixty-year-old Smith spoke of the situation of Virginia women in generalities that illuminate her own position as an intelligent and ambitious woman in a region and of a social class that steadfastly preserved ideals of domesticity. Outlining expectations placed on women, she stressed conservatism as "an attribute peculiarly cherished in Virginia, yet more if possible by the women than by the men."[18] Virginia women, she noted,

> smile when they are asked if they favor women's rights, so live they to bless and be blessed in the sunshine of domestic happiness, that if there be a yoke upon them they are perfectly unconscious of its existence; or, can it be that the yoke is softly lined with the velvet of courtesy and mutual respect, devotion and self-sacrifice, that its pressure can never gall. Let Virginia women long rest in their happy contentment, blind to any wrongs to be righted in the nature of their own lot. (409)

Today this wish for Virginia women might seem to drip with irony, but in 1893, in the context of a patriotic speech on behalf of the speaker's home state, it did not. Yet hardly had she affirmed an unreconstructed domesticity when she veered into an account of a Virginia woman pioneer in medicine, Oriana Moon—like herself born in 1834—followed by mention of the achievements in literature of female pupils at Hollins Institute and then by a review of women's education (and the support of it) in Virginia. She also praised Virginia women's endeavors in art and literature and their labor on behalf of the state's exhibit at the fair. In its mix of insistent domesticity and interest in women's intellectual and artistic achievements, Smith's talk resonates with the ambiguity of Hillern's *Only a Girl*, which Amanda Durff, we recall, had received just two years earlier. Smith cast about for a compromise, for the coexistence of domesticity, culture, and intellectual endeavors. Yet she was not willing to own up to the fact that her intellectual work allied her with women who were pushing for concrete rights. "I cannot imagine which part of my little essay you thought favored *Woman's Rights*," she exclaimed a year and a half later to her son Tucker. "I was perfectly unconscious of giving so false an impression of my views."[19]

Nevertheless, Smith's speech had concluded in praise of the experience of attending the World Exposition and the opportunity to converse there with "women of other lands and different training," offering a greeting from Virginia to "the genial, liberal women assembled here from all parts of the world" (411). She thus declared her allegiance to women who pushed out—even against—the boundaries of domesticity, feeling the pulse of the age and yet remaining under the spell of "the fair images of the women whom her mamma and grandmamma admired in their childhood" (408). As the Virginia woman grows older, Smith told the assembled, "her highest delight is to have pictured for her the life in which these lovely, revered beings moved. As she hears their virtues extolled, her eye kindles and her bosom dilates with the desire to be just such an [sic] one as they were, and to equal them would be to attain to the acme of her ambition" (408). Smith spoke of model Virginia women and had written of them in her essay "The Women of the Revolution," but the virtuous women of yore whose lives she longed to have pictured for her pleasure and emulation also populated the German fiction she translated.

Smith came to value her work as a translator. She saw translation as an exacting art, was critical of the work of other translators, and set standards for herself.[20] If she sometimes couched translation in terms of self-abnegation and labor to earn money for her family, she elsewhere displayed personal ambition in her wish to cultivate her skills and her striving for perfection.

She recognized, too, that translation required interpretation. Often one had to "cut loose from dictionaries and just interpret from one's own inner sense of the author's meaning," she wrote her son Harry in 1887: "Sometimes I have thought and thought over a passage and the elucidation will come like an inspiration as it were—and yet thankless task! The publishers as well as public *can make* believe *anybody* can translate and make no efforts to secure the best work. Now, I *never can succeed* to please myself, and always hope to translate the *next* one perfectly."[21] "Slavish literalism" was to be avoided. The translator needed temporarily to "lose his own identity and become imbued with the very spirit and life of his original, and thus clothe his impressions in such words as are the simple and spontaneous overflow of any cultivated mind seeking expression for a clearly defined train of thought."[22]

Smith worried about her lack of "technical knowledge of English grammar" and her usage, setting high expectations for herself and others.[23] "If publishers could only be made to perceive the difference between one translation & another," she grumbled in 1890. "Do you notice the quantity of translations advertised and yet no publisher has any to give to one so especially trained for the task as poor me?"[24] While Smith's translations were not reviewed nearly so often or prominently as Wister's, when they were, they were generally deemed acceptable. A review of *At a High Price* characterized her work fairly: "The translation is good on the whole, although in some places the meaning is a trifle obscure or awkwardly expressed."[25] Smith's renderings are competent, often truer to the word of the original than Wister's, but they lack the light, playful grace and daring that characterize the latter.

When this "intelligent and highly cultivated Christian lady" naïvely and determinedly set out from Pavilion V on the Lawn at the University of Virginia to earn money for her family through translation, she was ill-prepared for the Gilded Age book trade, which was industrializing and diversifying unimpeded by international copyright.[26] She had to learn how and to whom to sell her wares and how to talk to publishers in person in New York, which in 1896 she still referred to as "the hub of Yankeedom."[27] Over time, she became better schooled in the business side of translation.

In 1882 she thanked twenty-one-year-old Harry for doing business errands for her in Berlin, reflecting, "I used to suffer severely from disappointed hope, but long training has taught me to separate the business from the personal and to care little individually while I use equal diligence to ensure publication as ever." Smith's husband objected to her using Harry as her agent—Harry had not long been in Germany and did not yet speak good German—but Smith felt justified in introducing him to business and insisted that "no great harm was done [him]."[28] As she pushed Harry to become involved in her business, she also recognized that even after years of writing and translating she was handicapped by her sex.

In 1888 she wrote Harry, who was collaborating with her on a translation of Paul Lindau's *Spitzen*, of her recent exchange with the publisher S. S. McClure:

> I think I must enclose my portion ready of "Spitzen" or "Lace" in spite of your objections, for as you started the prospect with him, he would prefer doing business with you I am sure, and you see there's no prestige attached to me, as you flatteringly thought for although I spoke of you as my son he addressed me as *Miss*. Men can get better attention and terms too than women.[29]

Still, in 1890, when she sought to penetrate the schoolbook market with her historical novella *Lang Syne,* she proved a determined businesswoman, doggedly collecting endorsements from school superintendents nationwide.

Smith mainly worked with the aggressive publishers of cheap books for a mass reading public, the presses thought to be ruining the book trade with their shoddy products. When she published with the reputable, higher-end publisher Appleton, she had bad luck: although she was paid, the press misplaced her manuscript, which did not resurface until decades later. Whereas Wister's translations for Lippincott cost $1.50 a book, most of Smith's cost twenty-five cents or less and were thus available to a new class of reader.[30] In 1877 *Publishers' Weekly* supposed that these readers were "largely the *clientele* of the weekly story-papers" who by means of these cheap editions were being led into a "higher class of reading."[31]

From 1865 to 1919 new publishers entered the book trade who, like the publishers of magazines, had a sense for what the public enjoyed.[32] Smith's work appears with many of these new publishing houses in series that promise to fill leisure hours with pleasurable reading at affordable prices. While such series served clergymen who opposed the reading of novels as targets of disapprobation, their somewhat tarnished reputation owed perhaps more to the opposition of other publishers whose profits they diminished. In fact, their lists of authors overlap significantly with those published by more reputable presses.[33] Munro's much-pilloried Seaside Series, for example, included Austen, Carlyle, Cervantes, Cooper, Dickens, Hardy, Scott, de Staël, and Turgenev, alongside now-forgotten authors who were also published by, among others, Lippincott.

Of the entrepreneurs prepared to publish not merely reprints but also new translations as cheap books, Munro proved the most significant to Smith.

As she conceded, Munro, however niggardly, was "the only one to give [her] steady employment."[34] Of fifty German titles in the pocket edition of the Seaside Library, thirteen can with certainty be attributed to Smith.[35]

Munro founded his Seaside Library in May 1877 with the publication of Ellen Wood's *East Lynne*. The series, at first printed as quartos with two or three columns to the page, expanded at breakneck pace over the next decade; David Dzwonkoski describes the volumes as appearing "almost daily."[36] The titles in the series eventually numbered in the thousands, and on average, sales for each amounted to ten thousand copies, initially available at ten or fifteen cents apiece.

Later editions in the so-called pocket library were sized down to the handy twelvemo format. Their cover design reiterates the purpose of a "seaside library." The cover of *Gold Elsie* (1887), translated by Smith and her son nineteen years after Wister had first translated the book for Lippincott, resembles an upended crocodile suitcase bound with two buckled leather straps. Recalling a luggage tag, the label "Seaside Library. Pocket Edition" is slipped under one strap. A postcard with an image of a couple seated on a rocky shore with a lighthouse and sailboats in the distance is tucked under the other strap, evoking the vacation at the shore where, of course, the book owner would read the novel (see Figure 9.1).

While pirated editions—although Munro would have disputed the label—of English books remained most desirable for inclusion in the Seaside Library since they required only the cost of printing, there were already many editions of these same English books on the American market. Translations from the German and from other foreign languages, especially French, enlivened the list. In the specific case of books originally written in German, Munro occasionally reprinted British translations of German women's fiction, for example, *Raymond's Atonement*, Christina Tyrrell's translation of Werner's *Gebannt und erlöst*. However, the firm also calculated that the expanded variety and quantity of books offered by new American translations of popular German novels warranted paying a small translator's fee, thus providing one Mary Stuart Smith a dubious lifeline. The absence of international copyright was critical to the enterprise. In 1893 Munro's enterprise collapsed for multiple reasons: the panic and depression of 1893, the glutted market, poor management, and the passage of the international copyright law.

To make a profit, Munro and publishers like him kept costs down and cut corners where possible. As a translator, Smith keenly felt this economy. In letter after letter she complained about her honoraria.[37] Yet even as she became more assertive in asking for more money and tried mostly in vain to place her translations with better-paying publishers, she effectively resigned herself to

Figure 9.1 E. Marlitt, *Gold Elsie* (New York: Munro, 1887). Copy held by Rare Books and Manuscripts in The Ohio State University Libraries.

the conditions of the cheap book trade. The poor remuneration did not stop her from undertaking the next translation or from returning to Munro in the hopes that he would continue to be interested in new translated fiction to grow his Seaside Library. Nor did the incommensurate financial returns stop her in 1887 from encouraging her son, who was trying to establish himself as a lawyer in Kansas City, Missouri, to join her in the poorly paid enterprise.[38]

In her letters Smith presented herself as a pragmatist who earned money through translation, yet she repeatedly undermined this rationalization by complaining that her labor was poorly paid. "There is little money in literature, our humble unappreciated brand of translation especially," she wrote Harry, but then she justified working for paltry honoraria by outlining what even this little money could buy and claiming that intellectual labor translated into good works: "I always rate [translation work] by what the money accomplishes. Now our $15 will support Eliza's school at Kading 3 months."[39]

While Appleton paid Mrs. Chapman Coleman more than $3,000 in the late 1860s for her translations of Mühlbach, and Smith $600 for her translation in two volumes of *The Great Elector and His Times,* in the 1880s and 1890s Munro offered, by comparison, a mere pittance—$75 to $100.[40] Smith believed that original popular work written in English unjustly fared far better. In 1891, she fumed, "The N.Y. Ledger pays Mrs. Amelia Barr $25,000 for a novel & offers me as representative of W. Heimburg a better novelist $100. Too great a contrast is it not? They certainly should be ashamed."[41] Smith, who deemed translation a "high art," knew that sums of $75 to $100 did not honor the effort and artistry involved. Yet she translated on, continuing to defend translation as profitable.[42]

"I entirely agree with you," she wrote her son Tucker rather disingenuously; "it is ill-advised in me to allow myself to be so engrossed by the rather slavish art of translation. But you see there alone I find certain & tolerably remunerative employment. I *always* have some special task to accomplish."[43] Besides, "tolerably remunerative" did apply somewhat better to her current project—*The Pearl* for New York International News—for which she was to be paid $200, by comparison with $100 three years earlier for a Heimburg novel.[44] Earnings, small though they were, went for extras that made life more tolerable and supported her values—trips, sojourns at Chautauqua, help for her children, her church, the mission school in China honoring her deceased daughter. Her honoraria gave her greater freedom, keeping her from having to ask her penurious husband for money to do what she deemed vital. She planned to save the fee earned for *The Pearl* for a trip to California.

Her handwritten account of Harry's life testifies yet again to her conviction that her translation schemes turned the family's learnedness into cash.

She insists here that her son "used to accept gratefully this ill-paid tedious work [translation], saying he could not have paid his board without that aid."[45] Smith had felt justified in encouraging the impecunious Harry to translate. When in February 1887 she proposed collaboration, she pointed to translation as a source of extra income and a way of "looking busy" while he was waiting for work in his chosen profession of law: "You could get through your part in a month," she cajoled, "and thus look busy and pay your board by present work, while waiting for briefs."[46] One wonders whether Coleman offered her son, Chapman, similar advice about translating while he waited for gainful employment after the Civil War.

After Smith had experienced a boom in translation work only to have it fall off to next to nothing in the late 1890s, her ability to rationalize translation as profitable finally wore thin. She confessed to her son Tucker, who had advised her to cease translating: "It is well to be saved from one's self. I have sacrificed too much of my life to translation."[47] Her belated insight suggests that for all her rationalization, her persistent translating over decades had as much to do with the addictive challenge it presented as it did her earnings. As we shall see below, especially her correspondence with Harry reveals how wedded she became to this exacting, all-absorbing intellectual work.

Among complaints about the miserly honoraria for translation, there is only scant mention of the rights of the original authors. Her correspondence confirms that she established contact with two German novelists—Werner and Paul Lindau—and implies that both received compensation.[48] In February 1878 Smith mentioned her attempt to secure permission from Werner to "act for her."[49] While it is not clear in what capacity Smith could and would act, she does appear to have acquired some kind of consent from Werner through her publisher, Ernst Keil. Eight months after she had complained about a delay in receiving installments of *Die Gartenlaube* containing Werner's novel *Um hohen Preis*, she received an apologetic letter from Keil. Through Keil, Werner agreed as compensation to accept only a third of the "usual honorarium" ("des bisher üblichen Honorars") for her novel and gave Smith the right to include on the title page the designation "with permission of the authoress" ("Mit Genehmigung der Verfasserin").[50] A year later, the title page of *At a High Price* boasted that it was an "author's edition."[51] Likewise, when Smith's next published Werner translation, *What the Spring Brought*, appeared with Munro three years later in 1881, the title proclaimed "Translated with the author's permission by Mary Stuart Smith."[52] Two years later Smith was, however, dismayed to discover that a new serialized novel by Werner, *Der Egoist*, had already appeared as a book in Germany and in translation in England as *Partners* (both in 1882). She had written to Keil and

Werner, she told Harry, but thought that there was little hope "in securing its translation."⁵³ In 1885 Munro reprinted *Partners*, the British translation.

When Harry visited Werner in Leipzig in 1883, Smith averred that her only thought in urging him to do so was to give him the chance "to see a German literary woman, and maybe through her get access to literary society and see something of that phase of German life, than with any view to furthering my own schemes."⁵⁴ Six months later she assumed that she had, via her son's visit and her translations, secured a personal relationship with Werner and was emboldened to ask Harry to solicit help for his sister Lelia, an aspiring painter: "I have no doubt but that a lady like Miss Buerstenbinder [=Werner] might know of suitable quarters and would take an interest in helping Lelia if you would tell her of her work and plans. Literary & artistic people are apt to associate together," she conjectured, "and a sensible elderly woman like her would understand readily the needs of the situation. As a German she would like foreigners to form an agreeable impression of her home and your official position would assure her of its being right to befriend you."⁵⁵ While Smith translated Werner's novels throughout the 1880s, there is no further mention in her correspondence of contact with Werner or of an agreement or honorarium. Indeed, she disparagingly refers to Munro's publication of their translation of *St. Michael* as deemed by the world a "piratical undertaking," blaming Munro, however, and not herself.⁵⁶

Smith and Harry also made contact with Paul Lindau when they determined to translate *Spitzen* in 1888. Smith informed Harry in April that she had written to the "StaatZeitung [sic] for the first numbers of *Spitzen*."⁵⁷ By May she had procured advanced sheets from Lindau himself and, on Harry's advice, had secured his permission for the translation.⁵⁸ A year later, however, after the translation had appeared with Appleton, Smith suspected that Lindau was not happy with his honorarium since he had not written: "If he is affronted at getting so little I wonder how he thinks we feel."⁵⁹ Their tenuous relationship with him having deteriorated, Smith dismissed him "as not worth regarding more than an old stick" and suggested that they go ahead with their plans for a new translation of one of his works regardless of what he said: "He cannot retract his word, so let us use him, if he pleases, and pay his share, when he asks for it politely."⁶⁰ The agreements Smith had with Werner and Lindau were not contractually binding, and Smith honored them as suited her purposes. Until 1891 the United States' failure to sign on to international copyright supported her actions.⁶¹

In December 1890, when "the bill of International Copyright [was] threatening to pass," Smith and Harry worried over its impact on their work. As a lawyer Harry presumably understood better than his mother how it might impede their ability to translate contemporary authors. Smith continued to believe that merely forming a personal relationship with the authors to act as their agent in America would guarantee access to their works: "Why mourn over passage of International Copyright law?" she chided Harry. "It is the very thing for us, with two popular authors committed to us viz E. Werner & Lindau. The latter cannot eat his own words and his written permit is all we want, and he ought to be too thankful to have such respectable proxies if he did but know it."[62] The implied exclusive commitment of Werner guaranteeing Smith rights to her works—apparently based on informal agreements from the early 1880s and possibly only on the above-cited nonbinding letter from Keil—seems farfetched since two weeks previously Smith admitted to having lost Werner's address and since other translators had rendered Werner's works during the ten years following the publication of *What the Spring Brought*.[63] In any event, when Smith's *Clear the Track* (Werner's *Freie Bahn*) appeared in 1893 with the Federal Book Company after the passage of international copyright, that is, in the first full year in which international copyright went into effect, "Ernst Keil's Nachfolger," Werner's German publisher, was designated as the holder of the copyright of the translation.

Year after year Smith combed *Die Gartenlaube* for appropriate literature. She knew that she was not alone in mining the magazine for entertaining and wholesome fiction to translate, lamenting, for example, in 1890 the dearth of appropriate novels: "all in *Die Gartenlaube* are snapped up so soon & I know of no novel myself to which I incline."[64] Like Wister, she translated Marlitt, but she fastened in particular on Werner, in the end translating at least nine of her novels for book publication. If Munro had followed Lippincott's marketing strategies and had taken notice of the number of Werner translations Smith had completed for the Seaside Library, the publishing house might have featured Smith as "the translator of popular novels from the German by E. Werner." Instead her work was submerged in eclectic international lists of popular and classic literature and never advertised under her name.[65]

In 1887 Smith began a five-year collaboration with Harry that commenced with *Gold Elsie* (1887) and closed with Auerbach's *Villa on the Rhine* (1892). When their collaboration began, Smith had established at least a small beachhead as a translator and occasional writer, having published at least seven titles with Munro: six translations and her own *Art of Housekeeping*. In the case of their first collaboration, *Gold Elsie*, Smith happily wrote Harry, for once she did not have to "hawk about" a manuscript.[66] In February 1887 Munro had contacted her about a new translation of *Goldelse* for the "pitiful sum" of $75. She in turn called upon Harry, pointing out that he was "used to study" and that the task would interest him: "working 2 hours a day, she calculated, "you could get through your part in a month."[67] A few months later, Munro also asked Smith for a translation of *St. Michael*, this time promising her $100.[68]

Six of the translations that emerged from that five-year collaboration credit Harry, including *Gold Elsie*, in which case Harry is identified only by the designation "and son"—perhaps in imitation of "Mrs. Coleman and her daughters"—*Bride of the Nile* (1887); *The Owl-House* (1888); *Fairy of the Alps* (1889); and *A Judgment of God* (1889). The sixth of these translations, *Beacon Lights*, completed in 1891, did not appear until 1899, seven years after Harry's death. Smith's correspondence indicates that the two collaborated on several additional published translations of German fiction, including the above-mentioned *Villa on the Rhine*, *St. Michael* (1888), and Paul Lindau's *Lace* (1889).[69] Appleton did not credit either of them for *Lace*, but their letters reveal that the work is theirs; moreover, the copy held by the University of Virginia contains a handwritten notation under the author's name on the title page: "Translated by MS & G. H. Smith."[70] When *St. Michael* appeared without Harry's name, Smith wrote him an apologetic letter offering to put his name alone on *The Owl-House* "to make things square."[71] She did not follow through, perhaps upon Harry's demurral; *Owl-House* is attributed to them both. Harry died unexpectedly in February 1892, yet the failure to acknowledge his work on *Villa*, which appeared later that year, is peculiar in view of Smith's scrupulousness. We will return to this omission below.

The five years of collaboration were filled with translation projects, some of which never reached book publication. Smith's letters tell of futile attempts to place their "Lore von Tollen," implying that someone scooped them with Munro—Munro published an unattributed *Lenore von Tollen* in 1890.[72] They indicate as well that mother and son worked on Lindau's *Im Fieber* and possibly also on Heimburg's story "Unser Männe," which Smith suggested they translate as "Our Brownie."[73] The manic Smith also mentions other possible projects: Ida Boy-Ed's *Nicht im Geleise* ("Off the Track," which the Smiths could have found in the Deutsche Library, volume 224), Friedrich Adami's biography of Queen Luise, Hermann Jahnke's book on Bismarck, and juvenile books.[74]

Letters that emanated from this busy collaboration of mother and son offer insight into Smith's feelings about her activity as a translator. In Harry as collaborator, she had at last found someone with whom she could speak at length about this addictive work, and she wrote him with unparalleled intensity. She wished he were in Charlottesville with her, declaring that it would be "delightful . . . if we were near enough to hold consultations over our work and read our versions aloud to one another."[75] A few months later she sketched out the pleasures of a lengthy summer visit: "You and I could translate so nicely side by side about 3 hours a day, which used to work as you are, would only make your vacation more pleasant."[76]

Smith generally played a domineering role in Harry's life. There are hints that the sensitive son was smothered by his mother's predilections on many fronts. The year before their collaboration began she expressed at length her strong reservations about a young woman whom Harry wanted to marry.[77] No marriage took place. Four years later, in 1890, she instructed him to stop smoking in his current state of depression, also warning him that his depression likely came from overwork. He must beware, for "Satan takes advantages of such a condition of things to make his fiercest assaults."[78]

While Smith was ready to curtail Harry's professional work for the sake of his moral and spiritual well-being, she pushed him hard to translate, even when she knew that he found translation tedious. She hoped that once he got started, he would "find entertainment in it."[79] She cajoled him with the intellectual benefits of translation: "The practice of translating will certainly aid you in forming a good style of composition, and in acquiring facility in expressing your ideas."[80] When his pace did not suit her, she admonished him to work harder and faster. "So put on steam, my boy," she urged when they were working on *Gold Elsie*.[81] A month earlier she herself had excitedly turned over the running of the household to her daughter Mary "to clear the track for translating" with him.[82]

With Harry as collaborator Smith could strive toward the perfection she sought, discussing word choice and difficult passages. Their uncertainty about a line in Marlitt's *Goldelse* is telling of the challenge they faced as non-native speakers dependent on dictionaries. The original line reads "'Der Flederwisch hat uns noch gefehlt,' meinte er ärgerlich" ("This flibbertigibbet is all we need," he grumbled) and pertains to the unwelcome presence of an annoying but harmless young lady whose head is full of frivolous plans for a birthday celebration. The problematic word is "Flederwisch," which can mean feather duster (made of a goosewing, as Smith correctly notes) or used metaphorically. "About the meaning of Der Flederwisch etc.," Smith began in a letter to Harry, "it evidently means to show contempt for the newly arrived lady, as you observe the listeners both laughed. I find the meaning to be 'Goosewing used instead of a whisk for dusting'—Could it be?—'The duster has missed us again?' . . . I do not think this would have much sense for us Americans, though."[83] Smith's suggestion fortunately did not prevail. In 1868 Wister had rendered the line with feeling for the spirit of the German: "'That scatter-brain completes our misery,' he said with vexation."[84] The Smiths settled on "'The vixen is there!' he said, evincing his displeasure."[85]

Their rendering misses the eye-rolling humorous exasperation of the German expression "Das fehlte noch" (that's all we needed).

Although concerned with accuracy, Smith also did not hesitate to repackage her product for American readers. "I name my chapters, you do the same. It helps a novel amazingly," she instructed Harry.[86] Three years later she reminded him: "Let us always head our chapters. It quickens interest I'm convinced."[87] The original German novels have no such chapter titles, but the prescient Smith recognized that American readers were used to them and that as constituents of tables of contents they could sell books, titillate readers, and entice them to read on.

Mary Stuart Smith as Reader

Smith must have long wondered why her voluminous manuscript of *Der große Kurfürst und seine Zeit,* which she had completed in 1868 and for which she had been paid, had never been published. She herself had not forgotten it or what she saw as its potential appeal. Nearly twenty years later, in December 1887, she reminded Appleton about the manuscript. The time was ripe for its publication, she maintained, for, as she saw it, Mühlbach's historical novel addressed material that was in the news: "I wrote to Messers Appleton, reminding them of 'The Great Elector,'" she told Harry, "saying I thought the eyes of all the world being directed to the poor Crown Prince made it a peculiarly suitable time to bring it out. He replied that he saw no connection. I answered that to my mind the connection was a striking one. Prussia's First Frederick William and her last."[88]

Smith alluded here to Frederick's cancer of the larynx, which would kill him in June 1888 after he had reigned as emperor for only ninety-nine days. Although Appleton was unimpressed, Smith rightly saw that the family romance of illness corresponded to Mühlbach's brand of history writing. If the private pathos of the Hohenzollerns was newsworthy, then Smith had translated stories of Frederick's great-great-great-great-grandfather of equal pathos, and it was time to publish them: "The scene in the Old Palace at Berlin is thrilling," she wrote Harry. "I could think of nothing but the Young Elector and the Jewess who gave her life for him as I walked through those spacious halls, the first palace I had ever entered."[89] In recalling this particular episode from *The Youth of the Great Elector,* Smith thrilled to themes of love, conjugal loyalty, morality, and noble sacrifice. Her evaluation of the Great Elector novels and her thoughts about their potential appeal for American readers make visible that she, like Coleman and Wister, was also a reader, indeed an attentive reader of books by German women. Her active reading mattered in the selection and translation of German texts.

Smith had firm ideas about appropriate reading that were rooted in her Christian faith, her southern heritage, and her idealism. She liked Walter Scott's novels but was not entirely convinced by George Eliot's *Middlemarch*, which she found too long. Besides, she was unsure of "Mrs. Lewis's" piety.[90] Nowhere do her views become more explicit than in her violent reaction to the novels of Amélie Rives, an author who lived rather too close for comfort on an estate near Charlottesville and was thus a painful thorn in the proper Smith's flesh.

In April 1888 Rives's novella *The Quick or the Dead?* appeared in toto in *Lippincott's Magazine* in keeping with the magazine's year-old policy of foregoing serialization. Wister's translation of Werner's patriotic, chaste, and idealistic *Spell of Home* had appeared in February and would most certainly have met with Smith's approval. By contrast, Rives's novel describes a woman's physical longing for her dead husband and her sexual feelings for his living cousin who resembles him physically. The "quick or the dead" of the title refers to the deliberations of the protagonist as to whether she should remain a widow, true to her deceased husband, or marry his attractive cousin. The novella shocked the pious Smith, even as the American reading public rushed to buy the April issue. Smith was aghast. "Everybody *will* talk about Amélie Rives and 'The Dead or the Living,'" she wrote Harry in May 1888. Young men—presumably students at the University of Virginia—had remarked to her that Rives's writing tended "to lower the whole female sex in the eyes of men."[91]

Smith, who was collaborating with Harry on their translation of Marlitt's *Owl-House*, in which as always virtue is rewarded, asserted of Rives's fiction that there could be "no greater evil than Satan could desire a woman's pen to accomplish than this" and pronounced the author a "monster." There was surely no "other such coarse, vulgar minded woman in her state, born in her sphere of society." But in a paroxysm of southern patriotism, Smith went on to blame northern publishers for deliberately insulting the South by publishing books depicting southern women as sensual beings. She thought that Rives's novel could only be explained by her being in "the incipient stage of lunacy or an opium eater and crazed by the fulsome adulation of those cold-blooded Yankees cunningly pretending to admire her in order to send the keenest thrust yet given at the South whose greatest glory has hitherto been the virtue of her men and [*sic*] modesty and refinement of her women." Rives, "this deluded girl," Smith fumed, had disgraced herself and cast a reproach upon her country as hard to be removed as the blood from Lady MacBeth's hand. Oh the far-reaching wrong done the many generations of youth by the $1500 paid for that story (Harper $1000 for Virginia of Virginia) who can calculate, when you remember that the highest-toned Magazines in the Country endorse such writings, you know how young girls blindly follow fashions & will do whatever men admire and what will we come to? Miss Burney introduced the pure novel. Alas! if Miss Rives shall inaugurate the return to coarse vileness, profanity and even blasphemy—Let's all strive with all our might to stem the tide, and pray that this poor girl be converted & her publishers taught by money losses that the United States are a Christian people yet.[92]

The mention here of the "pure" novels of Fanny Burney suggests the reading Smith favored. While Rives's novels are frank and explicit about women's sexual feelings, Burney's courtship novel *Evelina* (1778), as Ruth Yeazell has argued, dissociates the self by rendering the modest heroine unconscious of her own desire. As Yeazell formulates it, Evelina "has internalized the prohibition against knowing her own desire—or at least against knowing it until her future husband 'speaks,' and thus speaks it for her."[93] When Evelina becomes conscious of her feelings, the narrative must labor to keep her from taking responsibility for them for the short time remaining before she marries. The novel thus supports a "taboo on woman's speaking her love."[94] In this respect Burney's novel displays an affinity with the German novels that Smith had translated so eagerly for Munro, for example, *Gold Elsie* and *The Old Mam'selle's Secret*.

Smith worried about the contents of the works she rendered and even wondered whether the translator might exercise censorship. Concerns arose especially with two male German authors whom she translated with Harry in the 1890s. Just as she believed Rives damaged the honor of the South, she felt Berthold Auerbach's *Villa on the Rhine* spread lies about the Confederacy. Initially Smith was excited by the request from the United States Book Company for a new translation of *The Villa on the Rhine*. She liked "its moral tendency," she told Harry in January 1891.[95] Five days later she was still pleased: "Auerbach is dead but a beautiful writer."[96] *Villa* was considered a "chef d'oeuvre," she noted. Thereafter she procured copies of Munro's German edition of the novel, and she and Harry began translating. By the end of the summer Smith had arrived at the final section of the novel, which consists of fictive letters, pro-Union and antislavery, written in the United States during the Civil War. Smith was outraged by the presentation of the South in them and did not want to mediate what she believed to be mendacities:

"and anybody looks over my writing after I am dead, I should bless them for expunging the sentence—and so I believe would Auerbach," she declared. "Neither you nor I can ever be poor enough to have to compromise principle. Hardy as we have worked we had better throw away the pittance promised than aid in perpetuating wrong done to our afflicted people."[97]

Auerbach's fictitious character wrote of the Confederacy having barbarously mistreated prisoners of war, but Smith insisted that she herself knew from eyewitnesses that this was not so. The original read, "Gerade die über die Grenzen der Menschlichkeit gehende Erbitterung, gerade die Rachsucht, mit der sie kämpfen und die Gefangenen behandeln sind mir Zeichen, daß sie wohl in [sic] den Sieg im Kriege glauben, aber nicht an einen Sieg in Frieden" (Precisely the bitterness, which surpasses the boundaries of humanity, precisely the spirit of revenge with which they fight and treat the prisoners are to me signs that they certainly believe in victory in war, but not in victory in peace [my translation]).[98] James Davis's authorized translation of 1874 omitted the reference to the treatment of prisoners of war, as did Charles C. Shackford's translation for Roberts Brothers (1869).[99] If Smith read either of these translations before reading the German—as the John W. Lovell Company suggested she should to save herself labor—she would have been all the more unprepared for the German original.[100] Despite Smith's dismay, the Smiths ultimately remained true to the original: "The very bitterness, which exceeds the bounds of all humanity, the very vengeance with which they fight and with which they treat their prisoners, are to me signs that they may hope to be victorious in battle but not in peace."[101]

Smith must have struggled with her conscience before giving in. In November 1891 she insisted on morality as important to the relationship and responsibility of the translator to and for the text: "As to stickling for morality being an insuperable obstacle to the translator, I do not believe it."[102] In the end she insisted on her obligation to voice what she saw as truth against the original text. A "translator's footnote" to a passage concerning Lincoln's assassination asserts that southerners were not responsible for either the murder or the practice of slavery. Instead, finding slavery "planted among them," they took the responsibility for Christianizing Africans and making of them "law-abiding men qualified for the franchise."[103]

Harry's death and Smith's outrage at the view of the South mediated in these final pages may explain the absence of Harry's name from the jointly translated book. Smith may have wished to avoid any stain on his honor by not identifying him as cotranslator of these offending passages. If so, she thereby commenced her labor to shape and preserve her son's memory, labor that would eventually culminate in a fifty-page manuscript and in the tallest grave marker on the family plot. Harry's obituary reported that he had finished translating a German book "a few days ago." "It is supposed," the obituary continued, "that his illness and death were the result of a too close attention to these engagements [translating and lawyering] which taxed too severely an already impaired state of health."[104] Smith, who pushed him so hard to translate, had reason to feel guilty and may have preferred not to see Harry's name on the dubious *Villa on the Rhine.*

Lindau's novels also disturbed Smith even as she devised schemes for making the author better known in America to help sell *Lace.* "Any questionable passages?" she worried when they were contemplating a second Lindau translation. "He is abler than the rest without doubt," she allowed, "but I do not want to compromise my character in any wise by translating a work whose moral may be misunderstood by the shallow."[105] Indeed, Lindau's *Lace* had presented a quandary to the pious Smith. For one thing, unlike the novels by women that Smith, Wister, and others had translated, it did not end happily but instead boasted a plot involving perjury, burglary, and adultery and ending in insanity and death. Smith wondered, "Can you not alter P. Lindau so as to winnow out any criminal tone to which neither of us should become a party."[106] While she was only too happy to be working with Appleton, who paid better than Munro, she urged Harry, who was translating the first part of the novel, not to read the "tragic end" of *Lace* until he had finished with his part.[107]

Smith worried about the effects of reading such literature on her depressive son. It may be telling, then, that the Smiths were not credited at all for *Lace,* especially since Smith otherwise saw to it that her name appeared on the title pages of her translations. The author of a Sunday school book and of patriotic historical fiction (*Lang Syne,* 1889), which she hoped would sell on the school textbook market, was perhaps not prepared to have her good name associated with a "criminal tone." When working on a second Lindau translation, Smith noted the effects of the fiction on her own state of mind: "It has a queer oppressive effect upon me, so weird, so vivid in its descriptions. I can see that horrible old professor and his poor victims as plainly as if I had known them actually."[108] She worried about the novel's unhappy ending: she wanted to translate the first part, "for, to tell the truth, I shrink from the tragic close."[109] Her shrinking from tragedy points again to the decades-long allure of German happy endings for American novel readers of her ilk. Smith had enough pain in real life; indeed, Harry died just a few weeks later.[110]

Although the Smiths began to translate male German authors whose books contained "questionable passages," Smith remained more at home in women's fiction in the vein of that generated by *Gartenlaube* authors. In 1888 she wrote Harry of liking Werner's *St. Michael*: "If it goes as well as it begins it promises to be E. Werner's *chef d'oeuvre*," she conjectured.[111] *St. Michael* adhered to Werner's successful pattern in its focus on a male character in need of redemption whose fate is tied to family and national politics, the sort of man Smith herself had described in her essay on women of the revolutionary war, a man whose "fairest achievements" were "prompted by the desire to please the woman who stands closest to his heart."[112] A novel that concludes with the Franco-Prussian War and thus the unification of Germany, *St. Michael* brings about the reconciliation of a grandfather and grandson and the unification of an aristocratic family fractured along religious lines (Catholic and Protestant), geographical lines (north and south), and class lines (the central character, Michael, is the product of a misalliance). In the end North German Michael, now Captain Rodenberg, marries the South German countess Hertha Steinruck following the German victory over France, in a united Germany and in a double marriage ceremony that appeases both Protestants and Catholics. We can easily imagine why the southerner Smith relished such fantasies of familial and national reunion and harmony. Without the burden of real experience of the Franco-Prussian War, American readers could believe in and cherish ideas of union in a far-off elsewhere that life at home in the fractured United States frustrated.

Harmony was on Smith's mind, and she must have relished in books the reconciliation of north and south that was not to be easily found in the American South, which, as she saw it, was ever vulnerable to insults from outsiders. A year later Smith, perhaps emboldened by her translation of Werner, published her own patriotic historical fiction, her one and only novella, *Lang Syne, or The Wards of Mt. Vernon*. The hundred-year anniversary of the commencement of Washington's presidency provided Smith, the southerner, with an opportunity to write patriotic historical fiction without having to confront the Civil War, yet the Lost Cause informs the work. *Lang Syne* concludes with a picture of wholeness set in Virginia not motivated by the specific story but redolent with nostalgia for the Old South. In the final scene Washington, returned from the war to his plantation, is greeted by "colored people of all ages." As the narrator emphasizes, "Assuredly without the setting of their dusky faces as a background, there would have been lacking a distinct element in what constituted a perfect picture of home life, whose absence must have been missed regretfully by Washington himself. For strong was the tie of affection that linked together the served and the servant in those old and well nigh forgotten days."[113] Indeed, as a letter to her son documents, Smith, like the Lost Causers, clung for years after the war to the fiction that slavery had been the "mildest domestic servitude the world ever saw and a substitute for which the whole world now seeks in vain" and remained sensitive to insults of "zealots and ignoramuses."[114]

Even as Smith hoped that she and Harry were translating a chef d'oeuvre when they took up *St. Michael,* she preferred Heimburg, her "favorite of all."[115] Heimburg won Smith's approval because she was "so much more evangelical in her spirit."[116] This taste for the evangelical is reflected in her own writing. When Smith wrote Harry's story after his untimely death, she worked the territory of the religiously colored domestic fiction that she preferred and produced an ending, albeit a sad one, worthy of that fiction. The death of Janie Harwood, Harry's fiancée, two weeks after Harry died provided promising material. Smith was certain, she wrote on the final page of the commemorative biography, that Harry "was welcomed by his Redeemer into the assembly of saints, and appointed to do nobler and higher work than could have been possible here below." Well schooled in sentimental German family romance, although of a happier sort, she concluded her account with a scene by Harry's coffin. Harry's fiancée placed "some lovely pale roses on his bosom. Her pathetic exclamation was 'Ah Harry, how could you go? You promised never to leave me.'" Smith then provided a pious and strangely hopeful, though lachrymose, coda, one as close to a happy ending as she could muster in view of the circumstances: "God heard that cry of anguish and permitted them to be speedily reunited in the better land."[117]

Smith's praise of Werner and Heimburg and her reservations about Lindau and Auerbach raise the issue of the worthiness of the enterprise of translating popular literature per se. Were such novels fit reading? Could reading of them be justified by their literary quality, their entertainment value, or their moral message? Smith had wrestled with these issues and in 1872 had made a public statement about worthy reading in the *Southern Review.* The journal editor, who did not entirely stand behind her assertions, framed her article with an asseveration of her piety and a disclaimer: "we do not wish to be understood as committing ourselves to the advocacy of novel-reading in any form or shape. We believe that the practice is, on the whole, decidedly pernicious."[118] Smith saw it differently and here said so in public.

Citing as premier examples Harriet Beecher Stowe and Charles Dickens, of whom she did not wholly approve, she maintained, "fiction is a power."[119] The power of fiction rests in its ability both to instruct and charm, she affirmed, relying on the well-worn argument *prodesse et delectare,* the European novel's oldest defense. She moreover enthusiastically cited the example of Charlotte Yonge, whose edifying Christian books she admired: "cold must be the heart that does not respond 'Amen' to the author's endeavor to exalt her species, by first seeking to engage their sympathies, albeit in behalf of a fictitious character" (449). Yonge, she noted approvingly, had outfitted an entire mission ship with her proceeds from the *Heir of Redclyffe*.

Advocacy of fiction's edificatory powers was perhaps to be expected in the *Southern Review*, but Smith also lauded the entertainment value of fiction. While she condemned sensation novels as "beneath notice, save as one of those agencies for evil," she asserted, "We think none will gainsay the position, that a first essential is the power to afford entertainment; for no one applies to fiction but with the hope of being amused; and if one must labor to read a novel, who does not esteem it labor misapplied?" (449–50). Entertainment, however, should not consist in fantasy. Smith demanded verisimilitude and insisted that characters should be lifelike; "in the most successful novels we have difficulty remembering that the characters are not real people," she observed. "When we do indulge in novel-reading, we love to be lifted, as if by an enchanter's rod, out of the every-day world into one in which ideal beings move to and fro, swaying . . . heart and mind, until becoming, as it were, for the time, an integral part of our very being" (450). Smith thus approximated in 1872 what Radway rediscovered in the twentieth century about the appeal of romance novels. Readers do not understand these novels with their happy endings and pleasurably idealized characters as belonging to a fantastical world apart but rather as contiguous with the world they know and as assimilable into their own experience

If Smith in 1872 provided the rationale for her own translations, her example also strongly suggests, like that of Coleman and Wister, that women's activity as translators can lead them to gain a sense of cultural agency, here an agency anchored in and supported by sentiment and virtue as articulated in popular novels by German women. Smith in fact came to feel that she had something to say to important men.

During his three years in Berlin (1882–85) where he enrolled as a student of civil engineering at the university and worked as vice consul general at the American consulate, Smith's son Harry was mentored by none other than Chapman Coleman, Ann Mary Coleman's son, who had served as First Secretary of Legation at Berlin since being appointed attaché by Grant in 1869. Smith presumably met Coleman himself when in 1884 she finally traveled to Germany and spent several weeks in Berlin with Harry, who had been given the use of the apartments of Consul Brewer and his family opposite the Tiergarten and within earshot of the famous Kroll gardens.

When six years later, in 1890, Smith published in *The Cosmopolitan* an essay on the New Berlin, overflowing with adulation for Prussia's Queen Louise, she felt enough of a connection to Coleman, who was still with the American legation, to contact him.[120] She wanted him to see to it that none other than the young German emperor, William II, received a copy of her essay. "Would it be wild," she asked Harry, "to send two copies to your friend Coleman asking him to present the others in the proper way, to the Emperor himself?"[121] Eighteen days later she informed Harry that she had sent off copies of her article to Berlin; she wished to instruct the emperor:

> I really feel a deep interest in all Queen Louisa's descendents, and I thought it could do a faulty young man, inclined to despotism no harm to be made aware of the reverence kindled in the hearts of Republicans by the virtues and heroic deeds of his predecessors. Even so humble an instrumentality might perchance kindle the desire to imitate them, and awaken kindly feelings toward the United States, whose people can admire goodness in king and emperor, while fondly clinging to the free institutions of their native land. What a visionary being I am surely, and yet when such impulses do come one fears not to yield to them.[122]

Smith had read and hoped to translate Friedrich Wilhelm Adami's popular biography of Queen Louise, William II's great-grandmother, who, as the epitome of feminine virtue, had become a highly sentimentalized German national icon.[123] Queen Louise spoke to Smith, as it were, and Smith wanted to speak back to Louise's great-grandson. Empowered by years of reading and translating, years of cultural mediation, Smith asserted in this letter the force of sentiment coupled with virtue and wielded by a woman to affect international relations by addressing the monarch *personally.*

That Smith operated here within a sense of expanded domesticity—domestic values extended into public life—becomes clear upon examination of the entire letter. In the same letter in which she expressed her wish to guide the German emperor, she described how she took a grandson strictly in hand. Francis Charles had pushed his sister, who fell and cut her forehead on the leg of Smith's desk, the desk in the *home* where she wrote and translated for the *public*. Smith moved swiftly to discipline the boy: "I took the little boy off to a room where we were by ourselves and made him kneel down and thank God for saving him from doing a greater mischief, and keep him from hurting his sister ever again. I am going to take him with me to meeting henceforth, to keep him from like escapades, if nothing else."[124] Francis Charles and William II, so Smith believed, both required a little feminine discipline.

A cranky writer for the *Literary World* had once declared, "Translations . . . are not wanted," and speculated that American readers were indifferent to foreign fiction, because "they cannot sympathetically enter into the lives and thoughts of persons who represent a society so different from their own."[125] Smith, however, saw the matter differently, believing translations of German sentimental fiction engendered in American readers precisely the sympathy that makes the foreign familiar. The Germany of the novels she translated, so Smith thought, at bottom shared her values. How, then, could she have imagined at the height of translating the "pure" novels of Marlitt, Heimburg, and Werner that she would live to see the United States go to war against a Germany that had "put aside all restraints of law and humanity"?[126]

CONCLUSION

> The historian must indeed be superficial, who, in making a philosophical estimate of the units which together constitute the individuality of any age, ignores its domestic relations, as an important factor in the great sum whose mysteries he is endeavoring to solve.
> —Mary Stuart Smith[1]

IN 1877 the anonymous author of a review essay of German novels in the original German found repeated occasion to generalize about Germans as a people. Among these assertions, those concerning Germans' failure to assimilate in America are particularly arresting. "That the peculiarities of German blood are not easily eradicated is patent to ordinary observation," the reviewer maintained, continuing,

> The Englishman or Irishman soon becomes absorbed into the body-politic, and the second generation are "more American than the Americans"; while the Germans, by their constantly recurring festivals of home origin, their observance of national and family anniversaries, with their frequent habit of costuming for balls and parties in garments, reminding them of their beloved Swabia, Bohemia or Westphalia, keep up those tender recollections which bind them to their native land and their relatives there. Whether from Berlin or Vienna, from the Danube or the Rhine, every German family strives to keep alive the memories, customs and speech of their fatherland.[2]

As this reviewer saw it, German migrants maintained their foreignness in the midst of a majority culture that was separate from their own. For those uncomfortable with Germans in their midst, such separation might have been welcome, for there would thus be no mistaking who was German and who was not.

German domestic fiction as it was Americanized through translation, publication, packaging, marketing, reviewing, and repeated reading, however, told a different story, one of assimilation. If, as Amy Kaplan argues, mid-nineteenth-century American women novelists tended to support the redrawing of domestic borders against the foreign in their delineation of domestic space as both familial and national, Gilded Age American *readers* welcomed foreign fiction into their homes once it had become palatably "Americanized."[3] Although originally written in a nationalizing context and although exhibiting elements alien to American culture, this fiction, as it turned out, could be made into an American product that both edified and entertained while supporting American domesticity and also sometimes gently pushing against domesticity's narrower definitions. It did so over several decades until the vogue ran out of steam in the new century. "We do not know how much of this taste for creditable, sympathetic German romance has lasted until now," the *New York Times* mused in 1907, unsure in this case whether the quality and appeal of this German romance were to be attributed to Annis Lee Wister's skill or the German originals: "Perhaps Mrs. Wister's own art and discretion lent a certain measure of literary dignity to the sentiment of some of her German originals which they did not possess in their first estate or which a less competent translator would have failed to convey."[4]

The German families presented to Americans in translation—from the Hohenzollerns to the Hellwigs—were families in turmoil, and the German world of these novels was filled, in the words of Agnes Hamilton, with people whom one would "not speak to in real life."[5] Yet even as these books showed family enmity in a harsh light, they invariably concluded with hope that the ideals prevailed, on which domesticity, affective individualism, the identity of the middle classes, and the liberal state relied. For the women who translated and read them in the Gilded Age, especially in the first three decades after the Civil War, they provided, in the formulation of Barbara Sicherman, "escape to" possibility, re-union, even adventure, within domestic spaces and escape *from* their own lives insofar as German fictions presented an alternate world in which the burden of the merely quotidian was absent. Those who read these novels could find entertainment, distraction, and edification in the privacy of reading as well as in the social experience of reading aloud and exchanging and gifting books. In German domestic fiction they went abroad to found a homeland for the time it took to read a book.

By the turn of the twentieth century, however, the interest in translating new popular German novels by women was diminishing. The several generations of German women writers who had produced this fiction were dead or near the end of their writing careers, as were the American women who translated them. Nevertheless, these somewhat old-fashioned novels continued to be reprinted, sold, and read for another ten to twenty years, proving with an afterlife of forty-five years in some cases not exactly to be ephemeral.[6]

Nearly thirty years after the mention by *The Nation* of "family likeness" in 1871, *The Independent* relied on the same conceit in characterizing Wister's translation of H. Schobert's *Picked Up in the Streets*: "It has a family resemblance to the weaker books in the dozen or so of translations from German novelists (exception being made Miss Marlitt) that the publishers have found popular light literature for American readers, especially of the gentler sex." The reviewer then offered the further examples of "Von [sic] Heimburg, Streckfuss, Werner and Von Reichbach [sic]."[7] *The Independent* was certainly correct to identify similarities among these novels, yet it bears considering that over the course of Americanization, of selection, translation, packaging—in uniform bindings, paratextual labeling, and so on—branding, marketing, and reviewing coupled with further labeling and categorizing, these novels had become somewhat more like one another and somewhat less like themselves.

If Alcott's displacement of the "h" and "ae" in Professor Bhaer's name can figure the transformations that took place in this German women's fiction as it was "Americanized" and yet still identified as German, then a concluding mention of Alcott can serve to characterize one last transformation that took place in the American reading and marketing of this literature. In 1908 *The Dial* marked Wister's death with a short notice asserting that "thousands of readers—especially young readers" were mourning Wister's passing: "To find another American writer who has made for herself such a place in girls' affections, one would have to go back to Louisa Alcott." Furthermore, the notice predicted, "By generations of children yet to come her versions of wholesome and homely German romances are likely to be read with all the delight that hailed their first appearance." Over the course of even this short notice "readers" have devolved into "children," and the article thus, with some exaggeration, mimics what appears to have happened with this German fiction in general: it began in Germany as reading for adults that could be enjoyed by the whole family because it was deemed "wholesome," and it was listed and reviewed as such, that is, adult reading, in America, too. Yet publishers—in imperial Germany as well as the United States—subsequently packaged it first and foremost for a female reading public. By the new century the literature previously marketed in that segment was seen as ever more childish as contemporary literature offered stronger stuff and as some women vigorously pushed the boundaries of gender restrictions in the work force, in education, in politics, and as writers. In the new century in America at least some of this

German fiction took its place beside other "classic" nineteenth-century international reading that was also popular—*Jane Eyre,* the novels of Jane Austen, Dumas, Scott, Eliot, Dickens, and others. These books, as classic novels, were taken up and read avidly by younger readers—indeed, were recommended to them—even if still read and esteemed by some adults.

An eighty-one-year-old Mary Stuart Smith, who had enthusiastically welcomed modern times in the automobile, nevertheless retained an allegiance to the reading of her younger years, to edification, entertainment, and the happy ending that projected harmony, reunion, and acknowledgment. She confessed to her husband in 1915: "I am *trying* to read the novel Janie has lent me, but they (I mean novels) of the day, rather disgust and revolt me— nothing inspiring or lofty about them."[8] Letters from her last years mention her wish to get hold of *Sunshine Jane* to amuse some friends and her desire to read the new novel by the author of *Pollyanna*.[9]

As for the feminized Germany mediated by this fiction, it hardly needs repeating that it was largely unlike the aggressive militarizing empire that would be at war with the United States in 1917. Nor was it much like the oppressive "severe, wooden character in tails with a full black beard and a medal on his chest," bearing the title "General Dr. von State" imagined by the young Thomas Mann and emblematic of the old order against which the young German moderns rebelled.[10] The Germany of women's novels translated into English for Americans' reading pleasure was instead not so different from the United States of women's wishing as the old castles, country estates, and sneering aristocrats might have led some to think.

For some American readers, the German regions of these books housed an ideal, in which femininity aided in the production of masculinity and an idea of nation in which the individual and the home mattered. German fiction in translation invited American readers to envision Germany as a place where some of their fondest wishes for real power of love, virtue, and sentiment could be pleasurably realized—even if arbitrarily and only in the imaginary. This was a power nineteenth-century American women were told they could and should wield, and some of them enjoyed traveling abroad, as it were, to do so. However, it was perhaps ultimately not so much German life that many of them encountered in their reading sojourns, but their alienated and sometimes idealized selves.

APPENDIX A

American Periodicals Cited

American Library Journal, The
American Literary Gazette and Publisher's Circle
American Magazine: A Monthly Miscellany Devoted to Literature, Science, The
American Socialist, The
Annual American Catalogue, The
Appleton's Journal
Art Amateur: A Monthly Journal Devoted to Art in the Household, The
Arthur's Illustrated Home Magazine
Athenäum
Atlantic Monthly, The
Belford's Magazine
Book Chat: A Monthly Review of Current Books and Magazines
The Boston Courier
Boston Herald
Boston Home Journal, The
Boston Saturday Evening Gazette, The
Bostonian: An Illustrated Monthly Magazine of Local Interest, The
British Quarterly Review, American Edition, The
Catholic World, The
Chautauquan, The
Chicago Tribune
Christian Advocate, The
Christian Examiner, The
Christian Union
Columbus Journal, The
Congregationalist, The
Cosmopolitan, A Monthly Illustrated Magazine
Critic, The
Current Literature: Magazine of Record and Review
Daily Inter Ocean, The
Daily Picayune
Dial: A Semi-Monthly Journal of Literary Criticism, Discussion and Information

Fashion Bazaar, The
Galaxy: A Magazine of Entertaining Reading, The
Galveston Daily News, The
Godey's Lady's Book
Good Housekeeping
Harper's New Monthly Magazine
Hours at Home: A Popular Monthly of Instruction and Recreation
International Review, The
Lippincott's Magazine of Literature, Science and Education
Literary World: A Monthly Review of Current Literature, The
Littell's Living Age
Louisville Courier Journal
Louisville Daily Journal
Medical Age: A Semi-Monthly Journal of Medicine and Surgery, The
Milwaukee Sentinel, The
Minneapolis Journal, The
Motion Picture News
Moving Picture World
Nassau Literary Magazine
Nation, The
National Quarterly Review, The
New Englander, The
New York Herald, The
New York Ledger, The
New York Observer and Chronicle
New York Times, The
New York Tribune, The
North American Review, The
Old Guard, The
Peterson's Magazine
Philadelphia Inquirer
Publishers' Trade List Annual, The
Publishers' Weekly: The American Book Trade Journal
Putnam's Monthly Magazine, or American Literature, Science, and Art
Round Table: A Saturday Review of Politics, Finance, Literature, Society and Art, The
Saturday Evening Post, The
Scribner's Monthly
Southern Farm and Home Magazine: A Magazine of Agriculture, Manufactures, and Domestic Economy
Southern Review, The
Southwestern Christian Advocate
St. Louis Globe-Democrat
St. Louis Republic, The
United Service: A Quarterly Review of Military and Naval Affairs
Weekly Review; Devoted to the Consideration of Politics, of Social and Economic Tendencies, of History, Literature, and the Arts

APPENDIX B

Late Nineteenth- and Early Twentieth-Century U.S. Library Catalogs and Finding Lists Consulted as an Index of Enduring Circulation

Boston Public Library. *Finding List of English Prose Fiction in the Public Library in the City of Boston which may be taken for home use.* Boston: Pub. by the trustees, 1903.

Brookline Public Library. *Catalogue of English Prose Fiction in the Brookline Public Library.* Brookline, Mass.: Pub. by the trustees, 1895.

Carnegie Library of Pittsburgh. *Classified Catalogue of the Carnegie Library of Pittsburgh. Part 6: Literature.* Pittsburgh: Pub. by the library, 1905.

Chicago Public Library. *Catalogue of English Prose Fiction and Juvenile Books in the Chicago Public Library.* Chicago: Pub. by the library, 1898.

Columbus Ohio Public School Library. *Catalogue of all the Books in the Circulating and Reference Departments.* Columbus, Ohio: Berlin Printing Company, 1897.

Enoch Pratt Free Library of Baltimore City. *Finding List. Central Library. English Prose Fiction including Fairy Tales.* 7th ed. Baltimore: Pub. by the library, 1908.

Los Angeles Public Library. *List of Novels and Tales in the English Language.* Los Angeles: Baumgardt Pub. Co., 1900.

Public Library of Cincinnati. *Finding List of English Prose Fiction.* Cincinnati: Pub. by the trustees, 1902.

Salem Public Library. *Class List No. 6 (Supplement).* Salem, Mass.: Pub. by the library, 1898.

San Francisco Free Public Library. *English Prose Fiction, including translations.* San Francisco: Pub. by the library, 1897.

Seattle Public Library. *Finding List of English Prose Fiction.* Seattle: Pub. by the library, 1903.

St. Louis Public Library. *English Prose Fiction, rev. and enl.* St Louis: Pub. by the library, 1903.

Withers Public Library (Bloomington, Ill.). *Finding List: Withers Public Library (Bloomington, Ill.).* Bloomington, Ill.: Lloyd & Miller, 1901.

APPENDIX C

Total German Novels Translated in America (1866–1917) by Woman Author

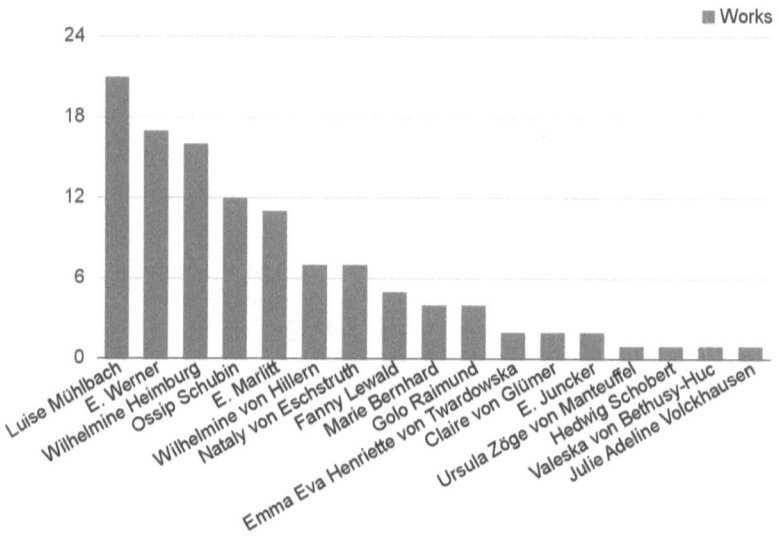

APPENDIX D

Total Number of Translations of German Novels in the United States (1866–1917) by Woman Author

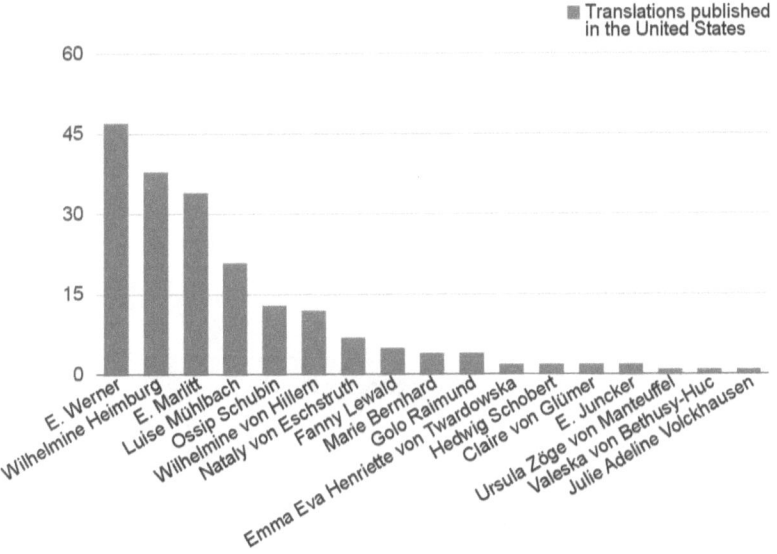

APPENDIX E

Total American Publications (1866–1917) by Woman Author
("American Publications" = editions, reprint editions, rebindings)

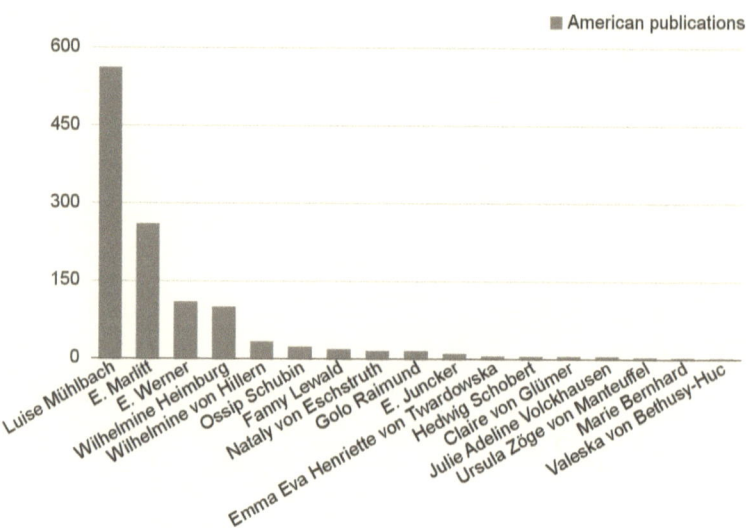

NOTES

Preface

1. "Three Percent: A Resource for International Literature at the University of Rochester." About us, http://www.rochester.edu/College/translation/threepercent/index.php?s=about (accessed 1 November 2009). A study of the economics of contemporary literary translation demonstrates, moreover, that, worldwide, the "number of translations *from* English is 22 times larger than (per head) of those *into* English." Victor Ginsburgh, Schlomo Weber, and Sheila Weyers, "The Economics of Literary Translation," *Poetics* 39.3 (June 2011): 231-32.

Chapter 1

1. Otto Heller, "Women Writers of the Nineteenth Century," in *Studies in Modern German Literature* (Boston: Ginn, 1905), 232.
2. Ibid., 252.
3. Ibid., 267.
4. As Jeffrey L. Sammons outlines, German-born Harvard professor Kuno Francke, in his twenty-volume edition of German classics translated into English, also lamented that Germany's best writers were neglected in America for the likes of "Zschokke, Gerstäcker, Auerbach, Spielhagen, not to mention the ubiquitous Mühlbach or Marlitt or Polko." Jeffrey L. Sammons, *Kuno Francke's Edition of* The German Classics *(1913–15): A Historical and Critical Overview* (New York: Peter Lang, 2009), 186. Sammons here quotes Kuno Francke and William Guild Howard, eds., *The German Classics of the Nineteenth and Twentieth Centuries: Masterpieces of German Literature Translated into English* (New York: German Publication Society, 1913–14), 9:268. Volume 9, which treats then contemporary authors, does not include any of the women authors to be examined here.
5. Heller, "Women Writers," 236–37.
6. Sarah Wadsworth traces market segmentation in the Gilded Age in, for example, juvenile fiction, books printed in other languages for immigrant communities, and the production of cheap books. Sarah Wadsworth, *In the Company of Books: Literature and Its "Classes" in Nineteenth-Century America* (Amherst: University of Massachusetts Press, 2006). Barbara Sicherman, who has done extensive biographical work on nineteenth-century women's reading, however, sees the actual practice of recreational reading as cross-

ing boundaries and taking many forms in this period, determined by "mundane seasonal considerations . . . , rituals of family life, ephemeral events such as traveling shows and public readings," political convictions, and "on occasion for emotional release and even transformation." She cautions against claims of cultural historians that "specific genres appealed to different classes." Barbara Sicherman, "Ideologies and Practices of Reading," in *The Industrial Book, 1840–1880,* ed. Scott E. Casper, Jeffrey D. Groves, Stephen W. Nissenbaum, and Michael Winship, vol. 3 of *A History of the Book in America* (Chapel Hill: University of North Carolina Press, 2007), 292–93, 296, respectively.

7. Richard H. Brodhead, *Cultures of Letters: Scenes of Reading and Writing in Nineteenth-Century America* (Chicago: University of Chicago Press, 1993), esp. 48–68.

8. W. M. Griswold, *A Descriptive List of Novels and Tales Dealing with Life in Germany* (Cambridge, MA: W. M. Griswold, Publisher, 1892).

9. Ibid., 712.

10. Ibid.

11. Bayard Quincy Morgan, *A Bibliography of German Literature in English Translation,* University of Wisconsin Studies in Language and Literature 16 (Madison, WI, 1922), 16.

12. Lillie V. Hathaway, *German Literature of the Mid-Nineteenth Century in England and America as Reflected in the Journals 1840–1914* (Boston: Chapman and Grimes, 1935), 108.

13. Ibid. Morgan likewise emphasizes the economic factor in the publication of translations, which is, in his view, "to a far greater extent controlled by purely economic considerations than is the publication of native literature" (*Bibliography of German Literature,* 10).

14. Hathaway, *German Literature,* 108. See 107–10 for her discussion of Marlitt, Werner, Hillern, Heimburg, Mühlbach, and other popular authors.

15. Henry Ward Beecher in *Descriptive Catalogue of Books, Bibles and Photograph Albums* (Philadelphia: Quaker City Pub. House, 1800), quoted by Louise Stevenson, "Homes, Books, and Reading," in Casper et al., *The Industrial Book,* 319.

16. William St Clair, *The Reading Nation in the Romantic Period* (Cambridge, UK: Cambridge University Press, 2004), 3.

17. Ibid., 7.

18. For a listing of Goethe as most frequently translated, see Henry A. Pochmann, compiler, and Arthur R. Schultz, ed., *Bibliography of German Culture in America to 1940;* 1953, rev. and corrected Arthur R. Schultz (Millwood, NY: Kraus International Publications, 1982), 344.

19. Charles Dudley Warner et al., eds., "Suggestions for Household Libraries," in *Hints for Home Reading: A Series of Chapters on Books and Their Use,* ed. Charles Dudley Warner et al. (New York: G. P. Putnam's Sons, 1880), 117–47. In addition to Goethe, the authors Schiller, Lessing, and Heine predictably turn up in various categories in these lists. The German male authors (listed mostly under the third-ranked list of fiction) include, for the most part, once prominent writers who, though not entirely forgotten, did not make the twentieth-century literary canon: Berthold Auerbach, Adelbert von Chamisso, Franz von Dingelstedt, Georg Ebers, Friedrich Baron de la Motte Fouqué, Gustav Freytag, Paul Heyse, and Ernst Reuter.

20. Fred B. Perkins, "What to Read," in *Hints for Home Reading,* 26.

21. *Catalogue of English Prose Fiction and Juvenile Books in the Chicago Public Library* (Chicago: Library Rooms, January 1889), 56 and 98, listings for Goethe and C. M. Mundt (Luise Mühlbach), respectively.

22. Peter Burke and R. Po-Chia Hsia, introd., *Cultural Translation in Early Modern Europe* (Cambridge: Cambridge University Press, 2007), 2. On translations as facts of the target culture as an assumption in the methodology and practice of descriptive translation studies, see Gideon Toury, *Descriptive Translation Studies and Beyond* (Amsterdam: John Benjamins Publishing Company, 1995), esp. 23–39.

23. *Classified Catalogue of the Carnegie Library of Pittsburgh 1895–1902 in Three Volumes* (Pittsburgh: Carnegie Library, 1907), vol. 2. See the respective alphabetical listings under "English Fiction" and "German Fiction."

24. John Tebbel, *The Expansion of an Industry, 1865–1919*, vol. 2 of *A History of Book Publishing in the United States* (New York: R. R. Bowker, 1975), Appendix C, 675–708.

25. John Tebbel, *Between Covers: The Rise and Transformation of Book Publishing in America* (New York: Oxford University Press, 1987), 178–79. W. D. Howells, "Novel-Writing and Novel-Reading: An Impersonal Explanation," in *Howells and James: A Double Billing* (New York: New York Public Library, 1958), 20.

26. Mary Kelley, *Private Women, Public Stage: Literary Domesticity in Nineteenth-Century America* (New York: Oxford University Press, 1984), 10–11.

27. On the reading of novels in the earlier part of the century, see the examples cited in Mary Kelley, *Learning to Stand and Speak: Women, Education, and Public Life in America's Republic* (Chapel Hill: University of North Carolina Press, 2006), 178–87.

28. Robert E. Cazden provides thorough documentation of the German-American book trade up to the Civil War. Robert E. Cazden, *A Social History of the German Book Trade in America to the Civil War* (Columbia, SC: Camden House, 1984). Cazden focuses on books in German, many of which were unauthorized reprints, that were sold and read in North America.

29. "On the Study of German in America," *Christian Examiner*, 87, no. 1 (July 1869): 2.

30. Ibid., 4. Jörg Nagler identifies the decade following the American Civil War and German unification as a "high point of German-American relations," relations that became increasingly strained over the course of the four decades preceding the First World War. Jörg Nagler, "From Culture to Kultur: Changing American Perceptions of Imperial Germany, 1870–1914," *Transatlantic Images and Perceptions: Germany and America since 1776*, ed. David E. Barclay and Elisabeth Glaser-Schmidt (Cambridge: Cambridge University Press, 1997), 131.

31. Hugh Ridley, *'Relations Stop Nowhere': The Common Literary Foundations of German and American Literature, 1830–1917* (Amsterdam: Rodopi, 2007).

32. Ibid., 13.

33. Henry A. Pochmann, *German Culture in America: Philosophical and Literary Influences, 1600–1900* (Madison: University of Wisconsin Press, 1957).

34. Hathaway (*German Literature*, 3) thanks the Germanist A. R. Hohlfeld for suggesting her topic and mentions Morgan as well in her acknowledgments.

35. Susan L. Mizruchi, for one, rethinks nineteenth-century American print culture as exhibiting a "newly formed multiculturalism in all its variety and complexity," one that was self-consciously addressed in American literature. Susan L. Mizruchi, *Multicultural America: Economy and Print Culture, 1865–1915* (Chapel Hill: University of North Carolina Press, 2008), 9.

36. Werner Sollors, ed., *Multilingual America: Transnationalism, Ethnicity, and the Languages of American Literature* (New York: University of New York Press, 1998); Marc Shell, ed., *American Babel: Literatures of the United States from Abnaki to Zuni* (Cambridge, MA: Harvard University Press, 2003); M. Lynn Weiss, ed., *Creole Echoes: The Francophone*

Poetry of Nineteenth-Century Louisiana, trans. Norman R. Shapiro (Urbana: University of Illinois Press, 2004).

37. Marc Shell and Werner Sollors, eds., *The Multilingual Anthology of American Literature: A Reader of Original Texts with English Translations* (New York: New York University Press, 2000).

38. Werner Sollors, ed., *An Anthology of Interracial Literature: Black-White Contacts in the Old World and the New* (New York: New York University Press, 2004).

39. Shelley Fisher Fishkin, "Crossroads of Cultures: The Transnational Turn in American Studies: Presidential Address to the American Studies Association," November 12, 2004," *American Quarterly* 57.1 (March 2005): 17–57.

40. Caroline F. Levander and Robert S. Levine, *Hemispheric American Studies* (New Brunswick, NJ: Rutgers University Press, 2008). See the editors' introduction, 1–17, for an articulation of their conceptual framework.

41. Werner Sollors, "German-Language Writing in the United States: A Serious Challenge to American Studies?" In *The German-American Encounter: Conflict and Cooperation between Two Cultures, 1800–2000*, ed. Frank Trommler and Elliott Shore (New York: Berghahn Books, 2001), 103–14; Winfried Fluck and Werner Sollors, eds., *German? American? Literature? New Directions in German-American Studies* (New York: Peter Lang, 2002).

42. American studies practiced in German-speaking contexts has also generated new work on German-American relations. Waldemar Zacharasiewicz, in *Images of Germany in American Literature* (Iowa City: University of Iowa Press, 2007), describes himself as "'the Americanist' at a major university [Vienna]" (vii). Likewise, a recent anthology focusing on the ways in which America figures in nineteenth-century German literature emerged from cooperation between professors of American studies and German studies at Dortmund, Germany. Cristof Hamann, Ute Gerhard, and Walter Grünzweig, eds., *Amerika und die deutschsprachige Literatur nach 1848: Migration—kultureller Austausch—frühe Globalisierung* (Bielefeld, Germany: transcript, 2009).

43. Greil Marcus and Werner Sollors, eds., *A New Literary History of America* (Cambridge, MA: Harvard University Press, 2009).

44. Casper et al., *The Industrial Book*, and Carl F. Kaestle and Janice A. Radway, eds., *Print in Motion: The Expansion of Publishing and Reading in the United States, 1880–1949*, vol. 4 of *A History of the Book in America* (Chapel Hill: University of North Carolina Press, 2009).

45. Meredith L. McGill, *American Literature and the Culture of Reprinting, 1834–1853* (Philidelphia: University of Pennsylvania Press, 2003), 2.

46. Meredith L. McGill, introd., *The Traffic in Poems: Nineteenth-Century Poetry and Transatlantic Exchange*, ed. Meredith McGill (New Brunswick, NJ: Rutgers University Press, 2008), 2.

47. Ibid., 3.

48. Ridley, 'Relations Stop Nowhere,' 119.

49. Lynne Tatlock and Matt Erlin, introd., *German Culture in Nineteenth-Century America: Reception, Adaptation, Transformation* (Rochester, NY: Camden House, 2005), xi.

50. Edith Grossmann, *Why Translation Matters* (New Haven, CT: Yale University Press, 2010), 49.

51. McGill, *American Literature*, esp. 45–75, 93–108.

52. See George Haven Putnam, "The Contest for International Copyright," in *American Literary Publishing Houses, 1638–1899*, ed. Peter Dzwonkoski, vol. 49.2 of *Dictionary*

of Literary Biography (Detroit, MI: Gale Research, 1986), 573-79; Aubert J. Clark, *The Movement for International Copyright in Nineteenth-Century America* (Washington, DC: Catholic University of America Press, 1960); and Richard Rogers Bowker, *Copyright, Its History and Its Law, Being a Summary of the Principles and Practice of Copyright with Special Reference to the American Code of 1909 and the British Act of 1911* (Boston: Houghton Mifflin, 1912). For discussions around the time of the beginning of the vogue of German novels by women, see, e.g., "International Copyright," *Atlantic Monthly* 20 (1867): 430-51; "International Copyright," *The Galaxy* 10 (1870): 811-18; Review of "Brief on Behalf of Authors and Publishers' in Favor of International Copyright, etc.," *North American Review* 114 (1872): 432-35.

53. Joseph S. Nye, Jr., *Soft Power: The Means to Success in World Politics* (New York: Public Affairs, 2004), 5. On soft power and German cultural transfer, see Eric Ames, "The Image of Culture—Or, What Münsterberg Saw in the Movies," in Tatlock and Erlin, *German Culture*, 23-24.

54. Brander Matthews, "Cheap Books and Good Books" (1887), in Dzwonkoski, *American Literary Publishing Houses*, 2:580.

55. Georg Jäger and Monika Estermann, "Geschichtliche Grundlagen und Entwicklung des Buchhandels im Deutschen Reich bis 1871," in *Das Kaiserreich 1871-1918*, vol. 1, pt. 1, of *Geschichte des deutschen Buchhandels im 19. und 20. Jahrhundert*, ed. Georg Jäger (Frankfurt am Main: Buchhändler-Vereinigung, 2001), 18.

56. Reinhard Wittmann, *Geschichte des deutschen Buchhandels. Ein Überblick* (Munich: C. H. Beck, 1991), 271.

57. Barbara Kasten, "Statistik und Topgraphie des Verlagswesens," in Jäger, *Das Kaiserreich 1871-1918*, vol. 2, pt. 1, 324, 326.

58. Morgan, *Bibliography*, 13, 16. Morgan's numbers include all books that he labels "German literature." Morgan's "literature," or rather his "humane letters," is a broadly inclusive category; it includes philosophy, works of art history, history, travel accounts, and biography, for example (10). The total number of book titles published in America in each of these years was 3,474, 4,437, and 8,141, respectively. See Tebbel, *Expansion of an Industry*, 678, 681, 693.

59. Comparing Morgan's calculations with Tebbel's lists yields a rough approximation at best since the categories are differently constructed. My estimate is based on a figure that eliminates from Tebbel's total for 1882 (3,474) titles in the categories theology and religion; law; education—language; medical, science, hygiene; social and political science; physical and mathematical science; useful arts; books of reference; sports, amusements, etc.; music books (chiefly singing books); and domestic and rural economies. Once these categories are removed, 2,018 titles remain. If one additionally eliminates the category humor and satire, the number falls to 1,983. I divided 140—the number of German titles listed by Morgan (itself an approximate number)—by that number.

60. Reinhard Wittmann, *Buchmarkt und Lektüre im 18. und 19. Jahrhundert. Beiträge zum literarischen Leben 1750-1800* (Tübingen: Max Niemeyer Verlag, 1981), 117. Tebbel, who bases his figures on a report in *Publishers' Weekly*, records total US production at 2,991 that same year (*Expansion of an Industry*, 677).

61. I thank Stephen Aiken, Perry Trolard, and Stephen Pentecost for creating these graphs based on the data assembled by student teams over the course of nearly two years in the Humanities Digital Workshop at Washington University. Stephen Pentecost generated the final forms of this and all other graphs included. Editions published in Great Britain are not included in these tallies, even though they too circulated in the United States.

62. This summary overview was undertaken to provide an index of marketing and circulation (and hence reading) of translations by a set of seventeen authors in the United States. For this purpose, therefore, any documented and dated imprint with a distinct title page is deemed a "publication," as are documented and dated iterations of translations with distinct covers marking them as uniquely marketed items. I am of course well aware of the differences among new editions, title editions, reprints, and rebinding. Despite our best efforts, there are certain to be more "publications" for each work than are documented in these graphs. The many such publications without dates could of course not be included in the timelines in these two graphs. The ongoing Lucile Project at the University of Iowa, which aims to recover the publishing history of Owen Meredith's *Lucile* (1860), provides a sense of how vigorously books were reedited, reprinted, and rebound in the nineteenth and early twentieth centuries. The project, which documents more than two thousand unique editions and issues of this text in the United States alone, demonstrates what an exhaustive search for unique copies of a popular book looks like and what collecting the data entails. See Sidney F. Hutner, *The Lucile Project*, University of Iowa, http://sdrc.lib.uiowa.edu/lucile/. Such an exhaustive search for unique copies of book publications of each translation in my dataset was not possible.

63. André Lefevere, *Translation, Rewriting and the Manipulation of Literary Fame* (London: Routledge, 1992), 11–25.

64. "On the Study of German in America," 2. See n. 29.

65. Ibid., 16–17.

66. "Recent Novels," *The Nation*, 19, no. 475 (6 August 1874): 92.

67. "Some German Literary Women," reprinted from the *New York Ledger* in the *Galveston Daily News*, December 14, 1895, 8.

68. Grossmann, *Why Translation Matters*, 55 and 14, respectively.

69. Ridley, 'Relations Stop Nowhere,' 121.

70. See, e.g., Lawrence Venuti, *The Translator's Invisibility: A History of Translation* (London: Routledge, 1995).

71. Kelley, *Learning to Stand and Speak*, 190; Kate Flint, *The Woman Reader, 1837–1914* (Oxford: Clarendon Press, 1993); Barbara Sicherman, *Well-Read Lives: How Books Inspired a Generation of American Women* (Chapel Hill: University of North Carolina Press, 2010).

72. "Advertisement for Schlesinger & Mayer, The Wabash-Avenue Book Store," *Chicago Daily Tribune*, December 7, 1902, 14.

73. Mary Stuart Smith to Gessner Harrison Smith, 24 February 1887, in Papers of the Tucker, Harrison, and Smith Families, Box 24, Small Special Collections Library, University of Virginia, Charlottesville, Virginia, hereafter abbreviated as THS Papers. Smith on more than one occasion, as in this letter, conflates the "Deutsche Library" with the "Seaside Library," calling it the "Seaside" or the "Deutsche Seaside." See her letters of 7 March 1887, 8 June 1887, 8 March 1888, Box 24.

74. Cazden describes the undertaking as "a series of cheap reprints published as a periodical to take advantage of favorable postal regulations" (*German Book Trade*, 376n81). Printed in newsprint-sized German black letter in quarto editions with triple columns, the Deutsche Library appeared semiweekly and could be purchased for ten to twenty cents an issue, depending on the number of pages, or for the annual subscription price of fifteen dollars. I thank Petra Watzke for compiling the data on the titles in the Deutsche Library.

75. I thank Brooke Shafar for compiling this census data. Source: Historical Census Browser, University of Virginia, Geospatial and Statistical Data Center. http://mapserver.lib.virginia.edu (accessed July 4, 2011).

76. These numbers were compiled with the help of Stephen Pentecost, using data supplied by "What Middletown Read?" Muncie Public Library, Center of Middletown Studies, Ball State University Library, http://www.bsu.edu/libraries/wmr/. The Muncie records run from November 5, 1891, through December 3, 1902, with a two-and-a-half-year hiatus from May 28, 1892, through November 5, 1894.

77. E. Marlitt, *The Old Mam'selle's Secret* (New York: Mershon Company, n.d.), front flyleaf. Exemplar owned by author.

78. E. Marlitt, *The Old Mam'selle's Secret* (Chicago: Donohue, Henneberry, n.d.), front flyleaf. Exemplar owned by author.

79. "What Middletown Read?" We cannot of course know who actually read the books when men and boys checked them out, but the same caveat pertains to female borrowers as well.

80. Mary Boykin Miller Chesnut, *Mary Chesnut's Civil War,* ed. C. Vann Woodward (New Haven, CT: Yale University Press, 1981), 661.

81. "Our Correspondents," *New York Herald,* May 1, 1873, 3.

82. Edith Wyatt, "A Matter of Taste," in *Every One His Own Way* (New York: McClure Phillips, 1901), 93–103, here 97.

83. Ibid., 103.

84. "The Prize Question in Fiction," *Publishers' Weekly* 9, no. 227 (May 20, 1876): 633–36.

85. For the books included in Munro's Seaside Library, I relied on the listing for the Seaside Library, Pocket Edition, supplied in the back matter of a late-century copy of E. Werner, *What the Spring Brought,* trans. Mary Stuart Smith [Pocket Edition] (New York: Munro, n.d.).

86. Robert Darnton, "What Is the History of Books?" *Daedalus* (Summer 1982): 65–83. This essay has been variously anthologized and amplified by Darnton, for example, in "Histoire du livre—Geschichte des Buchwesens: An Agenda for Comparative History," *Publishing History* 22 (1987): 35–41. Darnton returned to the essay again in 2007 in "'What Is the History of Books?' Revisited," *Modern Intellectual History* 4, no. 3 (2007): 495–508.

87. On the conversation between literary criticism and book history, see Leah Price, "Introduction: Reading Matter," *PMLA, Special Topic: The History of the Book and the Idea of Literature* 121, no. 1 (2006): 9–16.

88. See Robert Darnton, "First Steps Toward a History of Reading" (1986), in *Reception Study: From Literary Theory to Cultural Studies,* ed. James L. Machor and Philip Goldstein (New York: Routledge: 2001), 160–79.

89. Flint, in *The Woman Reader,* cautions against drawing hasty conclusions about reading practices by theorizing a "hypothetical woman reader." As she summarizes in her conclusion, she herself tries to illuminate reading practice as "at once pointing inwards and outwards, to the psychological and the socio-cultural," considering the "materiality of individual readers" as well as positionality (326–30).

90. "Distant reading," that is, analysis that focuses on units larger than an individual text as proposed and modeled by Franco Moretti, "Conjectures on World Literature," *New Left Review* 1 (January–February 2000): 54–68, and *Graphs, Maps, Trees: Abstract Models for Literary History* (London: Verso, 2005).

Chapter 2

1. On women's opportunities in the emergent mass market, see Lucia Hacker, *Schreibende Frauen um 1900: Rollen—Bilder—Gesten*, Berliner Ethnographische Studien 12 (Berlin: Hope, 2007), 95. Hacker's data is from Reinhard Wittmann, "Das literarische Leben 1848 bis 1880," *Buchmarkt und Lektüre*.

2. Ilsedore Rarisch, *Industrialisierung und Literatur. Buchproduktion, Verlagswesen und Buchhandel in Deutschland im 19. Jahrhundert in ihrem statistischen Zusammenhang* (Berlin: Colloquium Verlag, 1976), 66–67. See Jennifer Askey, "A Library for Girls: Publisher Ferdinand Hirt & Sohn and the Novels of Brigitte Augusti," *Publishing Culture and "Reading Nation": German Book History in the Long Nineteenth Century*, ed. Lynne Tatlock (Rochester, NY: Camden House, 2010), 161.

3. "Die Befürchtung liegt nahe, daß bei einer Gesamt-Assemblée der novellistischen Notabilitäten von heute nicht einmal auf jede Dame ein Herr kommen würde." E. Z., "Eine Heldin der Feder," *Die Gartenlaube*, no. 28 (1876): 465. Translations from the German are mine unless otherwise indicated.

4. Rudolf von Gottschall, *Die deutsche Nationalliteratur des neunzehnten Jahrhunderts*, 7th ed. (Breslau: Eduard Trewendt, 1902), 4:320.

5. William Whiston, "Our Monthly Gossip. Wilhelmine von Hillern," *Lippincott's Magazine of Popular Literature and Science*, 11, no. 22 (January 1873): 115.

6. Tebbel, *Between Covers*, 179.

7. Pochmann, *German Culture in America*, 346–47. In his brief summary of his data, Bayard Quincy Morgan (*Bibliography*, 17) remarks on the "insatiable appetite of the American public for narrative literature" satisfied by Heimburg, Marlitt, Werner, and others.

8. Kirsten Belgum, "Reading Alexander von Humboldt: Cosmopolitan Naturalist with an American Spirit," in Tatlock and Erlin, *German Culture*, 109.

9. The year 1858 is the date of birth listed by Pataky. Sophie Pataky, ed., *Lexikon deutscher Frauen der Feder* (1898; repr. Bern: Herbert Lang, 1971), 2:263.

10. *Encyclopaedia Britannica*, 11th ed., s.v. "German Literature."

11. "Our Correspondents," *New York Herald*, May 1, 1873, 3.

12. The best source for Mühlbach's views on her own writing and its reception is William H. McClain and Lieselotte E. Kurth-Voigt, "Clara Mundts Briefe an Hermann Costenoble. Zu L. Mühlbachs historischen Romanen," *Archiv für Geschichte des Buchwesens* 22, nos. 4–5 (1981), cols. 918–1250.

13. Brent O. Peterson, "Luise Mühlbach (Clara Mundt)," in *Nineteenth-Century German Writers to 1840*, ed. James Hardin and Siegfried Mews, vol. 133 of *Dictionary of Literary Biography* (Detroit: Gale Research, 1993), 204–6. Renate Möhrmann, however, refers to 290 novels in *Die andere Frau: Emanzipationsansätze deutscher Schriftstellerinnen im Vorfeld der Achtundvierziger Revolution* (Stuttgart: Metzler, 1977), 61.

14. Gottschall, *Die deutsche Nationalliteratur*, 4:80. Bayard Taylor, "Foreign Literature, Art, and Science, Prepared for Putnam's Magazine," *Putnam's Magazine* 13, no. 13 (January 1869): 108.

15. Heller, "Women Writers of the Nineteenth Century," 249.

16. Möhrmann, *Die andere Frau*, 60–84.

17. Peterson, "Luise Mühlbach," 207–8.

18. Robert Prutz, *Die deutsche Literatur der Gegenwart. 1848 bis 1858*, 2nd ed. (Leipzig: Voigt & Günther, 1860), 2:255.

19. Brent O. Peterson, *History, Fiction, and Germany: Writing the Nineteenth-Century Nation* (Detroit, MI: Wayne State University, 2005), 39. Peterson cites research by Alberto Martino, *Die deutsche Leihbibliothek: Geschichte einer literarischen Institution (1756–1914)* (Wiesbaden: Harrassowitz, 1990), 404, 410.

20. Lieselotte E. Kurth-Voigt and William H. McClain, "Louise Mühlbach's Historical Novels: The American Reception," *Internationales Archiv für Sozialgeschichte der deutschen Literatur* 6 (1981): 58. Kurth-Voigt and McClain provide here an extensive account of Mühlbach's American reception in both German and English.

21. Mühlbach mentions this unexpected payment in a letter to her German publisher. Luise Mühlbach to Hermann Costenoble, 13 July 1867, no. 76, in McClain and Kurth-Voigt, "Clara Mundts Briefe," col. 1107.

22. Tebbel, *Expansion of an Industry*, 204.

23. "Der freche Nachdruck in Nordamerika," *Deutsche Roman-Zeitung* 4, no. 45 (1867): col. 717.

24. *Putnam's Monthly Magazine of American Literature, Science, and Art* 11, no. 1 (January 1868): 128. Hathaway notes that there is "very little notice of [Mühlbach's novels] in the English journals and they do not seem to have been translated in England, nor were the many American translations reprinted there" (*German Literature*, 110).

25. Kurth-Voigt and McClain, "Louise Mühlbach's Historical Novels," 58.

26. "What the People Read," *Literary World* 4, no. 10 (March 1, 1874): 154.

27. Ibid., 153–54.

28. Rossiter Johnson, ed., *Authors Digest: The World's Great Stories in Brief* (1908; repr. New York: Authors Press, 1927), vol. 12, Lewald–Mühlbach.

29. Ernest A. Baker and James Packman, *A Guide to the Best Fiction: English and American Including Translations from Foreign Languages*, new and enlarged edition (London: George Routledge and Sons, 1932), 354–55.

30. Taylor, "Foreign Literature," 108.

31. Prutz, *Die deutsche Literatur der Gegenwart*, 2:255–56.

32. Gottschall, *Die deutsche Nationalliteratur*, 4:79–80.

33. Ibid., 4:82.

34. Rev. of *Berlin und Sanssouci oder Friedrich der Große und seine Freunde*, by Luise Mühlbach in *Deutsches Museum* 1, no. 9 (February 23, 1854): 325–27; reprt. in *Literaturkritik*, ed. Peter Uwe Hohendahl (Vaduz, Liechtenstein: Topos, 1984), 4:263, 265, respectively.

35. Ibid., 265.

36. Ibid., 266.

37. McClain and Kurth-Voigt, "Clara Mundts Briefe," col. 932.

38. "Literary Intelligence," *New York Times*, October 10, 1866, 2.

39. "Books of the Month," *Hours at Home* 4, no. 6 (April 1867): 572.

40. Hathaway reproduces a mordant review that appeared in the *New Englander* in 1867 that pronounces Mühlbach's novels a "heap of rubbish." Even Hathaway, who is ever ready to point out that popular literature by German women is third rate, allows that this review may "overshoot the mark" in its criticism. "Miss Muhlbach's [sic] Novels," *New Englander* 26, no. 101 (1867): 788, in *German Literature*, 110.

41. Rev. of *Frederick the Great and His Court*, by L. Mühlbach, trans. Mrs. Chapman Coleman and Daughters, *Catholic World* 4, no. 22 (1867): 579; Rev. of *Marie Antoinette and Her Son*, by L. Mühlbach, *Catholic World* 6, no. 35 (1867–68): 713.

42. Hathaway, "Miss Muhlbach's Novels," 788.
43. Rev. of the historical novels of Luise Mühlbach, *New York Times*, September 23, 1867, 2.
44. "Editor's Literary Record," *Harper's New Monthly Magazine* 41, no. 243 (August 1870): 459.
45. "New Publications," *Catholic World* 5, no. 26 (1867): 285.
46. "Books of the Month," *Hours at Home* 6, no. 4 (February 1868): 383; rev. of *The Story of a Millionaire*, by Luise Mühlbach, *The Nation* 15, no. 376 (September 12, 1872): 172.
47. John Esten Cooke, "Miss Mühlbach and Her System," *Appleton's Journal* 11 (1874): 169.
48. Rev. of *The Merchant of Berlin*, by L. Mühlbach, *Round Table* 5 (January 5, 1867): 12.
49. Rev. of *Frederick the Great and His Court. An Historical Novel*, by L. Mühlbach, *Catholic World* 4, no. 22 (January 1867): 579; "Notices of New Books," *New Englander* 26, no. 101 (October 1867): 788.
50. "Literary Intelligence. New Books," *New York Times*, October 10, 1866, 2.
51. "Literary Table," *Round Table* 8 (October 3: 1868): 230.
52. Kirsten Belgum, *Popularizing the Nation: Audience, Representation, and the Production of Identity in* Die Gartenlaube, *1853–1900* (Lincoln: University of Nebraska Press, 1998).
53. Ibid., 21.
54. "Blätter und Blüthen, " *Die Gartenlaube*, no. 44 (1894): 291.
55. Belgum, *Popularizing the Nation*, 16.
56. In 1874 Smith mentions her need to pay for her subscription to *Die Gartenlaube*. Mary Stuart Smith to Eliza L. C. Harrison, 17 February 1874. In 1888 she describes how she is translating Marlitt's *Eulenhaus* directly from her copy of *Die Gartenlaube*. Mary Stuart Smith to Gessner Harrison Smith, 14 February 1888. THS Papers, Boxes 18 and 24, respectively.
57. "Our Germans," *Chicago Tribune*, March 23, 1873, 10.
58. Brent O. Peterson, "E. Marlitt (Eugenie John) (5 December 1825—22 June 1887)," in *Nineteenth-Century German Writers, 1841–1900*, vol. 129 of *Dictionary of Literary Biography*, ed. James Hardin and Siegfried Mews (Detroit: Gale Research, 1993), 225.
59. "Das Geheimniß der alten Mamsell," *Die Gartenlaube*, no. 13 (1868): 208. By the end of the year it had been reprinted a fourth time. *Die Gartenlaube*, no. 46 (1868): 736.
60. Else Hofmann, daughter of Ernst Keil's successor, recounted in 1918, however, that Keil himself did not learn that Marlitt was a woman until he proposed to visit her at home in Arnstadt. Else Hofmann, *Eugenie Marlitt: Ein Lebensbild* [1918], ed. Fayçal Hamouda (Arnstadt: Edition Marlitt, 2005), 13–14.
61. In 1885 Friedrich Friedrich, in a controversial review in *Das Magazin für die Literatur des In- und Auslandes*, condemned Marlitt's novels as promoting a lurid sensuality because they were structured around delayed gratification, which in his view stimulated the reader "in hysterisch-krankhafter Weise" (in a hysterically sick manner). Later, Michael Kienzle identified Friedrich's review as sealing the long-enduring assessment of Marlitt as a "Trivialromanautorin" (woman author of trivial novels). Hans Arens, *E. Marlitt: Eine kritische Würdigung* (Trier: Wissenschaftlicher Verlag, 1994), 16–18.
62. Rudolf von Gottschall, "Die Novellisten der 'Gartenlaube,'" *Blätter für literarische Unterhaltung* 19 (May 5, 1870): 289–93. Repr. in *Deutschsprachige Literaturkritik 1870–1914: Eine Dokumentation*, ed. Helmut Kreuzer with the assistance of Doris Rosenstein (Frankfurt am Main: Peter Lang, 2006), 1:40–48.

63. Emma Goldman, *Living My Life* (New York: Knopf, 1931), 1:116.
64. Arens, *E. Marlitt*, 15.
65. Urzsula Bonter, *Der Populärroman in der Nachfolge von E. Marlitt: Wilhelmine Heimburg, Valeska Gräfin Bethusy-Huc, Eufemia von Adlersfeld-Ballestrem*, Epistemata Würzburger Wissenschaftliche Schriften Reihe Literaturwissenschaft 528 (Würzburg: Königshausen & Neumann, 2005), 95. Although she defends Marlitt against charges of writing fairy tales (see note 67), she specifically identifies Marlitt's happy endings as projecting an intact world.
66. Agnes Hamilton to Edith Trowbridge, 19 August 1895. Hamilton Family Papers, Schlesinger Library, Radcliffe Institute for Advanced Study, Harvard University. I thank Barbara Sicherman for generously directing my attention to this letter.
67. Lynne Tatlock, "Domesticated Romance and Capitalist Enterprise: Annis Lee Wister's Americanization of German Fiction," in Tatlock and Erlin, *German Culture*, 165. See also Bonter (*Populärroman*, 41–42), who explicitly takes up the issue of their resemblance to "Cinderella" and deftly enumerates the ways in which they do not in the least conform to that fairy tale.
68. For the enduring reading of Marlitt in Wilhelmine Germany, see Lynne Tatlock, "The Afterlife of Nineteenth-Century Popular Fiction and the German Imaginary: The Illustrated Collected Novels of E. Marlitt, W. Heimburg, and E. Werner," in Tatlock, *Publishing Culture*, 118-52. See especially 119 and 114n6 for Marlitt's works as recommended in advice books.
69. Rosa Mayreder, "Familienliteratur," *Das literarische Echo* 8 (1905–6), cols. 411–17; Ernst von Wolzogen, "Das Familienblatt und die Literatur," *Das literarische Echo* 9 (1907): cols. 177–85.
70. Ibid., col. 183. In 1902 *Die Gartenlaube* wrote its own history, reminding its readers that Marlitt's novels expressed the rapprochement of aristocracy and bourgeoisie in the spirit of the liberalism of the times. "Zur Geschichte der *Gartenlaube*," *Die Gartenlaube*, no. 8 (1902): 137.
71. "Zur Geschichte der *Gartenlaube*," 137, 900.
72. A notice in *Die Gartenlaube* comments that of the recent publications into English, French, Danish, Dutch, Swedish, and Italian, only the Danish and Dutch have not paid the author a fee. *Die Gartenlaube*, no. 5 (1876): 92. America is not mentioned here, and it is not clear whether "American" is subsumed under "English."
73. "The New York Mercantile Library," *Scribner's Monthly* 1, no. 4 (February 1871): 364. Louisa May Alcott's *Little Women* and *An Old Fashioned Girl* were, however, available in 250 copies and were "in constant circulation" (ibid.).
74. Morgan, *Bibliography*, 15. Morgan does not include in his tally the editions from the first decade of the new century, though they are listed under the entry for Marlitt.
75. Mühlbach's works, as historical fiction, enjoyed a somewhat different status from Marlitt's novels and were marketed somewhat differently by Appeton. They have been better preserved in libraries and thus in records such as Worldcat and the *National Union Catalogue*. My collecting of editions of *The Old Mam'selle's Secret* has to date enabled me to document 101 unique editions and reprint editions, and there is reason to suspect that more exist. Were one to undertake an equally thorough search for editions and reprint editions of the remaining nine novels, it is likely that Marlitt would come significantly closer to rivaling Mühlbach in the total number of publications.
76. Rev. of *The Old Mam'selle's Secret*, by E. Marlitt, trans. by A. L. Wister, *New York Times*, May 7, 1868, 2.

77. Rev. of *The Little Moorland Princess*, by E. Marlitt, trans. by A. L Wister, *The Nation* 15, no. 375 (5 September 1872): 157; Rev. of *The Little Moorland Princess*, by E. Marlitt, trans. by A. L. Wister, *Southern Farm and Home: A Magazine of Agriculture, Manufactures and Domestic Economy* 3, no. 6 (April 1872): 232.

78. "Some Novels," *Literary World* 7 (September 1, 1876): 48.

79. "Gold Elsie; from the German of E. Marlitt," *American Socialist* 4, no. 6 (February 6, 1879): 45.

80. "Blätter und Blüthen, E. Marlitt," *Die Gartenlaube*, no. 27 (1887): 450.

81. "E. Marlitt," *Die Gartenlaube*, no. 29 (1887): 476.

82. S. Baring-Gould, "Marlitt," reprinted from the *Gentleman's Magazine*, in *Little's Living Age* 176, no. 2276 (February 11, 1888): 352, 357, respectively.

83. Mary Stuart Smith, "E. Marlitt, the Novelist," *American Magazine* 7, no. 3 (January 1888): 369.

84. *At the Councillor's*, Marlitt's sixth full-length novel translated in North America, did not appear until later that same year, 1876, and thus did not come into consideration for the contest. "The Prize Question in Fiction," *Publishers' Weekly* 9, no. 127 (May 20, 1876): 634–36.

85. "What Middletown Read."

86. Rossiter Johnson, ed., "The Old Mam'selle' Secret," and "A Little Moorland Princess," in *Authors Digest*, 12: 180–202.

87. Johnson, *Authors Digest*, 20: 312.

88. According to Smith, "shrinking modesty seems to have been the motive that led Bertha Behrens, the sixteen-year-old daughter of a German army surgeon, to conceal her identity under the assumed name of Wilhelmine Heimburg when she came before the public as a writer, in the columns of a German woman's paper, viz, Victoria." Mary Stuart Smith, "W. Heimburg," *Current Literature* 24, no. 1 (July 1898): 21.

89. Bonter, *Populärroman*, 75. According to Bonter, the novel was serialized from May 20 to July 14, 1877, and then appeared in book form in Magdeburg in 1878.

90. "Kleiner Briefkasten," *Die Gartenlaube*, no. 42 (1878): 704.

91. "W. Heimburg," *Die Gartenlaube*, no. 39 (1884): 648; Adolf Hinrichsen, *Das literarische Deutschland*, 2nd ed. (Berlin, 1891), 88, quoted by Bonter, *Populärroman*, 76.

92. Theodor Fontane to Emilie Fontane, 8 June 1885, in Theodor Fontane, *Von dreissig bis achtzig. Sein Leben in seinen Briefen* (Leipzig: Dieterich, 1969), 323–34, cited by Bonter, *Populärroman*, 77.

93. Smith, "W. Heimburg," 21. The translation appeared in weekly installments in the *New York Tribune* (1881–82).

94. "A German Love Story," *Book Chat* 4, no. 7 (July 1889): 185.

95. Smith, "W. Heimburg," 21.

96. Morgan, *Bibliography*, 15.

97. "Fiction," *Literary World* 22, no. 7 (March 28, 1891): 112; Rev. of *A Sister's Love*, by W. Heimburg, *Nassau Literary Magazine* 46, no. 5 (December 1890): 863; Rev. of "Our Door Bell," as serialized in *Cosmopolitan*, *Milwaukee Daily Journal*, December 27, 1886; "Fiction," *Literary World* 22, no. 22 (October 24, 1891): 380; "Holiday Books," *Literary World* 20, no. 26 (December 21, 1889): 481.

98. Rev. of *Lucie's Mistake*, by W. Heimburg, *Nassau Literary Magazine* 46, no. 4 (October 1890): 213.

99. Rev. of *A Penniless Girl*, by W. Heimburg, *Literary World* 16, no.16 (August 8, 1885): 268.

100. "Fiction," *Literary World* 22, no. 18 (August 29. 1891): 293.

101. Rev. of *A Fatal Misunderstanding*, by W. Heimburg, *Literary World* 24, no. 16 (August 12, 1893): 258.

102. "The Books of 1884," *Publishers' Weekly* 27, no. 679 (January 31, 1885): 95; "The Books of 1890," *Publishers' Weekly* 39, no. 991 (January 1891): 152.

103. Heller, "Women Writers," 256.

104. Bonter, *Populärroman*, 77–78.

105. "E. Werner in Berlin und Rom," *Die Gartenlaube*, no. 27 (1872): 446. *Die Gartenlaube* complains here of an unauthorized translation of *Held der Feder* that has appeared in Italian translation in Rome.

106. Ernst Keil, "Eine literarische Freibeuterei," *Die Gartenlaube*, no. 44 (1873): 714–16.

107. The spine of *At a High Price* (Boston: Estes, 1879), for example, prominently displays the name "Ernest Werner." An anonymous review essay that appeared in 1877 in the *National Quarterly Review* refers to Elisabeth Werner throughout as "Ernst Werner." "German Novels and Novelists," *National Quarterly Review* 35, nos. 69–70, first series (July and October 1877): 83–104, 284–312.

108. "Eine Heldin der Feder," *Die Gartenlaube*, no. 28 (1876): 464–66.

109. Morgan, *Bibliography*, 15.

110. "The Books of 1883," *Publishers' Weekly* 25, no. 626 (January 26, 1884): 87. Of the eleven authors that merited mention here, five are German.

111. Heller, "Women Writers," 257.

112. For an account of the deceptions surrounding this pregnancy and the birth and subsequent death of the baby who was being underfed so that he would appear younger than he was, see Gisela Ebel, *Das Kind ist tot, die Ehre ist gerettet* (Frankfurt am Main: Tende, 1985).

113. Gottschall, *Die deutsche Nationalliteratur*, 4:341. Hillern briefly describes her education and many cultural contacts in Wilhelmine von Hillern, "Wilhelmine von Hillern," in *Bildende Geister: Unsere bedeutendsten Dichter und Schriftsteller der Gegenwart und Vergangenheit in charakteristischen Selbstbiographien sowie gesammelten Biographien und Bildern*, ed. Fritz Abshoff (Berlin: Peter J. Oestergard, 1905), 1:48.

114. *Und sie kommt doch!* was first serialized in *Die deutsche Rundschau* from October 1878 to September 1879, followed by its first book publication in March 1879. Maire Josephine Walshe, "The Life and Works of Wilhelmine von Hillern, 1836–1916" (PhD diss., State University of New York Buffalo, 1988), 179. The first English translation appeared in 1880 with Gottsberger in New York. Morgan, *Bibliography*, 253.

115. Hathaway, *German Literature*, 107–8. Hillern published only one novel in *Die Gartenlaube*. A feature article on her suggests, however, that she and her works interested Gartenlaube readers. "Die Tochter der Frau Birch-Pfeiffer," *Die Gartenlaube*, no. 36 (1872): 589–92.

116. Pochmann, *German Culture in America*, 347.

117. Wilhelmine von Hillern, *Höher als die Kirche: Edited with Introduction, Notes, Exercises, and Vocabulary*, ed. Eleonore Catherine Nippert (New York: F. S. Crofts, 1939); first published: New York: A. A. Knopf, 1928.

118. "Our Monthly Gossip. Wilhelmine von Hillern," *Lippincott's Magazine of Popular Literature and Science* 11, no. 22 (January 1873): 116.

119. *The Best Reading: Hints on the Selection of Books* (New York: G. P. Putnam and Sons, 1872), 83–84, 93.

120. "Literary Notes," *Appletons' Journal: A Magazine of General Literature* 9, no. 205 (February 22, 1873): 285.

121. "German sentimental novel" is the term used by the *Literary World* 22, no.18 (August 29, 1891): 293. The *New York Times* (May 1, 1881) recommended Wister's translation of *The Bailiff's Maid* as "wholesome, light reading for young people" and characterized her translations generally as from "safe and respectable" writers. In similar language, *Harper's* remarked of *The Little Moorland Princess* that "its moral tone is such that it can hardly fail to exert a healthful influence." "Editor's Literary Record," *Harper's New Monthly Magazine* 45, no. 267 (August 1872): 463.

122. Nancy Armstrong, *Desire and Domestic Fiction: A Political History of the Novel* (New York: Oxford University Press, 1987), 4.

123. Here and elsewhere I am, in using "region" rather than "province," mindful of Ian Duncan's distinction between the provincial as "defined by its difference from" the capital and the region which is "a place in itself." Ian Duncan, "The Provincial or Regional Novel," in *A Companion to the Victorian Novel*, ed. Patrick Brantlinger and William Thesing (Oxford: Blackwell: 2002), 318–35.

124. "Home town" is the historian Mack Walker's term for the dispersed towns in the German territories that were formative of the perceived individuality that characterized German regionalism in cultural production and German particularism in politics that persisted even after unification. See Mack Walker, *German Home Towns: Community, State, and General Estate, 1648–1871* (Ithaca, NY: Cornell University Press, 1971).

125. Armstrong, *Desire and Domestic Fiction*, 5.

126. Ibid., 1.

Chapter 3

1. Rev. of *Why Did He Not Die? or, The Child from the Ebräergang*, by Ad. von Volckhausen, *The Nation* 8, no. 317 (July 27, 1871): 63.

2. Ibid.

3. Ibid.

4. E. Marlitt, *Gold Elsie*, trans. A. L. Wister (Philadelphia: J. B. Lippincott, 1869), 3. All English quotations from *Gold Elsie* refer to this edition and translation unless otherwise indicated and will be cited parenthetically in the text.

5. See Kirsten Belgum, "E. Marlitt: Narratives of Virtuous Desire," in *A Companion to German Realism, 1848–1900*, ed. Todd Kontje (Rochester, NY: Camden House, 2002), 259–82, and on *Goldelse* in particular, see Belgum, *Popularizing the Nation*, 135–36.

6. Hans Arens passionately defends Marlitt against a German review from 1885 that objected to Marlitt's narrative structures: according to the reviewer, these were designed to arouse the reader in a "hysterically sick" manner by placing obstacles in the way of romantic union. Arens comes across as nearly as prudish as this contemporary reiewer when he insists that Marlitt's idea of love is completely unsexual and when he asserts that, to think otherwise, one would have to be a psychopath or an unscrupulous slanderer or have completely misunderstood the novels. In staking out his position, Arens has succumbed to a failure of the imagination and read only the surface narrative. Marlitt's novels do not promote sexual excess in the manner of sensation novels, although sexual excess is certainly present in them, only to be roundly condemned. Her works, true to the romance genre, are structured around the growing love of heroine and hero and make clear that the two

are drawn together by an unnamed, irresistible force. As discussed in chapter 4 below, the romance genre routinely erects obstacles to union to titillate readers. Moreover, in a culture that values reserve and restraint, small signs serve to indicate desire. Even as Marlitt's novels promote virtue and self-control on the surface, desire blossoms, the combination of text and subtext perfectly fulfilling the age-old dictum *prodesse et delectare*. For Arens's discussion, see *E. Marlitt*, 16–18.

7. The *British Quarterly Review* remarked that Marlitt had a *"penchant* for marrying brilliant young girls to grave middle-aged men." "Poetry, Fiction, and Belles Lettres," *British Quarterly Review, American Edition* 57 (April 1873): 300. She shares this tendency with her fellow German women writers, who perhaps copied this narrative pattern from her.

8. Gottschall ("Die Novellisten der 'Gartenlaube,'" 1:43) noted similarities between Herr von Walde and Brontë's Lord Rochester. He did not mention the similarities of the two Berthas.

9. The restoration of the community is reflected in the final description of the renovated castle. The renovated house is a favorite feature of Marlitt's domestic fiction. On the significance of the interior in Marlitt's *Im Hause des Kommerzienrats*, for example, see Kirsten Belgum, "Critique of the Parvenu Interior: Friedrich Spielhagen and Eugenie Marlitt," in *Interior Meaning: Design of the Bourgeois Home in the Realist Novel* (New York: Peter Lang, 1992), 103–27.

10. Rev. of *Gold Elsie*, by E. Marlitt, *The Nation* 7, no. 175 (October 29, 1868), 355–56.

11. Ibid.

12. "Some Novels," *Literary World* 7 (September 1, 1876): 48.

13. Rev. of *Gold Elsie*, by E. Marlitt, *British Quarterly Review, American Edition* 57 (April 1873): 300.

14. Advertisement, *Lippincott's Magazine* 24, no. 143 (November 1879): 17.

15. *Publishers' Weekly* 31, no. 801 (June 4, 1887): 736.

16. Mary Stuart Smith to Gessner Harrison Smith, 24 February 1887, in Papers of the Tucker, Harrison, and Smith Families, Box 24, Small Special Collections Library, University of Virginia, Charlottesville, Virginia.

17. Ibid.

18. John Tebbel describes rebinding and reprinting in the particular case of Grosset and Dunlap in *Expansion of an Industry*, 360–65.

19. There are likely more reprint editions than I have been able to document to date. Cf. the ongoing Lucile Project (Introduction, n. 61), which to date has established that, from 1860 to 1938, close to a hundred American publishers' brought out at least two thousand editions and issues.

20. *Finding List of English Prose Fiction in the Public Library of the City of Boston* (Boston: Published by the Trustees, 1903), 66, 92.

21. E. Marlitt, *Gold Elsie* (New York: Chatterton-Peck Company, n.d.).

22. Saidee E. Kennedy, "Adelaide's Skirts," *Little Folks for Youngest Readers, Little Listeners and Lookers at Pictures*, 1907, 357.

23. "Bei der Verfasserin der 'Gold-Else,'" *Die Gartenlaube*, no. 52 (1869): 827–29; "The Old Mam'selle's Secret. After the German of E. Marlitt. By Mrs. A. L. Wister," *New York Times*, May 7, 1868, 2.

24. Advertisement, *American Literary Gazette*, 297. The publication of *Secret* preceded *Gold Elsie* by approximately half a year. *Secret* was announced as "just published" on April

1, 1868, and *Gold Elsie* as "just ready" on October 8, 1868. Advertisement, *American Literary Gazette and Publishers' Circular* 10, no. 11 (April 1, 1868): 297; "Just Ready," *The Nation* 7, no. 171 (October 8, 1868): 298.

25. The novel was serialized in *Die Gartenlaube* in 1867 in nos. 21–38, that is, May to late September or early October.

26. "Annis Lee Wister Dead," *New York Times*, November 16, 1908, 9; "Funeral of Noted Translator Today," *Philadelphia Inquirer*, November 17, 1908.

27. Agnes Hamilton to Alice Hamilton, 10 August 1881; Agnes Hamilton to Edith Trowbridge, 19 August 1895, Hamilton Family Papers, Schlesinger Library, Radcliffe Institute for Advanced Study, Harvard University. Agnes's correspondent in the first of these, her cousin Alice, would be among the first North American women to audit classes at the University of Munich. Barbara Sicherman, *Alice Hamilton: A Life in Letters* (Cambridge, MA: Harvard University Press, 1984), 89.

28. Mark Twain, "The Awful German Language," in *A Tramp Abroad*, ed. Shelley Fisher Fishkin (New York: Oxford University Press, 1996), 603; Horst Kruse, "The Old Mamsell and the Mysterious Stranger: Mark Twain's Encounter with German Literature and the Writing of 'No. 44, The Mysterious Stranger,'" *American Literary Realism* 39, no. 1 (Fall 2006): 64–74.

29. Rev. of *The Old Mam'selle's Secret*, by E. Marlitt, *Lippincott's Magazine* 1 (1868): 680.

30. The quotation appeared, for example, in the back matter of Ouida's *Friendship*, along with advertisements for Susan Warner's *The Wide, Wide World*, three novels by Wilhelmine von Hillern, works by Baroness Tautphoeus, and other popular reading from the period. Ouida, *Friendship: A Story of Society* (Philadelphia: J. B. Lippincott, 1878), back matter.

31. *Catalog of "A. L. A." Library. 5000 Volume for a Popular Library Selected by the American Library Association and Shown at the World's Columbian Exposition* (Washington: Government Printing Office, 1893), 30, 36.

32. Rossiter Johnson, "Eugenie Marlitt," in *Authors Digest* 19: 312. The two plot summaries included are in volume 12:180–202 and include *Secret* and *The Little Moorland Princess*.

33. Charles Dudley Warner, ed., "Old Mamselle's Secret," *Library of the World's Best Literature, Ancient and Modern* (New York: J. A. Hill, 1896), 30:180.

34. *Classified Catalogue of the Carnegie Library of Pittsburgh 1895–1902 in Three Volumes* (Pittsburgh: Carnegie Library, 1907), 2:1897.

35. *Catalogue of English Prose Fiction and Juvenile Books in the Chicago Public Library* (Chicago: Chicago Public Library, 1898), 74, 145, as listed under John, E., and Wister, Annis L., Translations, respectively.

36. The title page of an exemplar dated 1868 announces itself as the third edition, suggesting that the number of reprint editions is far greater than I have been able to confirm. E. Marlitt, *The Old Mam'selle's Secret*, trans. A. L. Wister, 3rd edition (Philadelphia: J. B. Lippincott, 1868).

37. E. Marlitt, *The Old Mam'selle's Secret*, trans. Mary Stuart Smith, Seaside Pocket Edition 858 (New York: Munro, 1886).

38. "The Prize Question in Fiction," *Publishers' Weekly* 9, no. 227 (May 20, 1876): 634.

39. "Index to the Books of 1886," *Publishers' Weekly* 31, nos. 783–84 (January 29, 1887): 143.

40. E. Marlitt, *The Old Mam'selle's Secret*, trans. A. L. Wister, Lippincott's Series of Select Novels no. 75 (Philadelphia: J. P. Lippincott, 1887). On the importance of well-known antecedents to early film and the need for clarity, see, e.g., Charles Musser, *The Emergence of Cinema: The American Screen to 1907*, vol. 1 of *History of the American Cinema* (New York: Charles Scribner's Sons, 1990), 349, 352–53, 383, and Eileen Bowser, *The Transformation of Cinema, 1907–1915*, vol. 2 of *History of the American Cinema* (New York: Charles Scribner's Sons, 1990), 42–43, 52–53.

41. E. Marlitt, *The Old Mam'selle's Secret*, trans. E. H. (New York: Hurst and Company, n.d.).

42. "Old Mam'selle's Secret," *Moving Picture World* (7 December 1912): 1012; "Old Mam'selle's Secret," *Motion Picture News* (23 Nov 1912): 31–33.

43. Charlotte Brontë, *Johanna Eyre*, trans. Ernst Susemihl (Berlin: Duncker & Humblot, 1848). *Jane Eyre* was also adapted in 1856 for the German stage as *Die Waise von Lowood* by the popular playwright Charlotte Birch-Pfeiffer.

44. Gottschall, "Die Novellisten der 'Gartenlaube,'" 44.

45. Charlotte Brontë, *Jane Eyre* (New York: Alfred A. Knopf), 2:58.

46. E. Marlitt, *The Old Mam'selle's Secret* (Philadelphia: J. B. Lippincott, 1869), 211. Further page references to this edition appear in the body of the text.

47. Ulrich von Liechtenstein, "Lied 28," in *Frauendienst*, ed. Franz Viktor Spechtler (Göppingen: Kümmerle, 1897), 286, ll. 13–18. The two parts of the poem in the original Middle High German are found in Wister's translation on pp. 81 and 111, and both are translated on p. 112.

48. For a fuller discussion of this novel, see Lynne Tatlock, "Eine amerikanische Baumwollprinzessin in Thüringen. Transnationale Liebe, Familie und die deutsche Nation in E. Marlitts *Im Schillingshof*, " in Hamann et al., *Amerika und die deutschsprachige Literatur*, 105–25.

49. The third American translation appeared sixteen years later. E. Marlitt, *In the Schillingscourt*, trans. Hettie E. Miller, The Enterprise Series 52 (Chicago: E. A. Weeks, 1895).

50. Rev. of *In the Schillingscourt*, by E. Marlitt, *Literary World* 10, no. 22 (October 25, 1879): 342.

51. Steinestel's translation is very free, condenses the text, and does not observe the original chapter divisions. Her version consists of only thirty-four chapters. but it does not omit any of the events. Wister's consists of forty chapters. The German serialized and book versions and Miller's translation, however, consist of forty-one chapters.

52. Wister mistranslated the opening passage, which describes the mansion as a "Fremdling auf deutschem Boden" (foreigner on German soil), taking the "Fremdling" to be the architect and not realizing that the text anthropomorphizes the house here. E. Marlitt, *Im Schillingshof*, vol. 4 of E. *Marlitt's Gesammelte Romane und Novelle*, 2nd ed. (Stuttgart: Union Deutsche Verlagsgesellschaft, n.d.), 6; E. Marlitt, *In the Schillingscourt*, trans. Annis Lee Wister (Philadelphia: J. B. Lippincott Company, 1898), 6. Further page references to these editions appear in the body of the text, cited as M and W, respectively.

53. Joy Jordan-Lake, *Whitewashing Uncle Tom's Cabin: Nineteenth-Century Women Novelists Respond to Stowe* (Nashville, TN: Vanderbilt University Press, 2005), 63–96; Cheryl Thurber, "The Development of the Mammy Image and Mythology," in *Southern Women: Histories and Identities*, ed. Virginia Bernhard, Betty Brandeon, Elizabeth Fox-Genovese, and Theda Perdue (Columbia: University of Missouri Press, 1992), 87–108.

54. See Kenneth W. Goings, *Mammy and Uncle Mose: Black Collectibles and American Stereotyping* (Bloomington: Indiana University Press, 1994), figs. 1, 3, 4, 17, and 18, for examples of representations of African Americans with round faces and thick red lips.

55. E. Marlitt, *In the Schillingscourt*, trans. Emily R. Steinestel (New York: George Munro's Sons, n.d.), 91 and 102, respectively. Further page references to this edition appear in the body of the text, cited as S.

56. Drew Gilpin Faust, *The Creation of Confederate Nationalism: Ideology and Identity in the Civil War South* (Baton Rouge: Louisiana State University Press, 1988), 84.

57. Goings, *Mammy*, 9. On the origins of the myth of the Lost Cause in literature and popular culture, see also Rollin G. Osterweis, *The Myth of the Lost Cause, 1865–1900* (Hamdon, CT: Archon Books, 1973). On myths of the New South, see Paul M. Gaston: *The New South Creed: A Study in Southern Mythmaking* (New York: Alfred A. Knopf, 1970).

58. Goings, *Mammy*, 10. See below, chapter 9, for the southern translator Mary Stuart Smith's espousal of views associated with the Lost Cause.

59. Ibid, 9. Thurber also notes how the loving and loyal mammy as a product of the New South figured an idea of the antebellum South as it never was; the mammy demonstrated "that the South was capable of harmonious and loving relations.... The ideal mammy was presented as someone who loved unconditionally with forgiveness for the past" ("Development of the Mammy Image," 108).

60. For a discussion of paternalism and patriarchy as these pertain to southern planters as compared with Prussian Junkers, see Shearer Davis Bowman, *Masters and Lords: Mid-19th-Century U.S. Planters and Prussian Junkers* (New York: Oxford University Press, 1993), esp. ch. 5, 162–83. Bowman's study recalls that the idea of affective relationships between masters and those condemned to hereditary servitude was not foreign to the mid-century German-speaking world, when the paternalistic relationship of master and serf was on occasion nostalgically invoked as a social good characterizing an era, for example, when masters cared for workers when they reached old age (173–74).

61. Goings, *Mammy*, 8.

62. Belgum, "Narratives of Virtuous Desire," 259–82.

63. Todd Kontje, "Marlitt's World: Domestic Fiction in an Age of Empire," *Germany Quarterly* 77, no. 4 (2004): 416–17.

64. E. Marlitt, *In the Schillingscourt*, trans. Hettie E. Miller (Chicago: M. A. Donohue, n.d.), 471. Further page references appear in the body of the text, cited as HM.

65. Erika Dingeldey, *Luftzug hinter Samtportieren: Versuch über E. Marlitt* (Bielefeld: Aisthesis, 2007), 80.

66. "From J. B. Lippincott & Co., Philadelphia," *Arthur's Illustrated Home Magazine* 47, no. 12 (December 1879): 617.

67. For a discussion of the illustrations in the German edition, see Tatlock, "Afterlife," 118–52.

68. Marlitt, *Schillingscourt* (Donohue). Author's copy. The dedication is dated "Xmas 1911."

69. "Books," *Minneapolis Journal*, September 6, 1901, 5.

70. W. D. Howells, "Novel-Writing and Novel-Reading: An Impersonal Explanation," in *Howells and James: A Double Billing* (New York: New York Public Library, 1958), 19.

71. See Kelley, *Private Women, Public Stage*.

72. Rev. of *In the Schillingscourt*, by E. Marlitt, *The Nation* 29, no. 756 (December 25, 1879): 443–44.

73. "Romance," *Milwaukee Sentinel*, November 11, 1879, 7.
74. Ibid.
75. Rev. of *In the Schillingscourt*, *The Nation*, 444.
76. On the reading of German popular fiction by southern women, see below, chapters 7 and 9.
77. Copy owned by the author.
78. The formulation is Sicherman's in *Well-Read Lives*, 40.

Chapter 4

1. Mary Stuart Smith to Francis H. Smith, 8 July 1880, THS Papers, Box 19.
2. Scott Denham, Foreword, *W. G. Sebald: History—Memory—Trauma* (Berlin: Walter de Gruyter, 2006), 6. Contemporary Germans in turn tend to see the happy ending as quintessentially American and, in a more critical take, as part of the American culture industry, indeed, as the disneyfication of culture.
3. E. Werner, *Vineta: The Phantom City*, trans. Frances A. Shaw (Boston: Estes and Lariat, 1877), 411.
4. "Fiction," *Literary World* 10, no. 2 (May 24, 1879): 167.
5. Janice A. Radway, *Reading the Romance: Women, Patriarchy, and Popular Literature* (Chapel Hill: University of North Carolina Press, 1991), 207. Further page references to this work appear in the body of the text, cited as RR.
6. Pamela Regis, *A Natural History of the Romance Novel* (Philadelphia: University of Pennsylvania Press, 2003), 24, 22. Further page references appear in the body of the text.
7. Urszula Bonter maintains that Heimburg's spinster is modeled on Aunt Cordula in *The Old Mam'selle's Secret* (*Populärroman*, 79). But there are significant differences. Heimburg, unlike Marlitt, shifts full attention to the unfulfilled love of an elderly woman. If her novel is also devoted to revealing secrets, then it is to bring hidden emotional life to the surface and not to facilitate a young woman's romance.
8. W. Heimburg, *The Pastor's Daughter*, trans. Mrs. J. W. Davis (Chicago: Donohue Brothers, n.d.), 32.
9. Bonter, *Populärroman*, 82–88.
10. Ibid., 93–104.
11. "Authors and Books," *The Bostonian* 3, no. 4 (January 1896): 404.
12. Notice of Behrens, Bertha, *Beetzen Manor: A Romance*, trans. Elsie Lathrop (New York: International News Co., 1895), in *The Annual American Catalogue 1895* (New York: Publishers' Weekly, 1895), 17.
13. "Recent Fiction," *The Critic* 15, no. 385 (1891): 263.
14. W. Heimburg, *A Sister's Love: A Novel*, trans. Margaret P. Waterman (New York: Worthington, 1890), 174. For continuity I use the title *Her Only Brother* in my discussion of this text. Further page references to this edition appear in the body of the text.
15. Morgan, *Bibliography*, 231.
16. "Recent Fiction," *The Critic* 15, no. 385 (1891): 263; "Recent Publications," *Daily Picayune*, November 25, 1888, 14; Advertisement, *Southwestern Christian Advocate*, November 27, 1890, 5, col. D.
17. Griswold, *Descriptive List*, 733–34.

18. In his book on songs for St. Martin's Day, Wilhelm Jürgensen identifies several versions of this song from areas around Hanover and Altmark, three of which are very close to Heimburg's lines. Wilhelm Jürgensen, *Martinslieder: Untersuchung und Texte, Wort und Brauch.* Volkskundliche Arbeiten namens der Schlesischen Gesellschaft für Volkskunde 6 (Breslau: M. & H. Marcus, 1910), 111–13.

19. Griswold, *Descriptive List,* 733.

20. Ibid., 734.

21. W. Heimburg, *Herzenskrisen* (Berlin: O. Janke, 1887). Griswold incorrectly lists this novel as *Zwei Freundinnen* (*Descriptive List,* 729).

22. "Fiction," *Literary World* 21, no. 17 (August 16, 1890): 267.

23. W. Heimburg, *Lucie's Mistake,* trans. J. W. Davis (New York: R. F. Fenno, 1899), 292.

24. Ibid., 188.

25. Mary Stuart Smith's mention of "Lore von Tollen" in letters to her son suggests that the two had also translated (or wished to translate) the novel but failed to place it. Mary Stuart Smith to Gessner Harrison Smith, 24 July 1889 and 6 August 1889, in THS, Box 25.

26. Griswold, *Descriptive List,* 740–41.

27. W. Heimburg, *Lora: The Major's Daughter,* trans. J. W. Davis (Chicago: Donohue Brothers, n.d.), 3. Further page references to this edition appear in the body of the text.

28. F[anny] Lewald, *Hulda, or The Deliverer: A Romance,* trans. A. L. Wister (Philadelphia: J. B. Lippincott, 1876), 43. Further page references to this edition appear in the body of the text.

29. "Fanny Lewald (Germany, 1811–1889). Hulda (1875)," in *Authors Digest* 12: 1–10.

30. "Recent Novels," *The Nation* 19, no. 475 (August 6, 1874): 92.

31. Claire von Glümer, *A Noble Name, or Dönninghausen* (Philadelphia: J. B. Lippincott, 1888), 326–27. Further page references to this edition appear in the body of the text.

32. "Some New Novels," *The Independent* 34, no. 1777 (December 21, 1882): 13.

33. "Recent Fiction," *The Independent* 36, no. 1859 (July 17, 1884): 11.

34. Ursula Zöge von Manteuffel, *Violetta. A Romance,* trans. A. L. Wister (Philadelphia: J. B. Lippincott, 1886), 368.

35. "New Novels by Popular Authors. Violetta," *Lippincott's Monthly Magazine* (January 1887): A38.

36. "Talk about Books," *The Chautauquan* 7, no. 2 (November 1886): 128.

37. "Recent Fiction," *The Critic* 140 (September 4, 1886): 112.

38. Rev. of *Violetta,* by Ursula Zöge von Manteuffel, *Literary World* 17, no. 15 (July 24, 1886): 253.

39. "Recent Fiction," *The Critic,* 112.

40. "Charming Summer Novels," *The Dial* 7, no. 75 (July 1886): 55.

41. I thank Lisabeth Hock for a critical reading of this section in progress and for sharing her own work in progress on Hillern's *Arzt der Seele.*

42. *The Galaxy* characterized *Arzt* as treating "the Woman Emancipation question in a spirit decidedly against the view of its votaries." Rev. of *Arzt der Seele,* by Wilhelmine von Hillern, *The Galaxy* 9, no. 4 (April 1870): 577. A review essay of ten German novels objected strenuously to *Arzt* as "the work of a conservative who has not chosen to discuss the question on its merits." Anon., "German Novels and Novelists," *National Quarterly Review* 35, no. 70, first series (October 1877): 307.

43. Fourteen years after the novel first appeared in English translation, Lippincott was

still advertising the book in such terms, quoting from two reviews. See, e.g., "The Works of Wilhelmine von Hillern," in Louisa Parr, *Dorothy Fox* (Philadelphia: Lippincott, 1884), back matter.

44. E. A. McCobb, "Of Women and Doctors: *Middlemarch* and Wilhelmine von Hillern's *Ein Arzt der Seele*," *Neophilologus* 68 (1984): 585.

45. Wister's translation corresponds to the serialized version in its adherence to the division of the novel into three parts, with the first chapter in each of these parts numbered 1. The German book version of the novel is by contrast divided into four volumes, each of which restarts chapter numbering with number 1. It splits part two of the original serialized version in half. Compare Wilhelmine von Hillern, *Ein Arzt der Seele*, 4 vols. (Berlin: O. Janke, 1869) with Wilhelmine von Hillern, *Ein Arzt der Seele, Deutsche Roman-Zeitung* (1869), 1: 161–94; 241–72; 321–56; 401–30, 481–512, 561–90, 641–90, 721–48, 825–38, 899–912; 2: 31–64, 105–44, 187–224, 265–306.

46. Advertisement, *New York Times*, May 7, 1870, 7.

47. *Catalog of A. L .A. Library: 5000 Volumes for a Popular Library*, 27, 36.

48. Warner, *World's Best Literature*, 30:347–48. The claim in this entry that the book's "exaggeration and sentimentality do not appeal to the English reader" (348) is refuted by the many editions and widespread availability of the book in America over forty years.

49. Rev. of *Only a Girl*, by Wilhelmine von Hillern, *Harper's New Monthly Magazine* 41, no. 243 (August 1870): 459.

50. "The Second Wife," *Literary World* 5, no. 3 (August 1874): 39.

51. Wilhelmine von Hillern, *Only a Girl*, trans. A. L. Wister (Philadelphia: J. B. Lippincott, 1887), 167. Further page references to this edition appear in the body of the text.

52. German feminist Hedwig Dohm remarked in 1874 that intellectual women were generally thought to have "hard features, a long nose, flat-heeled boots, [and] character quirks" and to be elderly. Patricia M. Mazón, *Gender and the Modern Research University: The Admission of Women to German Higher Education, 1865–1914* (Stanford, CA: Stanford University Press, 2003), 55. In 1872 German anatomist Theodor von Bischoff argued that university study would make women barren. Ibid., 89.

53. The grounds cited for rejecting Ernestine are historically accurate, corresponding to those that dominated the discussion in the 1870s in the German Reich as it moved from having no formal policy on women's admission to study to policies banning women at almost all German universities by 1879. See Mazón, *Gender and the Modern Research University*, esp. 85–114.

54. "German Novels and Novelists," 311. See n. 42.

55. To this day women remain underrepresented in areas of science in industrialized countries and find it difficult to balance "domestic with professional responsibilities." Sandra Harding, *Sciences from Below: Feminisms, Postcolonialities, and Modernities* (Durham, NC: Duke University Press, 2008), 104.

56. McCobb, " Of Women and Doctors" 577.

57. Janice Radway, "Readers and their Romances," in *Reception Study: From Literary Theory to Cultural Studies*, ed. James L. Machor and Philip Goldstein (New York: Routledge, 2001), 243.

58. Natalie Davis, "Women on Top," in *Society and Culture in Early Modern France: Eight Essays* (Stanford, CA: Stanford University Press, 1975), 144.

59. Wister, who was not a native speaker of German, may not have known the meaning of "Querkopf" and thus merely inferred the meaning from context. Whether she

deliberately altered the meaning or misunderstood it, either scenario involves an act of interpretation. Wilhelmine von Hillern, *Ein Artz der Seele* (Berlin: Otto Janke, 1869), 4: 235–36). Further page references to this edition appear in the body of the text.

60. Wilhelmine von Hillern, *Ernestine: A Novel,* trans. Sabine Baring-Gould (London: Thos. De La Rue, 1879), 2:299. The New York publisher W. S. Gottsberger reissued Baring-Gould's 1879 translation in 1881.

61. Sicherman, *Well-Read Lives,* 1.

62. As Sicherman points out, "remaining single was, with few exceptions, a virtual condition for a middle-class woman to have a career." Ibid., 2. Of the 164 borrowers of *Only a Girl* (1891–1902) in Muncie, Indiana, 128 are identifiably female ("What Middletown Read").

63. Lippincott advertised Werner as "Author of the 'Hero of the Pen'" on the title page of the first edition of *At the Altar* (1872). I have not, however, found evidence that *Hero* had been published in English by the time of the publication of *At the Altar.* Likewise, an advertisement in the *New York Times* announces *At The Altar* as by the author of "Hermann" and "Hero of the Pen," even though *Hermann* had not yet appeared in book form in English. "New Publications," *New York Times,* September 7, 1872, 8.

64. "Recent Novels," *The Nation* 15, no. 376 (September 12, 1872): 171.

65. E. Werner, *At the Altar,* trans. J. S. L. (Philadelphia: J. B. Lippincott, 1872), 320. Further page references to this edition appear in the body of the text.

66. "Books," *Christian Union* 6, no. 20 (November 20, 1872): 428, and "Recent Novels," 172 (see n. 64).

67. "New Publications," *New York Times,* October 12, 1872, 3.

68. "The Latest Novels and New Books," *The Independent* 35, no. 1824 (November 15, 1883): 12.

69. "The Books of 1883," *Publishers' Weekly* 25, no. 626 (January 26, 1884): 87.

70. E. Werner, *Banned and Blessed,* trans. A. L. Wister (Philadelphia: J. B. Lippincott, 1890), 390, 375. Further page references to this edition appear in the body of the text.

71. David Blackbourn, *The Conquest of Nature: Water, Landscape, and the Making of Modern Germany* (New York: W. W. Norton, 2006), 175. Werner's works do not figure among Blackbourn's historical examples, yet they testify eloquently to the affirmation of the conquest of nature that he depicts here.

72. Francke and Howard, *German Classics.* Muriel Almon's translation of Storm's novella appears in volume 11. On Storm's presence in this volume, see Sammons, *Kuno Francke's Edition,* 188–89. Theodor Storm, "The Rider on the White Horse," trans. Margarita Münsterberg, in *German Fiction,* ed. William Allan Neilson, Harvard Classics of Shelf Fiction 15 (New York: P. F. Collier, 1917), 185–91.

73. Advertisement for E. Werner's *A Lover from Across the Sea,* in Edward A. Robinson and George H. Wall, *The Gun-Bearer* (New York: Robert Bonner's Sons, 1894), unnumbered back page. The reference to the "German domestic love-story" in this advertisement suggests that "German" served as a kind of branding.

74. Alison Light, "'Returning to Manderley': Romance Fiction, Female Sexuality, and Class," in *Feminism and Cultural Studies,* ed. Morag Shiach (Oxford: Oxford University Press, 1999), 372. Further page references for Light's work are included in the body of the text.

75. Making a case for Marlitt's novels as belonging to German realism, Belgum argues that realism should be understood broadly to include "the perceived importance of desire

on the part of nineteenth-century readers, female as well as male." After all, milestones of nineteenth-century German realism feature male heroes who achieve their heart's desire. See Belgum, "Narratives of Virtuous Desire," 277.

76. Nataly von Eschtruth, *The Erl Queen*, trans. Emily S. Howard, The Snug Corner Series (New York: Wm. L. Allison Company, n.d.), fly leaf and verso of the book cover of author's copy. Further page references to this edition appear in the body of the text.

77. Rev. of *The Erl Queen*, by Nataly von Eschstruth, *Peterson's Magazine* 102, no. 2 (August 1892): 176; "Books! Books! Books! For Christmas Holidays," *Chicago Daily Tribune*, December 17, 1895, 4.

78. "Recent Fiction," *The Critic* 18, no. 553 (September 24, 1892): 164.

79. In 1900 Schlesinger Mayer's Washington Avenue Bookstore advertised the *Erl Queen*, along with Heimburg's *Lora: The Major's Daughter*, and her *Chaplain's Daughter* and other English and American books as "girls' books." "Schlesinger Mayer. The Wabash Avenue Bookstore," *Chicago Daily Tribune*, December 1, 1900,15.

Chapter 5

1. "Romance," Rev. of *In the Schillingscourt*, *Milwaukee Sentinel*, November 11, 1879, 7. As Mary Kelley points out, the majority of the popular works by the American "literary domestics" featuring "dreams of romantic love" as courtship also "stopped short of the altar." Kelley, *Private Women, Public Stage*,259.

2. Rosa Mayreder, "Familienliteratur," cols. 411–17, esp. col. 413, and Ernst von Wolzogen, "Das Familienblatt und die Literatur," cols. 177–85.

3. "Recent Fiction," *The Critic* 40 (July 15, 1882): 191.

4. By November 1879 *The Second Wife* was in its twelfth edition. Advertisement, *Lippincott's Magazine* 24, no. 143 (November 1879): 17.

5. Stanley Cavell, *Pursuits of Happiness: The Hollywood Comedy of Remarriage* (Cambridge, MA: Harvard University Press, 1981), 1. Further page references to Cavell are contained in the body of the text.

6. "A German Novel," *American Socialist* 3, no. 10 (March 7, 1878): 77.

7. "Literary Notices," *Godey's Lady's Book and Magazine* 89, no. 531 (September 1874): 280.

8. Rev. of *The Second Wife*, *Literary World* 5, no. 3 (August 1, 1874): 39.

9. Ruth-Ellen Boetcher Joeres, *Respectability and Deviance: Nineteenth-Century German Writers and the Ambiguity of Representation* (Chicago: University of Chicago Press, 1998), 228. Joeres cites Tania Modleski, *Loving with a Vengeance: Mass-Produced Fantasies for Women* (New York: Methuen, 1982) as Modleski responds to Fredric Jameson, "Reification and Utopia in Mass Culture," *Social Text* 1 (Winter 1979): 130–48. Further page references to Joeres's book are contained in the body of the text.

10. E. Marlitt, *The Second Wife: A Romance*, trans. A. L. Wister (Philadelphia: J. B. Lippincott, 1875), 121. All further page references to this edition appear in the body of the text.

11. "Books and Authors," *Christian Union* 10, no. 1 (July 8, 1874): A8.

12. My copy of *A Brave Woman* contains the date December 25, 1896, and the inscription "Paulina S. Schwarz from her teacher, Miss Florence J. Pepin." E. Marlitt, *A Brave Woman, with fifty photogravure illustrations*, translated by Margaret P. Waterman (New

York: Wm. L. Allison Company, n.d.). The verso of the title page contains the notation "copyright, 1891, by Worthington Co."

13. "Literary Notices," *Godey's Lady's Book* (see n. 7).

14. Rev. of *The Second Wife, Literary World,* 39.

15. The plot of *Jane Eyre* itself contains elements of the novel of remarriage, insofar as the first wedding ceremony of Mr. Rochester and Jane is interrupted with the dreadful news that he already has a wife. For nine chapters the couple is split apart until a chastened and maimed Mr. Rochester is able to propose a second time since his first wife has died.

16. Barbara Sicherman, "Sense and Sensibility: A Case Study of Women's Reading in Late-Victorian America," in *Reading in America,* ed. Cathy N. Davidson (Baltimore, MD: Johns Hopkins University Press, 1989), 208.

17. Ibid., 212.

18. E. Marlitt, *The Second Wife* (Chicago: Donohue, Henneberry, n.d.). Copy owned by author. The book is also signed in another hand: "Myrtle Fuchs," but it is unclear whether Myrtle Fuchs was the original owner, the "Mamma" intended in the dedication.

19. The *Literary World* announced on May 1, 1874, that Osgood would issue the novel "in time for the summer demand." "Literary News," *Literary World* 4, no. 12 (May 1, 1874): 190. E. Werner, *Good Luck!* translated by Frances A. Shaw (New York: A. L. Burt, n.d.), 1. Further page references to this edition appear in the body of the text. In 1876 Estes and Lauriat purchased the plates and remainders of J. R. Osgood including E. Werner's *Good Luck!* and reissued the novel. Raymond L. Kilgour, *Estes and Lauriat. A History; 1898–1914* (Ann Arbor: University of Michigan Press, 1957), 73.

20. "Healthy Light Literature. Which should be in every Library," *American Library Journal* 1, no. 10 (June 30, 1877): 352.

21. "Minor Book Notices," *Literary World* 4, no. 12 (May 1, 1874): 188.

22. Leland's translation of Heine's *Reisebilder* (Pictures of Travel) had appeared in its fifth revised edition in New York in 1866 and by 1882 had gone through four more editions. Morgan, *Bibliography,* 239.

23. By contrast, in Marlitt's *Countess Gisela,* which was serialized in *Die Gartenlaube* in 1869, the same year in which Bebel's Workers' Party was founded, there is no need for strikes. The conditions of the workers have been improved by the skillful management of Berthold, the benevolent absentee owner who has worked his magic from afar in opposition to the local government. Berthold has expanded the foundry into "dimensions hitherto undreamed of"; where there was once a single chimney, there are now fourteen. The factory is providing work for the needy and unemployed in the area, wages are very high, and "every possible attention [is] paid to the comfort of the work-people." He has also founded a "popular library, a savings bank, and several other benevolent institutions." E. Marlitt, *Countess Gisela,* trans. A. L. Wister (Philadelphia: J. B. Lippincott, 1869), 140 and 142, respectively. Workers parties are thus superfluous in this paternalistic fantasy of affective individualism, one shared by Werner's novel as well.

24. Emile Zola's *Germinal,* with its coal-mining setting and more critical view of management, would not be published until a decade later in 1885.

25. Worker relations become an issue repeatedly in Werner's novels, always with the plea for better conditions for the workers brought about by the iron will and ethical stance of an individual man. Those who exploit their workers are repudiated, but the workers are expected to see the greater wisdom of benevolent men who rule over them. In *Freie Bahn* (1893; *Clear the Track,* 1893), Egbert, the energetic and intelligent self-made engineer,

flirts with socialism for a time but ultimately repudiates it to become the heir apparent of Eberhard, the owner of the Odensburg works and his longtime benefactor. Although Egbert leaves the corrupt socialist party, he does not give up all of his socialist principles when he returns to the fold. Surprisingly, the factory owner concedes, "I am no longer the old blockhead who supposed that, alone, he could stem the tide of a new era. . . . I can summon to my side a young, fresh force that is in sympathy with the present." E. Werner, *Clear the Track! A Story of Today*, trans. Mary Stuart Smith (New York: The Federal Book Company, n.d.), 319. Werner's factory owner thus reflects the strategy of imperial Germany, guided by Bismarck, to outflank the socialists and split the liberals through the implementation of social legislation including insurance for illness (1883), accidents (1884), and invalidity and old age (1889). See David Blackbourn, *The Long Nineteenth Century: A History of Germany, 1780–1918* (New York: Oxford University Press, 1998), 346. It is possible that Werner read Elizabeth Gaskell's *North and South* in English or as *Margarethe* in German translation, where she would have encountered a scene with a lone factory owner facing an angry mob. Werner musters far less sympathy for the workers than does Gaskell.

26. "Blätter und Blüthen," *Die Gartenlaube*, no. 40 (1893): 687. The tenth volume in the collection did not put in an appearance until 1896. See the announcement of its recent publication in *Die Gartenlaube*, no. 45 (1896): 772.

27. E. Marlitt, *Goldelse*, vol. 8 of *E. Marlitt's Gesammelte Werke* (Stuttgart: Union deutsche Verlagsgesellschaft, 1890), back advertising pages. The identical advertisement for the Werner series recurs repeatedly in volumes from both the Heimburg and the Marlitt series.

28. "Minor Book Notices," 188 (see n. 21).

29. Smith claimed in 1898 that her translation of *Lumpenmüllers Lieschen*, commissioned by George Ripley and Whitelaw Reid, "introduced W. Heimburg to American readers through the columns of the New York Tribune." Mary Stuart Smith, "W. Heimburg," *Current Literature* 24, no. 1 (July 1898): 22. Her translation ran weekly in the *Tribune* from October 26, 1881, through February 15, 1882. In 1882 *The Critic* alluded to *Lieschen* in connection with "standard novels at cheap rates" supplied by the *Tribune*. "Recent Fiction," *The Critic* 40 (15 July 1882): 191.

30. Dickey's translation and Smith's rendering for the *Tribune* both begin with what becomes chapter 2 of the 1879 German book publication of *Lumpenmüllers Lieschen* (Leipzig: Keil, 1879) as does the original serialization in *Die Gartenlaube*, indicating that the magazine served as the source of both of these translations. Lathrop's translation, by contrast, contains the later-added first chapter. A notice in *Publishers' Weekly* announces that *A Maiden's Choice* is in preparation for the *International Library* for the fall. *Publishers' Weekly* 40, nos. 1025–26 (September 26, 1891): 392.

31. "Lenox and Summer Series. Paper Publications," *Publishers' Weekly* 49, no. 1251 (January 25, 1896): 210. Other favorites appearing in Fenno's series were books by Balzac, Barrie, Collins, Daudet, Doyle, Fothergill, Hardy, and Ouida, as well as novels by the German writers Marlitt and Georg Ebers.

32. *Die Gartenlaube* announced the publication of *Lumpenmüllers Lieschen* in Heimburg's collected works in issue no. 26 (1891): 448.

33. The illustrated German edition appeared in May or June 1891; Worthington's illustrated edition appeared sometime in the fall of 1891.

34. Mary Stuart Smith to Gessner Harrison Smith, 30 April 1888, in THS Papers, Box 24.

35. "Recent Fiction," *The Critic* 40 (July 15, 1882): 192, and "Literary Notes," *The Critic* 31 (March 11, 1882): 74.

36. "Editorial Notes," *United Service: A Quarterly Review of Military and Navel Affairs* 7, no. 1 (July 1882): 114; "Book Table," *Godey's Lady's Book and Magazine* 123, no. 737 (November 1891): 443. The former notice appears in a publication targeting male readers. It includes a list of "novels and romances" that are classified as summer reading for "lovers of light reading." While this listing in a men's journal might be evidence for men's reading of this literature, it is also possible that the notice suggested to men books that they could buy for the women in their lives.

37. Rev. of *A Maiden's Choice*, by W. Heimburg, *Peterson's Magazine* 100, no. 5 (November 1891): 461.

38. W. Heimburg, *A Maiden's Choice*, translated by Elise L. Lathrop (New York: R. F. Fenno & Company, 1899). Author copy. The dedication is written twice more in a different hand—"Ada B. Parker from Marie L. Bartholomew" and "Ada B. Parker / Port Gibson / New York / from Mrs. Bartholomew"—as if Ada B. Parker had a sentimental wish to remember the gift-giver. The illustrations in the Worthington edition are poor-quality reproductions of the illustrations by R. Wehle that appear in *Lumpenmüllers Lieschen* (1891), volume 2 of the ten-volume illustrated collected novels and novellas of Heimburg published by Keils Nachfolger/Union Deutsche Verlagsgesellschaft. All further page references to this edition of Lathrop's translation appear in the body of the text.

39. Notice, *Publishers' Weekly* 40, nos. 1025–26 (September 26, 1891): 392.

40. "Recent Fiction," *The Critic* 40 (July 15, 1882): 191.

41. "Current Fiction," *Literary World* 29, no. 14 (July 9, 1898): 219.

42. Michael Koser points out that the treatment of the paper mill in the novel presents early capitalism as an idyll in which social and economic disparities are bridged by personal bonds. Michael Koser, Afterword, *Lumpenmüllers Lieschen*, by Wilhelmine Heimburg, Das Schmökerkabinett (Frankfurt am Main: Fischer, 1974), 247–48.

43. "Recent Fiction," *The Critic* 17, no. 517 (January 16, 1892): 35.

44. "Recent Fiction," *The Critic*, 191 (see n. 40).

45. The insistence on Christmas and the Christmas tree as a quintessentially German holiday circulated in imperial Germany in descriptions of encounters with the alien, for example, in newspaper accounts and memoirs of the Franco-Prussian War. As Frank Becker points out, the celebration of Christmas 1870 offered the opportunity for Germans to express their love of family and home anew. Newspapers—and later on, memoirs—abounded with reports of official and improvised Christmas celebrations in the field. See Frank Becker, *Bilder von Krieg und Nation. Die Einigungskriege in der bürgerlichen Öffentlichkeit Deutschlands 1864–1913* (Munich: R. Oldenbourg Verlag, 2001), 367. A governess's story from 1908 offers a further example. She describes for the readers of a girls' magazine her experience of Christmas among Russians, concluding with the statement that foreigners are incapable of understanding the meaning of the Christmas tree, "the ancient property" of the Germans. E. Kothe, "Unser Weihnachtsbaum in der Fremde," *Töchter-Album*, ed. Thekla von Gumpert (Berlin: Carl Flemming Verlag, [1908]), 54:507.

46. The novel elsewhere signals Heimburg's reading of Freytag's best-selling *Soll und Haben*, when a character speaks of family affairs as "in a perfect chaos—Jews, money-lenders" with mortgage upon mortgage (*A Maiden's Choice*, 148).

47. The *Gartenlaube* serialization concluded in October 1874. The *New York Times* announced the publication of *Broken Chains* on December 8, 1874 ("New Publications," 7).

48. The *Literary World* spoke of "fine characterization in the book" but then asserted, "its general effect is unpleasant," without explaining why. The reviewer may have found the original marriage too degrading to be redeemed. "Minor Book Notices," *Literary World* 5, no. 9 (February 1, 1875): 141.

49. E. Werner, *Broken Chains*, trans. Frances A. Shaw, Osgood's Library of Novels 46 (Boston: James R. Osgood and Company), 30. Further page references to this edition appear in the body of the text.

50. W. Heimburg, *Misjudged* (Chicago: Donohue, n.d.). Exemplar advertised on abebooks.com

51. "Fiction," *Literary World* 22, no. 18 (August 29, 1891): 293.

52. "Recent Fiction," *The Critic* 16, no. 410 (November 7, 1891): 248.

53. "Literature. Book Reviews," *The Congregationalist* 36 (September 3, 1891): 3.

54. "A New Novel by W. Heimburg," *New York Times*, July 15, 1891, 3.

55. W. Heimburg, *Misjudged*, trans. J. W. Davis, Snug Corner Series (Chicago: M.A. Donohue, n.d.). Author's copy. Further page references to this edition appear in the body of the text.

56. Heimburg may have borrowed from Marlitt's *Countess Gisela* in adding a bronze foundry to an iron foundry to forge a wedding of art and industry. In *Countess Gisela* Marlitt recounts how the addition of a bronze foundry to an iron works has transformed the "productions of the establishment" from a "most primitive" kind to "artistic specimens of bronze-castings." Marlitt, *Countess Gisela*, 140.

57. Thomas Mann, *Buddenbrooks* (New York: A. A. Knopf, 1924); Thomas Mann, "Tristan," in *Stories from the Dial* (New York: Dial Press, 1924), 248–321; Thomas Mann, "Tonio Kröger," trans. Bayard Quincy Morgan, in vol. 19 of Francke and Howard, *German Classics*, 184–250; Thomas Mann, "Tonio Kröger," in *Death in Venice and Other Stories*, trans. Kenneth Burke (New York: Knopf, 1925), 193–284.

58. W. Heimburg, *Gertrude's Marriage*, trans. J. W. Davis, Snug Corner Series (Chicago: Donohue Brothers, n.d.), 307. This edition claims on its title page to be illustrated but contains no pictures.

59. "Minor Notices: Three Summer Novels," *Literary World* 20, no. 11 (May 25, 1889): 177.

60. "Talk about New Books," *Catholic World* 49, no. 289 (April 1887): 112.

61. Advertisement, *Christian Union* 40, no. 20 (November 14, 1889): 618; advertisement, *The Independent* 41, no. 2138 (November 21, 1889): 22; advertisement, *The Art Amateur: A Monthly Journal Devoted to Art in the Household* 22, no. 1 (December 1889): 9.

62. Advertisement, *Christian Union* 18, no. 2 (July 10, 1878): 2.

63. McCobb, "Of Women and Doctors," 571–86.

64. "A German Love Story," *New York Times*, July 22, 1878, 3.

65. "Colonel Dunwoddie, and Other Novels," *Atlantic Monthly* 42, no. 254 (December 1878): 702.

66. *Saturday Evening Post* 57, no. 51 (July 13, 1878): 3; "Recent Fiction," *Literary World* 9, no. 4 (September 1, 1898): 57.

67. Notice of the copyright appeared in *Publishers' Weekly* 69, no. 1793 (June 9, 1906): 1647.

68. E. Juncker, *Margarethe or Life-Problems: A Romance*, trans. A. L. Wister (Philadelphia: J. B. Lippincott Company, 1887), 228.

69. Moritz von Reichenbach, *The Eichhofs: A Romance*, trans. A. L. Wister (Philadelphia: J. B. Lippincott, 1902). In 2010 a Zurich bookseller on abebooks.com advertised it in a set dated 1900–1909.

70. In 1902, for example, it is advertised in the *New York Times*, alongside several novels by Marlitt, in a popular library available from A. D. Matthews' Sons as one of "the best books ever." Display ad, *New York Times*, June 15, 1902, 24. The 1902 edition is the last edition I have been able to document.

71. "Literary Notes," *The Critic* 1, no. 7 (April 9, 1881): 102.

72. "News and Notes," *Literary World* 12, no. 9 (April 23, 1881): 154.

73. Rev. of *The Eichhofs*, by Moritz von Reichenbach, *The Independent* 33, no. 1696 (June 2, 1881): 12.

74. "Current Fiction," *Literary World* 12, no. 11 (May 21, 1881): 182.

75. Bethusy-Huc wrote *Die Eichhoffs* just a few years after the appearance of *Anna Karenina* (1877). In its flirtation with and avoidance of adultery and its inclusion of a character named Wronsky, the novel may signal a debt to Tolstoy. The Russian novel had, however, not yet been translated into German.

76. Moritz von Reichenbach, *The Eichhofs: A Romance*, trans. A. L. Wister (Philadelphia: J. B. Lippincott Company, 1888), 317. All further page references to this edition appear in the body of the text.

77. "Current Fiction," *Literary World* 12, no. 11 (May 21, 1881): 182.

78. "Literary Notes," *The Critic* 31 (March 11, 1882): 74. See, e.g., "Mrs. A. L. Wister's Translations from the German," *Literary World* 25, no. 7 (April 7, 1894): 98. The last dated edition I have found is from 1902. Raimund's novel appeared in volume 1 of the 1882 *Deutsche Roman-Zeitung*. The *Roman-Zeitung* ran from October to October, which means that volume 1 (1882) actually began in October 1881. *50 Jahre Deutsche Roman-Zeitung. Festschrift zum fünfzigjährigen Jubiläum 1863–1913* (Berlin: Otto Janke [1913]), 22.

79. Advertisement, *Literary World* 13, no. 14 (July 15, 1883): 2.

80. "Current Fiction," *Literary World* 13, no. 14 (July 15, 1882): 230.

81. Ibid.

82. "Recent Fiction," *The Critic* 41 (July 29, 1882): 201.

83. Golo Raimund, *From Hand to Hand: A Novel*, trans. A. L. Wister (Philadelphia: J. B. Lippincott, 1882), 371. Further page references to this edition appear in the body of the text.

84. In her study of European realism, Lilian R. Furst contrasts "insistently acknowledged background" and "omnipresent context for the action" with the realist evocation of place as a "dynamic set of circumstances." *All Is True: The Claims and Strategies of Realist Fiction* (Durham, NC: Duke University Press, 1995), 176. Furst concludes that the realist evocation of place is achieved "more through enactment than through description" (188).

Chapter 6

1. Kontje, "Marlitt's World," 408–26.
2. On *Gartenlaube* fiction as transhistorical, see Tatlock, "Afterlife," 118–52.
3. W. Heimburg, *Two Daughters of One Race*, trans. D. M. Lowrey (New York: Worthington, 1889), 329. Subsequent page references to this edition appear in the body of the text.

4. Furst, *All Is True*, 176.

5. E. Werner, *Hero of the Pen*, trans. Frances A. Shaw (Boston: W. F. Gill, 1875); *Hero of the Pen*, trans. Mary Stuart Smith (New York: Munro, 1883); and *The Quill-Driver*, trans. H. E. Miller (Chicago: Weeks, 1895). A fourth translation appeared in Great Britain: *Hero of the Pen*, trans. S. Phillips (London: Sampson Low, Marston, Searle, and Rivington, 1878). Smith may have published a translation in a periodical already in 1873. In a letter to her aunt she mentions having received payment for a translation of *Hero of the Pen* in 1873 but does not say from whom. Mary Stuart Smith to Mary Jane Harrison, 19 May 1873, in THS Papers, Box 17.

6. "Our Book Sale," advertisement, *Chicago Daily Tribune*, December 12, 1897, 36.

7. "Gill's Library of Select Novels by Eminent Authors," *Christian Union* 12, no. 21 (November 24, 1875): 429.

8. E. Werner, *Hero of the Pen*, trans. Frances A. Shaw (New York: R. Worthington, 1880), 7. Further page references to this edition appear in the body of the text.

9. Twenty years later, when *The Quill-Driver* appeared, the war had become even more remote. A notice in *Publishers' Weekly* reprinted in *Annual American Catalogue 1895* speaks of the "German wars of 1866," confusing the Austro-Prussian War of 1866 with the Franco-Prussian War of 1870–71. *Annual American Catalogue 1895* (New York: Office of the Publishers' Weekly, 1895), 214.

10. William A. Harris, "The Mission of Woman," *Southern Review* 9, no. 20 (October 1871): 938.

11. Peter Gay, "An Experiment in Denial: A Reading of the *Gartenlaube* in the Year 1890," in *Traditions of Experiment from the Enlightenment to the Present*, ed. Nancy Kaiser and David E. Wellbery (Ann Arbor: University of Michigan Press, 1992), 149. Further page references to this essay appear in the body of the text.

12. E. Werner, *Flames* (Chicago: Donohue, Henneberry, 1891), 6. The preface is signed "Lake View, August 3, 1890." Subsequent page references to this edition appear in the body of the text.

13. Smith mentions wanting to start work on *Flammenzeichen* in a letter to her son and cotranslator. Mary Stuart Smith to Gessner Harrison Smith, 17 November 1890, in THS, Box 26.

14. Mary Stuart Smith to George Tucker Smith, 27 September 1897, in THS, Box 30.

15. Advertisement, Frederick Loeser & Co., *New York Times*, January 20, 1912, 6.

16. E. Werner, *His Word of Honor: A Copyright Translation* (New York: Street and Smith, 1892).

17. C. L. H., "Book Notices," *Belford's Magazine* 7, no. 39 (August 1891): 447.

18. Mary Stuart Smith to Gessner Harrison Smith, 9 December 1890, in THS, Box 26.

19. E. Werner, *The Northern Light*, trans. D. M. Lowrey (New York: Robert Bonner's Sons, 1891), 9. Further page references to this edition appear in the body of the text.

20. "Flammenzeichen," *Die Gartenlaube*, no. 13 (1890): 412.

21. Mary Stuart Smith to Gessner Harrison Smith, 17 November 1890, in THS, Box 26.

22. Theodor Storm, *Viola Tricolor, and, Curator Carsten*, trans. Bayard Quincy Morgan and Frieda M. Vogt (London: Calder, 1936).

23. In 1898 the readership of the *Berliner Illustrirte Zeitung* responded to a questionnaire asking which period of history was the unhappiest of the century. The unequivocal answer was the "Franzosenzeit 1806–1812" (time of the French occupation). "Die Bilanz des Jahrhunderts," *Berliner Illustrierte Zeitung*, December 25, 1898, 48.

24. Part 2 of *Debit and Credit* involves the restoration of a run-down estate on Polish soil and the defense of that estate against Polish rebels. Poles are depicted either as gallant but irresponsible aristocrats or dull peasants. Germans who have "gone native" are portrayed in a negative light. Gustav Freytag, *Soll und Haben* (Leipzig, 1855).

25. Advertisement, *Publishers' Weekly* 11, no. 280 (May 26, 1877): 554.

26. E. Werner, *Vineta, the Phantom City,* trans. Frances A. Shaw (Boston: Estes and Lauriat, 1877), 217.

27. Frank Mayo and John G. Wilson, *Nordeck: A Play in Five Acts* (Chicago: H. McAllaster, 1883), 4.

28. "Mayo as Nordeck," theater poster, International Poster Center http://www.postersplease.com/index.php?FAFs=d8c844d24a81b05a677558d05f8b7cff&FAFgo=/Auctions/LotDetail&LotID=17370&sr=0&t=C&ts=&AID=113 (accessed June 22, 2010).

29. "Mr. Frank Mayo's Triumph," *New York Times,* May 19, 1885, 5.

30. Joseph Duane Fike, "Frank Mayo: Actor, Playwright, and Manager" (PhD diss., University of Nebraska, Lincoln, 1980). Chapter 4 documents Mayo's productions of *Nordeck,* and chapter 5 describes Mayo's discouraging years with *Nordeck* and his surprising success with his Mark Twain adaptation.

31. "What the Press Says about the New Features," *Lippincott's Magazine* 39 (January 1887): unnumbered page. The notice quotes Julian Hawthorne in *New York World.*

32. For information on Whitney, see L. L. Stroebe, "Marian P. Whitney. In Memoriam," *Monatshefte* 38, no. 6 (October 1946): 372–74.

33. E. Werner, *Heimatklang,* ed. Marian P. Whitney (New York: Henry Holt and Company, 1903), iii.

34. E. Werner, "The Spell of Home," trans. A. L. Wister, *Lippincott's Monthly Magazine,* February 1888, 210.

35. Ibid., 214.

36. "Advertisement for Schlesinger & Mayer, The Wabash-Avenue Book Store," *Chicago Daily Tribune,* December 7, 1902, 14. The *Publishers' Trade List Annual* lists editions of *The Price He Paid* for that year with both Rand and Street. A. H. Leypoldt, *The Publishers' Trade List Annual* 30 (New York: Office of the Publishers' Weekly, 1902), 1046.

37. E. Werner, *The Price He Paid: A Special Translation* (New York: F. M. Lupton, 1891), 293. Although this book advertises itself as a "special translation," it is in fact a new edition of Tyrrell's *No Surrender* with a frontispiece depicting the duel that constitutes the climax of the novel. All further page references to this edition appear in the body of the text.

38. Rev. of *At a High Price,* by E. Werner, *The Independent* 31, no.1584 (April 10, 1879): 10.

39. Ibid.

40. Rev. of *The Price He Paid,* by E. Werner, *Medical Age* 14, no. 20 (October 26, 1896): 631.

41. "Fiction," *Literary World* 27, no. 23 (November 14, 1896): 381.

42. Rev. of *The Price He Paid,* by E. Werner, *Annual American Catalogue 1891* (New York: Office of the Publishers' Weekly, 1892), 201.

43. As Jeffrey L. Sammons outlines (*Kuno Francke's Edition,* 189–90), Raabe was included in volume 11 of Kuno Francke's *German Classics* alongside Theodor Storm and Friedrich Spielhagen. The work included is a deeply abridged version of Raabe's *Der Hun-*

gerpastor (1864). Raabe's narrative style challenges the translator, just as it did nineteenth-century German readers with whom he became increasingly unpopular.

44. Wilhelm Raabe, *Eulenpfingsten*, in *Sämtliche Werke* (Göttingen: Vandenhoeck & Ruprecht, 1956), 11: 446.

45. Drew Gilpin Faust, *Mothers of Invention: Women of the Slaveholding South in the American Civil War* (Chapel Hill: University of North Carolina Press, 1996), 153.

46. Advertisement, Frederick Loeser & Co., *New York Times*, December 1, 1917, 6.

47. L. Mühlbach, *Mühlbach's Historical Romances in Twenty Volumes* (New York: The University Society, n.d.). Exemplars owned by author.

48. Peterson, *History, Fiction, and Germany*, 39, 282–83n30.

49. Ibid., 97–145.

50. "New Publications," *Catholic World* 5, no. 26 (1867): 285.

51. "Maunderings," *Old Guard* 6, no. 4 (April 1868): 291.

52. Cooke, "Miss Mühlbach and Her System," 169.

53. Munro, for one, saw to it that Marlitt, Heimburg, Werner, and Mühlbach all appeared in English translation in his Seaside Library. An advertising page inserted in the front matter of an edition of *What the Spring Brought* contains three lists: one of Heimburg's works contained in the Seaside Library, Pocket Edition, one of Werner's works, and one of Mühlbach's works. E. Werner, *What the Spring Brought*, trans. Mary Stuart Smith (New York: George Munro, n.d.).

54. "Literary Intelligence: New Books," *New York Times*, October 10, 1866, 2.

55. Luise Mühlbach, *Frederick the Great and His Court*, trans. Mrs. Chapman Coleman and her Daughters (New York: The University Society, n.d.), 180. Further page references to this edition appear in the body of the text.

56. Peterson, *History, Fiction, and Germany*, 118.

57. L. Mühlbach, *The Youth of the Great Elector: An Historical Romance*, trans. Mary Stuart Smith (New York: The Marion Company, 1915), 344–45. Further page references to this edition appear in the body of the text.

58. L. Mühlbach, *The Reign of the Great Elector* (New York: The University Society, n.d.), 99. Further page references to this edition appear in the body of the text.

59. Other editions place the image in the chapter "Love's Sacrifice," where Rebecca recapitulates the story of her marriage. See L. Mühlbach, *The Youth of the Great Elector: An Historical Romance*, trans. Mary Stuart Smith (New York: D. Appleton and Company, 1905), 274.

60. E. Marlitt, *The Second Wife: A Romance*, trans. A. L. Wister (Philadelphia: J. B. Lippincott, 1875), 85.

61. Mary Stuart Smith, "The Women of the Revolution," in *Lang Syne, or The Wards of Mount Vernon* (New York: John B. Alden, 1889), 97.

Part Three

1. Smith, "The Women of the Revolution," 131.

2. Mary Austin, *Earth Horizon: Autobiography* (Boston: Houghton Mifflin, 1932), 100–102, quoted in Sicherman, *Well-Read Lives*, 43.

3. Louisa May Alcott, *Little Women, or, Meg, Jo, Beth and Amy*, introd. Anna Quindlen (Boston: Little, Brown, 1994), 352.

4. Ibid., 332. Patricia Meyer Spacks, for example, observes that subjecting Jo to a father figure "was something of a sell." Patricia Meyer Spacks, *The Female Imagination* (New York: Alfred A. Knopf, 1975), 101. For an interpretation of Alcott's decision to marry Jo to Professor Bhaer that frames it more progressively, as, among other things, a deliberate decision not to capitulate to the conventions of romance that would dictate marriage to the young, handsome, and rich Laurie, see Barbara Sicherman, "Reading Little Women: The Many Lives of a Text," in *U.S. History as Women's History: New Feminist Essays*, ed. Linda K. Kerber, Alice Kessler-Harris, and Kathryn Kish Sklar (Chapel Hill: University of North Carolina Press, 1995), 245–66.

5. Louisa May Alcott, *Jo's Boys and How They Turned Out: A Sequel to "Little Men"* (Boston: Little, Brown, 1953), 48.

6. Michel Espagne and Michael Werner, eds., *Qu'est-ce qu'une littérature nationale? Approches pour une théorie interculturelle du champ littéraire*, Philologiques 3 (Paris: Editions de la Maison des Sciences de l'Homme, 1994); Robert Darnton, "First Steps Toward a History of Reading," 160–79.

Chapter 7

1. Damon R. Eubank, *In the Shadow of the Patriarch: The John J. Crittenden Family in War and Peace* (Macon, GA: Mercer University Press, 2009), 1.

2. Ibid., 1–2.

3. Eubank's family biography of J. J. Crittenden and his children makes a good case for Crittenden's powerful presence as pater familias and outlines the not-always-beneficial pressures that he imposed on his children, particularly the male children. The Crittenden family serves as a cogent example of tragic familial rifts that ensued especially in border states during the American Civil War. While Eubank includes Coleman in this biography, the boys, who played prominent public roles, figure more centrally. Coleman's correspondence provides information on the family and thus serves as an important source for Eubank's study. Eubank has, however, not taken full measure of Coleman herself or given the translations or her biography of her father any more than passing attention. In fact, he does not mention them by name and refers instead incorrectly to "works on the campaigns of Frederick the Great" translated "years earlier" for Ulysses Grant. Ibid., 161. Francis Hudson Oxx, *The Kentucky Crittendens: The History of a Family Including the Genealogy of Descendants in Both the Male and Female Lines, Biographical Sketches of Its Members and Their Descent from Other Early Colonial Families* (n.p.: n.p., 1940), 145–46.

4. Ann Mary Crittenden (Coleman) to John J. Crittenden, 5 May 1828, 18 December 1827, 4 January 1828, in John Jordan Crittenden Papers, Rare Book, Manuscript, and Special Collections Library, Duke University, Durham, North Carolina, hereafter abbreviated as JJC Papers.

5. Anonymous, *Louisville Daily Journal* September 20, September 27, October 3, 1861. Cited by Eubank, *Shadow of the Patriarch*, 46.

6. Coleman's daughter Florence had married in 1855 and did not accompany the family. Coleman's ostensible reason for a sojourn in Europe was to be able to live more cheaply, yet staying in Louisville would have been a financially wiser choice. It is clear from her correspondence even before her husband's death that she was bored with her lot there, even though she was considered a queen of Louisville society and lived at a premier

address. See, e.g., John J. Crittenden to Ann Mary Coleman, 9 May 1849, JJC Papers. In this letter Crittenden tried to console his disappointed daughter when her brother, not her husband, received an appointment to Liverpool, England.

7. John J. Crittenden to Ann Mary Coleman, 17 September 1857, JJC Papers.

8. J. J. Crittenden to his daughter, Mrs. A. M. Coleman, 10 February 1857, in *The Life of John J. Crittenden, with selections from his correspondences and speeches*, edited by his daughter, Mrs. Chapman Coleman (Philadelphia: J. B. Lippincott, 1871), 2: 137.

9. Ibid., April 1863, JJC Papers.

10. Ibid.

11. Albert D. Kirwan, *John J. Crittenden: The Struggle for the Union* (Lexington: University of Kentucky Press, 1962), 467.

12. Eubank, *Shadow of the Patriarch*, 40. Oxx, *The Kentucky Crittendens*, 146. Oxx writes of Coleman's "first and most difficult mission for the Confederacy" as follows: "Before she left Paris for New York she agreed to help transmit some dispatches from William Mason, the Confederate minister to France, to Jefferson Davis in Richmond. With the important documents sewed between the double soles of her shoes, she reached Louisville in safety. At this point, suspicion being aroused at the provost's headquarters, she changed shoes with Judith Venable. Miss Venable succeeded in getting through the Union lines alone . . . and delivered the papers to the Confederate authorities in Richmond." Ibid.

13. Ibid., 147.

14. Ann Mary Coleman to John J. Crittenden, 5 April 1863, JJC Papers.

15. Ibid.

16. Ibid., 18 May 1863, JJC Papers.

17. Kirwan, *John J. Crittenden*, 447.

18. Will of Chapman Coleman, JJC Papers. In late February or early March 1865 Coleman brazenly wrote to Jefferson Davis personally, requesting that her only remaining son, Chapman, be assigned some lighter duty. The letter was eventually referred to Nathan Bedford Forrest, but before he could react to it Lee and Johnston had surrendered their armies. Siegel Auctions, Item No. 2454, Letter, 6 March 1865, http://www.siegelauctions.com/1997/786/ya7864.htm (accessed August 29, 2010).

19. Her circumstance as widow and sole supporter of her unmarried daughters in wartime mirrors that of Mühlbach, whose works she would soon translate. Mühlbach suffered financially from the economy and disrupted communication and publishing in wartime, in her case during the Austro-Prussian War (1866) and Franco-Prussian War (1870–71).

20. Ann Mary Coleman to Patrick Joyes, 25 April 1864, 19 September 1864, in Joyes Family Additional Papers, 1820–1891 (J89b) Filson Historical Society, hereafter cited as Joyes Family Additional Papers 1820–1891 (J89b).

21. Ann Mary Coleman to Patrick Joyes, 2 July 1865, Joyes Family Additional Papers 1820–1891 (J89b).

22. John J. Crittenden to Ann Mary Crittenden Coleman, 18 November 1831, JJC Papers.

23. Gerard R. Wolfe, *The House of Appleton* (Metuchen, NJ: Scarecrow Press, 1981), 128. Tebbel also writes (*Expansion of an Industry*, 203–4) that the decision to publish a series of Mühlbach novels resulted from William Worthen Appleton's reading of Adelaide de Vendel Chaudron's *Joseph II*, which had been published in the Confederacy in 1864. Tebbel does not provide his sources for this account. The first version of this anecdote in

book form appears in Samuel C. Chew, *Fruit among the Leaves: An Anniversary Anthology* (New York: Appleton-Century-Crofts, 1950), 32. The same story was repeated yet again most recently in George E. Tylutki, "D. Appleton and Company (New York: 1838–1933). D. Appleton (New York; 1831–1838)," in Dzwonkoski, *American Literary Publishing Houses*, 1:25. Tylutki, however, corrects Chew's erroneous date of Appleton's publication of Chaudron's translation of *Joseph II and His Court* to 1867. Lieselotte E. Kurth-Voigt and William H. McClain rely on Tebbel in their work on Luise Mühlbach's American reception: "Louise Mühlbach's Historical Novels." Although Wolfe, Tebbel, and Tylutki correct some errors in Chew's account, their histories accept the gist of the story uncritically, as do Kurth-Voigt and McClain.

24. Cathleen A. Baker pinpoints the date of publication of Chaudron's four-volume translation as May 19, 1864. Cathleen A. Baker, *The Enterprising S. H. Goetzel: Antebellum and Civil War Publisher in Mobile, Alabama* (The Legacy Press, www.thelegacypress.com, 1985–2010), 17.

25. Wolfe, *House of Appleton*, 128.

26. *Joseph II and His Court* with Appleton was not announced as "just published" until February 16, 1867. Advertisement, *Round Table* 5 (February 16, 1867): 110.

27. Chew, *Fruit among the Leaves*, 32. There are many points here that demand further scrutiny. For one, in 1865 Chaudron's publisher, S[igismund] H[einrich] Goetzel, had published a second novel by Mühlbach that is never mentioned in this account, namely, *Henry the Eighth and His Court or Catherine Parr*, translated by Henry Niles Pierce. Appleton issued a new edition of it in the very same year in which he reprinted Chaudron's translation, 1867. Goetzel was still trying to sell both volumes, for which he had secured new US copyrights after the conclusion of the Civil War, as an advertisement in the *American Literary Gazette and Publishers' Circular* indicates. *American Literary Gazette and Publishers' Circular* 6, no. 1 (1 November 1865): 30. A subsequent advertisement informs the public that *Joseph II and His Court* "and the other publications of S. H. Goetzel, Mobile," are "for sale by Collins & Brother" in New York. Advertisement, *American Literary Gazette and Publishers' Circular* 6, no. 3 (December 1, 1865): 118. As I outline below, Chaudron belatedly tried to place additional translations with Appleton but was scooped by the Colemans. When Chew alludes to "other translators," however, he may have in mind Amory Coffin, whose translation of *The Merchant of Berlin* appeared with Appleton very early in 1867 (although in some later editions the copyright date is listed as 1866, contemporary publications list the publication date as 1867, as does the volume itself), described as a "companion volume to Frederick and his Court . . . and of Joseph and his Court." "Books of the Month," *Hours at Home: A Popular Monthly of Instruction and Recreation* 4, no. 3 (January 1867): 285. See also "List of Some Recent Publications," *North American Review* 104, no. 214 (January 1867): 215, where *Merchant* is entered with a publication date of 1867 just below *Frederick the Great and His Court* (listed with the publication date 1866).

28. D. Appleton to Ann Mary Coleman, 8 May 1866, JJC Papers.

29. "Announcements," *American Literary Gazette and Publishers' Circular* 7, no. 3 (June 1, 1866): 61.

30. D. Appleton to Ann Mary Coleman, 8 May 1866, JJC Papers.

31. "Announcements," *Round Table* 4, no. 55 (September 22, 1866): 125.

32. "Literary Table," *Round Table* 4, no. 56 (September 29, 1866): 139. The *New York Times* published an account by S. H. Goetzel, the publisher, concerning the publication of *Joseph II*. According to this account, Goetzel, who had since 1859 had a copy of the

novel, contacted Chaudron to translate it for monthly serialization in a planned magazine publication. Wartime vicissitudes impeded the project and therefore Goetzel opted for publishing the translation of the book as a novel instead. Goetzel concluded his account with an emphatic assertion: "This is the true statement of the manner by which MUHLBACH's German productions were introduced into the United States." "New Publications," *New York Times*, January 30, 1867, 2. This account was apparently intended to correct the erroneous and highly romanticized version that had appeared two weeks earlier, according to which,

> While the war was in progress, a lady of Mobile received by one of the steamers which succeeded in running the blockade, a copy of *Joseph II and His Court*. She had the enterprise to translate it, and a publisher at Raleigh, North Carolina, we believe, brought it out. Although poorly printed and on dingy paper, it had an extensive sale, both on account of its intrinsic merit and the scarcity of reading matter in the South. Copies of the work afterward found their way to the North and attracted the attention of lovers of light literature of the more substantial sort. Shortly Messieurs Appleton & Co. determined to republish all of Mrs. MUHLBACH's productions and commencing but a month or two ago with *Frederick the Great and his Court*, they now follow up that volume with *The Merchant of Berlin*, and promise to give fourteen more volumes of the same prolific writer. ("Literary Intelligence," *New York Times*, January 14, 1867, 2)

Although erroneous, the version with Chaudron as "steel magnolia" prevailed, no doubt in part because Appleton began advertising *Joseph II* with a quotation from the erroneous and romantic version from the *New York Times*—obviously an appealing story with which to sell books. See advertisement, *Christian Advocate* 40, no. 5 (January 31, 1867): 40; advertisement, *American Literary Gazette and Publishers' Circular* 8, no. 7 (February 1, 1867): 227. Over the course of approximately two years a garbled account gradually emerged, according to which *Joseph II* was a huge success from the start, well known nationwide (apparently even during the Civil War), a success that ushered in the Mühlbach series. The *Round Table*, as mentioned above, had pointed out in 1866 upon the appearance of *Frederick the Great and His Court* that Chaudron's translation of *Joseph II* was regrettably *not* that well known.

33. "Literary Table," 139 (see n. 32).

34. Ann Mary Coleman to Patrick Joyes, 6 December 1866, Joyes Family Additional Papers 1820–1891 (J89b).

35. Advertisement, *American Literary Gazette and Publishers' Circular* 8, no. 8 (February 15, 1867): 225; "Announcements," *American Literary Gazette and Publishers' Circular* 8, no. 11 (April 1, 1867): 327. These two novels were, respectively, the fourth and fifth novels by Mühlbach published by Appleton.

36. *Frederick the Great and His Relations*, *The Merchant of Berlin*, *Louisa of Prussia*, *Napoleon in Germany*, and *Frederick the Great in Bohemia*. The first and last of these titles are reproduced incorrectly in this announcement. "Announcements," *Round Table* 4, no. 62 (November 10, 1866): 245.

37. For an outline of the creation of nationalist Frederick myths in nineteenth-century Germany, containing many examples that originate in the 1850s, see Peterson, *History, Fiction, and Germany*, 97–145.

38. Appleton to Ann Mary Coleman, New York, 13 August 1867, JJC Papers. "Nearly

ready" was a bit of an exaggeration. The novel, translated by Chaudron, in the end the sixteenth in Appleton's series of historical novels, did not appear until late November 1868. See advertisement, *American Literary Gazette and Publishers' Circular* 12, no. 2 (November 16, 1868): 59, where it is announced for publication on November 21, 1868.

39. *Goethe and Schiller: An Historical Romance* was announced in the *American Literary Gazette and Publishers' Circular* on August 1, 1868. "Fiction," *American Literary Gazette and Publishers' Circular* 11, no. 7 (August 1, 1868): 162.

40. Kurth-Voigt and McClain ("Louise Mühlbach's Historical Novels," 61) point out that it would have been possible for Chapman Coleman, who joined the American Legation in Berlin in 1869, to have met Mühlbach sometime before her death in 1873.

41. Ulysses S. Grant to Mrs. Mary Coleman & daughters, 3 October 1866, JJC Papers. The gift had already been acknowledged on Grant's behalf by Adam Badeau (1831–95). Adam Badeau to Ann Mary Coleman, 3 September 1866, JJC Papers.

42. Robert E. Lee to Ann Mary Coleman, 12 April 1867, JJC Papers.

43. See Ann Mary Coleman, "A Grant Retirement Bill," unpublished manuscript, JJC Papers.

44. An announcement of the Phelps von Rottenburg marriage that appeared in the *New York Times* confirms that Chapman was still in Berlin as First Secretary of the Legation, having served twenty-four years there. The article inaccurately implies that he had held this title the entire time. *New York Times*, June 1, 1893, 2. As letters held in the JJC Papers to Alexander H. Stephens (1816–83), former vice-president of the Confederacy and Georgia congressman, testify, Coleman had vigorously campaigned beginning in the late 1870s for a promotion for her son. In 1884 Chapman was offered the post of First Secretary of Legation in Peking, which he turned down (possibly on her advice), but finally in the same year he received the coveted promotion in Berlin. Chapman Coleman to Ann Mary Coleman, 20 September 1884, JJC Papers.

45. *The Life of John J. Crittenden*, 1: v.

46. Ibid., 1: vii.

47. For a list of members and a description of the founding and procedures of the Literary Society, see Helen Nicolay, *Sixty Years of the Literary Society* (Washington, DC: privately printed, 1934).

48. Among Coleman's papers, held in the JJC Papers, are a number of manuscripts, indicated as presentations to the Literary Society.

49. Mary T. Tardy, *The Living Female Writers of the South* (Philadelphia: Claxton, Remsen and Haffelbinger, 1872), 56.

50. Ibid., 57.

51. "A Famous Woman," *Courier Journal*, February 14, 1891, 8.

52. See Coleman's correspondence with Joyes, Joyes Family Additional Papers 1820–1891 (J89b).

53. Ann Mary Coleman to Patrick Joyes, 19 October 1888, Joyes Family Additional Papers 1820–1891 (J89b).

54. Ibid., 4 November 1888, Joyes Family Additional Papers 1820–1891 (J89b).

55. Ann Mary Coleman to Morton Joyes, 25 June 1889, Joyes Family Additional Papers 1820–1891 (J89b).

56. Ann Mary Coleman to Patrick Joyes, 25 November 1867, Joyes Family Additional Papers 1820–1891 (J89b).

57. Ibid., 3 December 1867, Joyes Family Additional Papers 1820–1891 (J89b).

58. Sophie, Comtesse de Ségur, *Fairy Tales for Little Folks*, trans. Mrs. Chapman Coleman and her daughters (Philadelphia: Porter and Coates, 1869); Otto Müller, *Charlotte Ackermann: A Theatrical Romance, Founded upon Interesting Facts in the Life of a Young Artist of the Last Century*, trans. Mrs. Chapman Coleman and her daughters (Philadelphia: Porter and Coates, 1871), translation of Otto Müller, *Charlotte Ackermann. Ein Hamburger Theater-Roman aus dem vorigen Jahrhundert* (Frankfurt am Main: Meinger Sohn & Cie., 1854).

59. *Der Grosse Brockhaus*, 15th edition (1932), s.v. "Müller, Otto."

60. Appleton & Co. to Ann Mary Coleman, 13 August 1867, JJC Papers.

61. Ann Mary Coleman to Florence Joyes, 17 April 1872, Joyes Family Additional Papers 1820–1891 (J89b). This unidentified manuscript was never published as far as I have been able to determine. Whether it was the unpublished translation of Honoré de Balzac's novel *La dernière fée* (1823), titled *The Last Fairy* and held in the JJC Papers, is a matter for speculation.

62. Tebbel, *Expansion of an Industry*, 204.

63. Ann Mary Coleman to Patrick Joyes, 6 December 1866, Joyes Family Additional Papers 1820–1891 (J89b). On Appleton's earnings, see Tebbel, *Expansion of an Industry*, 204.

64. Appleton to Mrs. Chapman Coleman, 8 May 1866, JJC Papers.

65. Appleton & Co. to Ann Mary Coleman, 13 August 1867, JJC Papers.

66. "A Famous Woman," 8 (see n. 51). In an undated list of accounts, the $3,761 received from Appleton is divided among Coleman, her three daughters, and Chapman. Joyes Family Additional Papers 1820–1891 (J89b).

67. Luise Mühlbach, *Berlin and Sans-Souci, or Frederick the Great and His Friends*, trans. Mrs. Chapman Coleman and her daughters (New York: The University Society, n.d.), 19.

68. L[uise] Mühlbach, *Frederick the Great and His Court*, trans. Mrs. Chapman Coleman and her daughters (New York: The University Society, n.d.), 220 and 235, respectively.

69. Ibid., 205.

70. Mühlbach, *Berlin and Sans-Souci*, 56.

71. "Maunderings," *Old Guard* 6, no. 4 (April 1868): 291.

72. Cooke, "Miss Mühlbach and Her System," 171.

73. Goings, *Mammy*, 9.

74. Ibid.

75. Ann Mary Coleman to John J. Crittenden, 18 May 1863, JCC Papers.

76. Coleman, *Life of John J. Crittenden*, 2:365.

77. Drew Gilpin Faust has shown that white Confederate women became disabused of the romance of war "in the face of the unrelenting pressure of real war" as ever more sacrifices were demanded of them. If Coleman, too, had been disenchanted, that disenchantment ebbed as time passed, but then Coleman sympathized with the South, yet lived in the North where conditions were not as dire. "Altars of Sacrifice: Confederate Women and the Narratives of War," in *Divided Houses: Gender and the Civil War*, ed. Catherine Clinton and Nina Silber (New York: Oxford University Press, 1992), 171–99, esp. 181–86. For Faust's account of suffering in and after the war, see *This Republic of Suffering: Death and the American Civil War* (New York: Alfred A. Knopf, 2008).

78. J. J. Crittenden to Ann Mary Coleman, 2 July 1859, in *Life of John J. Crittenden*, 2:178.

79. Rev. of *For My Own Sake,* by Marie Bernhard, *Boston Herald,* quoted in an advertisement in Marie Bernhard, *The Pearl,* The Authors Library 6 (New York: International News Company, 1894).

Chapter 8

1. Previously Wister had published only Georg Blum and Ludwig Wahl, *Seaside and Fireside Fairies,* trans. Annis Lee Wister (Philadelphia: Ashmead and Evans/Lippincott, 1864). Duodecimo or twelvemo is a book composed of pages of a size (5 by 7 ¾ inches) formed by folding a single printer's sheet into twelve leaves. *American Heritage Dictionary,* s.v. "duodecimo" and "twelvemo." This chapter draws heavily on my essay "Domesticated Romance and Capitalist Enterprise: Annis Lee Wister's Americanization of German Fiction," in Tatlock and Erlin, *German Culture,* 153–82.

2. On the back inside cover of the June issue of *Lippincott's Magazine* 5 (1870) readers are alerted to the availability of the eighth edition of *The Old Mam'selle's Secret* (1868), as well as the sixth edition of *Gold Elsie* (1868) and the fifth edition of *Countess Gisela* (1870).

3. "Mrs. Annis Lee Wister Dead," *New York Times,* November 16, 1908, 9.

4. Horace Howard Furness, *The Letters of Horace Howard Furness,* ed. Horace Howard Furness Jayne (Boston: Houghton Mifflin, 1922), 1:350.

5. Ossip Schubin, *Countess Erika's Apprenticeship,* trans. A. L. Wister (Philadelphia: J. B. Lippincott, 1891), 6.

6. Untitled notice, *New York Times,* June 1, 1907, BR352.

7. "'My advice, worthless in all cases according to my estimation of it, is always 'destroy.' All this accumulation teaches me the same lesson. I have kept all my father's letters but I think I shall burn them before I go abroad. Carrie Thomas' I destroy regularly. You & I differ in this I know. But when the dear hands that have penned & the brains that created have left my mortal sight & I see before me these [perishable?] pen-strokes I always want to say 'Oh take this too—it has no right to permanence.'" Annis Lee Wister to Howard Horace Furness, 5 August 1896, Furness MSS, Annenberg Rare Book and Manuscript Library, Van Pelt-Dietrich Library, Philadelphia, Pennsylvania (hereafter cited as Furness MSS).

8. Pochmann, *German Culture in America,* 336. As the preface to Wister's translation of *Struwwelpeter* reports, "This translation of *Slovenly Peter* was made about sixty-five years ago by a young girl, Annis, daughter of Dr. William Furness. . . . Her father gave a copy to his friend [Ralph Waldo] Emerson for his children." E. E. F., preface to *Slovenly Peter,* by Heinrich Hoffmann, trans. Annis Lee Furness (Boston: Houghton Mifflin, n.d.). Testimony of Furness's friendship with Emerson is preserved in *Records of a Lifelong Friendship, 1807–1882. Ralph Waldo Emerson and William Henry Furness,* ed. H[orace] H[oward] F[urness] (Boston: Houghton Mifflin, 1910).

9. W. S. W. Ruschenberger, *A Sketch of the Life of Caspar Wister, M.D. Reprinted from the Transactions of the College of Physicians of Philadelphia, November 5, 1890* (Philadelphia: Wm. J. Dornan, 1891). Annis Lee is mentioned only once by name in this thirty-four-page sketch.

10. Catherine Clinton, *Fanny Kemble's Civil Wars* (New York: Simon and Schuster, 2000), 245–47.

11. Jones Wister, *Jones Wister's Reminiscences* (Philadelphia: J. B. Lippincott, 1920), 22.

12. John Tebbel, *The Creation of an Industry, 1630–1865*, vol. 1 of *A History of Book Publishing in the United States* (New York: R. R. Bowker, 1972), 376.

13. Ibid., 375; Belgum, *Popularizing the Nation*, 132; Peterson, "E. Marlitt (Eugenie John)," 225.

14. Inside front cover of the January issue of *Lippincott's Magazine* 1 (1868) and front cover of the January issue of *Lippincott's Magazine* 3 (1869), respectively.

15. "Over Yonder," trans. Mrs. B. Elgard, *Lippincott's Magazine* 3 (1869): 200–210, 300–310, 414–32; "Magdalena," *Lippincott's Magazine* 4 (1869): 211–25, 319–27, 441–48. No translator is listed for *Magdalena*. Marlitt's *Thüringer Erzählungen* appeared with Keil in 1869 (Peterson, "E. Marlitt," 223).

16. "Only No Love," trans. Mrs. A. L. Wister, *Lippincott's Magazine* 3 (1869): 638–49 and 4 (1869): 86–98.

17. See Peterson, "E. Marlitt," 223–24, for a listing of the first book publications and the first publications of the translations.

18. Ruschenberger, *Life of Caspar Wister*, 26. While Ruschenberger gives his age as fourteen, Caspar is listed in the Philadelphia Register of Deaths as thirteen years of age. Register of Deaths, no. 335, 1869, Philadelphia City Archives, Philadelphia, Pennsylvania. He died on December 14, 1869. *Philadelphia Inquirer*, December 15, 1869.

19. The *American Literary Gazette and Publishers' Circular* announced the publication of the Hackländer novel on May 16, 1870. "Announcements," *American Literary Gazette and Publishers' Circular* 15, no. 2 (May 16, 1870): 44. The *New York Times* gave notice of the 544-page *Only a Girl* on May 7, 1870, as "just ready." Advertisement, *New York Times*, May 7, 1870, 7. On April 15, 1871, the *American Literary Gazette and Publishers' Circular* announced that *Why Did He Not Die?* "will be ready in a few days." Advertisement, *American Literary Gazette and Publishers' Circular* 16, no. 12 (April 15, 1871): 266.

20. "Announcements," *American Literary Gazette and Publishers' Circular* 18, no. 2 (November 15, 1871): 44.

21. Undated and unsigned note, Furness MSS. Wister is described here as a sixty-six-year-old woman, which indicates that the note was written either in 1896 or 1897.

22. Alert to women's oppression in patriarchal Germany, the German author Gabriele Reuter pointed out the irony of exhausted women's therapeutic drinking of water enriched in iron in a country that fancied itself built of "iron and blood." Gabriele Reuter, *Aus guter Familie*, 6th ed. (Berlin: Suhrkamp, 1897), 359.

23. Annis Lee Wister to S. Weir Mitchell, 31 December [no year], Mitchell Papers, College of Physicians of Philadelphia, Philadelphia, Pennsylvania (hereafter cited as Mitchell MSS).

24. In two anthologies Luise F. Pusch examines the frustration of the daughters and sisters of famous men, pointing out that these real women lived the dreary fate of Virginia Woolf's hypothetical "Judith Shakespeare." Their brothers and fathers, while encouraging a modicum of literacy, consistently overlooked, thwarted, or devalued the talents of their sisters and daughters. Luise F. Putsch, ed., *Schwestern berühmter Männer* (Frankfurt am Main: Insel, 1981) and Luise F. Putsch, ed., *Töchter berühmter Männer* (Frankfurt am Main: Insel, 1988).

25. Annis Lee Wister to Henry Lea, 1 October 1890, Furness MSS.

26. Annis Lee Wister to Mrs. E. M. Hieslaven, 18 August [no year], Historical Society of Pennsylvania, Philadelphia, Pennsylvania. The address on Wister's stationary is 1303 Arch Street, Wister's home during the period when she completed most of her transla-

tions. The letter must have been written before 1883, when she moved into the new house at 1322 Locust Street, designed by her brother Frank Furness.

27. Annis Lee Wister to Miss Dickinson, 27 January [no year], letter owned by author. As in the case of the previous letter, the address on the stationary is 1303 Arch Street. The letter must therefore have been written before 1883. This same sentiment is echoed in a short notice in *The Dial* two decades or more later. *The Dial* claims that when Wister ceased translating in 1891, "she excused herself from further labors of the sort on the plea that the daughter of her father (the late William H. Furness, D.D.) and the sister of her brother (Dr. Horace Howard Furness) ought to be engaged in worthier work than translating German love stories for American girls to read." Notice, *The Dial* 43, no. 513 (November 1, 1907): 278.

28. Review quoted in "Popular Translations from the German by Mrs. A. L. Wister," in an advertising supplement in *Lippincott's Magazine* 49 (January–June 1892): 46.

29. Quoted by Joan Shelley Rubin, *The Making of Middlebrow Culture* (Chapel Hill: University of North Carolina Press, 1992), 10.

30. On the German canon, see Jeannine Blackwell, "German Literary History and the Canon in the United States," in *German Studies in the United States: A Historical Handbook*, ed. Peter Uwe Hohendahl (New York: Modern Language Association of America, 2003), 143–65.

31. Annis Lee Wister to S. Weir Mitchell, 24 November 1888, MSS 2/0241-03 Ser. 4.3, Box 9, Letters from Annis Lee Wister to S. W. Mitchell, Mitchell MSS.

32. Warner et al., *Hints for Home Reading*, title page. The lists of recommended books are to be found on pp. 117–47.

33. Sicherman, "Reading and Middle-Class Identity," 138.

34. Untitled notice, *New York Times*, June 1, 1907, BR352.

35. "Recent Fiction," *The Critic* 2, no. 27 (July–December 1884): 4.

36. Appleton was one of the few American publishers' to make royalty payments to foreign authors in the 1870s. Tylutki, "D. Appleton and Company," 1:23.

37. Peter Jaszi and Martha Woodmansee, "Copyright in Transition," in Kaestle and Radway, *Print in Motion*, 94.

38. See Putnam, "Contest for International Copyright," 2:573–79; Clark, *Movement for International Copyright*; Bowker, *Copyright*.

39. "International Copyright," *Atlantic Monthly* 20 (1867): 430–31.

40. *Die Gartenlaube*, no. 14 (1872): 236.

41. Meredith McGill, "Copyright," in Casper et al., *The Industrial Book*, 162.

42. "Translators and Translating," *Publishers' Weekly* 14, no. 344 (August 17, 1878): 174.

43. Inside back cover of the January issue of *Lippincott's Magazine* 5 (1870).

44. See *Countess Gisela. From the German of Marlitt*, by Mrs. A. L. Wister (Philadelphia: J. B. Lippincott, 1869); *The Little Moorland Princess, Translated from the German of E. Marlitt*, by Mrs. A. L. Wister (Philadelphia: J. B. Lippincott, 1872); *The Second Wife. A Romance, From the German of E. Marlitt by Mrs. A. L. Wister* (Philadelphia: J. B. Lippincott, 1875).

45. See, e.g., *In the Schillingscourt: A Romance. From the German of E. Marlitt*, by Mrs. A. L. Wister (Philadelphia: J. B. Lippincott, 1898). The fourth edition of *The Old Mam'selle's Secret* displays Wister's name only on the spine. *Old Mam'selle's Secret. After the German of E. Marlitt. By Mrs. A. L. Wister*, 4th ed. (Philadelphia: J. B. Lippincott, 1869).

46. Marlitt, *Little Moorland Princess*, fly leaf.

47. Rev. of *In the Schillingscourt*, by E. Marlitt, *The Nation* 29, no. 756 (1879): 443.
48. "New Books," *New York Times*, May 1, 1881, 10.
49. Notice, *The Dial* 43, no. 513 (November 1, 1907): 278.
50. Ibid.
51. *List of books sent by home and foreign committees to the Library of the Woman's Building, World's Columbian Exposition, Chicago, 1893*, compiled for the United States World's Columbian Commission Board of Lady Managers under the direction of Edith E. Clarke (Chicago 1893), 52, col. 2. http://digital.library.upenn.edu/women/clarke/library/library.html (accessed December 10, 2009). Sarah Wadsworth summarizes the importance of this exhibit: "A signal achievement in women's history and in cultural history more broadly, the resulting library gathered under one roof more than 7,000 volumes authored, illustrated, edited, or translated by women." Sarah Wadsworth, Preface, Special Issue, *Libraries and Cultures* 41, no. 1 (Winter 2006): 1. I thank Katrin Völkner for alerting me to this journal's special issue.
52. "Books of the Month," *Lippincott's Magazine* 50 (1892): 820. All of Marlitt's works were reissued in Germany in an illustrated edition as *Marlitt's gesammelte Romane und Novellen* from 1888 to 1890. The mention of illustrations from the German editions in 1892 therefore probably refers to these illustrations. Moreover, the fact that Lippincott advertised an edition of Marlitt's works with these illustrations from German sources in 1892 after the United States had passed an international copyright law implies that the American firm had worked with Keils Nachfolger/Union Deutsche Verlagsgesellschaft. I have, however, not been able to locate any of the illustrated Wister translations of Marlitt mentioned in this advertisement and have therefore not been able to confirm the German origins of the illustrations or in fact the existence of this ten-volume edition. For information on the German edition of the illustrated, collected works of Marlitt, see Tatlock, "Afterlife," 118–52.
53. A "transaction" in the language of the Muncie database refers to a checkout of a book. The numbers were compiled with the help of Stephen Pentecost, using data from "What Middletown Read."
54. Frank Luther Mott, *Golden Multitudes: The Story of Best Sellers in the United States* (New York: Macmillan, 1947), 52.
55. I acquired these eleven volumes from an American antiquarian bookseller. I know nothing about Amanda A. Durff, their first owner.
56. Janice A. Radway, *A Feeling for Books: The Book-of-the Month Club, Literary Taste, and Middle-Class Desire* (Chapel Hill: University of North Carolina Press, 1997), 148.
57. Ibid., 147.
58. Rev. of *Why Did He Not Die? or, The Child from the Ebräergang*, by Ad. von Volckhausen, trans. by Mrs. A. L. Wister, *The Nation* 8, no. 317 (July 27, 1871): 63.
59. "Fiction," *Literary World* 10, no. 2 (May 24, 1879), 166.
60. Review of *In the Schillingscourt*, by E. Marlitt, *Literary World* 10, no. 22 (October 25, 1879): 342.
61. *Publishers' Weekly* 29, no. 742 (1886): 526.
62. Advertisement, *Lippincott's Magazine* 24 (November 1879): 17.
63. H. C. Walsh, "Book-Talk," *Lippincott's Magazine* 41 (1890): 289.
64. Advertisement, *The Dial* 7, no. 82 (February 1887), advertising page.
65. "Book Table," *Godey's Lady's Book and Magazine* 117, no. 701 (November 1888): 422.
66. "Our Recent Books," *Lippincott's Magazine* 42 (1889): 137.

67. Schubin, *Countess Erika's Apprenticeship*, 6.

68. Ibid.

69. Advertisement, *New York Times*, November 2, 1907, BR698.

70. My copy, dated 1907, with a copyright date of November 1907 as well, claims to be a second edition, indicating at least short-term success. Adolf Streckfuss, *The Lonely House*, trans. by Mrs. A. L. Wister, 2nd ed. (Philadelphia: J. B. Lippincott, 1907). Wister is advertised on the title page principally by means of her translations of Marlitt: "Translator of 'The Old Mam'selle's Secret,' 'Gold Elsie,' 'The Second Wife,' 'The Happy-Go-Lucky,' etc." Eichendorff's *Happy-Go-Lucky* (Aus dem Leben eines Taugenichts) also famously ends happily: "und es war alles, alles gut!" (and all, all was well!).

71. Streckfuss, *Lonely House*, front matter.

72. Rev. of *The Lonely House*, by Adolf Streckfuss, *New York Observer and Chronicle* 85, no. 48 (November 28, 1907): 703.

73. "Literature of the Day," *Lippincott's Magazine* 1 (1868): 680–81.

74. These words echo Thomas Wentworth Higginson's discussion of stylistic attributes such as "simplicity," "freshness," and "choice of words" as the qualities that elevate books to the "domain of pure literature." Thomas Wentworth Higginson, "Literature as an Art," *Atlantic Monthly* 20 (1867): 745–55; quoted by Rubin, *Making of Middlebrow Culture*, 13.

75. Advertisement, *Lippincott's Magazine* 22 (1888): 19. Lippincott here quotes the *Boston Courier*.

76. Promotion for *The Owl's Nest*, *Publishers' Weekly* 34, nos. 868–69 (1888): 287.

77. Rev. of *A Penniless Girl*, by W. von Heimburg, *The Independent* 37, no. 1895 (March 26, 1885): 12.

78. "A German Novel," *Literary World* 15, no. 16 (August 9, 1884): 16.

79. Review of *Misjudged*, by W. Heimburg, trans. Mrs. J. W. Davis, *Literary World*, August 22, 1891, 293.

80. E. Marlitt, *The Lady with the Rubies*, trans. A. L. Wister (Philadelphia: J. B. Lippincott, 1885), 333; E. Marlitt, *Die Frau mit den Karfunkelsteinen* (Leipzig: Ernst Keil's Nachfolger, n.d.), 326. Further page references to these editions appear in the body of the text.

81. The first two expressions in quotations can be read in a review of *A Penniless Girl*, by W. Heimburg, in *The Independent* 37, no. 1895 (March 26, 1885): 12. "Rehabilitate" refers to the above-quoted "A German Novel," 16 (see n. 78).

82. "New Publications," *Arthur's Illustrated Home Magazine* 47, no. 6 (June 1879): 314.

83. Sarah B. Wister, "Art-Experiences of an Ignoramus," *Lippincott's Magazine* 15 (1875): 712.

Chapter 9

1. "Translators and Translating," *Publishers' Weekly* 14, no. 344 (August 17, 1878): 174.

2. Ibid.

3. Mary Stuart Smith to George Tucker Smith, 23 July 1894, THS Papers, Box 28.

4. During the final year of the Civil War, the average income of professors "did not exceed one hundred dollars in value." Philip Alexander Bruce, *History of the University of Virginia, 1819–1919* (New York: Macmillan, 1921), 3:321.

5. Mary Stuart Smith to Gessner Harrison Smith, 26 November 1890, THS Papers, Box 26.

6. David Marvel Reynolds Culbreth, *The University of Virginia: Memoirs of Her Student-Life and Professors* (New York: Neale, 1908), 384. The Baptist minister John A. Broadus, who must have known Smith since his time as chaplain of the University of Virginia in the mid-1850s, wrote her of seeing Murillo's painting on his visit to the *Gemäldegalerie* in Dresden and the resemblance he saw to her, and then, in good Protestant fashion, repudiated the Mary worship in the images of the Madonna collected in the gallery. John A. Broadus to Mary Stuart Smith, 1 December 1870, THS Papers, Box 16.

7. Mary Stuart Smith to Francis H. Smith, 8 July 1880, THS Papers, Box 19.

8. Francis H. Smith (1829–1928), professor of natural philosophy; Gessner Harrison (1807–62), professor of ancient languages; George Tucker (1775–1861), professor of moral philosophy.

9. Notice of this public performance appears in the *Daily Inter Ocean*, which reported on the events of the fair. "To-day's World's Fair Programme," *Daily Inter Ocean* 91 (June 23, 1893): col. A.

10. Her contribution to *Harper's Cook Book Encyclopaedia*, furthermore, is documented in a brief notice for the work in the *New York Times*. "Notes and News," *New York Times*, November 8, 1902, BR14. See also Mary Stuart Smith to Mary Jane Harrison, 18–29 May 1873, THS Papers, Box 17, one of several letters documenting her contributions to Harper's *Bazar*.

11. Mary Stuart Smith to Frank H. Smith, 11 September 1871, THS Papers, Box 17.

12. Mary Stuart Smith to Gessner Harrison Smith, 28 March 1890, THS Papers, Box 26.

13. Ibid., 3 June 1887, THS Papers, Box 24.

14. Mary Stuart Smith to George Tucker Smith, 11 December 1896, THS Papers, Box 30. Tucker was born in 1866, which confirms the timeframe of 1868 for the translation.

15. Rosalie, who was sick, complained that her mother was only reading German and never talked. Rosalie Smith to Gessner Harrison Smith, 9 May 1888, THS Papers, Box 24.

16. Mary Stuart Smith to Francis H. Smith, Thursday Morning, 2 July 1896, THS Papers, Box 30.

17. Charles W. Kent, "Mary Stuart Smith [1834—]," in *Library of Southern Literature* (New Orleans: Martin and Hoyt, 1909), 11:4947.

18. Mary Stuart Smith, "The Virginia Woman of Today," in *The Congress of Women: Held in the Women's Building. World's Columbian Exposition, Chicago, U.S.A., 1893*, ed. Mary Kavanaugh Oldham Eagle (Chicago: Monarch Book Company, 1894), 409. Further references to this speech are cited within the text.

19. She may refer here to the speech held at the Chicago Exposition, which had appeared in print a few months earlier. Mary Stuart Smith to George Tucker Smith, 17 February 1895, THS Papers, Box 29.

20. The English translator Clara Bell came in for harsh criticism when Smith and her son were producing a new translation of Georg Ebers's *Nilbraut*. Smith found it "wretchedly poor" but then admitted a few days later that "trying [to translate] oneself makes one take more indulgent views of the efforts of others." Mary Stuart Smith to Gessner Harrison Smith, 3 June and 8 June 1887, THS Papers, Box 244.

21. Ibid., 9 April 1887, THS Papers, Box 24.

22. Quoted by Charles W. Kent, "Mary Stuart Smith," 11:4949. Kent identifies the source merely as "one of her early essays."

23. Mary Stuart Smith to Gessner Harrison Smith, 9 December 1890, THS Papers, Box 26.

24. Ibid., 3 November 1890, THS Papers, Box 26.

25. "Contemporary Literature," *International Review,* August 1879, 227. Reviews of *At a High Price* disagreed on the quality of Smith's skill as a translator. Two regional newspapers display this spread, ranging from a blistering criticism of this "miserable translation which has left the German idioms and positions of words as far as possible from colloquial English" to praise of "Mary Stuart Smith who seems to have the rare faculty of conveying the spirit of the author, as well as his [sic] matter and ideas." Rev. of *At a High Price,* by E. Werner, *Milwaukee Daily Sentinel,* April 26, 1879, 8, col. A; "New Books," *St. Louis Globe-Democrat,* March 24, 1879, 3, col. C.

26. Editor's Note, *Southern Review* 10, no. 22 (April 1872): 60.

27. Mary Stuart Smith to George Tucker Smith, 30 August 1898, THS Papers, Box 30. Smith found herself speaking of Tucker's return "home" to New York from the Spanish-American War and ruefully noted how "liberalizing" war had been for her to be able to call the "hub of Yankeedom" home.

28. Mary Stuart Smith to Gessner Harrison Smith, 12 December 1882, THS Papers, Box 21.

29. Ibid., 23 May 1888, THS Papers, Box 24.

30. Barbara Sicherman ("Reading and Middle-Class Identity," 141) designates as "cheap books" books priced at five, ten, and twenty cents. Smith's earliest translations for Munro are priced at twenty cents.

31. *Publishers' Weekly,* October 6, 1877, 396.

32. Tebbel, *Expansion of an Industry,* 307.

33. Sicherman maintains that, given the significant number of "classic books" available in "cheap libraries," the idea that reading *contents* were stratified along class lines needs to be questioned. Sicherman, "Ideologies and Practices of Reading," 296–97.

34. She not only translated for Munro but also wrote weekly articles for his *Fashion Bazar,* as this letter documents. Mary Stuart Smith to Gessner Harrison Smith, dated "Monday morning or Sunday night near 1 AM" [May 1888], THS Papers, Box 24.

35. Two additional Smith translations appeared in the regular Seaside Series.

36. David Dzwonkoski, "George Munro (New York: 1868–1893), George Munro and Company (New York: 1864–1868), George Munro's Sons (New York: 1893–1906), George Munro Publishing House (New York: 1906–1908)," in Peter Dzwonkoski, *American Literary Publishing Houses,* 1:315.

37. A letter from Margaret J[unkin] Preston makes clear that Smith has complained about the honoraria for translating: "I am sorry to hear you say that you find your work of translation an ill-paid service; I had an idea that German translation was more or less profitable, and I believe your specialty lies in that language." Preston went on to say that she found literature generally to be unprofitable and that she had earned little from her books. Margaret J. Preston to Mary Stuart Smith, 8 April 1887, THS Papers, Box 24.

38. Mary Stuart Smith to Gessner Harrison Smith, 24 February 1887, THS Papers, Box 24.

39. "Eliza's school" was a Christian school established in China in memory of Smith's daughter Eliza Smith Walker, who died suddenly when pregnant with her first child on September 2, 1880. Mary Stuart Smith to Gessner Harrison Smith, undated letter, THS Papers, Box 45.

40. Smith reported to Harry that a Mrs. Serte had told her that Mrs. Coleman received $5,000 for her translation; she thought that the honorarium had been $1,000. Mary Stuart

Smith to Gessner Harrison Smith, Monday 11.20 [May 1888], THS Papers, Box 24. See chapter 6 for Coleman's earnings.

41. Ibid., April 1, [1891], THS Papers, Box 26.

42. Ibid., 9 December 1890, THS Papers, Box 26.

43. Mary Stuart Smith to George Tucker Smith, 13 March 1894, THS Papers, Box 28.

44. Ibid., 6 March 1994, THS Papers, Box 28; Mary Stuart Smith to Gessner Harrison Smith, April 1, [1891], THS Papers, Box 26.

45. Mary Stuart Smith, "Record of What she can write down, in brief, of the main incidents of her beloved and lamented Harry's Life" [sic], undated manuscript, 49, in THS Papers, Box 56. After Harry's death, Smith for a time tried to remake her son Tucker, who was serving in the navy as a physician, into a man of letters and the confidant that Harry had been. She urged him to write a story for a contest and tried to interest him in her new translation, Marie Bernhard's *The Pearl*, which she falsely characterized as a "nautical story," simply because the heroine's true love is at sea (and out of sight) for most of the novel. See, e.g., Mary Stuart Smith to George Tucker Smith, 2 July 1894, THS Papers, Box 28.

46. Mary Stuart Smith to Gessner Harrison Smith, 24 February 1887, THS Papers, Box 24.

47. Ibid., 9 June 1898, THS Papers, Box 31.

48. Smith also described herself as "a representative of W. Heimburg," but none of her letters confirms any kind of contact or agreement with the author or with Keil. Mary Stuart Smith to Gessner Harrison Smith, April 1, [1891], THS Papers, Box 26.

49. Mary Stuart Smith to Lelia Smith, 12 February 1878, THS Papers, Box 19.

50. Ernst Keil to Mary Stuart Smith, 1 November 1878, THS Papers, Box 19.

51. E. Werner, *At a High Price*, trans. Mary Stuart Smith (Boston: Estes and Lauriat, 1879), title page.

52. E. Werner, *What the Spring Brought*, trans. Mary Stuart Smith (New York: George Munro, 1881), title page.

53. Mary Stuart Smith to Gessner Harrison Smith, 1 January 1883, THS Papers, Box 21.

54. Ibid., 30 January 1883, THS Papers, Box 21.

55. Ibid., 25 June 1883, THS Papers, Box 21. In an earlier letter she pushed Harry to pay a second visit to Werner. Ibid., 5 June 1883, THS Papers, Box 21.

56. Ibid., 9 May 1888, THS Papers, Box 24.

57. Ibid., "Monday morning or Sunday night" [May 1888], THS Papers, Box 24.

58. Ibid., Monday 11.20 [May 1888], THS Papers, Box 24.

59. Ibid., 6 August 1889, THS Papers, Box 25.

60. Ibid., 29 November 1891, THS Papers, Box 27.

61. The position of Munro on international copyright, which when passed contributed to the demise of his company, was somewhat contradictory. But if his position shifted, it was consistently taken with an eye to his own undertakings. He had proposed "a royalty payment system as early as 1879" and ten years later demanded a copyright law that would favor his product (Dzwonkoski, 316). Yet he also fought copyright when it threatened his enterprise. He sometimes paid "conscience money" to authors whom he reprinted. As we have seen, Smith's letters indicate that at least small sums were paid to Werner and Lindau. Raymond Howard Shove points out, furthermore, that "while it is not improbable that Munro did pay many of the foreign authors whose works appeared in the *Seaside Library,*

the amounts paid were undoubtedly small in most cases," and he quotes Munro who grumbled on one occasion that "the foreign author . . . was never satisfied. To sell books at low prices, Munro could not pay a hefty honorarium and still make a profit." Raymond Howard Shove, *Cheap Book Production in the United States, 1870 to 1891* (Urbana: University of Illinois Library, 1937), 59.

62. Mary Stuart Smith to Gessner Harrison Smith, 26 December 1890, THS Papers, Box 26.

63. Ibid., 9 December 1890, THS Papers, Box 26. In fact, a second translation of *Frühlingsboten*, titled *The Master of Ettersberg*, appeared with Street and Smith in 1891.

64. Mary Stuart Smith to Gessner Harrison Smith, 9 November 9, 1890, THS Papers, Box 26.

65. Munro did, however, sometimes advertise the offerings in the Seaside Library by grouping the works under their respective authors' names; foreign authors are not, however, necessarily identifiable as foreign.

66. "Hawking about" is Smith's expression for this "trying" task. Mary Stuart Smith to Gessner Harrison Smith, 3 June 1887, THS Papers, Box 24.

67. Ibid., 24 February 1887, THS Papers, Box 24.

68. Ibid., 28 May 1887, 3 June 1887, THS Papers, Box 24.

69. Smith's *An Insignificant Woman* (1891) also appeared in Bonner's Ledger Library in this time period, but Smith's letters contain no indication that Harry collaborated with her on this translation.

70. Paul Lindau, *Lace: A Berlin Romance*, Appleton's Town and Country Library 30 (New York: Appleton, 1889). Alderman Library, University of Virginia, Call No. PT2423. L75621889.

71. Mary Stuart Smith to Gessner Harrison Smith, 30 April 1888, THS Papers, Box 24.

72. Ibid., 24 July 1889, 6 August 1889, 13 August 1889, THS Papers, Box 25.

73. Ibid., 19 November 1891, THS Papers, Box 26.

74. Ibid., 6 August 1889, THS Papers, Box 25; 30 April 1888, THS Papers, Box 24; November 1890, THS Papers, Box 26; [22 December] 1887, THS Papers, Box 24.

75. Ibid., 24 February 1887, THS Papers, Box 24.

76. Ibid., 28 May 1887, THS Papers, Box 24.

77. Ibid., 21 June 1886, THS Papers, Box 24. Smith feared that the young woman, thanks to the resources of an aunt, had been raised with expensive tastes and a lack of a work ethic: "While the mother has toiled and labored, the daughters have been brought up to consider the first duty of youth to be enjoyment and the ornamentation of society."

78. Ibid., 30 April 1890, THS Papers, Box 26.

79. Ibid., 7 March 1887, THS Papers, Box 24.

80. Ibid., 17 October 1887, THS Papers, Box 24.

81. Ibid., 1 April 1887, THS Papers, Box 24.

82. Ibid., 7 March 1887, THS Papers, Box 24.

83. Ibid., 9 April 1887, THS Papers, Box 24.

84. E. Marlitt, *Gold Elsie*, trans. A. L. Wister (Philadelphia, PA: Lippincott, 1869), 181.

85. E. Marlitt, *Gold Elsie*, trans. Mary Stuart Smith and Son (New York: Munro, 1887), 151. I thank Lisa Iacobellis, Rare Books and Manuscripts in The Ohio State University Libraries, for copying this passage for me from the copy of the Smiths' translation held at The Ohio State University and for providing me with scans of select pages of the novel.

86. Mary Stuart Smith to Gessner Harrison Smith, 1 April 1887, THS Papers, Box 24.

87. Ibid., 25 November 1890, THS Papers, Box 26.

88. Ibid., 15 December [1887], THS Papers, Box 24. Smith mentions here that the manuscript was completed nineteen years earlier and that she was paid for her work. In April 1868 she noted that she had worked on the translation of the "Great Elector" all winter and has seven hundred pages to go. Mary Stuart Smith to Mary Jane Harrison, 18 April 1868, THS Papers, Box 16.

89. Mary Stuart Smith to Gessner Harrison Smith, 15 December [1887], THS Papers, Box 24.

90. Mary Stuart Smith to Eliza L. C. Harrison, 7 September 1873, THS Papers, Box 17.

91. Mary Stuart Smith to Gessner Harrison Smith, Monday Morning or Sunday night, near 1 A.M., [May] 1888, THS Papers, Box 24.

92. Ibid. Rives's *Virginia of Virginia* appeared with Harper and Brothers in the same year as *The Quick or the Dead?* appeared in *Lippincott's Magazine*. It recounts the passion of an uneducated white southern woman for an Englishman. Virginia speaks dialect and plots the death of her rival. Although she does sacrifice herself to save the Englishman's favorite horse, she sorely undermines cherished ideas of southern womanhood.

93. Ruth Bernard Yeazell, *Fictions of Modesty: Women and Courtship in the English Novel* (Chicago: University of Chicago Press, 1984), 126–27.

94. Ibid., 128.

95. Mary Stuart Smith to Gessner Harrison Smith, 7 January 1891, THS Papers, Box 26.

96. Ibid., 12 January 1891, THS Papers, Box 26.

97. Ibid., 11 September 1891, THS Papers, Box 26.

98. Berthold Auerbach, *Das Landhaus am Rhein,* Die Deutsche Library 75 (New York: George Munro, 1882), 2:74. I thank Kirsten Belgum for pointing me to this sentence. On the function of America in Auerbach's *Villa on the Rhine,* see Kirsten Belgum, "'Wie ein Mensch sich selbst bilden kann.' Zur Funktion von Amerika in Auerbachs *Landhaus am Rhein,*" in Hamann et al., *Amerika und die deutschsprachige Literatur,* 59–82.

99. Berthold Auerbach, *The Villa on the Rhine* (New York: Henry Holt and Company, 1874), 2: 980.

100. John W. Lovell Company to Mary Stuart Smith, 5 January 1891, THS Papers, Box 26. Here the suggestion is made that by looking at previous translations her "labors might be lessened" and that she could both improve on them and obtain some ideas from them.

101. Berthold Auerbach, *The Villa on the Rhine,* trans. Mary Stuart Smith (New York: International Book Company), 2: 445.

102. Mary Stuart Smith to Gessner Harrison Smith, 20 November 1891, THS Papers, Box 26.

103. Auerbach, *Villa,* trans. Smith, 2:457.

104. Printed obituary inserted in the diary of Eliza L. C. Harrison (1808–93; mother of Mary Stuart Smith), THS Papers, Box 45. The publication information has been cut off the obituary.

105. Mary Stuart Smith to Gessner Harrison Smith, November 1890, THS Papers, Box 26.

106. Ibid., 29 March 1888, THS Papers, Box 24.

107. Ibid., 10 February [1889], THS Papers, Box 25.

108. Ibid., 9 January 1892, THS Papers, Box 26.

109. Ibid., 29 November 1891, THS Papers, Box 26.

110. The Smiths' translation of Lindau's novella *Im Fieber*, if ever completed, was not published as a book.

111. Mary Stuart Smith to Gessner Harrison Smith, 7 February 1888, THS Papers, Box 24.

112. Smith, "The Women of the Revolution," 97.

113. Smith, *Lang Syne*, 91–92.

114. Mary Stuart Smith to Gessner Harrison Smith, 19 October 1891, THS Papers, Box 27.

115. Ibid., 17 March 1888, THS Papers, Box 24.

116. Ibid., 13 April [1888], THS Papers, Box 24.

117. Smith, "Harry's Life," 50.

118. Editor's Note, *Southern Review* 10, no. 22 (April 1872): 460.

119. [Mary Stuart Smith], Rev. of *Askaros Kassis, the Copt. A Romance of Modern Egypt*, by Edward De Leon, *Southern Review* (April 1872): 446. Further citations of this article appear in the body of the text. Her feelings about *Uncle Tom's Cabin* surface again in her correspondence from the 1890s when she writes of a performance of *Uncle Tom's Cabin* that is to take place in Charlottesville. She has heard from the students that they are going to break it up and piously avers, "Colored people are so easily wrought up. It is very wicked to try and excite them and young people generally in this way," referring to the fact that the play was not allowed to be performed in Lynchburg. Mary Stuart Smith to George Tucker Smith, 14 February 1894, THS Papers, Box 28.

120. Mary Stuart Smith, "Berlin, the City of the Kaiser," *The Cosmopolitan* 8, no. 5 (March 1890): 515–28. The publication date of this essay obscures the fact that it was actually written around May 1888. Smith mentions having sent it first to Frank Leslie, where it lay fallow for two months only to be rejected. Mary Stuart Smith to Gessner Harrison Smith, "At night," 11 July [1888], THS Papers, Box 25.

121. Ibid., 24 February 1888, THS Papers, Box 25.

122. Ibid., 14 March 1890, THS Papers, Box 26.

123. Ibid., 30 April 1888, THS Papers, Box 24.

124. Ibid., 14 March 1890, THS Papers, Box 26.

125. "Translations," *Literary World*, March 1, 1874, 152.

126. Woodrow Wilson, "An Address to a Joint Session of Congress," April 2, 1917, *The American Presidency Project* http://www.presidency.ucsb.edu/ws/index.php?pid=65366 (accessed August 25, 2010).

Conclusion

1. Smith, "The Women of the Revolution," 97.

2. Anonymous, Rev. Essay, *National Quarterly Review* 35, no. 70, first series (October 1877): 301–2.

3. Amy Kaplan, "Manifest Domesticity," in *No More Separate Spheres!* ed. Cathy N. Davidson and Jessamyn Hatcher (Durham, NC: Duke University Press, 2002), 203.

4. Untitled notice, *New York Times*, June 1, 1907, BR352.

5. Agnes Hamilton to Edith Trowbridge, 19 August 1895. Hamilton Family Papers, Schlesinger Library, Radcliffe Institute for Advanced Study, Harvard University.

6. The American interest in this fiction thus extended beyond the typical time that, according to Franco Moretti, "normal literature remains in place," namely, twenty-five to thirty years (*Graphs, Maps, Trees*, 20). The activity of translation itself was concentrated within a thirty-five-year range with some outliers.

7. "Recent Fiction," *The Independent* 40, no. 2063 (June 14, 1888): 17.

8. Mary Stuart Smith to Francis H. Smith, 11 August 1915, THS Papers, Box 42.

9. Mary Stuart Smith to Eleanor Smith Kent, 15 June 1914, 14 August [1917], THS Papers, Box 41 and 43, respectively. The second letter does not designate the year but is listed in THS as from 1917.

10. Thomas Mann, *Betrachtungen eines Unpolitischen. Gesammelte Werke* (Frankfurt am Main: S. Fischer, 1983), 247; quoted by Hermann Glaser, *Die Kultur der Wilhelminischen Zeit: Topographie einer Epoche* (Frankfurt am Main: S. Fischer, 1984), 236.

BIBLIOGRAPHY

The American Heritage Dictionary, s.v. "duodecimo" and "twelvemo."
Ames, Eric. "The Image of Culture—Or, What Münsterberg Saw in the Movies." In Tatlock and Erlin, *German Culture,* 21–41.
Arens, Hans. *E. Marlitt: Eine kritische Würdigung.* Trier: Wissenschaftlicher Verlag, 1994.
Armstrong, Nancy. *Desire and Domestic Fiction: A Political History of the Novel.* New York: Oxford University Press, 1987.
Askey, Jennifer. "A Library for Girls: Publisher Ferdinand Hirt & Sohn and the Novels of Brigitte Augusti." In Tatlock, *Publishing Culture,* 155–78.
Baker, Cathleen A. *The Enterprising S. H. Goetzel: Antebellum and Civil War Publisher in Mobile, Alabama.* The Legacy Press, www.thelegacy press.com, 1985–2010.
Becker, Frank. *Bilder von Krieg und Nation. Die Einigungskriege in der bürgerlichen Öffentlichkeit Deutschlands 1864–1913.* Munich: R. Oldenbourg Verlag, 2001.
Belgum, Kirsten. *Interior Meaning: Design of the Bourgeois Home in the Realist Novel.* German Life and Civilization 9. New York: Peter Lang, 1992.
——. "E. Marlitt: Narratives of Virtuous Desire." In *A Companion to German Realism, 1848–1900,* edited by Todd Kontje, 259–82. Rochester, NY: Camden House, 2002.
——. *Popularizing the Nation: Audience, Representation, and the Production of Identity in "Die Gartenlaube," 1853–1900.* Lincoln: University of Nebraska Press, 1998.
——. "Reading Alexander von Humboldt: Cosmopolitan Naturalist with an American Spirit." In Tatlock and Erlin, *German Culture,* 107–27.
——. "'Wie ein Mensch sich selbst bilden kann.' Zur Funktion von Amerika in Auerbachs *Landhaus am Rhein.*" In Hamann et al., *Amerika und die deutschsprachige Literatur,* 59–82.
Blackbourn, David. *The Conquest of Nature: Water, Landscape, and the Making of Modern Germany.* New York: W. W. Norton, 2006.
——. *The Long Nineteenth Century: A History of Germany, 1780–1918.* New York: Oxford University Press, 1998.
Blackwell, Jeannine. "German Literary History and the Canon in the United States." In *German Studies in the United States: A Historical Handbook,* edited by Peter Uwe Hohendahl, 143–65. New York: Modern Language Association of America, 2003.
Bonter, Urszula. *Der Populärroman in der Nachfolge von E. Marlitt: Wilhelmine Heimburg, Valeska Gräfin Bethusy-Huc, Eufemia von Adlersfeld-Ballestrem.* Epistemata Würzburger Wissenschaftliche Schriften Reihe Literaturwissenschaft 528. Würzburg: Königshausen & Neumann, 2005.

Bowker, Richard Rogers. *Copyright, Its History and Its Law, Being a Summary of the Principles and Practice of Copyright with Special Reference to the American Code of 1909 and the British Act of 1911*. Boston: Houghton Mifflin, 1912.

Bowman, Shearer Davis. *Masters and Lords: Mid-19th-Century U.S. Planters and Prussian Junkers*. New York: Oxford University Press, 1993.

Bowser, Eileen. *The Transformation of Cinema, 1907-1915*. Vol. 2 of *History of the American Cinema*. New York: Charles Scribner's Sons, 1990.

Brodhead, Richard H. *Cultures of Letters: Scenes of Reading and Writing in Nineteenth-Century America*. Chicago: University of Chicago Press, 1993.

Bruce, Philip Alexander. *History of the University of Virginia, 1819-1919*. New York: Macmillan, 1921.

Burke, Peter, and R. Po-Chia Hsia. Introduction to *Cultural Translation in Early Modern Europe*, 1-4. Cambridge: Cambridge University Press, 2007.

Casper, Scott E., Jeffrey D. Groves, Stephen W. Nissenbaum, and Michael Winship. *The Industrial Book, 1840-1880*. Vol. 3 of *A History of the Book in America*. Chapel Hill: University of North Carolina Press, 2007.

Cavell, Stanley. *Pursuits of Happiness: The Hollywood Comedy of Remarriage*. Cambridge, MA: Harvard University Press, 1981.

Cazden, Robert E. *A Social History of the German Book Trade in America to the Civil War*. Studies in German Literature, Linguistics, and Culture 1. Columbia, SC: Camden House, 1984.

Chew, Samuel C. *Fruit among the Leaves: An Anniversary Anthology*. New York: Appleton-Century-Crofts, 1950.

Clark, Aubert J. *The Movement for International Copyright in Nineteenth-Century America*. Washington, DC: Catholic University of America Press, 1960.

Clinton, Catherine. *Fanny Kemble's Civil Wars*. New York: Simon and Schuster, 2000.

Culbreth, David Marvel Reynolds. *The University of Virginia: Memoirs of Her Student-Life and Professors*. New York: Neale, 1908.

Darnton, Robert. "First Steps Toward a History of Reading" (1986). In Machor and Goldstein, *Reception Study*, 160-79.

———. "Histoire du livre—Geschichte des Buchwesens: An Agenda for Comparative History." *Publishing History* 22 (1987): 35-41.

———. "What Is the History of Books?" *Daedalus* (Summer 1982): 65-83.

———. "'What Is the History of Books?' Revisited." *Modern Intellectual History* 4, no. 3 (2007): 495-508.

Davis, Natalie. "Women on Top." In *Society and Culture in Early Modern France: Eight Essays*, 124-51. Stanford, CA: Stanford University Press, 1975.

Denham, Scott. Foreword to W. G. Sebald. *History—Memory—Trauma*, 1-6. Berlin: Walter de Gruyter, 2006.

Dingeldey, Erika. *Luftzug hinter Samtportieren: Versuch über E. Marlitt*. Bielefeld: Aisthesis, 2007.

Duncan, Ian. "The Provincial or Regional Novel." In *A Companion to the Victorian Novel*, edited by Patrick Brantlinger and William Thesing, 318-35. Oxford: Blackwell, 2002.

Dzwonkoski, David. "George Munro (New York: 1868-1893), George Munro and Company (New York: 1864-1868), George Munro's Sons (New York: 1893-1906), George Munro Publishing House (New York: 1906-1908)." In *American Literary Publishing*

Houses 1638–1899, edited by Peter Dzwonkoski, 315–16. *Dictionary of Literary Biography*, vol. 49.1. Detroit, MI: Gale Research Co., 1986.

Ebel, Gisela. *Das Kind ist tot, die Ehre ist gerettet*. Frankfurt am Main: Tende, 1985.

Encyclopaedia Britannica, 11th ed., s.v. "German Literature."

Espagne, Michel, and Michael Werner. *Qu'est-ce qu'une littérature nationale? Approches pour une théorie interculturelle du champ littéraire*. Philologiques 3. Paris: Editions de la Maison des Sciences de l'Homme, 1994.

Eubank, Damon R. *In the Shadow of the Patriarch: The John J. Crittenden Family in War and Peace*. Macon, GA: Mercer University Press, 2009.

Faust, Drew Gilpin. "Altars of Sacrifice: Confederate Women and the Narratives of War." In *Divided Houses: Gender and the Civil War*, edited by Catherine Clinton and Nina Silber, 171–99. New York: Oxford University Press, 1992.

——. *The Creation of Confederate Nationalism: Ideology and Identity in the Civil War South*. Baton Rouge: Louisiana State University Press, 1988.

——. *Mothers of Invention: Women of the Slaveholding South in the American Civil War*. Chapel Hill: University of North Carolina Press, 1996.

——. *This Republic of Suffering: Death and the American Civil War*. New York: Alfred A. Knopf, 2008.

Fike, Joseph Duane. "Frank Mayo: Actor, Playwright, and Manager." PhD dissertation, University of Nebraska, Lincoln, 1980.

Fishkin, Shelly Fisher. "Crossroads of Culture: The Transnational Turn in American Studies: Presidential Address to the American Studies Association, November 12, 2000." *American Quarterly* 57, no. 1 (March 2005): 17–57.

Flint, Kate. *The Woman Reader, 1837–1914*. Oxford: Clarendon Press, 1993.

Fluck, Winfried, and Werner Sollors, eds. *German? American? Literature? New Directions in German-American Studies*. New York: Peter Lang, 2002.

Furst, Lilian R. *All Is True: The Claims and Strategies of Realist Fiction*. Durham, NC: Duke University Press, 1995.

Gaston, Paul M. *The New South Creed: A Study in Southern Mythmaking*. New York: Alfred A. Knopf, 1970.

Gay, Peter. "An Experiment in Denial: A Reading of the *Gartenlaube* in the Year 1890." In *Traditions of Experiment from the Enlightenment to the Present*, edited by Nancy Kaiser and David E. Wellbery, 147–64. Ann Arbor: University of Michigan Press, 1992.

Ginsburgh, Victor, Schlomo Weber, and Sheila Weyers. "The Economics of Literary Translation." *Poetics* 39, no. 3 (June 2011): 228–46.

Glaser, Hermann. *Die Kultur der Wilhelminischen Zeit: Topographie einer Epoche*. Frankfurt am Main: S. Fischer, 1984.

Goings, Kenneth W. *Mammy and Uncle Mose: Black Collectibles and American Stereotyping*. Bloomington: Indiana University Press, 1994.

Gottschall, Rudolf von. *Die deutsche Nationalliteratur des neunzehnten Jahrhunderts*. 7th ed. Breslau: Eduard Trewendt, 1902.

——. "Die Novellisten der 'Gartenlaube.'" *Blätter für literarische Unterhaltung* 19 (5 May 1870): 289–93. Reprinted in *Deutschsprachige Literaturkritik 1870–1914: Eine Dokumentation*. Edited by Helmut Kreuzer with the assistance of Doris Rosenstein. 3 vols. Frankfurt am Main: Peter Lang, 2006.

Griswold, M. W. *A Descriptive List of Novels and Tales Dealing with Life in Germany*. Cambridge, MA: W. M. Griswold Publishers, 1892.

Grossmann, Edith. *Why Translation Matters* . New Haven, CT: Yale University Press, 2010.
Hacker, Lucia. *Schreibende Frauen um 1900: Rollen—Bilder—Gesten.* Berliner Ethnographische Studien 12. Berlin: Hope, 2007.
Hamann, Cristof, Ute Gerhard, and Walter Grünzweig, eds. *Amerika und die deutschsprachige Literatur nach 1848: Migration—kultureller Austausch—frühe Globalisierung.* Bielefeld, Germany: transcript, 2009.
Harding, Sandra. *Sciences from Below: Feminisms, Postcolonalities, and Modernities.* Durham, NC: Duke University Press, 2008.
Hathaway, Lillie V. *German Literature of the Mid-Nineteenth Century in England and America as Reflected in the Journals, 1840–1914.* Boston: Chapman and Grimes, 1935.
Heller, Otto. "Women Writers of the Nineteenth Century." In *Studies in Modern German Literature,* 229–95. Boston: Ginn, 1905.
Hofmann, Else. *Eugenie Marlitt: Ein Lebensbild* [1918], edited by Fayçal Hamouda. Arnstadt: Edition Marlitt, 2005.
Howells, W. D. "Novel-Writing and Novel-Reading: An Impersonal Explanation." In *Howells and James: A Double Billing,* 5–24. New York: New York Public Library, 1958.
Hutner, Sidney F. *The Lucile Project.* University of Iowa, http://sdrc.lib.uiowa.edu/lucile/.
Jäger, Georg, and Monika Estermann. "Geschichtliche Grundlagen und Entwicklung des Buchhandels im Deutschen Reich bis 1871." In *Das Kaiserreich 1871–1918,* 17–41. Vol. 1, pt. 1, of *Geschichte des deutschen Buchhandels im 19. und 20. Jahrhundert.* Frankfurt am Main: Buchhändler-Vereinigung GmbH, 2001.
Jaszi, Peter, and Martha Woodmansee. "Copyright in Transition." In Kaestle and Radway, *Print in Motion,* 90–101.
Joeres, Ruth-Ellen Boetcher. *Respectability and Deviance: Nineteenth-Century German Writers and the Ambiguity of Representation.* Chicago: University of Chicago Press, 1998.
Jordan-Lake, Joy. *Whitewashing Uncle Tom's Cabin: Nineteenth-Century Women Novelists Respond to Stowe.* Nashville, TN: Vanderbilt University Press, 2005.
Jürgensen, Wilhelm. *Martinslieder: Untersuchung und Texte, Wort und Brauch.* Volkskundliche Arbeiten namens der Schlesischen Gesellschaft für Volkskunde 6. Breslau: M. & H. Marcus, 1910.
Kaestle, Carl F., and Janice A. Radway, eds. *Print in Motion: The Expansion of Publishing and Reading in the United States, 1880–1949.* Vol. 4 of *A History of the Book in America.* Chapel Hill: University of North Carolina Press, 2009.
Kaplan, Amy. "Manifest Domesticity." In *No More Separate Spheres!* edited by Cathy N. Davidson and Jessamyn Hatcher, 184–207. Durham, NC: Duke University Press, 2002.
Kasten, Barbara. "Statistik und Topographie des Verlagswesens." In *Das Kaiserreich 1871–1918,* 300–367. Vol. 1, pt. 2 of *Geschichte des deutschen Buchhandels im 19. und 20. Jahrhundert.* Frankfurt am Main: Buchhändler-Vereinigung GmbH, 2001.
Kelley, Mary. *Learning to Stand and Speak: Women, Education, and Public Life in America's Republic.* Chapel Hill: University of North Carolina, 2006.
———. *Private Women, Public Stage: Literary Domesticity in Nineteenth-Century America.* New York: Oxford University Press, 1984.
Kent, Charles W. "Mary Stuart Smith [1834—]." In *Library of Southern Literature* 11, 4957–50. New Orleans: Martin & Hoyt, 1909.

Kilgour, Raymond L. *Estes and Lauriat: A History, 1898-1914*. Ann Arbor: University of Michigan Press, 1957.

Kirwan, Albert D. *John J. Crittenden: The Struggle for the Union*. Lexington: University of Kentucky Press, 1962.

Kontje, Todd. "Marlitt's World: Domestic Fiction in an Age of Empire." *German Quarterly* 77, no. 4 (2004): 408–26.

Koser, Michael. Afterword to *Lumpenmüllers Lieschen*, by Wilhelmine Heimburg. Frankfurt Am Main: Fischer, 1974.

Kruse, Horst. "The Old Mamsell and the Mysterious Stranger: Mark Twain's Encounter with German Literature and the Writing of 'No. 44, The Mysterious Stranger.'" *American Literary Realism* 39, no. 1 (Fall 2006): 64–74.

Kurth-Voigt, Lieselotte E., and William H. McClain. "Louise Mühlbach's Historical Novels: The American Reception." *Internationales Archiv für Sozialgeschichte der deutschen Literatur* 6 (1981): 52–77.

Lefevere, André. *Translation, Rewriting, and the Manipulation of Literary Fame*. London: Routledge, 1991.

Levander, Caroline F., and Robert S. Levine. Introduction to *Hemispheric American Studies*, 1–17. New Brunswick, NJ: Rutgers University Press, 2008.

Light, Alison. "'Returning to Manderley': Romance Fiction, Female Sexuality, and Class." In *Feminism and Cultural Studies,* edited by Morag Shiach, 371–94. Oxford: Oxford University Press, 1999.

Machor, James, and Philip Goldstein. *Reception Study: From Literary Theory to Cultural Studies*. New York: Routledge, 2001.

Marcus, Greil, and Werner Sollors, eds. *A New Literary History of* America. Cambridge, MA: Harvard University Press, 2009.

Martino, Alberto. *Die deutsche Leihbibliothek: Geschichte einer literarischen Institution (1756-1914)*. Wiesbaden: Harrasowitz, 1990.

Matthews, Brander. "Cheap Books and Good Books" (1887). In *American Literary Publishing Houses 1638-1899*, edited by Peter Dzwonkoski, 580–86. *Dictionary of Literary Biography*, vol. 49.2. Detroit, MI: Gale Research Co., 1986.

Mazón, Patricia M. *Gender and the Modern Research University: The Admission of Women to German Higher Education, 1865-1914*. Stanford: Stanford University Press, 2003.

McClain, William H., and Lieselotte E. Kurth-Voigt. "Clara Mundts Briefe an Hermann Costenoble. Zu L. Mühlbachs historischen Romanen." *Archiv für Geschichte des Buchwesens* 22, nos. 4/5 (1981): cols. 918–1250.

McCobb, E. A. "Of Women and Doctors: *Middlemarch* and Wilhelmine von Hillern's *Ein Arzt der Seele*." *Neophilologus* 68 (1984): 571–86.

McGill, Meredith L. *American Literature and the Culture of Reprinting, 1834-1853*. Philadelphia: University of Pennsylvania Press, 2003.

———. "Copyright." In Casper et al., *The Industrial Book*, 158–77.

———. Introduction to *The Traffic in Poems: Nineteenth-Century Poetry and Transatlantic Exchange,* edited by Meredith McGill, 1–12. New Brunswick, NJ: Rutgers University Press, 2008.

Mizruchi, Susan L. *Multicultural America: Economy and Print Culture, 1865-1915*. Chapel Hill: University of North Carolina Press, 2008.

Möhrmann, Renate. *Die andere Frau: Emanzipationsansätze deutscher Schriftstellerinnen im Vorfeld der Achtundvierziger Revolution*. Stuttgart: Metzler, 1977.

Moretti, Franco. "Conjectures on World Literature." *New Left Review* 1 (January-February 2000): 54-68.
———. *Graphs, Maps, Trees: Abstract Models for Literary History.* London: Verso, 2005.
Morgan, B. Q. *A Bibliography of German Literature in English Translation.* University of Wisconsin Studies in Language and Literature 16. Madison: University of Wisconsin Press, 1922.
Mott, Frank Luther. *Golden Multitudes: The Story of Best Sellers in the United States.* New York: Macmillan, 1947.
Musser, Charles. *The Emergence of Cinema: The American Screen to 1907.* Vol. 1 of *History of the American Cinema.* New York: Charles Scribner's Sons, 1990.
Nagler, Jörg. "From Culture to Kultur: Changing American Perceptions of Imperial Germany, 1870-1914." In *Transatlantic Images and Perceptions: Germany and America since 1776,* edited by David E. Barclay and Elisabeth Glaser-Schmidt, 131-54. Cambridge: Cambridge University Press, 1997.
Nicolay, Helen. *Sixty Years of the Literary Society.* Washington, D.C.: privately printed, 1934.
Nye, Joseph S., Jr. *Soft Power: The Means to Success in World Politics.* New York: Public Affairs, 2004.
Osterweis, Rollin G. *The Myth of the Lost Cause, 1865-1900.* Hamdon, CT: Archon Books, 1973.
Oxx, Francis Hudson. *The Kentucky Crittendens: The History of a Family Including the Genealogy of Descendants in Both the Male and Female Lines, Biographical Sketches of Its Members and Their Descent from Other Early Colonial Families.* N.p.: n.p., 1940.
Pataky, Sophie, ed. *Lexikon deutscher Frauen der Feder,* 1898. Rpr. Bern: Herbert Lang, 1971. 2 vols.
Peterson, Brent O. "E. Marlitt (Eugenie John) (5 December 1825-22 June 1887)." In *Nineteenth-Century German Writers,* 225-28. *Dictionary of Literary Biography, 1841-1900,* vol. 129. Detroit, MI: Gale Research Co., 1993.
———. *History, Fiction, and Germany: Writing the Nineteenth-Century Nation.* Detroit, MI: Wayne State University, 2005.
———. "Luise Mühlbach (Clara Mundt)." In *Nineteenth-Century German Writers to 1840,* edited by James Hardin and Siegfried Mews, 204-10. *Dictionary of Literary Biography,* vol. 133. Detroit, MI: Gale Research Co., 1993.
Pochmann, Henry A. *German Culture in America: Philosophical and Literary Influences, 1600-1900.* Madison: University of Wisconsin Press, 1957.
Pochmann, Henry A., compiler, and Arthur R. Schultz, ed. *Bibliography of German Culture in America to 1940.* 1953, revised and corrected by Arthur R. Schultz. Millwood, NY: Kraus International Publications, 1982.
Price, Leah. "Introduction: Reading Matter." *PMLA, Special Topic: The History of the Book and the Idea of Literature* 121, no. 1 (2006): 9-16.
Prutz, Robert. *Die deutsche Literatur der Gegenwart. 1848 bis 1858,* 2nd ed. Leipzig: Voigt & Günther, 1860.
Putnam, George Haven. "The Contest for International Copyright." In *American Literary Publishing Houses 1638-1899,* edited by Peter Dzwonkoski, 573-79. *Dictionary of Literary Biography,* vol. 49.2. Detroit, MI: Gale Research Co., 1986.
Putsch, Luise F., ed. *Schwestern berühmter Männer.* Frankfurt am Main: Insel, 1981.
———, ed. *Töchter berühmter Männer.* Frankfurt am Main: Insel, 1988.

Radway, Janice A. *A Feeling for Books: The Book-of-the Month Club, Literary Taste, and Middle-Class Desire*. Chapel Hill: University of North Carolina Press, 1997.

———. "Readers and Their Romances." In Machor and Goldstein, *Reception Study*, 213–45.

———. *Reading the Romance: Women, Patriarchy, and Popular Literature*. Chapel Hill: University of North Carolina Press, 1991.

Rarisch, Ilsedore. *Industrialisierung und Literatur. Buchproduktion, Verlagswesen und Buchhandel in Deutschland im 19. Jahrhundert in ihrem statistischen Zusammenhang*. Berlin: Colloquium Verlag, 1976.

Regis, Pamela. *A Natural History of the Romance Novel*. Philadelphia: University of Pennsylvania Press, 2003.

Ridley, Hugh. *'Relations Stop Nowhere': The Common Literary Foundations of German and American Literature, 1830–1917*. Amsterdam: Rodopi, 2007.

Rubin, Joan Shelley. *The Making of Middlebrow Culture*. Chapel Hill: University of North Carolina Press, 1992.

Sammons, Jeffrey L. *Kuno Francke's Edition of* The German Classics *(1913–15): A Historical and Critical Overview*. New Directions in German-American Studies 6. New York: Peter Lang, 2009.

Schultz, Arthur R. ed. *Bibliography of German Culture in America to 1940*; 1953, revised and corrected by Arthur R. Schultz. Millwood, NY: Kraus International Publications, 1982.

Shell, Marc, ed. *American Babel: Literatures of the United States from Abnaki to Zuni*. Cambridge, MA: Harvard University Press, 2003.

Shell, Marc, and Werner Sollors, eds. *The Multilingual Anthology of American Literature: A Reader of Original Texts with English Translations*. New York: New York University Press, 2000.

Shove, Raymond Howard. *Cheap Book Production in the United States, 1870 to 1891*. Urbana: University of Illinois Library, 1937.

Sicherman, Barbara. *Alice Hamilton: A Life in Letters*. Cambridge, MA: Harvard University Press, 1984.

———. "Ideologies and Practices of Reading." In Casper et al., *The Industrial Book*, 279–302.

———. "Reading and Middle-Class Identity in Victorian America: Cultural Consumption, Conspicuous and Otherwise." In *Reading Acts: U.S. Readers' Interactions with Literature, 1800–1950*, edited by Barbara Ryan and Amy M. Thomas, 137–60. Knoxville: University of Tennessee Press, 2002.

———. "Reading Little Women: The Many Lives of a Text." In *U.S. History as Women's History: New Feminist Essays*, edited by Linda K. Kerber, Alice Kessler-Harris, and Kathryn Kish Sklar, 245–66. Chapel Hill: University of North Carolina Press, 1995.

———. "Sense and Sensibility: A Case Study of Women's Reading in Late-Victorian America." In *Reading in America*, edited by Cathy N. Davidson, 71–89. Baltimore: Johns Hopkins University Press, 1989.

———. *Well-Read Lives: How Books Inspired a Generation of American Women*. Chapel Hill: University of North Carolina Press, 2010.

Sollors, Werner, ed. *An Anthology of Interracial Literature: Black-White Contacts in the Old World and the New*. New York: New York University Press, 2004.

———. "German-Language Writing in the United States: A Serious Challenge to American Studies?" In *The German-American Encounter: Conflict and Cooperation between Two*

Cultures, 1800–2000, edited by Frank Trommler and Elliott Shore, 103–14. New York: Berghahn Books, 2001.

———, ed. *Multilingual America: Transnationalism, Ethnicity, and the Languages of American Literature.* New York: University of New York Press, 1998.

Spacks, Patricia Meyer. *The Female Imagination.* New York: Alfred A. Knopf, 1975.

St Clair, William. *The Reading Nation in the Romantic Period.* Cambridge: Cambridge University Press, 2004.

Stevenson, Louise. "Homes, Books, and Reading." In Casper et al., *The Industrial Book,*, 319–31.

Tatlock, Lynne. "The Afterlife of Nineteenth-Century Popular Fiction and the German Imaginary: The Illustrated Collected Novels of E. Marlitt, Wilhelmine Heimburg, and E. Werner." In Tatlock, *Publishing Culture,* 118–52.

———. "Eine amerikanische Baumwollprinzessin in Thüringen. Transnationale Liebe, Familie und die deutsche Nation in E. Marlitt's *Im Schillingshof.*" In Hamann et al., *Amerika und die deutschsprachige Literatur,* 105–25.

———. "Domesticated Romance and Capitalist Enterprise: Annis Lee Wister's Americanization of German Fiction." In Tatlock and Erlin, *German Culture,* 153–82.

———, ed. *Publishing Culture and the "Reading Nation": German Book History in the Long Nineteenth Century.* Rochester, NY: Camden House, 2010.

Tatlock, Lynne, and Matt Erlin, ed. *German Cultures in Nineteenth-Century America: Reception, Adaptation, Transformation.* Rochester, NY: Camden House, 2005.

Tebbel, John. *Between Covers: The Rise and Transformation of Book Publishing in America.* New York: Oxford University Press, 1987.

———. *The Creation of an Industry, 1630–1865.* Vol. 1 of *A History of Book Publishing in the United States.* New York: R. R. Bowker, 1972.

———. *The Expansion of an Industry, 1865–1919.* Vol. 2 of *A History of Book Publishing in the United States.* New York: R. R. Bowker, 1975.

"Three Percent: A Resource for International Literature at the University of Rochester." http://www.rochester.edu/College/translation/threepercent/index.php?s=about, accessed 1 November 2009.

Thurber, Cheryl. "The Development of the Mammy Image and Mythology." In *Southern Women: Histories and Identities,* edited by Virginia Bernhard, Betty Brandeon, Elizabeth Fox-Genovese, and Theda Perdue, 87–108. Columbia: University of Missouri Press, 1992.

Toury, Gideon. *Descriptive Translation Studies and Beyond.* Amsterdam: John Benjamins Publishing Company, 1995.

Tylutki, George E. "D. Appleton and Company (New York: 1838–1933). D. Appleton (New York; 1831–1838)." In *American Literary Publishing Houses 1638–1899,* edited by Peter Dzwonkoski, 23–27. *Dictionary of Literary Biography,* vol. 49.1. Detroit, MI: Gale Research Co., 1986.

Venuti, Lawrence. *The Translator's Invisibility: A History of Translation.* London: Routledge, 1995.

Wadsworth, Sarah. *In the Company of Books: Literature and Its "Classes" in Nineteenth-Century America.* Amherst: University of Massachusetts Press, 2006.

———. Preface to Special Issue of *Libraries & Cultures* 41, no. 1 (Winter 2006): 1–4.

Walker, Mack. *German Home Towns: Community, State, and General Estate, 1648–1871.* Ithaca, NY: Cornell University Press, 1971.

Walshe, Maire Josephine. "The Life and Works of Wilhelmine von Hillern, 1836–1916." PhD dissertation, State University of New York Buffalo, 1988.
Weiss, M. Lynn, ed. *Creole Echoes: The Francophone Poetry of Nineteenth-Century Louisiana*. Translated by Norman R. Shapiro. Urbana: University of Illinois Press, 2004.
"What Middle Town Read." Muncie Public Library, Center for Middletown Studies, Ball State University Library, http://www.bsu.edu/libraries/wmr.
Wister, Jones. *Jones Wister's Reminiscences*. Philadelphia: J. B. Lippincott, 1920.
Wittmann, Reinhard. *Buchmarkt und Lektüre im 18. und 19. Jahrhundert. Beiträge zum literarischen Leben 1750–1800*. Tübingen: Max Niemeyer Verlag, 1981.
———. *Geschichte des deutschen Buchhandels. Ein Überblick*. Munich: C. H. Beck, 1991.
Wolfe, Gerard R. *The House of Appleton*. Metuchen, NJ: Scarecrow Press, 1981.
Yeazell, Ruth Bernard. *Fictions of Modesty. Women and Courtship in the English Novel*. Chicago: University of Chicago Press, 1984.
Zacharasiewicz, Waldemar. *Images of Germany in American Literature*. Iowa City: University of Iowa Press, 2007.

INDEX

acknowledgment, as element of the happy ending, 108, 121–23, 131, 133, 139, 148–50, 154–55, 191, 194, 266
actress: role of in German novels, 95–99; and social death, 96, 99
adaptation of German literature, 172; film, 65; theater, 172; translation as, 12, 149, 172, 225, 233–35
affect in German novels, appeal to, 56–57, 69, 76–77, 82, 94, 186–87, 194. *See also* affective attachment; affective individualism; affective community; sentimentality
affective attachment: between master and slaves, 75–77, 257, 290n60; to language and literature, 173; marriage as, 154; to stories, 212
affective community, 77, 137
affective individualism, 170, 180, 182, 264, 296n23
Aimard, Gustave, 23
A. L. Burt Publishing Company, 23, 59, 64, 79, 128–29, 166
Alcott, Louisa May, 33, 218, 227–28, 265; *Jo's Boys*, 304; *Little Women*, 164, 196, 216, 265, 283n73, 304n4; *An Old Fashioned Girl*, 215, 283n73
Americanization, 12, 20, 215, 224–29, 264–65. *See also under* translation
American Library Association, 63, 104
American Studies, new approaches to, 9–11, 276n42
"amusement fiction" (*Unterhaltungsliteratur*), 3, 34

Andersen, Hans Christian, 23, 99, 104
Anna Amalia, Princess of Prussia (Amelia), 186–87
anti-Catholicism, German, 77, 112–14, 157, 193. *See also Kulturkampf*
anti-French sentiment, German, 77, 154, 168
anti-Pietism, German, in novels, 157
anti-Polish sentiment, German, 171
anti-Semitism, German, 150
Anti-Socialist Laws, German, 174–75
Appleton, D., and Company. *See* D. Appleton and Company
Appleton, Daniel, 203–6, 210
Appleton, William Henry, 224
Appleton, William Worthen, 203, 305n23
Appleton's Journal, 35, 48
Arminius (Hermann), 159
Armstrong, Nancy, 48–49, 182
Arnim, Bettina von, 30
artists, male, as plot element, 72, 78, 139–45
artists, women, as plot element, 100–101, 107
assimilation, 11, 27, 77, 97, 263–64
Auerbach, Berthold, 36, 255, 258, 273n4, 274n19; *Villa on the Rhine* (*Das Landhaus am Rhein*), 249–50, 254–56
Augustus William, Prince of Prussia, 186
Austen, Jane, 80, 160, 243, 266; *Persuasion*, 87; *Pride and Prejudice*, 80
Austin, Mary, 195
authorship: anxiety of, 222; destabilized

332 Index

by translation 12, 225–29, 233; individualism of, 12

Bach, Johann Sebastian, as national signifier, 68–69, 71, 77
bad-brother plot, 87–88, 93–94, 149–50, 157
Balzac, Honoré de, 23, 65, 181, 297n31, 309n61
Baring-Gould, S. (Sabine), 110–11, 166, 294n60
Barrie, J. M. (James Matthew), 297n31
Bebel, August, 132, 296n23
Beethoven, Ludwig van, as national signifier, 61, 77
Behrens, Bertha. *See* Heimburg, Wilhelmine
Bernhard, Marie, 29, 270–72; *The Pearl* (*Die Perle*), 246, 317n45
Bethusy-Huc, Valeska Gräfin von (Valeska von Reiswitz und Kaderžin, Gräfin von Bethusy-Huc), 30, 230, 270–72; *The Eichhofs* (*Die Eichhofs*), 122, 148–51, 300n70
Birch-Pfeiffer, Charlotte, 46, 289n43
Bismarck, Otto von, 113, 164–65, 171, 175, 250, 297n25. *See also* anti-Catholicism; *Kulturkampf*
Bjørnson, Bjørnstjerne, 23
Black Beauty (Anna Sewell), 80
Blackmore, R. D. *See Lorna Doone* (R. D. Blackmore)
Blum, Georg, and Ludwig Wahl, *Seaside and Fireside Fairytales* (selections from *See und Strand* and *Märchen*), 310n1
Böhlau, Helene, 30; *Halbtier!*, 87
Boisgobey, Fortuné du (Fortuné Hippolyte Auguste Castille), 23
book covers, 24, 64, 66–67, 85–86, 203, 217, 226–28; as display, 8, 228; and marketing, 134, 226, 228, 244–45, 277n67; targeting girls and women, 8, 21, 59–60, 111, 141–42, 166, 228
book history, 9–10, 24

book inscriptions: by gift giver, 119, 129, 134, 290n68, 295n12, 298n38; by owner, 21, 82, 119, 141, 228, 296n18
book production, growth of in Imperial Germany, 13–14, 28
books, cheap, 19–20, 59, 64, 225, 228, 243–46, 273n6, 278n74, 316n30, 317–18n61. *See also* Munro, George, and Company
books as gifts, 119–20, 134, 207, 219, 227, 264, 298n38, 308n41. *See also* book inscriptions
Braddon, Mary Elizabeth, 42
branding, 107, 155–56, 265, 294n73
British literature, 6, 9, 11, 16, 19, 49, 59, 71, 219; reprinting of in the United States, 6, 13, 23, 219.
British translations of literature by German women, 43, 109–10, 177, 244, 248
Brontë, Charlotte, 33, 80; influence of on E. Marlitt, 39, 56, 65, 126–29, 287; *Jane Eyre*, 39, 42, 56, 65, 126–28, 287n8, 289n43
Burnett, Frances Hodgson, 208
Burney, Fanny, 254; *Evelina*, 254
Bürstenbinder, Elisabeth. *See* Werner, Elisabeth
Burt, A. L. *See* A. L. Burt Publishing Company

Caldwell, H. M. *See* H. M. Caldwell Company
Carlyle, Thomas, 243
Cavell, Stanley, 26, 121–23, 126
Cervantes, Miguel de, 23, 243; *Don Quixote*, 23
Chamisso, Adelbert von, 274n19
Chatterton-Peck Company, 59–60
Chaudron, Adelaide de Vendel, 203–6, 211, 305n23, 306n24, 306–7n32, 308n28
cheap editions. *See* books, cheap
Cherbuliez, Victor, 23
Chesnut, James, Jr. (General), 22

Chesnut, Mary Boykin Miller, 22
Chicago World's Fair. *See* World's Columbian Exposition
Civil War, U.S.: comfort in reading after, 76, 78, 180, 200, 213, 257, 264; economic effects of, 27, 219, 237, 247, 314n4. *See also* Confederate Nationalism; Lost Cause; *and under* Coleman, Ann Mary (Mrs. Chapman Coleman, née Crittenden); Smith, Mary Stuart (née Harrison); *In the Schillingscourt under* Marlitt, E. (Eugenie John), works of,
Clark, Given and Hooper, 59, 64
Claudius, Wilhelm, 80
Coleman, Ann Mary (Mrs. Chapman Coleman, née Crittenden): and D. Appleton and Company, 204–6, 209–11, 305–6n23; and earnings from translation, 209–11; and family division during the Civil War, 199–202, 304n3; and her sons, 200–202, 206–7, 305n18; impecunity of, 202, 209–10, 305n19; and John J. Crittenden, 200–202, 207–8, 213–14; *Life of John J. Crittenden*, 207–8, 213; possession of copyright by, 210–11; and romantic view of history, 200, 202, 212–13; skill of as translator, 211–12; and social connections, 27, 199–200, 207–8; sojourns in Europe of, 200–201, 205–6, 304n6; southern sympathies of, 27, 180, 200–202, 207–8, 212–13, 305n12, 309n77; and translation with her daughters, 202–3, 206, 209–12; and Ulysses S. Grant, 22, 207, 304n3. *See also under* Mühlbach, Luise (Clara M. Mundt)
Coleman, Ann Mary (Mrs. Chapman Coleman, née Crittenden), works translated by: *Berlin and Sans-Souci, or Frederick the Great and His Friends*, 207, 211; *Charlotte Ackermann*, 210; *Fairy Tales for Little Folks*, 210; *Frederick the Great and His Court*, 204–5, 306n27, 306–7n32; *Frederick the Great and His Family*, 205. *See also under* Mühlbach, Luise (Clara M. Mundt), works of
Coleman, Chapman (husband of Ann Mary Coleman), 199, 200–202, 209
Coleman, Chapman (son of Ann Mary Coleman and Chapman Coleman), 200–202, 205–7, 259–60, 305n18, 308n40, 308n44, 309n66
Coleman, Eugenia (daughter of Ann Mary and Chapman Coleman), 202, 209
Coleman, John Crittenden (son of Ann Mary and Chapman Coleman), 201–2
Collins, Wilkie, 6, 99, 297n31
colonialism, 65, 126, 157
comedy, 149, 179; high, 117; New, 123; of remarriage, 122–23, 126; Old, 123
"communications circuit," 24
Confederate Nationalism, 25, 76. *See also* Lost Cause
Conkey, W. B. *See* W. B. Conkey Company
Cooke, John Esten, 35–36, 182
copyright, international, 13, 32, 224–25, 242, 244, 248–49, 313n52, 317n16. *See also* pirate printing; reprinting; *and under* Coleman, Ann Mary (Mrs. Chapman Coleman, née Crittenden); Stowe, Harriet Beecher; and Wister, Annis Lee (née Furness)
Costenoble, Hermann, 281n21
cousin marriage, 89, 95, 139, 170–74, 189, 253
Craik, Dinah Maria. *See* Mulock, Dinah Maria
Crittenden, George (brother of Ann Mary Coleman), 199
Crittenden, John. J., 27, 199–201, 207–8, 213–14, 304n3, 304n6
Crittenden, Thomas (brother of Ann Mary Coleman), 199
cultural transfer, 3, 6, 11–12, 24, 156, 219, 277n53

Danish-German War in German novels, 160, 173–74
Dante Alighieri, 181
D. Appleton and Company, 33, 180, 203–6, 250, 252, 305–6n23, 306–7n32, 307–8n38; and authors' honoraria, 32, 243, 248, 312n36; and international copyright, 224; and translators' honoraria, 209–10, 246, 256, 309n66. *See also under* Coleman, Ann Mary (Mrs. Chapman Coleman, née Crittenden)
Darnton, Robert, 24, 196, 279n86
Daudet, Alphonse, 23, 65, 114, 297n31
Davis, Jefferson, 199, 305n12
Davis, Mrs. J. W. (translator), 85, 92–93, 141
dedications, book. *See* book inscriptions
Deutsche Library, Die. *See under* Munro, George, and Company
Deutsche Roman-Zeitung, 47, 96, 103, 146, 151, 230, 300n78
Deutsche Rundschau, Die, 47
Deutsches Museum, 34
Dickens, Charles, 33, 41, 65, 160, 181, 243, 258, 266; *Oliver Twist*, 59
Dickey, Katharine S. (translator), 134, 297n30
Dingelstedt, Franz von, 274n19
"distant reading," 25, 279n90
divorce in German fiction, 73, 77, 123, 140, 143, 153, 158, 167, 184; American disapproval of, 80, 121
Dohm, Hedwig, 293n52
domestic fiction, German: adaptation for the American stage, 172; adventure within, 56, 85, 163, 241, 264; Americanization of, 264 (*see also* Americanization); as genre sought by Americans in German literary production, 16–17, 20, 23, 96, 223, 230, 249; German historical fiction as, 182–84, 189, 191, 193–94; and national culture, 50, 54, 61, 79–80, 155; popular literature by women defined as, 25, 48–50; and remarriage, 121–22 (*see also* remarriage); as wholesome reading, 44, 48, 129, 215, 258–59, 265, 286n121
domesticity in novels: and agency, 57, 121–23, 143–44, 159; ahistoricity of, 158; linked to the nation, 26, 54, 140, 158–59, 190–91, 257, 264; and literary work, 100, 196; men fashioned to support, 133, 143–44, 148; pushing the boundaries of, 5, 144, 260, 264; supported within novels, 57, 99, 144, 150, 240–41, 264. *See also* masculinity in novels; *and under* femininity
Donohue, M. A., and Company. *See* M. A. Donohue and Company
Donohue brothers, 85
Donohue, Henneberry, and Company, 59, 64, 128–29, 165
Doyle, Arthur Conan, 65, 207, 297n31
Droste-Hülshoff, Annette von, 16
Droz, Gustave, 23
Dumas, Alexandre (père), 23, 32, 35, 65, 181, 266; *The Count of Monte Cristo* 23, 80; *Monsieur de Chauvelin's Will*, 237

E. A. Weeks and Company, 59, 64, 80, 128, 160
Ebers, Georg, 274n19, 297n31, 315n20; *Bride of the Nile* (*Die Nilbraut*), 250, 315n20
Ebner-Eschenbach, Marie von, 16
Eichendorff, Joseph von, *The Happy-Go-Lucky* (*Der Taugenichts*), 150, 223, 314n70
Elgard, Mrs. B. (translator), 219
Eliot, George (Mary Anne Evans), 41, 62, 65, 160, 181, 266; *Middlemarch*, 103, 147, 253; *Silas Marner*, 80
Elizabeth Christine, Queen of Prussia, 183–86, 189, 211
Emerson, Ralph Waldo, 6, 181, 218, 223, 310n8
Empire Publishing Company, 64
Ernst Keil's Nachfolger, 249, 313n52. *See also* Keil, Ernst

Eschstruth, Nataly von, 16–17, 29, 270–72; *The Erl Queen* (*Die Erlkönigin*), 119–20
Estes and Lauriat, 64, 129, 171, 174, 296n19
Europe: American longing for, 200, 214, 235; American suspicion of, 13, 102, 200
European novels, popular in America, 23
Evans, Edward Payson, 8
Excelsior Publishing Company, 64
exoticism, 18, 32, 56, 74, 81, 88, 126, 182, 193

femininity: of books, 228; constitutive of masculinity, 131–32, 141, 266; deviation from codes of, 103–7, 110, 124, 152–53; importance of to marriage, 121, 132, 141, 149, 153, 215; models of in novels, 88, 105, 149, 260; and national history, 77, 134, 149, 160, 163, 169, 260, 266; reinscription within, 56, 77, 153, 160, 163; and virtue, 119, 138, 215, 260, 266. See also gender; masculinity in novels; separate spheres; Woman Question, The
Fenno, R. F. See R. F. Fenno and Company
Feuillet, Octave, 23
Fielding, Henry, 181
Fishkin, Shelley Fisher, 10
Flaubert, Gustave, 181
Fleming, May Agnes, 42
F. M. Lupton Publishing Company, 59, 128, 177; Bijou Series, 64; Stratford Series, 64
Fontane, Meta, 222
Fontane, Theodor, 5, 43, 116; *Frau Jenny Treibel*, 46; *Unterm Birnbaum*, 43
Fothergill, Jessie, 65, 297n31
Francke, Kuno, *The German Classics of the Nineteenth and Twentieth Centuries*, 116, 145, 273n4, 302n43
Franco-Prussian War, 157, 159, 298n45, 301n9, 305n19; as plot element, 78, 94, 151, 158, 160–61, 164–65, 168–69, 257
Frankfurt Parliament, 178
Frederick II of Prussia (Frederick the Great), 31, 180–89, 193–94, 200, 204, 206–7, 212–15, 304n3; as German national icon, 182, 205–6
Frederick III (Emperor), 252
Frederick William, Elector of Brandenburg (The Great Elector), 180, 188–93, 252
Frederick William I of Prussia, 181–83, 252
Frederick William III of Prussia, 162
French literature in translation, 6, 19, 23–24, 32, 65, 209, 237, 244. See also entries for pertinent authors
Freytag, Gustav, 36, 274n19; *The Ancestors* (*Die Ahnen*), 139; *Debit and Credit* (*Soll und Haben*), 170, 298n46, 302n24
Friedrich, Friedrich, 282
friendships, portrayal of women's, 91–92
Frye, Northrup, 122
Furness, Frank (brother of Annis Lee Wister), 27, 217, 312n26
Furness, Helen Kate (née Rogers; wife of Horace Howard), 218
Furness, Horace Howard (brother of Annis Lee Wister), 27, 216–18, 220, 223, 312n27
Furness, William Henry (father of Annis Lee Wister), 217–18, 310n8, 312n27

Gaboriau, Émile, 23
Garfield, James, 208
Gartenlaube, Die, 37–38; complaints of about unauthorized translations, 225, 285n105; and German national identity, 37, 61, 164–65, 170; and German women writers, 5, 25, 28–29, 38–43, 45, 47, 159; liberalism of, 37, 40, 75, 175, 283n70; as source of fiction for translation, 20, 38, 62, 128, 170, 247, 249, 282n56, 297n30. See also Keil, Ernst

Gaskell, Elizabeth, 297n25
Gautier, Théophile, 23
Gay, Peter, 164–65, 167, 170
gender, 168; complementary roles, 163, 194; and domestic fiction, 49, 182; and history, 159; and nationality, 159–63, 194; play with grammatical, 79, 191; and reading, 21–22; and science, 104, 106, 124; and the slave system, 76; transgression of norms of, 103, 105–6, 109, 111, 124, 151–53. *See also* masculinity in novels; separate spheres; *and under* femininity; marketing strategies
George M. Hill Company, 64, 128
George Munro and Company. *See* Munro, George, and Company
German-American Studies, 10, 276n42
German literature, read in the original in the USA, 7, 12. *See also* Deutsche Library, Die, *under* Munro, George and Company; *Heimatklang* under Werner, Elisabeth; *Höher als die Kirche* under Hillern, Willhelmine
German national imaginary, 25, 54, 61, 159
German Studies, 9–10, 276n42
German women's fiction, used for German instruction in the USA, 12, 47, 173
Germany, imperial: depictions of in fiction, 113, 131–33, 151, 157–59, 170, 175–76, 178–79; feminized images of, 4, 79, 158, 164, 194, 266
Gerstäcker, Friedrich, 273n4
Glümer, Claire von, 29, 99, 227, 230, 270–72; *A Noble Name* (*Dönnighausen*), 96, 99–103
Goethe, Johann Wolfgang von, 6–7, 29, 42, 116, 238, 274n18; *Clavigo*, 97; *Elective Affinities* (*Die Wahlverwandtschaften*), 97, 147; "Der Erlkönig," 119; *Faust*, 23, 97, 146; *Iphigenia on Tauris* (*Iphigenie auf Tauris*), 97; *Wilhelm Meister's Apprenticeship* (*Wilhelm Meisters Lehrjahre*), 97, 99–100, 147

Goetzel, Samuel, 203, 306n27, 306–7n32
Goldman, Emma, 39
Gottschall, Rudolf von, 28, 34, 39, 46, 65
Grant, Ulysses S., 22, 207, 259, 304n3
Griswold, W. M., 4–5, 18, 89–90, 99, 154, 157
Grosset and Dunlap, 59, 287n18
Guy Livingston (George Alfred Lawrence), 215

Hackländer, Friedrich Wilhelm, 220, 311n19; *Enchanted and Enchanting*, 220
Hamilton, Agnes, 39, 62, 129, 264
Hamilton, Alice, 62, 129, 288n27
Handel, George Frideric, 68
Harder, Ludwig, 230
Hardy, Thomas, 6, 93, 160, 243, 297n31; *The Mayor of Casterbridge*, 71
Harris, Rev. William A., 164
Harrison, Gessner (father of Mary Stuart Smith), 238, 315n8
Harte, Bret, 6
Hartner, E. (Emma Eva Henriette von Twardowska), 29, 230, 270–72
Hathaway, Lillie V., 5–6, 9, 47, 275n34, 281n24
Hawthorne, Nathaniel, 65, 181
Hay, M. C., 42
Haydn, Franz Joseph, 68
Hayes, Rutherford B., 208
Hecker, Friedrich, 175
Hector, Annie French (Mrs. Alexander), 42
Heimburg, Wilhelmine (Bertha Behrens), 40, 42–48, 86–87, 94; collected works of, 297n32; influence of E. Marlitt on, 291n7, 299n56; influence of Gustav Freytag on, 139, 298n46; popularity in the United States, 16, 29, 43–44, 270–72; published by George Munro, 23, 303n53; use of pseudonym by, 42, 284n88. *See also under* Smith, Mary Stuart (née Harrison); Wister, Annis Lee (née Furness)
Heimburg, Wilhelmine, works of: *Antons*

Erben, 86; *Beetzen Manor*, 86; *Cloister Wendhusen* (*Kloster Wendhusen*), 86–87; *Defiant Hearts* (*Trotzige Herzen*), 134, 136; *A Fatal Misunderstanding*, 44; *For Another's Fault* (*Um fremde Schuld*), 93; *Gertrude's Marriage* (*Trudchens Heirat*), 122, 145; Her *Only Brother/A Sister's Love: A Novel* (*Ihr einziger Bruder*), 86–88, 90, 93, 156; *An Insignificant Woman: A Story of Artist Life/Misjudged* (*Eine unbedeutende Frau*), 122, 141–46; *Lora, the Major's Daughter/Lenore von Tollen* (*Lore von Tollen*), 61, 87, 91, 93, 150, 295; *Lore Lotte*, 43; *Lottie of the Mill / Lizzie of the Mill/A Tale of an Old Castle/ A Maiden's Choice* (*Lumpenmüllers Lieschen*), 42–43, 122–23, 133–34, 136–39, 297nn29–30, 298n38; *Lucie's Mistake/ Friendship's Test/ Hortense/ My Heart's Darling* (*Herzenskrisen*), 44, 86, 91–93 122; *The Owl-House/The Owl's Nest* (*Das Eulenhaus*), 42–43, 45; *A Penniless Girl* (*Ein armes Mädchen*), 44, 314 n81; *Der Stärkere*, 86; *The Story of a Clergyman's Daughter/The Pastor's Daughter* (*Aus dem Leben meiner alten Freundin*), 42, 85–86, 291n7, 295n79; *Two Daughters of One Race* (*Die Andere*), 157–58; "Unser Männe," 250; *Wie auch wir vergeben*, 86

Heine, Heinrich, 274n19; *Die Harzreise*, 130–31, 296n22

Heller, Otto, 3–5, 8, 31, 39, 42, 44, 46, 173

Henry, Prince of Prussia, 186

Heyse, Paul, 274n19

Hill, George M. *See* George M. Hill Company

Hillern, Wilhelmine von, 22, 29–30, 46–48, 53, 226–27, 230, 270–72, 285n13, 288n30

Hillern, Wilhelmine von, works of: *By His Own Might* (*Aus eigner Kraft*), 48, 112; *Geier-Wally: A Tale of the Tirol* (*Die Geier-Wally*), 47–48; *Higher than the Church* (*Höher als die Kirche*), 12, 47; *The Hour Will Come: A Tale of an Alpine Cloister* (*Und sie kommt doch!*), 285n114; *Only a Girl/ Ernestine; a Novel* (*Ein Arzt der Seele*) (*see under* Wister, Annis Lee [née Furness], works translated by); *A Twofold Life* (*Ein Doppelleben*), 47

historical fiction, German: as domestic fiction, 48–49, 180, 182–83; and family relations, 26, 48, 61, 68, 70, 94, 138, 167–68, 171, 174, 183–86, 189; historical figures at the center of, 29, 31–36, 181–93; inclusion of women in, 85, 106, 170, 184–85, 194; inviting comparison with U.S. history, 78, 180, 200, 202, 212–14; pretention of, 29, 33–34, 215; romance in, 31, 158, 160–63, 170, 174, 182, 188; spousal fidelity in, 191–93, 252

H. M. Caldwell Company, 59, 64

Hoffmann, Heinrich, *Slovenly Peter* (*Struwwelpeter*), 310n8

Holmes, Mary Jane, 42

Home Book Company, 64

home towns, German, depiction of, 54, 79, 94, 286n124. *See also* regionalism

honoraria: foreign author's, 32, 225, 247–48, 318n61; translator's, 13, 32, 204–5, 209–10, 239, 244, 246–48, 316n37. *See also* royalties, authors'

Hugo, Victor, 23, 181; *Les Misérables*, 23; *Notre-Dame de Paris*, 39

Humboldt, Alexander von, 29

Hurst and Company, 59, 64, 128

illustrations, 37, 80, 134, 206, 227, 231, 298n38, 299n58, 313n52

incest, avoidance of in fiction, 89, 163

industrial age, depictions of, 131–32, 144, 157, 296n23, 296–97n25

Ingersoll, Robert G., 82

inscriptions. *See* book inscriptions

International Book Company, 64

international copyright. *See* copyright, international

James, Alice, 222
James, George Payne Rainsford, 32
James, Henry, 16, 35; *Daisy Miller,* 102; *The Portrait of a Lady,* 102
Jameson, Fredric, 124, 295n9
Janke, O. *See* O. Janke
J. B. Lippincott and Company: competition with publishers of cheap books, 58–59, 63–64, 71–72, 79–80, 128, 173, 243–44; and international copyright, 225, 313n52; marketing strategies of, 223–24, 235, 249; price of novels published by, 64, 243; as publisher of E. Juncker in translation, 147; as publisher of E. Marlitt in translation, 36, 41, 54, 58–59, 62–64, 219–20, 224–27, 231, 313n52; as publisher of E. Werner in translation, 45, 114, 172–73, 294n63; as publisher of Fanny Lewald in translation, 96; as publisher of Ossip Schubin in translation, 231; as publisher of Valeska von Bethusy-Huc in translation, 149; as publisher of Wilhelmine Heimburg in translation, 134, 292–93n43; as publisher of Wilhelmine von Hillern in translation, 47, 103, 112. See also *Lippincott's Magazine;* and under Wister, Annis Lee (née Furness)
Jefferson, Thomas, 199, 238
Jewett, Sarah Orne, 6
Jews in German novels, 150, 156, 189, 192–93, 298n46. *See also* anti-Semitism, German
Johnson, Andrew, 22, 207
Johnson, Rossiter, 33, 63, 99
John W. Lovell Company, 58, 64, 79, 255
Joseph II (Holy Roman Emperor), 31. *See also under* Mühlbach, Luise
Joyes, Patrick (son-in-law of Ann Mary Coleman), 202, 205, 209
Juncker, E. (Else [Kobert] Schmieden), 29, 230, 270–72; *Margarethe; or, Life-Problems (Lebensrätsel),* 122, 145–47

Keil, Ernst, 37, 40, 219, 225, 247, 249, 317. *See also* Ernst Keil's Nachfolger

Keller, Gottfried, 5, 116
Kemble, Fanny, 218
Kinkel, Johann Gottfried, 175
Kipling, Rudyard, 65
Kirschner, Aloisia. *See* Schubin, Ossip
Kock, Paul de, 32
Kraszewski, Józef Ignacy, 24
Kulturkampf, 77, 113. *See also* anti-Catholicism, German

Lafayette, Marie Joseph Paul Yves Roch Gilbert Du Motier, Marquis de, 199
Laird and Lee Publishing Company, 59
La Motte Fouqué, Friedrich Heinrich Karl, Freiherr de, 29, 274n19
Lassalle, Ferdinand, 131
Lathrop, Elise L. (translator), 123, 134, 297n30
Lawrence, George Alfred. See *Guy Livingston* (George Alfred Lawrence)
Lea, Henry, 222
Lee, Robert E., 22, 207
Lesage, Alain-René, 23
Lessing, Gotthold Ephraim, 274n19; *Emilia Galotti,* 97
Lewald, Fanny, 16, 23, 30, 230, 270–72; *Hulda; or the Deliverer (Die Erlöserin),* 7, 96–99, 101–2, 156, 220
Lewis, Matthew Gregory, 33
liberalism in German novels by women, 39, 139, 148, 170, 176, 180, 194, 264, 283n70; linked to regional vision of Germany, 49; understood in America as countering determinism, 167
Lindau, Paul, 247–49, 256, 258, 317n61; *Im Fieber,* 250, 320n10; *Lace (Spitzen),* 243, 248, 250, 256
Lippincott, J. B. and Company. *See* J. B. Lippincott and Company
Lippincott's Magazine: decision to print novels in toto in lieu of serialization, 172–73, 253; information for would-be tourists in, 235; promotion of Annis Lee Wister's translations in, 47, 62, 233, 220, 225–26, 229, 310n2; translations in as selling point, 219
London, Jack, 33

Longfellow, Henry Wadsworth, 33, 65, 99
Lorna Doone (R. D. Blackmore), 166
Lost Cause, 25, 76, 81, 257, 290nn57–59. *See also* Confederate Nationalism
Loti, Pierre, 33
Louisa Ulrika (Ulrica) of Prussia, 186
Louise, Queen of Prussia, 61, 93, 259–60
Louise Henriette of Orange (Louisa Henrietta), 189–91
Lovell, John W. *See* John W. Lovell Company
Lovell, Coryell and Company, 59, 64
Lowell, James Russell, 16
Lowrey, D. M., 165–66, 169
Lucile Project, The, 278n62, 287n19
Lupton, F. M. *See* F. M. Lupton Publishing Company
Lytton, Edward Robert Bulwer (pseud. Owen Meredith), 278n62

M. A. Donohue and Company, 59, 64, 80, 141
Mann, Thomas, 145, 266
Manteuffel, Ursula Zöge von (Frau von Trebra-Lindenau), 30, 102, 230, 270–72; *Violetta*, 95–96, 99–102, 111, 157, 229–30
Manzoni, Alessandro, 33; *The Betrothed*, 23–24
Maria Theresa of Austria (Empress), 214
marketing: age-specific, 59, 265; and boxed sets, 63, 146, 227; and classification of German novels as summer reading, 53, 102, 134, 141–42, 166, 298n36 (*see also* Seaside Library *under* Munro, George, and Company); and creation of identifiable genre of German fiction, 30, 48, 102, 265; gendered, 8, 21–22, 111, 119–20, 134, 166, 223, 228; and publication of German books in series alongside literary classics, 4, 6, 64–65, 160, 180–81; and translator's name, 63, 149, 151, 224, 227–28, 233, 235, 249. *See also* book covers; branding; *and under* J. B. Lippincott and Company;

Mühlbach, Luise (Clara M. Mundt); Wister, Annis Lee (née Furness)
Marlitt, E. (Eugenie John), 38–42, 53–55, 297n31; and age disparity in fictional couples, 55, 287n7; criticism of, 39–40, 273n4, 274n14, 282n61; defense of, 286n6, 294–95n75; illustrated editions of the works of, 313n52; international popularity of, 6–7, 16, 22–23, 29–30, 40–43, 46, 72, 224, 270–72, 280n7; and *Lippincott's Magazine*, 219, 311n15; and national culture, 68–70, 78–79; published in the Seaside Library, 23, 58–59, 128, 245, 249, 303n53; as purveyor of happy endings, 39, 45, 57–58, 70, 84, 94, 104, 109, 127–28, 215, 283n65; rate of production, 230; and serialization in *Die Gartenlaube*, 38, 40, 47, 61–62, 71, 128, 219; use of pseudonym by, 38, 282n60. *See also under* Brontë, Charlotte; Heimburg, Wilhelmine (Bertha Behrens); J. B. Lippincott and Company
Marlitt, E. (Eugenie John) works of: *At the Councillor's; or, a Nameless History* (*Im Hause des Kommerzienrats*), 41, 58, 157, 284n84, 287n9; *The Bailiff's Maid* (*Amtmanns Magd*), 286n121; *Countess Gisela* (*Die Reichsgräfin Gisela*), 38, 40, 154, 157, 226, 296n23, 299n56, 310n2; *Gold Elsie* (*Goldelse*), 38, 54–62, 65, 80–81, 105, 109, 126–27, 181, 215–16, 286n5, 287–88n24, 310n2 (*see also under* Smith, Mary Stuart [née Harrison], works translated with Gessner Harrison Smith; *In the Schillingscourt* (*Im Schillingshof*), 71–82, 95, 121, 154, 159, 213, 229, 289nn48–49, 289n52, 312n45; *The Lady with the Rubies* (*Die Frau mit den Karfunkelsteinen*), 234; *The Little Moorland Princess/ The Princess of the Moor* (*Das Haideprinzeßchen*), 38, 41–42, 80, 156, 220, 225, 286n121, 288n32; *Magdalena* (*Die Zwölf Apostel*), 219; *The Old Mam'selle's Secret* (*Das*

Geheimnis der alten Mam'sell),
14–15, 23, 39, 41–42, 57, 61–71,
95, 98, 126, 128, 159, 181, 215–17,
227, 283n75, 287–88n24, 288n36,
291n7; *Over Yonder* (*Blaubart*) 219;
The Owl-House/The Owl's Nest (*Das Eulenhaus*), 41–43, 45, 229, 233, 253,
282n56; *The Second Wife/A Brave Woman* (*Die zweite Frau*), 16, 22–23,
62, 80, 104, 122, 124–29, 140, 146,
157, 193, 220
marriage in German novels: and class difference, 39, 68–70, 94–102, 113, 136–39, 145–47, 171, 174, 257; critical portraits of, 107–8; dynastic, 183–84, 186, 189–91, 212; interethnic, 74–79, 82, 97, 167, 170–71, 173; interfaith, 113, 192–93, 257; as "narrative essential," 84; reconciliation of with art, 144–45; reconciliation of with women's intellectual aspirations, 106–11, 124; women's choice and, 108. *See also* cousin marriage; divorce in German fiction; domesticity in German novels; marriage of convenience in German novels; remarriage, novels of
marriage of convenience in German novels, 72, 77–78, 121–22, 125, 129–31, 136, 138, 152, 171
Marryat, Frederick, 33
Martineau, Harriet, 33
masculinity in novels, 46, 106, 131–32, 148–51, 154, 163; female determined and enabled, 55, 78, 126–27, 129, 133, 141, 143–44, 148, 189–90; and national history, 26, 79, 153, 159–60, 164, 189–92; redeemed, 132, 143. *See also under* Werner, E. (Elisabeth Bürstenbinder)
Matthews, Brander, 13
Maupassant, Henri René Albert Guy de, 181
Mayo, Frank, 172, 302n20
Mayreder, Rosa, 39, 121
McClure, Samuel Sidney, 243
McGill, Meredith, 11–12

Melville, Herman: *Moby Dick*, 33; *Typee*, 33
Menzel, Adolph, 144, 206
Meredith, George, 33
Meredith, Owen. *See* Lytton, Edward Robert Bulwer
Mershon Company, 59, 64, 128
Meyer, Conrad Ferdinand, 5
military, German: civilian volunteers in, 157, 168; male redemption through service in, 78–79, 160, 167–69
Mill, John Stuart, 104
Miller, Hettie E., 79–80
Mitchell, Silas Weir, 217–18, 222; and the rest cure, 222
Modleski, Tania, 124, 259n9
Moon, Oriana, 241
Moretti, Franco, 279n90, 321n6
Morgan, Bayard Quincy: bibliography of German literature in translation in America, 5, 9, 14, 40, 44–45, 275n34, 277nn58–59, 280n7, 283n74
Mühlbach, Luise (Clara M. Mundt), 6–7, 16, 29–36, 159, 179–80, 281n24, 305n19, 307n8; classification of fiction of, 35–36, 48, 182–83; gender of readers of, 22; marketing of, 30, 180–81, 283n75, 303n53; reception of, 32–36, 40, 180–83, 193, 280n12, 281n20; and remuneration of for the American translations of her works, 32, 281n21
Mühlbach, Luise (Clara M. Mundt), works of: *Berlin and Sans-Souci, or Frederick the Great and His Friends* (*Berlin und Sans-Souci oder Friedrich der Große und seine Freunde*), 33–34, 181, 184, 186–87, 204–5, 207, 211; *Deutschland in Sturm und Drang*, 181; *Frederick the Great and His Court* (*Friedrich der Große und sein Hof*), 32, 35, 181, 183–88, 204–5, 211; *Frederick the Great and His Family* (*Friedrich der Große und seine Familie*), 181, 186–87, 205; *Goethe and Schiller: An Historical Romance* (*Goethe und Schiller*), 206, 308n39;

Henry the Eighth and His Court or Catherine Parr (*König Heinrich VIII. und sein Hof, oder: Katharina Parr*), 33, 306n27; *Joseph II and His Court* (*Kaiser Josef II. und sein Hof*), 22, 32, 203–4, 305–6n23, 306n26, 306–7n32; *Marie Antoinette and Her Son* (*Marie Antoinette und ihr Sohn*), 33; *Mohammed Ali and His House* (*Mohammed Ali und sein Haus*), 32, 206; *Mohammed Ali's Nachfolger*, 32; *Queen Hortense* (*Königin Hortense: ein napoleonisches Lebensbild*) 35, 205–6; *The Reign of the Great Elector* (*Der große Kurfürst und sein Volk* [pt. 2 of *Der große Kurfürst und seine Zeit*]), 188, 190–93, 303n59; *The Youth of the Great Elector* (*Der junge Kurfürst* [pt. 1 of *Der große Kurfürst und seine Zeit*]), 188–90, 252. *See also under* Coleman, Ann Mary (Mrs. Chapman Coleman, née Crittenden), works translated by; Smith, Mary Stuart (née Harrison), works translated by

Müller, Otto, *Charlotte Ackermann*, 210

Mulock, Dinah Maria, 99; *John Halifax Gentleman*, 39, 71

Muncie Public Library, 21–22, 42, 111, 227, 278–79n76, 294n62, 313n53

Mundt, Clara M. *See* Mühlbach, Luise

Mundt, Theodor, 31

Munro, George, and Company: Deutsche Library, Die, 20, 58, 254, 278n74, 319n98; and international copyright, 317–18n61; *New York Fashion Bazar*, 239; as publisher of cheap books, 59, 64, 243, 245–46, 316n30; and reprinting, 243–44, 248, 317–18n61; Royal Series, 71; Seaside Library, 23, 58, 64, 173, 177, 243–44, 246, 303n53, 318n65. *See titles of individual works published with* Munro; *and under* Heimburg, Wilhelmine (Bertha Behrens); *and* Smith, Mary Stuart (née Harrison)

Mutual Book Company, 64

national canon, German, 4, 6, 30, 83, 115–17, 170, 223, 274n19. *See also* Francke, Kuno, *The German Classics of the Nineteenth and Twentieth Centuries*

nationalism: American, 13; German, 25, 50, 78, 137, 140, 159, 161, 181, 188, 307n37; Polish, 171. *See also* Confederate Nationalism, National Liberals; *and under* domestic fiction; femininity; masculinity in novels; Werner, E. (Elisabeth Bürstenbinder)

National Liberals, German, 49, 175, 182, 206

national literature, German formation of compared with American, 8–9

New York Publishing Company, 59

Ohnet, Georges, 23
O. Janke, 32, 47, 205, 230
Oswald, E. (Bernhardine Schulze-Smidt), 230
Ouida. *See* Ramée, Maria Louise de la

paperback edition, 64. *See also* Seaside Library *under* Munro, George, and Company

pirate printing, 13, 24, 32, 244. *See also* copyright, international

Plato, 181
Poe, Edgar Allan, 181
Polko, Elise, 273n4

popular literature, international appeal of, 3, 9–13, 16–17, 22, 84. *See also* Ridley, Hugh

Porter and Coates, 64, 210
Poynter, Eleanor Frances, 42
pseudonyms, German women novelists' use of, 29–30, 38, 42, 45, 100, 148

Raabe, Wilhelm, 5, 302–3n43; *Eulenpfingsten*, 178–79

racial and ethnic stereotyping in German novels, 73–74, 77, 90, 167–68

Radway, Janice, 84, 108, 112, 117–18, 228, 259
Raimund, Golo (Bertha [Heyn] Frederich), 30, 122, 230, 270–72; *From Hand to Hand* (*Von Hand zu Hand*), 122, 151–54, 159, 230; *A New Race* (*Ein neues Geschlecht*), 230
Ramée, Maria Louise de la (pseud. Ouida), 42, 65, 80, 215, 297n31; *Friendship*, 288n30
Reade, Charles, 62, 99, 166
readers of German novels in translation, American: age of, 25, 59, 85, 101, 120, 265–66; ethnicity of, 21; gender of, 21–22, 25, 31, 111–12
reading pleasure: and active female protagonists, 54–55, 89, 102, 104, 129, 163; and delayed gratification, 25; erotic, 55, 80, 125, 127–28; and gender politics, 117–18; legitimacy of, 36, 223, 258–59; and the solving of mysteries, 54, 61, 81, 124, 126
realism, proximity of romance to, 97, 117–18
rebinding, 59, 278n62, 287n18
regionalism, rootedness of German fiction in, 49, 61, 65, 71, 102, 112, 116, 156–58, 215. *See also* home towns, German, depiction of
Reichenbach, Moritz von. *See* Bethusy-Huc, Valeska Gräfin von (Valeska von Reiswitz und Kaderžin, Gräfin von Bethusy-Huc)
remarriage, novel of: acknowledgment within, 121–23, 126, 131, 133, 139, 148–50, 154, 185, 191, 194; free choice within, 123, 154–55; *Jane Eyre* as, 296n15; and Luise Mühlbach's historical novels, 184–85, 188, 191; narrative patterns of, 121–23, 129, 138, 145, 147–49, 151–55; and reconciliation of desire and economic necessity, 26, 91, 122–23, 127–29, 131, 134, 138, 143–45; status of women and, 123. *See also* divorce in German fiction; marriage in German novels
reprinting in America, 11–15, 265, 272,
275n28, 277–78n62; of novels by E. Marlitt, 40–41, 54, 58–59, 63–64, 79–80, 128, 225, 283n75, 287n19, 288n36; of novels by E. Werner, 45, 112, 129, 160, 174, 177; of novels by Luise Mühlbach, 33, 181, 204; of novels by Wilhelmine Heimburg, 44–45, 85–86, 146; of novels by Wilhelmine von Hillern, 47, 103. *See also under* Munro, George, and Company
Reuter, Ernst, 274n19
Reuter, Gabriele, 30; *Aus guter Familie*, 87, 311n22
revolutions of 1848: legacy of in German fiction, 174–75, 177–79
R. F. Fenno and Company, 59, 134, 174, 297n31
Rhine River and the national imaginary, 160–62, 164
Ridley, Hugh, 8–9, 11, 17
ritual death as element of romance, 26, 84, 88, 92, 97, 112
Rives, Amélie, 254; *The Quick or the Dead?*, 253–54; *Virginia of Virginia*, 319n92
Rodde, Dorothea, 106, 108
romance novels: and female subjectivity, 25, 117; narrative elements of, 84, 112, 117–18, 259
romance tradition, European, 182
Rostopchine, Sophie Feodorovna, Comtesse de Ségur: *Fairy Tales for Little Folks*, 210
royalties, authors', 13, 312n36, 317n61. *See also under* honoraria

Sand, George, 23, 31
Schiller, Friedrich, 29, 181, 274n19; *Kabale und Liebe*, 97–98
Schlegel, Dorothea, 30
Schlink, Bernhard, *The Reader* (*Der Vorleser*), 83
Schmid, Christoph von, 29
Schmieden, Else [Kobert]. *See* Juncker, E.
Schobert, Hedwig Harnisch, 30, 230, 270–72; *Picked Up in the Streets*, 265

Schopenhauer, Arthur, 107
Schubert, Franz, 77
Schubin, Ossip (Aloisia Kirschner), 30, 227, 230–31, 270–72; *Countess Erika's Apprenticeship* (*Gräfin Erikas Lehr- und Wanderjahre*), 217, 230–31
Schulze-Smidt, Bernhardine. *See* Oswald, E.
Schurz, Carl, 175, 208
science and gender in novels. *See under* gender
Scott, Walter, 41, 160, 181, 243, 266; historical novels of, 35–36, 182, 253; *Ivanhoe*, 71, 192
Sears and Company: American Home Classics, 64
Seaside Library. *See under* Munro, George, and Company
Sebald, W. G.: *Austerlitz*, 83; *The Emigrants* (*Die Ausgewanderten*), 83; *Rings of Saturn* (*Die Ringe des Saturns*), 83; *Vertigo* (*Schwindel, Gefühle*), 83
sentimentality: and the appeal of German novels, 58, 119, 141, 215, 234–35, 293n48; and domestic fiction, 48, 191; heightened in translation, 74; of novel readers, 82, 258–59, 266; as perceived German national trait, 44, 68, 137, 145; and public affairs, 260–61; satire of German bourgeois, 46
separate spheres, 164, 240. *See also* gender
serialized fiction: as constrained by its format, 173, 253; as selling point for magazines, 38, 219; translated from off the page, 71–72, 165, 128, 293n45, 297n30, 298–99n47.
Sewell, Anna. *See Black Beauty* (Anna Sewell)
Shakespeare, William, 27, 216, 218, 223; *Henry IV, part 2*, 192
Shaw, Frances A. (translator), 129, 131, 139, 160–61, 163, 171, 296n19
Shell, Marc, 9–10
Sigel, Franz, 175

Smith, Francis (husband of Mary Stuart Smith), 238–39, 240, 242, 246, 266, 315n8
Smith, George Tucker (son of Mary Stuart and Francis Smith), 239, 241, 246–47, 315n14, 316n27, 317n45
Smith, Gessner Harrison, "Harry" (son of Mary Stuart and Francis Smith), 169, 242–43, 246–60, 316n40, 317n45, 317n55, 318n69. *See also* Smith, Mary Stuart (née Harrison), works translated with Gessner Harrison Smith
Smith, Mary Stuart (née Harrison): business sense of, 242–43, 246–47, 316n27; and E. Werner (Elisabeth Bürstenbinder), 247–49, 257–58; and George Munro and Company, 165–66, 243–50, 256, 316n30, 316n34; and Gessner Harrison Smith (Harry), 242–43, 248–57, 258–60, 317n45, 317n55; hostility toward the American North, 242, 253; and Paul Lindau, 248, 256; and remuneration for translation, 210, 237, 244, 246–47, 316–17n40; skill of as translator, 18, 191, 242, 316n25; sources of translations of, 20, 37, 247, 249–50, 282n56, 297n30; taste in reading of, 134, 252–54, 256–57, 258, 266; and the University of Virginia, 237–40; views of on Amélie Rives, 253–54; views of on fiction, 258–59; views of on slavery and race, 255, 257–58, 320n119; views of on translation, 239–42, 246–47; views of on The Woman Question, 240–41; and Wilhelmine Heimburg, 246, 250, 258, 317n48
Smith, Mary Stuart (née Harrison), works of: *The Art of Housekeeping*, 249; *At a High Price*, 174–78, 237, 242, 247, 285n107, 316n25; *Clear the Track*, 249; *The Great Elector* (=*The Youth of the Great Elector* and *The Reign of the Great Elector*), 180, 188–93, 237–39, 246, 249, 252, 319n88; *Heirs*

of the Kingdom, 239, 256; *Hero of the Pen*, 160–64, 301n5; *An Insignificant Woman*, 122, 141, 318n69; *Lang Syne, or The Wards of Mt. Vernon*, 243, 256–57; *Monsieur de Chauvelin's Will*, 237; *The Old Mam'selle's Secret*, 63–64, 254; *A Tale of an Old Castle* (aka *Lieschen, a Tale of an Old Castle*), 43, 133–34, 297n29; *What the Spring Brought*, 247, 249, 279n85, 303n53

Smith, Mary Stuart (née Harrison), works translated with Gessner Harrison Smith: *Beacon Lights*, 165, 169, 250, 301n13; *The Bride of the Nile*, 250, 315n20; *The Fairy of the Alps*, 250; *Gold Elsie*, 58–59, 244–45, 249–52, 254; *A Judgment of God*, 250; *Lace*, 243, 250, 256; *The Owl-House*, 41, 250, 253; *St. Michael*, 248, 250, 257–58; *The Villa on the Rhine*, 249–50, 254–56.

social death as element of romance, 95–96, 99, 102

soft power, 13

Solger Reinhold, 175

Sollors, Werner, 9–10

Sophia Dorothea of Hanover, Queen of Prussia, as portrayed in historical fiction, 183–84, 186

Southworth, E. D. E. N. (Emma Dorothy Eliza Nevitte), 80, 99, 208

Spielhagen, Friedrich von, 273n4, 302n43

Spitzweg, Carl, 161

Staël, Madame de (Anne-Louise-Germaine), 23, 243

St Clair, William, 5–6

Steinestel, Emily R. (translator), 71–74, 79, 289n51

Stevenson, Robert Louis, 65, 160, 166

Storm, Theodor, 302n43; *Carsten Curator*, 170; *Der Schimmelreiter*, 115–16, 294n72

Stowe, Harriet Beecher, 258; and international copyright, 225; *Uncle Tom's Cabin*, 320n119

Streckfuss, Adolf, 230, 265; *Castle Hohenwald* (*Die von Hohenwald*), 235; *The Lonely House; after the diaries of Herr Professor Döllnitz* (*Das einsame Haus: Nach den Tagebüchern des Herrn Professor Döllnitz*), 231, 314n70

Sue, Eugène, 23, 32

Süskind, Patrick, *Perfume: The Story of a Murderer* (*Das Parfum: Die Geschichte eines Mörders*), 83

Syndicate Trading Company, 59

Tardy, Mary T., 208

Tarkington, Booth, 18; *Alice Adams*, 137

Tautphoeus, Jemima Montgomery, Baroness, 62, 288n30

Taylor, Bayard, 31, 33

Taylor, Zachary, 199

Tebbel, John, 7, 11, 203, 287n18

Tennyson, Alfred, 65, 157

Thackeray, William Makepeace, 33, 35, 41, 62, 160; *The History of Henry Esmond*, 71

theater in novels, 100–101; and aesthetic education, 98–99; and social death, 95

transatlantic literary studies, 11

translation: as addiction, 220, 247, 250; as art, 231, 239, 241–42, 246, 264; and authorship, 63, 149, 225–28, 233, 235; as cottage industry, 211; foreignized, 17–18; and interpretation, 79, 109–11, 123, 130–31, 169, 177, 242, 255; as middle-class women's labor, 202, 216, 218–19, 237; naturalized, 17, 233; and the Other, 17; rates of for German fiction, xi, 14–16, 40, 43, 47, 270–72. *See also under* adaptation of German literature

Trenck, Friedrich, Freiherr von der, literary treatment of, 186–87, 212

Trollope, Anthony, 33, 99, 224–25

Tucker, George (grandfather of Mary Stuart Smith), 239, 315n8

Turgenev, Ivan Sergeyevich, 124, 181, 243

Twain, Mark (Samuel Langhorne Clemens), 62, 99, 302n30; "The Awful

German Language," 62; *The Mysterious Stranger*, 62
Twardowska, Emma Eva Henriette von. *See* Hartner, E.
Tyrrell, Christina (translator), 134, 174, 177, 244, 302n37

Ulrich von Liechtenstein: *Frauendienst*, 70
University of Virginia, 237–38, 240, 242; and the status of women, 27, 253
Unterhaltungsliteratur. *See* "amusement fiction"

values, middle-class: German novels as purveyors of, 5, 12–13, 18–19, 48–49, 57, 79, 82, 124, 139, 261
Varnhagen, Rachel, 30
Venuti, Lawrence, 18
Verdi, Giuseppe, *La Traviata*, 96
Vernes, Jules, 23
Volckhausen, Julie Adeline Voigt, 30, 53, 270–72; *Why Did He Not Die? or, The Child from the Ebräergang* (*Das Kind aus dem Ebräergang*), 112, 220
Voltaire (François-Marie Arouet), 181
Vosmaer, Carl, 24

Wagner, Richard, 29, 140
Wahl, Ludwig. *See* Blum, Georg and Ludwig Wahl: *Seaside and Fireside Fairytales* (selections from *See und Strand* and *Märchen*)
Walker, Eliza Smith (daughter of Mary Stuart and Francis Smith), 246, 316n39
Warner, Charles Dudley, 63, 274n19, 293n48
Waterman, Margaret P. (translator), 89–90
W. B. Conkey Company, 59, 64
Weeks, E. A. *See* E. A. Weeks and Company
Werner, E. (Elisabeth Bürstenbinder): and *Die Gartenlaube*, 29, 37, 45–47, 133, 164–65, 170, 247, 285n105; and the literary production of masculinity, 46, 114–16, 129, 131–33, 141, 151, 159–64, 168–89; and nationalistic themes, 61, 140, 159, 161, 163–64, 168–69, 171–74, 194, 253, 257; popularity of in the United States, 6, 16, 23, 29, 45–46, 172, 249, 265, 270–72, 280n7; use of pseudonym, 45. *See also* revolutions of 1848, treatment of the legacy of in German literature; *and under* Smith, Mary Stuart (née Harrison)
Werner, E. (Elisabeth Bürstenbinder), works of: *The Alpine Fairy/The Fairy of the Alps* (*Die Alpenfee*), 156–57, 250; *At the Altar* (*Am Altar*), 112–15; *At a High Price/At a High Price, or The Price He Paid/No Surrender/The Price He Paid* (*Um hohen Preis*), 174–78, 237, 242, 247, 285n107, 316n25; *Banned and Blessed/Raymond's Atonement* (*Gebannt und erlöst*), 46, 111–12, 114–17, 132; *Beacon-Fires/Beacon Lights/Flames/His Word of Honor/The Northern Light/The Sign of Flame* (*Flammenzeichen*), 160, 164–70, 174, 250, 301n13; *Broken Chains/Riven Bonds* (*Gesprengte Fesseln*), 122, 139–41, 145, 298n47; *Clear the Track* (*Freie Bahn*), 157, 249, 296–97n25; *Fata Morgana*, 157; *Good Luck!/Good Luck, or, Success and How He Won it /She Fell in Love with Her Husband* (*Glück auf!*), 130–33; *Hermann*, 159; *Hero of the Pen/The Quill-Driver* (*Ein Held der Feder*), 45, 160–64, 170, 285n105, 294n63, 301n5; *Partners* (*Der Egoist*), 247–48; *Saint Michael/St. Michael* (*Sankt Michael*), 229, 248, 250, 257–58; *The Spell of Home* (*Heimatklang*), 172–74, 253; *Vineta; or the Phantom City* (*Vineta*), 160, 170–72, 174; *What the Spring Brought* (*Frühlingsboten*), 247, 249, 279n85, 303n53

Werner Company, 64
Wharton, Edith, 136
Whitney, Marian P., 173, 302n31
Wichert, Ludwig Ernst, 220, 230
Wilde, Oscar, 181
Wilhelmina, Princess of Hesse-Kassel, 186
William I (Emperor), 102, 181
William II (Emperor), 164, 166, 260
William L. Allison Company, 59, 64, 128
Wilson, John G., *Nordeck*, 172
Wister, Annis Lee (née Furness): connections of, 216–18; and copyright protection, 147, 225–26; and death of her son, 220; displacement of the original author by, 63, 225–26, 228, 233–34; and feelings about her translation, 222–23, 312n27; and Henry Lea, 222; marketing of translations of by J. P. Lippincott and Company, 36, 63, 96, 102–3, 151, 225–33, 314n70; reputation of, 27, 96, 216–17, 224–27, 231, 233, 236, 239, 264; and selection of works to translate, 53, 95–96, 102, 107, 111, 147, 151, 229–31, 233; and Silas Weir Mitchell, 217–18, 222–23; skill of as translator, 18, 73–74, 79, 109–11, 151, 224, 234–35; source of translated works of, 20, 230; work habits of, 220–21; and work with Horace Howard Furness, 217–18.
Wister, Annis Lee (née Furness), works translated by: *The Alpine Fairy*, 156–57; *At the Councillor's; or, a Nameless History*, 41, 58, 157, 284n84; *The Bailiff's Maid*, 286n121; *Banned and Blessed*, 46, 111–12, 114–17, 132; *Castle Hohenwald*, 235; *Countess Erika's Apprenticeship*, 217, 230–31; *Countess Gisela*, 40, 226, 310n2; *The Eichhofs*, 122, 148–51, 300n70; *Enchanted and Enchanting*, 220; *From Hand to Hand*, 122, 151–54, 159, 230; *Gold Elsie*, 54–59, 61–62, 80–81, 215–16, 219, 233, 287–88n24, 310n2, 314n70; *The Green Gate*, 220; *The Happy-Go-Lucky, or Leaves from the Life of a Good for Nothing*, 223, 314n70; *Hulda; or the Deliverer*, 7, 96–99, 100–102, 111, 156, 220, 230; *In the Schillingscourt*, 71–82, 121, 229, 289n52, 312n45; *The Lady with the Rubies*, 234; *The Little Moorland Princess*, 41–42, 220, 225, 286n121, 288n32; *The Lonely House; after the diaries of Herr Professor Döllnitz*, 231–33; *Margarethe; or Life-Problems*, 122, 145–47, 151, 157, 230; *A New Race*, 230; *A Noble Name*, 96, 99–103; *The Old Mam'selle's Secret*, 39, 41–42, 57, 61–71, 128, 215–17, 219, 227, 233, 312n45, 314n70; *Only a Girl*, 7, 47–48, 103–11, 230, 292n42, 293n45, 293–94n59, 294n62, 311n19; *Only No Love*, 219, 226; *A Penniless Girl*, 44, 233; *Picked Up in the Streets*, 265; *Saint Michael*, 229; *Seaside and Fireside Fairy Tales*, 310n1; *The Second Wife*, 16, 23, 62, 124–29, 220, 295n12, 314n70; *Slovenly Peter*, 310n8; *The Spell of Home*, 172–74, 253; *Violetta*, 96, 99–102, 111, 230, 292; *Why Did He Not Die? or The Child from the Ebräergang*, 112, 220, 311n19. See also under *Lippincott's Magazine*
Wister, Caspar (husband of Annis Lee Wister), 218
Wister, Caspar (son of Annis Lee and Caspar Wister), 220, 311n18
Wister, Owen, 217–18
Wister, Sarah B., 218, 235
Wolzogen, Ernst von, 40
Woman Question, The, 102, 104, 107, 111, 157
women and science in novels. *See under* gender
women's rights, 103, 240
women writers: exclusion of from national canons 3–4, 6, 30; increase in production of, 28; new opportunities

for, 25, 28, 38; prejudices against, 34, 39–40; prominence in North America of German, xi, 11, 16, 23, 29, 54. *See also under* Gartenlaube, Die
Wood, Ellen (Mrs. Henry Wood), *East Lynne*, 42, 71, 244
working class, literary portrayals of, 49
World's Columbian Exposition, 104, 227, 239–41, 315n19
Wyatt, Edith, "A Matter of Taste," 22–23
Wyss, Johann David, 29
Wyss, Johann Rudolf, 29

Yates, Edmund Hodgson, 215
Yonge, Charlotte M., 80, 99, 258; *The Heir of Redclyffe*, 64, 128, 259

Zöge von Manteuffel, Ursula (Frau von Trebra-Lindenau). *See* Manteuffel, Ursula Zöge von (Frau von Trebra-Lindenau)
Zola, Emile, 114; *Au Bonheur des Dames*, 46; *Germinal*, 296n24
Zschokke, Heinrich, 273n4

www.ingramcontent.com/pod-product-compliance
Lightning Source LLC
Chambersburg PA
CBHW030105010526
44116CB00005B/104